AIR CARRIER OPERATIONS

Mark J. Holt • Phillip J. Poynor

Iowa State Press
A Blackwell Publishing Company

Mark J. Holt, a pilot for a major airline based in Atlanta, soloed at age sixteen. He holds an ATP pilot certificate with Boeing 757/767 and BAE Jetstream 41 type ratings and a Flight Engineer (Turbojet) certificate. His professional flying career includes extensive flight and ground instructing experience and service as a check airman for a large regional airline. Mark also served nine years as an electronics/radar technician for the U.S. Air Force Air National Guard.

Phillip J. Poynor, J.D., associate professor of aviation at the State University of New York at Farmingdale is the FAA/Industry 2001 Flight Instructor of the Year. He holds an ATP pilot certificate and is an active flight and ground instructor. He has been captain qualified on Part 135 carriers and has taught courses on Air Carrier Operations and Advanced Systems for many years. Phil is an attorney with a practice limited to aviation matters. He was a staff attorney in the flight operations department of a major, international airline. He began his flying career over 25 years ago and has been instructing for more than 20 years. He is a NAFI Master CFI. Phil received the Excellence in Pilot Training Award from the National Air Transportation Association in 1998 and the Chancellor's Award for Excellence in Teaching from SUNY in 1994. He also owns and operates a large, independent flight school, is on the Board of Directors of the National Association of Flight Instructors, and is a member of the NATA Flight Training Committee.

Iowa State Press
A Blackwell Publishing Company
2121 State Avenue, Ames, Iowa 50014

Orders: 1-800-862-6657
Office: 1-515-292-0140
Fax: 1-515-292-3348
Web site: www.iowastatepress.com

Authorization to photocopy items for internal or personal use, or the internal or personal use of specific clients, is granted by Iowa State Press, provided that the base fee of $.10 per copy is paid directly to the Copyright Clearance Center, 222 Rosewood Drive, Danvers, MA 01923. For those organizations that have been granted a photocopy license by CCC, a separate system of payments has been arranged. The fee code for users of the Transactional Reporting Service is 0-8138-0788-3/2002 $.10.

∞ Printed on acid-free paper in the United States of America

First edition, 2002

Library of Congress Cataloging-in-Publication Data
Holt, Mark J.
      Air carrier operations/Mark J. Holt, Phillip J.
Poynor—1st ed. p.cm.
Includes bibliographical references and index.
      ISBN 0-8138-0788-3
1.Aeronautics, Commercial, 2. Airlines—Management.
3. Airlines—Law and legislation—United States. I. title.
TL552 h65 2002
387.7—dc21
                        2001006205

The last digit is the print number: 9 8 7 6 5 4 3 2 1

AIR CARRIER OPERATIONS

Contents

Acknowledgements

The authors would like to thank, first and foremost, the individuals who spent their valuable time reviewing our manuscript and offering suggestions and information.

Athena Janke and Rusty Bell offered their expertise, and we are grateful to them. Dave Rosenbaum, at Iowa State Press, offered invaluable support during the development of this text, and his efforts are greatly appreciated. Greg N. Brown "got the ball rolling" on this text and generously offered his design and graphic arts expertise in the production of several figures in this book. We would also like to thank Captain "Billy" Walker and Captain Al Spain of JetBlue Airways and Captain Dave Young of Delta Air Lines for allowing us access and use of company flight, maintenance, and operation specifications manuals.

Others who contributed inspirational and moral support include Becky Holt and a number of undergraduate students enrolled in the aviation program at the State University of New York at Farmingdale.

Our special thanks to Dave English for allowing us the use of the snippets that begin each chapter. These come from his wonderfully whimsical book of great quotations of flight, *Slipping the Surly Bonds,* and help lighten and enliven what can otherwise be a pretty mind-numbing subject.

To all these folks, thanks for your help!

RAs	resolution advisories
RCLM	runway centerline markings
RNAV	area navigation
RVR	runway visual range
RVV	runway visibility value
SATCOM	satellite communication system
SDF	simplified directional facility
SIGMET	significant meteorological information
sm	statute mile
TAF	terminal area forecast
TAs	traffic alerts
TCAS	traffic alert and collision avoidance system
UTC	Universal Coordinated Time
VFR	visual flight rules
VNAV	vertical navigation equipment
VOR	VHF omnirange
VOR/DME	VHF omnidirectional range/distance measuring equipment
VORTAC	VHR omnirange radio/tactical air navigation
WAT limit	weight-altitude-temperature limits

Preface

I confess that in 1901, I said to my brother Orville that man would not fly for fifty years.

—Wilbur Wright, 1908

Air Carrier Operations is an introductory text that attempts to introduce the student to the significant regulations impacting airline operations. Although it is primarily intended for an air carrier flight operations course, it could be used as part of a general air carrier operations course as well. This book is intended for use in sophomore or junior level courses. At this juncture in their studies, most college students of aviation disciplines have been exposed to very little of the restrictive regulations that make up modern airline operations. Whether Part 121 airline or Part 135 charter operator, these companies live or die by their compliance with the applicable Federal Aviation Regulations or FARs (14 CFR). Surprisingly, aviation students are largely unexposed to the layers of regulations in a Part 61 flight-training program or, at best, minimally exposed to them in a Part 141 pilot school.

The purpose of this book, then, is to examine the multitude of regulations governing an air carrier. It will focus primarily on Part 121 air carriers, though we necessarily discuss Part 119 and relevant portions of parts 135, 91, and 61 of the FARs. We approach this discussion assuming that the student has some background in piloting or maintenance and has been exposed to introductory courses in aviation. These introductory courses are often found in the freshman or sophomore year and have titles such as General Aeronautics or Introduction to Aviation and are often conducted as a private pilot ground school. Due to the nature of air carrier operations, a large portion of this text focuses on Instrument Flight Rules (IFR) flight operations. Consequently, we recommend students complete the Instrument Rating before undertaking study of this book.

We do not attempt to explain every regulation in all of its nuances. Rather, we try to paint a mosaic that explains as much the why as it does the what, leaving the student with a clear understanding of why some of the complex rules are as they are. For this reason, we don't quote excessively from the regulations. We do try to give the appropriate reference so the student may read it on his or her own, and it is essential that the student do this as part of the study of this book. Therefore, the student should acquire a copy of the current FARs that includes at a minimum Parts 1, 61, 91, 119, 121, and 135 (14CFR1, 61, 91, 119, 121, 135). These are available in various forms from various publishers and also in a subscription format as well.

When we reference a regulation in the text, it is important that the student pull out his or her copy of the regulations and read the text of that rule at the same time the explanation is read. That way he or she gets not only the "big picture" from our text but also the detail and wording from the actual regulation. If there is ever a conflict between our statement of the rule and the actual rule, obviously the rule governs. In addition to learning about that particular rule, the student will also develop the skills needed to properly read and interpret the FARs. This is a skill that will surely be needed as s/he gets further into his or her professional career.

This book is designed to assist the student in his or her first serious foray into the FARs by explaining what something means and why it is done then allowing the student to get the full meaning of the rule by reading it for him- or herself. At the conclusion of the book, the student will have been exposed to the entirety of FAR Part 121. We don't expect an expert level of understanding after one pass through this text. It is reasonable to expect at the conclusion of this book that the student should have an appreciation of the variety of regulatory issues involved in air carrier operations and be able to identify the appropriate and applicable regulations pertaining to them. He or she should then be able to read the regulations and apply them with an understanding of what they require. With this in mind, it is suggested that any testing in a course based on this text be open book Federal Air Regulations (FARs) testing.

Another use we anticipate for this book is as a review or introduction of Part 121 regulations to the airline pilot candidate. Whether the pilot is going for an employment interview or starting an initial training class with a 121 carrier, this book can provide a quick study so the pilot will be prepared. In recent times, with airline pilot hiring running at record levels, pilots are going to the airlines with ever decreasing experience levels while the training programs more or less assume that pilots have been exposed to this material somewhere. Increasingly, that is not true. Pilots that have not gone through collegiate training programs (e.g., many military pilots or civilian flight school trained pilots) have probably never seen most of the material in this book. This book can enable the pilot to get a head start on the interview process or initial training class. Such pilots should pay particular attention to chapters 2, 8, 9, 10, 11, and 12 as these chapters are most directly related to the operational issues most likely to be asked about in an interview or addressed in the indoctrination and initial training programs.

Organization of the Text

In organizing this text we decided for ease of correlation to the FARs that we would follow the general layout of the subparts to Part 121. Within the subparts, we intentionally do not attempt to present the rules in numerical order. In some cases that might make sense, but in many others the flow of the material in the FARs is confusing and misleading. We have tried to reorganize the material so that related rules are discussed at the same time. We want the reader to be able to put the disjointed pieces together and grasp the interrelationships that so often exist in the FARs. For this reason each chapter pretty much stands on its own legs. If a reader is especially interested in a particular area (operational rules, for example), he or she could go directly to chapter 12, which covers Subpart T, Operations. Again, for the most part, the reader can start his or her journey through this book at any point and end it at any point and still get the full value of the effort made.

If an unfamiliar term is used in the text, check the glossary. We have included an extensive glossary of new terms that are introduced in the book. If you don't find the term in our glossary, another place you can try is the Pilot/Controller Glossary found in the Aeronautical Information Manual (AIM).

Abbreviations

ACARS	automated communication and reporting system
AD(s)	airworthiness directive(s)
ADF	automatic direction finder
ADI	attitude director indicator
AFD	Airport Facility Directory
AFGS	automatic flight guidance system
AFM	airplane flight manual
AQP	advanced qualification program
ARINC	Aeronautical Radio, Inc. (commercially subscribed radio frequency)
ARTS	aircrew records tracking system
ATC	air traffic control
ATIS	Airport Terminal Information Services
ATP	airline transport pilot
CAA	Civil Aviation Authority
CASE	Coordinating Agencies for Suppliers Evaluation
CDFTRS	crewmember duty and flight time record system
CFM	company flight manual
CFR	Code of Federal Regulations
CL	centerline lights
CRM	crew resource management
CVR	cockpit voice recorder
DA/DH	decision altitude/decision height
DFDR	digital flight data recorder
DME	distance measuring equipment
DO	director of operations
DOT	Department of Transportation
DRM	dispatcher resource management
ETA	estimated time of arrival
ETOPS	extended range twin engine operations
FCC	Federal Communications Commission
FDR	flight data recorder
FL	flight level
FMC(S)	flight management computer (system)
FOM	flight operations manual
FOQA	flight operations quality assurance
FSDO(s)	fight standards district office(s)

GMM	general maintenance manual
GMT	Greenwich mean time
GOM	general operations manual
GPS	global positioning system
GPWS	ground proximity warning system
HAA	height above airport
HAT	height above touchdown
HGS	heads-up guidance system
HIRL	high intensity runway lights
ICAO	International Civil Aviation Organization
IFR	instrument flight rules
ILS	instrument landing system
IMC	instrument meteorological conditions
INS	inertial navigation system
JAA	European Joint Aviation Authorities
LAHSO	land and hold short operations
LOC/BC	localizer back course
LOFT	line oriented flight training
LRCS(s)	long-range communication system(s)
LRNS(s)	long-range navigation system(s)
MDA	minimum descent altitude
MEA GAP	gap or break in navigation signals at the minimum enroute altitude
MEL	minimum equipment list
MIS	maintenance irregularity summary report
MLS	microwave landing system
MNPS	minimum navigation performance standards
MRR	maintenance reliability report
MSL	mean sea level
NAMNPS	North Atlantic Minimum Navigation Performance Standards
NAVAIDS	navigation aids
NDB	nondirectional beacon
NOTAMs	Notices to Airmen
NTSB	National Transportation Safety Board
NWS	U.S. National Weather Service
OEI	one engine inoperative
OSHA	Occupational Safety and Health Administration
PA	public address system
PANS-OPS	Procedures for Air Navigation Services—Aircraft Operations (ICAO)
PMI	principal maintenance inspector
POI	principal operations inspector

AIR CARRIER OPERATIONS

What Is an Air Carrier?

You cannot get one nickel for commerical flying.

—Inglis M. Uppercu
Founder of the first American airline
to last more than a couple of months

As we begin this study of air carriers we first need to answer the deceptively simple question: What is an *air carrier*? What do they do? How are they different from us flying around in our training airplanes or perhaps our private aircraft? In this chapter that's the question we seek to answer. We also will introduce the parts of the Federal Aviation Regulations (14 CFR) that apply to air carriers. These regulations will then form the basis for study of the rest of the book.

What Is an Air Carrier?

To understand what is meant by the term "air carrier," first we must understand what is meant by "term of art." Then we can understand the phrase "air carrier" as a term of art. A term of art is simply a term that has a meaning beyond that understood by the layman. That is, it has a special meaning within the context of the trade in which it is used. To understand the term "air carrier" we need to look back at several hundred years of British common law theory and principles to understand the concept of *carriage*. Black's Law Dictionary defines carriage as

> . . . Transportation of persons either for pleasure or business, . . . drawn over the ordinary streets and highways of the country.

In other words, carriage was the simple act of carrying or transporting persons. This concept has been expanded through the centuries to include carrying or transporting both persons and goods. Early in the development of the concept of carriage, it was discerned that there are different types or levels of carriage. If you take your TV in your car to be repaired, is that carriage? If you take your friend's TV in your car to be repaired, is that carriage? What if you take your friend to the TV repair shop to pick up the TV, is that carriage? More important, is there any legal difference between these examples?

Private vs. Common Carriage

As British culture developed from a completely agrarian base to more of a centralized and industrial base, the law began to recognize that there were differences in carriage based on the differences in what was being done. In the law of *torts*, which is the law of compensating for civil wrongs, the law developed the concept of *duty to care*. Duty to care is essentially the level of responsibility which a person (or company) has toward others to protect them from harm. Older common law carved out a number of differing levels of duty depending upon the relationship between the people involved and the circumstances surrounding their interaction.

For example, what responsibility do you have toward my car and me if I park it in the lot at your mall? Is that different from the responsibility you have toward my car and me if I park it in your driveway to attend a party at your house? Further, is that different from the responsibility you have to my car and me if I park it in your pay parking lot? Finally, what if I deliver it to your employee (say a valet in a restaurant) and he or she parks it? Is the responsibility changed? In such situations, British (and later American) common law drew distinctions among these transactions. The law said that in the first example, you have a gratuitous bailment with little (but some degree of) duty to care. This proceeds along a continuum until in the last two examples the law would hold that you have a bailment for hire and therefore a much higher duty to care. Our common law heritage is wonderful at drawing arcane distinctions between very slightly differing sets of facts. In modern times, many courts have eliminated these distinctively different standards of care, but with respect to carriage the arcane lines of care are still deeply drawn in the sand.

With respect to *carriage*, the distinction drawn was first between *private carriage* and *public carriage*. Private carriage is that carriage arranged between two parties—the carrier and the carried (or between some other small numbers of parties and the carrier). In this case, the carrier is simply carrying the persons or property of this small number, and it may be *gratuitous* (meaning there is no compensation exchanged for the carriage) or it may be *for hire* (which means money *or some other medium of exchange* has changed hands). So in the examples above where you were taking your friend or your friend's TV to the repair shop, you have an example of private carriage. If you received no money or other tangible rewards, then you have a *gratuitous private carriage*. On the other hand, if you received money or tangible (or in some cases even intangible) rewards for the carriage, then you have *private carriage for hire*.

Public carriage, on the other hand, implies a willingness to deal with many people who have a need to have something or someone taken someplace. Although it is possible some good Samaritan might do this for free, it is much more likely that the application of the concept of public carriage will be to someone that is engaging in the business of carrying people or things in hopes of making a dollar. Therefore, we will speak only of *public carriage for hire*. Note that it is not necessary that the person make money off of the transportation alone for it to be carriage for hire. What if I owned a resort in a very remote location and, as a service to my guests, provided air transportation into and out of the resort? Would that be public carriage for hire or gratuitous public carriage? FAA and NTSB decisions have held that this is public carriage for hire.

Again, looking at this example as a continuum, what lies further out than the above example of the resort operator? What if there was a resort area with many resorts (such as Aspen, CO) and you saw an opportunity to make money by starting a bus line (or an airline) to take anyone who wishes from Denver to Aspen. This willingness to take anyone in your public carrier for hire has now moved you the highest level, that of the *common carrier*. Black's Law Dictionary defines a common carrier as

. . . those that undertake to carry all persons (or cargo) indifferently who may apply for passage, so long as there is room and there is no legal excuse for refusal.

In other words, the *common carrier* is a person or company who will carry anyone so long as they have the money to pay the fare (tariff). General indicators of *common carriage* include

- *Holding out* to the public of willingness to
- Perform *carriage of all comers* (persons or goods)
- From *place to place*
- For *compensation or hire*.

We've dwelt at length on the distinctions between private and common carriage. What difference does it make? The difference is in the liability which the law places on the carrier. Private carriage has some liability. For example, all of you who drive know that you have to maintain minimum insurance on your car. If you injure someone and it can be proved that you were negligent, the injured party may recover damages against you for injuries that you caused. However, if someone were injured in your car through no fault of yours, recovery in a lawsuit would be quite difficult.

On the other hand, as a common carrier, your *duty to care* is much higher. Our common law background has held you to a much higher standard of care that approaches that of an *insurer*. What is an insurer? An insurer is someone who has responsibility to make sure or secure, to guarantee, to ensure safety to anyone. An insurer is completely responsible for the liability for breeches of safety and security of anyone with whom it has a contract. In other words, a common carrier is nearly totally responsible for the safety and security of the passengers and freight in its care.

Why is the duty to care so high for a common carrier? Again, the origins are found in the early British common law cases. To understand, picture yourself back in that agrarian British society. Bandits roam the highways (highwaymen). Travel is by horse or stagecoach. In that environment, passengers were truly put at the complete disposal of the carrier. Other than perhaps packing a weapon, the passenger could not protect him- or herself from the various travails and dangers that might lurk along the highways in the course of traveling. He or she *had to rely* on the protection of the carrier and its agents. The law therefore placed this responsibility squarely on the shoulders of the carrier. This concept has continued to modern times and forms the conceptual basis for the regulation of the public transportation industries.

Our common carriers, be they taxicabs, buses, trains, boats, or airplanes, are held to the highest standard of care found in tort law. They are virtually insurers of the safety and security of the passengers who entrust their lives and property to the carriers every day. In addition to the responsibility that the civil law (through the torts system) places on the common carrier, the government at its various levels seeks to assure that the common carrier recognizes and lives up to this extraordinary level of duty to care. This is done through any number of regulations under the local, state, and federal regulatory and administrative law systems. For aviation, this takes the form of federal regulation of air carriers by the Federal Aviation Administration, found primarily in chapter 14 of the *Code of Federal Regulations* (14 CFR), parts 61, 91, 119, 121, and 135.

FAA Tests of Common Carriage

(If it looks like a duck and quacks like a duck . . .)

Above, we saw that there were four tests to determine common carriage. These are essentially the tests the FAA uses in determining if an individual or company is acting as a common carrier (that is, as an air carrier).

Holding out to the Public of Willingness to Carry

To be considered a common carrier, the carrier must *hold itself out to the public*. That is, it must let the public know that it is available for carriage. While advertising is not the only way a carrier may hold out to the public, it is probably the most common way of doing so. Flyers, notices, and newspaper, television, and radio ads certainly qualify as a holding out. However, so would word of mouth, promotions, and public appearances where the carrier states its willingness to carry people or goods if the carrier institutes these things.

Perform the Carriage for All Comers

Earlier we saw that one of the early definitions of common carrier included a willingness to transport anyone. A common carrier is interested in carrying anyone; a private carrier is interested only in limited carriage. There are a number of private carriers. One example is a corporate aircraft operated for only one corporation. Another example includes operators that carry automobile parts from the parts manufacturers to the assembly plants. In this case the carrier serves only one contract, namely the carmaker operating the assembly plant.

So, how many contracts may an operator have and remain in private carriage? There is no hard and fast rule, but in FAA Advisory Circular 120-12A covering private versus common carriage relating to large aircraft, the FAA has stated that if an operator is operating as many as three contracts, it will be held to be private carriage. Conversely, the advisory circular says that as few as 18 to 24 contracts are considered to be common carriage. What about four or five contracts? Well, at present, that issue has not been definitively decided, but anyone considering operating more than three contracts as private carriage is doing so at considerable peril of being held to the common carriage standards.

From Place to Place

This of course is central to the idea of carriage; that is, you actually take people or goods someplace. That's why sightseeing rides aren't generally viewed as common carriage. In a sightseeing flight, no one is going anyplace.

For Compensation or Hire

Common carriage requires that the person providing the service be hired to provide the service. If there is no hiring, then it is gratuitous private carriage and does not become subjected to regulation as a common carrier. However, hiring can have some very unusual considerations. The first example: "I'll pay you a hundred bucks to take me to Altoona" clearly includes transportation (carriage) for hire ($100). It's an "exchange thing." You give me transportation; I'll give you money. Nearly everyone would understand this to be transportation for hire. What about the following example?

You, an aspiring airline pilot and broke college student, want to get flight time. You know a lot of your fellow students like to ski, so you put a sign in your dorm bulletin board which reads

> WANTED: Skiers to share expenses of flights to ski country. Will take you and one friend to Sugarbush MT any weekend. Your share: $100 each. Call Phil at . . .

We will see that this will probably be held to constitute common carriage under the FARs. This is one of the many ways small operators can run afoul of the regulations in Part 135 and be found to be common carriers. Students often ask, "But how would the FAA catch this?" The usual enforcement action for this kind of activity normally arises out of one of two situations. The first is a post-accident/incident investigation and the second is in ramp checks at popular tourist/visitor destination airports.

FAR Implications of Common Carriage

Before beginning a discussion of the ramifications of the FARs on common carriage, we need to look at the structure of the FARs. Actually, it's not the FARs at all (except to every pilot and aviation professional!). It's actually chapter 14 of the Code of Federal Regulations (14 CFR). (We have used and will continue to use the familiar term FARs.) You may have seen references such as 14 CFR 61.105. A pilot would probably refer to this as "Part 61, section 105," or even more simply as FAR 61.105. 14 CFR is broken down into a number of "parts" such as *Part 61: Pilots and Flight Instructors* or *Part 91: Operating Rules*. We will begin with a discussion of Part 1: Definitions.

Part 1 of the FARs doesn't define common carrier. That is a term of art carried down through years of British and American common law. It does define *air carrier*.

> *"Air Carrier" means a person who undertakes directly by lease, or other arrangement, to engage air transportation.*
> FAR 1.1

This begs the question: What is *air transportation*?

> *"Air Transportation" means interstate, overseas, or foreign air transportation or the transportation of mail by aircraft.*
> FAR 1.1

This is somewhat circular in reasoning but basically says if you are carrying people in interstate, overseas, or foreign transportation or if you are carrying any mail (even intrastate), you are providing air transportation. So, if you are doing these things, you are an air carrier.

A third definition we need to have is that of *commercial operator*.

> *"Commercial Operator" means a person who, for compensation or hire, engages in the carriage by aircraft in air commerce of persons or property, other than as an air carrier or foreign air carrier.... Where it is doubtful that an operation is for*

"compensation or hire," the test applied is whether the carriage by air is merely incidental to the person's other business or is, in itself, a major enterprise for profit. FAR 1.1

Why do we care about all these fine points? Simply put, we care so we can comply with all of the appropriate regulations. For any of this to apply, we must first find that the proposed operation is common carriage. If it isn't, FAR parts 121 and 135 don't apply. We would first apply the four point test. What about our example from above of advertising for skiers? The four point test for common carriage:

1. Holding out? Yes, the sign.
2. Transport persons or property? Yes, that's why you advertised.
3. From place to place? Yes, home airport to Vermont.
4. Carriage for compensation? Yes, you are being paid.

So under these tests, you have a common carriage situation; now what? Some of you who are pilots are probably saying to yourselves, "Wait a minute. I know Part 61 allows a private pilot to "share expenses" of a flight. I'll just change the $100 to a pro rata share and then this is ok to do." Well, let's look at FAR 61.113.

61.113 Private Pilot Privileges and Limitations—Pilot in Command
(a) *Except as provided in paragraphs (b) through (g) of this section, no person who holds a private pilot certificate may act as pilot in command of an aircraft that is carrying passengers or property for compensation or hire; nor may that person, for compensation or hire, act as pilot in command of an aircraft.*
(c) *A private pilot[1] may not pay less than the pro rata share of the operating expenses of a flight with passengers provided the expenses involve only fuel, oil, airport expenditures, or rental fees.*

On the surface, this may allow you to perform this flight. However, the facts we assumed still seem to indicate a common carrier. The dilemma is that the FAA will look at this and see common carriage. One of the tests they will use to determine if it is common carriage or not is what is sometimes referred to the ***independent interest*** test. That means that you as the pilot would have an independent interest in going on this trip even if the "paying passenger" were to cancel at the last minute. Would you still go to Sugarbush Mountain if 2 hours before departure the passenger said he had an unexpected assignment to do and couldn't go skiing this weekend? If not, that is a strong indicator that this is not a sharing of expenses situation, but rather an exercise of common carriage.

One of the authors is an avid fan of his college football team, the Texas Tech Red Raiders. (Go Big Red!) Since owning a flight school and teaching college he has flown his Piper Seneca from New York out to Columbus (to watch his team lose to Ohio State), to Raleigh-Durham (to watch them lose to North Carolina State), to Athens, Georgia (to watch them lose to Georgia), to Happy Valley (to watch them lose to Penn State) (and others he's too ashamed to mention). Finally, he trekked to Arizona and watched them beat Air Force in the Copper Bowl. Flying back that evening to Texas, it was very mellow; Tech had won, the night sky over the southern Rockies was beautiful, the peaks were snow covered; life was good. Then it occurred to him. He had spent more money flying his airplane all over the country watching Texas Tech try to win a football game than he had spent going to Texas Tech! That's dedication and probably a little insanity.

But, the point is, what do you think? If he had placed an ad asking for someone to accompany him to a game and share expenses would he have gone had that person backed out at the last minute? Well, nearly every one of these trips was made by the author alone, so clearly he would have. A cancellation would not have affected his decision to bear the full costs of the trip. FAA would say that he had an independent interest in making the trip. That would take him out of common carriage and allow him to use the relief provision of FAR 61.113(c) and have a pro rata sharing of expenses with any other insane football fans that might like to come along. But if, like the skiing trip, he cancelled at the loss of the passenger, FAA would probably hold this type of flight to be covered under the common carriage rules. So what? What difference does it make?

The short answer is, it makes a huge difference. When conducting flights for compensation or hire, the FARs set forth two general types of requirements. The first is a requirement that the pilot hold at least a commercial pilot certificate; this is necessary for the *pilot to be compensated or hired*. Many aspiring airline pilots upon receipt of their commercial certificate rush right out and put up ads just like we described. In the New York area, it's very common to see ads for skiing and flying to the casinos in Atlantic City. Their thinking is, "I'm now a commercial pilot so I can finally charge money to carry passengers for hire." In fact, FAR 61.133 would seem to support that point of view:

61.133 Commercial Pilot Privileges and Limitations
(g)   *Privileges.*
  (1)   *General. A person who holds a commercial pilot certificate may act as pilot in command of an aircraft—*
    (i)   *Carrying persons or property for compensation or hire, provided the person is qualified in accordance with this part and with the applicable parts of this chapter that apply to the operation; and*
    (ii) *For compensation or hire, provided the person is qualified in accordance with this part and with the applicable parts of this chapter that apply to the operation.*

What is the difference between (i) and (ii)? On the surface, they may appear to mean the same thing. But, a closer look reveals that (i) covers passengers paying (compensating or hiring the aircraft) regardless of whether the pilot gets paid; (ii) covers the pilot being paid, regardless of whether the passengers are paying for the trip.

So, if you have a commercial pilot certificate you're all set to start charging, right? Well, not so fast. Notice that 61.113 simply says that you, the pilot, may act as pilot in command of the aircraft. But, both (i) and (ii) have that little clause at the end that nobody reads that says

. . . in accordance with this part and the applicable parts of this chapter that apply to the operation.
FAR 61.133

What is the significance of this clause? Simply stated, it means that if you are otherwise found to be a common carrier and not entitled to the sharing expenses provision of part 61.113(c) you need to have an air carrier certificate to comply with those pesky "applicable parts of this chapter that apply to the operation." What parts are those?

Meet FAR parts 119, 121, and 135. These provisions of the FARs set up the requirements to hold air carrier certificates if you are an air carrier (a common carrier) as previously defined and discussed. FAR 61.133 only addresses the issue of whether you may pilot the aircraft when used for carriage for compensation or hire. There is a second, unrelated requirement, which is independent of the pilot question. That requirement examines the need to hold a certificate. If you are conducting flights carrying passengers or cargo for compensation or hire and the company (or you) don't hold the required *air carrier operating certificate*, you are committing multiple, major FAR violations.

The requirement to have an operating certificate is found in FAR Part 119.

119.1 Applicability

(a) *This part applies to each person operating or intending to operate civil aircraft—*
>   (1) *As an air carrier or commercial operator, or both, in air commerce or*
>   (2) *When common carriage is not involved, in operations of U.S. registered civil airplanes with a seat configuration of 20 or more passengers, or a maximum payload capacity of 6,000 pounds or more.*

FAR 119.5 sets forth the specific requirements for air carriers to obtain a certificate and operations specifications prior to initiating service.

(g) *No person may operate as a direct air carrier or as a commercial operator without, or in violation of, an appropriate certificate and appropriate operations specifications.*

So, if it is your intent to operate as either a commercial operator or direct air carrier (see definitions in 119.3), you must first obtain the appropriate certificate and operations specifications. But how do we know what kind of certificate is needed? That is, do we need to operate under Part 135 or Part 121? The answer to this question is found by looking in Subpart B, specifically FAR 119.21 and the definitions of FAR 119.3.

FAR 119.21 paragraph (a) says an operator must conduct its operations under Part 121 if it is a domestic operation, a flag operation, or a supplemental operation, while commuter operations and on-demand operations fall under Part 135. These terms are all defined in 119.3. To simplify these terms a bit:

A ***domestic operation*** is any *scheduled* operation that is operated entirely within the 48 contiguous United States. This includes those flight legs of an international trip which are entirely within the 48 contiguous United States. For example, the Los Angeles to New York leg of a Los Angeles–New York–London flight would be domestic operations. These are flights that are conducted in sophisticated aircraft. This includes turbojets, airplanes with more than nine passenger seats or a payload capacity in excess of 7,500 pounds.

A ***flag operation*** is any *scheduled* operation that operates between any point within Alaska or Hawaii and any point outside of Alaska or Hawaii. It is one that operates between any point within the 48 contiguous United States and any point outside the 48 contiguous United States, or that operates between two points which are completely outside the 50 United States. As with domestic operations, these are also flights that are conducted in sophisticated aircraft. This includes turbojets, aircraft with more than nine passenger seats or a payload capacity in excess of 7,500 pounds.

A ***supplemental operation*** is one that conducts charter type (nonscheduled) operations. That is, the place and time of departure and arrivals are negotiated between the operator and the customer. They don't operate on a fixed schedule. The distinction between on-demand and supplemental has to do with the size of the aircraft used. A supplemental operator uses aircraft having more than 30 seats and/or aircraft with more than 7,500 pounds payload capacity.

A ***commuter operation*** is an operation that conducts scheduled operations (five or more round-trips per week) in non-turbojet aircraft which have nine or fewer passenger seats or a payload capacity of 7,500 pounds or less.

An **on-demand operation** is an operation conducting nonscheduled operations in aircraft of 30 seats or less if common carriage or 20 seats or less if non–common carriage.

To recapitulate, if an operation is a domestic, flag, or supplemental operation, then the carrier must hold a Part 121 certificate [119.21(a)(1,2, or 3)]. If it is a commuter or on-demand operation, then the carrier must hold a Part 135 certificate [119.21(a)(4,5)]. There is language that allows a Part 121 carrier to conduct its commuter operations under Part 121 if it elects to do so.

Most of the balance of this book will explore the ins and outs of FAR Part 121 applicable to domestic, flag, and supplemental [FAR 119.21(a)(1) through (3)] operators. We will occasionally contrast a Part 135 rule with a Part 121 rule, but the focus of the book will be Part 121.

Part 121: Subpart A: General
(14 CFR 121.1 through 121.15)

This subpart of Part 121 sets forth the very basics of what is applicable to a domestic, flag, or supplemental carrier. 121.1 is used to determine the applicability of Part 121 to various persons and activities. The obvious application of Part 121 to domestic and flag carriers and their employees and contractors is stated. Also covered is the not so obvious application of the drug and alcohol testing provisions of Part 121 to nonstop sightseeing flights in small aircraft that cover less than 25 miles from the departure airport. 121.1 also extends coverage of Part 121 to the persons (passengers) aboard 121 aircraft.

We mentioned earlier that should you operate an aircraft in operations that require an air carrier certificate but don't possess one, you are committing major, multiple violations of the FARs. To see how this works, take a look at 121.4 (or 135.7 for commuter and on-demand operators). These rules, entitled Applicability of Rules to **Unauthorized Operators**, provide that in this case, the FAA will treat your operation *as if you had a certificate* and then violate you for all of the provisions applicable to a certificate holder. Since there are literally hundreds of provisions and each violation has a potential civil penalty of $10,000, even a single flight can result in potential fines in the millions of dollars as well as certificate action against any airmen involved in the operation. It pays to know if your proposed operation requires a 121 or a 135 certificate.

Another question that comes up in regard to flag operations (or certain domestic operations at foreign airports (i.e., Canada and Mexico) is what rules are followed in the other country? 121.11 covers that rule by stating you will follow local air traffic and airport rules except if the 121 rule is more restrictive and may be followed without violating the local rules. Conversely, a foreign carrier operating in the United States is not subject to Part 121 rules but is required to follow our air traffic and general operating rules. Fortunately, International Civil Aviation Organization (ICAO) rules significantly standardize these operational and air traffic rules, but a pilot must pay particular attention to the local rules when operating in foreign airspace.

121: Subpart E: Approval of Routes: Domestic and Flag Operations
(14 CFR 121.91 through 121.107)

Unlike our flying under Part 91, a domestic or flag carrier can't simply fly anywhere it wishes to fly. Subpart E provides the basis for certificating the routes of the carrier. This certification process looks at the adequacy of airports and other facilities and then approves those routes and airports for use. A basic concept is that we can only use approved routes and facilities in 121 operations. 121.93 and 121.95 set up the requirements for route approvals and 121.97 sets the requirements for airport approvals. Some of the significant items for approval of airports are airport safety and security; runway, clearway, and stop-way information; displaced thresholds; obstacles; instrument procedures; and special information. This information must be maintained and distributed by the carrier to the appropriate personnel.

Part 121 air carriers must have the ability to communicate with their aircraft at any point on the route structure. This is done to assure that the carrier retains *operational control* of the aircraft at all times. We will discuss operational control later in the text, but for now it's the concept that the carrier, not the crew, is the final determinant of how the aircraft is operated. Certainly that is done in consultation with the pilot in command, but ultimately decisions regarding how the aircraft is operated are decisions of the carrier, not the individual pilot. Of course the pilot in command retains emergency authority to deal with situations that require immediate decisions. 121.99 establishes the communications requirements for being able to contact an aircraft at any point on the route structure in a rapid and reliable fashion. This system must be independent of any system operated by the U.S. government (e.g., flight service or air traffic control networks).

Part 121 carriers perform their flight planning in a function called *dispatch*. Dispatch is a department in the airline that is responsible for all flight planning and control. A dispatcher is a certificated airman and works with the crew and other departments such as maintenance and meteorology to assure compliance with all operational rules. 121.107 sets forth the requirements for flag and domestic operators to have adequate numbers of conveniently located dispatch centers to ensure proper operational control of each flight. 121.101 sets forth the requirements to have sufficient weather reporting facilities to ensure reports and forecasts for the operation. Domestic carriers must use either U.S. National Weather Service (NWS) forecasts and reports or forecasts and reports prepared by a source approved by the NWS. Flag carriers must use sources approved by the *Administrator* (of the FAA).

Approved by the Administrator

That's the first (but certainly not the last) time the phrase "approved by the Administrator" appears in this book. Does this term mean the Administrator has to look at every carrier's weather service and approve it? Clearly she would be a busy gal if that were the case. When the FARs refer to approval by the Administrator (or similar phrases) what it means is approval by the Administrator *or a person who has been delegated authority to issue the approval by the Administrator.* In most operational areas including flight operations and maintenance, that means the approval has been delegated to the *flight standards* organization of FAA. The Associate Administrator for Flight Standards in Washington, DC, heads this organization. He or she delegates authority to the regional flight standards organizations, which, in turn, delegate the authority to local *flight standards district offices (FSDOs)*. These are the offices you may have had contact with if you are a pilot or student pilot. They control certification of pilots and enforcement of operational regulations. At the airline, each carrier is assigned a *principal operations inspector (POI)* and a *principal maintenance inspector (PMI)*. These inspectors have overall responsibility for surveillance of the carrier and assuring compliance of the carrier with all regulations.

Finally, 121.105 requires that the carrier have adequate numbers of servicing and maintenance facilities available to it for the necessary and proper servicing of the aircraft in its operations.

121: Subpart F: Approval of Areas and Routes: Supplemental Operations
(14 CFR 121.111 through 121.127)

Subpart F of Part 121 for supplemental operations is similar to Subpart E for domestic and flag operations in that it specifies the routes and areas of operations. Since charter departure and destination airports are negotiated between the airline and customer, they don't operate so much according to a set schedule/route as do domestic or flag carriers. Therefore, the FAA also approves *areas of operations* for supplemental carriers.

The major distinction between flag and domestic carriers and supplemental carriers is seen in the area of operational control. As we saw earlier, flag and domestic operators are required to conduct dispatch of their aircraft. That is, the flight crew and the certificated dispatcher must agree before every flight how the flight is to be conducted, and during flight deviations from the plan must, generally speaking, be agreed upon as well. Looking at 121.125 we can see that supplemental operators needn't dispatch their aircraft; rather, they must provide for **flight following**. Flight following is significantly different from dispatching in several ways. First, as stated above, dispatching requires the use of certificated airmen holding a dispatcher's certificate. 121.127(b) merely requires that the supplemental carrier show that the persons performing the function of operational control be able to perform their required duties. That is, the carrier, not the FAA certificate, determines the fitness of the operational control personnel. Supplemental operators must perform operational control but need not dispatch their aircraft. That means the pilot in command solely determines the suitability for flight and has ultimate responsibility for all planning decisions.

To support this method of operations, the FAA requires that the carrier have adequate facilities to properly maintain operational control of the aircraft. That control can be performed in a number of different ways. The supplemental carrier is left to its own devices to determine how, under its operational need, it can meet the operational control requirements. This system is the flight following system described in FARs 121.125 and 121.127. The purpose of this system is to keep the managers of the operation informed as to the safe progress and needs of the carrier's flights so that those personnel can maintain operational control.

Summary

In this chapter we have seen the relationship between the common law concept of common carriers and the very high duty to care. We have seen how that has been translated into a federal regulatory structure to assure that U.S. air carriers are operated so as to achieve that very high duty to care. The FAA requires that carriers specifically implement the various provisions of the FARs so as to assure compliance. This is done through a document called **operations specifications**, and these specifications are the subject of the next chapter.

Notes

1. Even though FAR 61.113 says "Private Pilot Privileges and Limitations," it has significant application to Commercial (and even Airline Transport) Pilots. When a pilot is

performing an operation that doesn't require the privileges of a higher certificate, s/he uses the privileges of the lower certificate. Even though those privileges aren't specifically spelled out under the higher certificate Privileges and Limitations section, s/he may use any of the privileges of a lower certificate. When a commercial pilot wants to use the "expense sharing" authority, s/he must use the provisions of 61.113.

2. The only authority in the FAR for sharing expenses in this manner is found in 61.113. If the pilot is receiving money from a passenger to take him someplace in an airplane that is not owned or leased by the passenger, there are only two ways this can be done: (1) Have an operating certificate and commercial pilot certificate or (2) use the expense sharing provisions of 61.113.

Important Terms or Concepts from this Chapter

Administrator	FAR 91
Air carrier	Flag operation
Air transportation	Flight following
Carriage	Flight standards
Carriage of all comers	Flight standards district office (FSDO)
Code of Federal Regulations (CFR)	Holding out
Commercial operator	Independent interest
Common carriage	Insurer
Common carrier	On-demand operation
Commuter operation	Operational control
Compensation or hire	Place to place
Dispatch	Principal maintenance inspector (PMI)
Domestic operation	Principal operations inspector (POI)
Duty to care	Private carriage
FAR 1	Public carriage
FAR 119	Supplemental operation
FAR 121	Test for common carriage
FAR 135	Torts
FAR 61	Unauthorized operator

Chapter 1 Exam

1. The concept of common carriage is derived from
    a. Federal Aviation Regulations.
    b. Federal statutes.
    c. British common law.
    d. State statutes.

2. Private carriage is distinguished from common carriage primarily by
   a. The lack of an exchange of money for transportation (carriage).
   b. The amount of money charged for the transportation (carriage).
   c. Contracts between parties as opposed to carriage on an individual basis.
   d. Transportation (carriage) of only one or very small numbers of parties.

3. Which of the following is not an element of common carriage?
   a. Having a license or certificate.
   b. Performing carriage for anyone (persons or goods).
   c. From place to place.
   d. For compensation or hire.

4. Holding out to the public would include
   a. Advertising.
   b. Flyers in a campus student union.
   c. Statements on a web page.
   d. All of the above.

5. In analyzing a situation where a private pilot is accused of acting illegally as a common carrier, the FAA will, among other tests, look to see if the pilot
   a. Was paid only for the fuel, oil, and aircraft rental.
   b. Had an independent interest in taking the trip.
   c. Advertised the availability of his or her services.
   d. Used his or her personal aircraft or paid money for a rental aircraft.

6. As a commercial pilot, acting individually and without further certificates, you may
   a. Charge a hunter to take him to the deep north woods of Alaska.
   b. Charge a fellow student half of the costs to take him home to visit his girlfriend.
   c. Charge a gas company to perform pipeline aerial spotter patrols.
   d. Charge an acquaintance to take her to the Atlantic City casinos.

7. A company must operate under 14 CFR 121 if it is
   a. A domestic operation.
   b. A commuter operation.
   c. An on-demand operation.
   d. None of the above.

8. A company operating small corporate size jets between Los Angeles and Mexico City on a scheduled basis would need to hold
   a. A domestic operating certificate.
   b. A flag operating certificate.
   c. A supplemental operating certificate.
   d. An on-demand operating certificate.

9. Assume you were operating as an on-demand air carrier but didn't have an operating certificate. The potential penalty for this would be a $10,000 fine for
   a. Each flight conducted for compensation or hire.
   b. Conducting flights without a certificate.
   c. Each section of Part 135 for each flight conducted.
   d. You wouldn't be fined; you would be required to obtain a certificate before continuing and your pilot certificate could be suspended.

10. Operational control is the concept that
    a. The carrier, not the crew, is the final determinant of how the aircraft is operated.
    b. The carrier knows where all of its aircraft are and relies on the crew to advise it of what they intend to do.
    c. The crew, acting for the carrier, determines how best to operate the flight.
    d. The pilot in command is solely responsible for the conduct of the flight.

Operations Specifications: Development and Application

*Federal Aviation Regulations are worded either by the most stupid
lawyers in Washington, or the most brilliant.*

—Anon.

In the last chapter we saw how, historically, air carriers were held to the highest standard
of care and, as a result, a large body of federal regulatory authority developed to assure
that they perform to that high standard. They are subject to regulation in FARs parts 119,
121, and 135. In this chapter we will see how the FAA requires the carriers to formulate a
plan and a document to identify exactly how the carrier will comply with a wide variety
of regulations. This process results in the creation of an ***operations specifications*** (***ops
specs***) document. In a nutshell this is the document created by the carrier and FAA
wherein the carrier specifically explains (or identifies) how it will conduct operation of
its aircraft in accord with the FARs.

Part 119: Certification: Air Carriers and Commercial Operators

The study of air carrier rules must begin with FAR Part 119. Why do we have Part 119 any-
way? The FAA instituted FAR 119 in 1996 to further bring the air carriers of both parts 121
and 135 under the umbrella of "One Level of Safety." Prior to that date, regional airlines
(19 seats or less) operated under the then much less restrictive Part 135 while aircraft
larger than that were operated under the most restrictive provisions that were found in
FAR Part 121. One Level of Safety was a major effort of the Airline Pilots Association and
other pilot labor groups (unions) that was picked up by the FAA; it sought to have a completely uniform set of operating rules for all scheduled air carriers *regardless of the size of
the aircraft.*

We saw some of Part 119 in chapter 1. Now we will examine the specific requirements
that a carrier has to obtain, maintain, and conduct its operations in accord with its operations specifications. FAR 119.33 establishes the specific requirement that Part 121 and
Part 135 ***direct air carriers***[1] be United States citizens (including corporate "citizens"),
obtain an ***air carrier certificate***, and develop and maintain operations specifications.
These operations specifications must contain "the authorizations, limitations and certain
procedures under which each kind of operation is to be conducted."

Operations Specifications

Once it has been determined that a proposed operation (or series of operations) requires an air carrier certificate, we must then move our attention to either FAR Part 121 or FAR Part 135. These parts prescribe the rules to be followed by commercial operators, air carriers operating large aircraft (Part 121) or small aircraft (Part 135). These parts of the FARs establish specific rules for air carriers that are substantially more restrictive than FAR Part 91: General Operating Rules. All operators of all aircraft must comply with the general rules of FAR Part 91. Then, in addition, Part 121 or Part 135 adds additional rules that apply exclusively to the certificated, direct air carriers.

Prior to the implementation of Part 119, the FARs recognized the substantially different operating capabilities and environments that exist for large and small aircraft. With the implementation of Part 119, the dividing line between Part 135 and Part 121 operations was moved to considerably smaller aircraft. As we have seen in chapter 1, domestic and flag operators must comply with Part 121 while commuter and on-demand operators must comply with Part 135. All of these operators must have operations specifications.

As we saw above in FAR 119.33 a person may not operate as a direct air carrier unless that person obtains operations specifications that prescribe the authorizations, limitations, and procedures under which each kind of operation must be conducted. FAR 119.7 tells us specifically what the operations specifications must contain:

> *(a)*   *Each certificate holder's operations specifications must contain*
>   *(1)*   *The authorizations, limitations, and certain procedures under which each kind of operations, if applicable, is to be conducted; and,*
>   *(2)*   *Certain other procedures under which each class and size of aircraft are to be operated.*

Since each operator must have a set of operations specifications, what must go into them? The answer to this question is found in FAR 119.49 Contents of Operations Specifications. This provision breaks down the contents of the ops specs into three categories, depending upon what type of carrier is involved. FAR 119.49(a) covers domestic, flag, and commuter carriers; FAR 119.49(b) covers supplemental carriers; and FAR 119.49(c) establishes the requirements for on-demand operations. While these requirements are similar in nature, there are differences between the different classes of carriers. Let's look at domestic, commuter, and flag carriers for example.

Each certificate holder conducting domestic, flag or commuter operations must obtain Operations Specifications containing all of the following:

> *(1)*   *The specific location of the certificate holder's principal base of operations . . .*
> *(2)*   *Other business names under which the certificate holder may operate (DBA or "Doing business as") . . .*
> *(3)*   *Reference to the economic authority issued by the Dept. of Transportation, if required*
> *(4)*   *Type of aircraft,*
>   *Registration markings and serial numbers of each aircraft . . .,*
>   *Each regular and alternate airport to be used in scheduled operations,*

Except for commuter operations, each provisional and refueling airport
[All the items in (4) may be kept current on a list, which is incorporated by reference into the ops specs.]
The certificate holder may not conduct any operation using any aircraft or airport not listed.

(5)   *Kinds of operations authorized*
(6)   *Authorization and limitations for routes and areas of operations*
(7)   *Airport limitations*
(8)   *Time limitations (or standards for determining time limitations) for over-hauling, inspecting and checking airframes, engines, propellers, rotors, appliances and emergency equipment*
(9)   *Authorization for the method of controlling weight and balance of aircraft*
(10) *Interline equipment interchange requirements, if relevant*
(11) *Aircraft wet lease information required by FAR119.53(c)*
(12) *Any authorized deviation and exemption granted from any requirement of this chapter*
(13) *Any other item the administrator determines necessary.*

FAR 119.49(a)

There, in a nutshell, is the content of the operations specifications (or ops specs). But, what are ops specs? In a very real sense, they are nothing more than the carrier telling the FAA how it intends to comply with the requirements of the Federal Aviation Regulations. The FAA Air Carrier Inspector's Handbook, Order 8400.10 explains it well:

Within the air transportation industry there is a need to establish and administer safety standards to accommodate many variables. These variables include a wide range of aircraft; varied operator capabilities; the various situations requiring different types of air transportation; and the continual, rapid changes in aviation technology. It is impractical to address these variables through the promulgation of safety regulations for each and every type of air transport situation and the varying degrees of operator capabilities. Also it is impractical to address the rapidly changing aviation technology and environment through the regulatory process. Safety regulations would be extremely complex and unwieldy if all possible variations and situations were addressed by regulation. Instead, the safety standards established by regulation should usually have a broad application which allows varying acceptable methods of compliance.

The op specs provide an effective method for establishing safety standards that address a wide variety of variables. In addition, op specs can be adapted to a specific operator's class and size of aircraft and type and kind of operation. Operations specifications can be tailored to suit an individual operator's needs. Only those authorizations, limitations, standards, and procedures that are applicable to an operator need to be included.

Perhaps the best way to understand the concept of op specs is to look at a sample Part 121 jet carrier's op specs outline. Specific detailed examples of the provisions will be given in the text.

U.S. Department of Transportation Federal Aviation Administration
Operations Specifications

Table of Contents

PART A: General

		HQ CONTROL DATE	EFFECTIVE DATE	AMENDMENT NUMBER
1.	Issuance and Applicability	04/09/99	03/16/00	1
2.	Definitions and Abbreviations	03/30/00	02/16/01	2
3.	Airplane Authorization	02/01/00	03/16/00	1
4.	Summary of Special Authorizations	11/20/96	02/21/01	8
5.	Exemptions and Deviations	07/19/96	12/04/00	3
6.	Management Personnel	02/10/98	12/01/00	2
7.	Other Designated Persons	02/10/98	12/01/00	2
8.	Operational Control	04/28/98	03/16/00	1
9.	Airport Aeronautical Data	04/29/98	03/16/00	1
10.	Aeronautical Weather Data	04/29/98	03/16/00	1
11.	Approved Carry-on Baggage Program	01/11/98	03/16/00	
22.	Approved Exit Seat Program	05/08/98	03/16/00	1
23.	Authorization to Use an Approved Procedure for Determining Operations During Ground Icing Conditions	02/10/98	03/16/00	1
25.	Approved Computer-based Record Keeping System	04/23/98	03/16/00	1
27.	Land and Hold Short Operations	08/11/00	02/16/01	2
30.	Part 121 Supplemental Operations	11/05/97	03/16/00	1
31.	Authorized to Make Arrangements with Training Centers, Air Agencies, and/or Other Organizations for Certificate Holder Training	12/04/97	03/16/00	1
47.	Telegraphic/Emergency Airworthiness Directives	12/13/99	03/16/00	0

Print Date: 02/21/2001
CERTIFICATE NO.: YENA761K
Aeromech Airways Corporation

U.S. Department of Transportation Federal Aviation Administration
Operations Specifications

Table of Contents

PART B: En Route Authorizations, Limitations, and Procedures

	HQ CONTROL DATE	EFFECTIVE DATE	AMENDMENT NUMBER
31. Areas of En Route Operation	02/01/00	03/16/00	1
32. En Route Limitations and Provisions	07/09/99	03/16/00	1
34. IFR Class I En Route Navigation Using Area Navigation Systems	03/27/98	03/16/00	1
35. Class I Navigation in the U.S. Class A Airspace Using Area or Long-Range Navigation Systems	07/01/97	03/16/00	1
36. Authorized to Conduct Class II Navigation Using Long-Range Navigation Systems (LRNS)	12/04/98	03/16/00	1
45. Extended Overwater Operations Using a Single Long-Range Communication System	12/09/98	08/09/00	0
50. Authorized Areas of En Route Operations	09/12/97	08/09/00	2

Print Date: 02/23/2001
CERTIFICATE NO.: YENA761K
Aeromech Airways Corporation

U.S. Department of Transportation Federal Aviation Administration
Operations Specifications

Table of Contents

PART C: Airplane Terminal Instrument Procedures and Airport Authorizations and Limitations

U.S. Department of Transportation Federal Aviation Administration
Operations Specifications

Table of Contents

PART D: Aircraft Maintenance

Print Date: 05/09/2001
D085-1
CERTIFICATE NO.: YENA761K
Aeromech Airways Corporation

U.S. Department of Transportation Federal Aviation Administration
Operations Specifications

E096.	Weight and Balance Control Procedures	HQ Control:	01/29/99
		HQ Revision:	01b

The following procedures have been established to maintain control of weight and balance of the certificate holder's aircraft operated under the terms of these specifications (identified below) and to ensure that these aircraft are loaded within the gross weight and center of gravity limitations.

a. Procedures by which either actual or approved average passenger and crew weights may be used are in the operator's weight and balance control program.
b. Procedures by which either actual or approved average baggage weights may be used are in the operator's weight and balance control program.
c. The actual passenger and baggage weights shall be used in computing the weight and balance of charter flights and other special service involving the carriage of special groups.

d. All aircraft shall be weighed in accordance with the procedures for establishing individual or fleet aircraft weights outlined in the operator's weight and balance control program.

e. The following loading schedules and instructions shall be used for routine operations:

Aircraft M/M/S/	Type of Loading Schedule	Loading Schedule Instructions	Weight and Balance Control Procedures
A-320-232	Computer	FCOM—Vol. 2 (data) Vol. 3 (procedures) SOM—Chapter 17	Aeromech Weight and Balance Manual, Revision 00 dated 12/03/99

Document references by volume, chapter, etc.

Print Date 02/11/2001
CERTIFICATE NO.: YENA761K
Aeromech Airways Corporation

Now that you have seen the table of contents and a sample section of this carrier's ops specs, let's take a closer look at what they contain. They contain all the material needed to comply with FAR 119.49(a). They are broken down into five subchapters:

A. General
B. En Route Authorizations, Limitations, and Procedures
C. Airplane Terminal Instrument Procedures and Airport Authorizations and Limitations
D. Aircraft Maintenance
E. Weight and Balance Control Procedures

The following description of the table of contents and the material contained therein lays the foundation for the discussion in the rest of the text. Note that Section E: Weight and Balance Control Procedures is a single ops specs section, so we have included the entire section as an example of what one looks like.

Part A: General

Issuance and Applicability
Contained in this section of the op specs is a discussion of who the carrier is, business names, principal place of business, certificate number, and similar items.

Definitions and Abbreviations
This portion contains definitions of certain aeronautical terms such as Category I instrument approach, certificate holder, and operational service volume (of a NAVAID).

Airplane Authorization
This section lists the *types of aircraft* that FAA has approved for use by the carrier.

Summary of Special Authorizations and Limitations

This section lists the special authority that the carrier may have or doesn't have. Typical issues would be authority such as domestic operations to certain foreign airports (e.g., Canada), lower than standard takeoff minimums under Part 121, ferry flight, minimum equipment list usage, North Atlantic operations (NAT/OPS), and extended-range operations with twin engine aircraft (ETOPS). The op specs will clearly spell out if the carrier has or is prohibited from using these special authorizations.

Exemptions or Deviations

Any carrier may apply for exemptions (waivers) from the requirements of the FARs. If these exemptions have been granted, they will be listed under the exemptions and deviations section. These would be exemptions specific to that carrier. For example, this carrier has been granted the "People's Express" exemption (to be discussed in chapter 11), which allows it to disregard the qualifiers in the terminal airdrome forecast in certain circumstances.

Management Personnel

This is a listing of the required management positions and the name of each person filling that position. In chapter 3 we will explore the specific management personnel requirements. This section also specifically lists which management position is responsible for application and modification of various sections of the op specs for the company.

Other Designated Persons

This section lists other persons that, while not specifically spelled out by the FARs, are still essential to the company. Examples are who you serve with process in the event of a lawsuit or other legal action and who is authorized to apply for and receive operations specifications for the carrier.

Operational Control

This is a very important issue with the FAA. It wants to know exactly who is in control of planning and operation of company aircraft and how that control is exercised. This is a major conceptual difference between Part 91 operations and Part 121 or Part 135 operations. As an air carrier, operation of a flight is a collaborative process and the company retains the right (and responsibility) to direct the planning and operation of the flight.

Airport Aeronautical Data

What kind of regular and provisional or refueling airports are to be used. Usually, the list of specific airports will be contained in the company operations manual or flight manual and will be incorporated by reference into the op specs. On scheduled flights, the company may only operate into those airports listed. Another important issue discussed here is that of producing and distributing performance analysis charts for each runway at each airport. This takeoff and landing data is runway specific for a Part 121 carrier and is usually contained in the aircraft or operating manuals.

Aeronautical Weather Data

What source of official weather data does the carrier intend to employ? How is it going to be disseminated to affected personnel? What procedures are in effect to assure all of this happens in a timely manner?

Approved Carry-on Baggage Program
If the company intends to allow carry-on baggage, it must describe how that system will work. How will bags be assured to fit in the allocated space?

Part 121 Domestic Operations to Certain Airports Outside the 48 Contiguous States
Under certain circumstances, carriers are permitted to use the domestic rules of Part 121 even though the operation meets the requirements of flag operations. For example, most flights to Canada may be permitted to operate under domestic rules. However, before a carrier may do this, it must list in the op specs the city pairs (routes) on which it will use the domestic rules.

Approved Exit Seat Program
The company must spell out how it will comply with the FAA requirement to have able-bodied persons seated next to emergency exits. These people must be given the opportunity to decline to assist in the event of an evacuation.

Authorization to Use an Approved Procedure for Determining Operations During Ground Icing Conditions
The company must state how it will comply with required de-icing and anti-icing requirements of the FAA including how it will compute holdover times.

Approved Computer-based Record Keeping System
The company must address how it will keep the records required by Part 121. It will spell out if computers are to be used, how audits will be performed, where and how backups will be maintained, and other similar items.

Land and Hold Short (LAHSO) Operations
If the company is authorized to conduct LAHSO operations, the specific runway configurations that may be used will be listed in the op specs. This may include incorporation by reference to the Airport Facility Directory (AFD). The section also contains the technical details as to how the LAHSO operations are to be conducted.

Part 121 Supplemental Operations
If the carrier is authorized to conduct nonscheduled (supplemental) operations, this section will specify the geographic area where this is permitted. It will state that it may conduct supplemental operations at its regular airports using domestic or flag rules as applicable.

Authorized to Make Arrangements with Training Centers, Air Agencies, and/or Other Organizations for Certificate Holder Training
The carrier may be authorized to use other airlines or private providers such as Flight Safety, International, SimuFlite or other Part 142 simulator training facilities to conduct its required training program. If so, the details are spelled out in the op specs.

Telegraphic Emergency Airworthiness Directives (ADs) Notification Requirements
This section spells out the procedure to be followed in the event the FAA issues an emergency airworthiness directive applicable to the carrier's airplanes. Further, it identifies exactly who is responsible for processing the AD after receipt from FAA and who is to acknowledge receipt of the AD to the issuing FAA office.

Part B: En Route Authorizations, Limitations, and Procedures

Areas of En Route Operation

IFR operations on and off airways are defined along with the operational criteria that must be used to operate off airway. This includes the use of Class I navigation (navigation within the service volume of the navigation aid) and Class II navigation (navigation outside the service volume of the navigation aid), if authorized.

En Route Limitations and Provisions

This section establishes that the carrier's aircraft will be operated in a manner that assures the position may be reliably fixed sufficiently to comply with air traffic control. If operating using Class II navigation, the aircraft must be able to reliably fix its position at least once an hour.

IFR Class I En Route Navigation Using Area Navigation Systems

If the carrier is authorized to use any form of area navigation (VOR/DME RNAV, GPS, INS, FMCS, etc.), it will be spelled out in this section. In addition the ops specs will identify exactly which equipment is authorized for use for Class I navigation.

Class I Navigation in U.S. Class A Airspace Using Area or Long-Range Navigation Systems (LRNS)

If the carrier is authorized to conduct operations in U.S. Class A airspace, using any form of long-range navigation equipment, as discussed above, it will be stated here.

Authorized to Conduct Class II Navigation Using Long-Range Navigation Systems (LRNS)

If the carrier seeks to perform navigation using multiple long-range navigation systems, that will be authorized in this section. In addition, the section will specify in which Class II airspace it is authorized to be used. For example, it may not be authorized to be used in the North Atlantic Minimum Navigation Performance Standards (NAMNPS) airspace.

Extended Overwater Operations Using a Single Long-Range Communication System

The operator may be authorized to conduct extended overwater operations with only a single long-range communications system. This provision will establish what equipment is authorized to be used and the geographic areas where the single system is permitted.

Authorized Areas of En Route Operations, Limitations, and Provisions

This section identifies the specific areas where the carrier is authorized to conduct en route operations. For example, this carrier is permitted to operate in the western Atlantic Ocean outside of MNPS airspace and the 48 contiguous United States and the District of Columbia.

Part C: Airplane Terminal Instrument Procedures and Airport Authorizations and Limitations

Terminal Instrument Procedures

This section establishes under what authority an approach must have been issued in order for the carrier to use it. For example, this carrier must use approaches that are developed by the carrier (and approved by FAA), approved U.S. Part 97 civil approaches, approved U.S. military approaches, or foreign approaches approved under either ICAO PANS-OPS (Procedures for Air Navigation Services—Aircraft Operations) or the JAA JAR-OPS-1 document of the European Joint Aviation Authorities (JAA).

Basic Instrument Approach Procedure Authorizations: All Airports
The carrier lists all of the approaches that are approved by FAA for use by the carrier.

Straight-in Category I Approach Procedures Other than ILS, MLS, or GPS and IFR Landing Minimums: All Airports
This section describes the lowest operational minimums applicable to the carrier's operations. It also lists the penalties paid (in terms of minimums) for inoperative equipment. Examples from this section of the operations specifications are discussed in more detail in chapters 11 and 12.

Limitations and Provisions for Instrument Approach Procedures and IFR Landing Minimums
If a captain is a low time captain, he may fall into the category of "high minimums" captain. That means the FAA raises the approach minimums over the published minimums until such time as he has sufficient experience to no longer be considered a high minimums captain. This section establishes the increases to the approach minimums and also requires additional runway to be available under certain conditions for high minimums captains.

Alternate Airport IFR Weather Minimums
The carrier may use *standard* or *derived alternate minimums* in its operations. A derived alternate minimum is a method of determining alternate airport weather minimums other than by the standard alternate minimums required by Part 91. For example, see FAR 91.169(c), which requires that an airport have forecast weather of 600 foot ceiling and 2 miles visibility for a precision approach or 800 foot ceiling and 2 miles visibility for a nonprecision approach in order to list the airport as a required alternate airport. If the carrier wishes to use derived alternate minimums, then the approved method for determining the alternate minimums must be given.

IFR Takeoff Minimums, Part 121 Airplane Operations: All Airports
Part 91 establishes IFR takeoff visibility minimums for Part 121 and Part 135 operators (e.g., see FAR 91.175(f)). The company may be authorized to conduct reduced minimums takeoffs. If so, the method of computing the amount of reductions and the applicable conditions will be given.

Flight Control Guidance Systems for Automatic Landing Operations Other than Categories II and III
Modern flight management equipment often permits automatic approach and landing to be performed even on Category I approaches. If this is permitted for this carrier the terms and conditions allowing it will be spelled out in this section. It will require specific training for the crew before they are permitted to use the automatic landing capability of the aircraft.

Published RNAV Instrument Approach Operations Using an Area Navigation System
If the carrier is permitted to perform RNAV approaches (including FMCS), it will be spelled out here. The crew must be specifically trained on how to use this equipment.

Turbojet Airplane Takeoff Operations with Tailwind Components of 10 Knots or Less
If the approved airplane flight manual (AFM) allows for tailwind takeoffs, it may be approved. The limits placed on this will include a maximum tailwind component of 10 knots.

Airports Authorized for Scheduled Operations

The carrier will list airports it intends to use for operations. This includes regular, refueling, provisional and alternate airports. A regular airport is one it intends to serve with scheduled service. A refueling airport is one to which aircraft may be dispatched only for the purposes of refueling. A provisional airport is one that is used to provide scheduled service to a community when the regular airport serving that community is unavailable. An alternate airport is one where the carrier's aircraft may land if a landing at the intended airport becomes impractical.

Autopilot Engagement After Takeoff and During Initial Climb for Auto Flight Guidance System (AFGS) Operations

This provision allows the pilot to engage the autopilot at a lower than standard altitude. Normally parts 121, 125, and 135 require that the autopilot not be engaged below 500 feet. If the system is fully operational and the crew trained, it may engage the autopilot below 500 feet with this ops specs provision.

IFR Approach Procedures Using Vertical Navigation

If the carrier has vertical navigation equipment (VNAV), this provision allows it to conduct nonprecision approaches using the VNAV for vertical guidance.

Category I, ILS, MLS, or GLS Approach Procedures and IFR Landing Minimums: All Airports

Sets minimums for this type of approach and outlines what equipment and limitations are applicable to the carrier.

Category I IFR Landing Minimums: Circle-to-Land Approach Maneuver

This provision limits the use of circling approach procedures to a minimum of 1,000 foot ceiling and 3 miles visibility (or higher published minimums). This is common for air carriers to limit circling approaches to VFR conditions.

Category I IFR Landing Minimums: Contact Approaches

The carrier cannot conduct contact approaches unless the pilot in command has received special training in the procedures to be used.

Terminal Visual Flight Rules, Limitations, and Provisions

The carrier is authorized to conduct visual approach procedures and charted visual flight procedures within B, C, and D airspace and in some E airspace.

IFR Lower than Standard Takeoff Minimums, 14 CFR Part 121 Airplane Operations

Part 91 sets minimum visibilities for instrument departures. Standard takeoff minimums are 1 statute mile for two engine aircraft and 1/2 statute mile for three or more engine aircraft. These values can be substantially reduced with training and certain equipment such as runway lighting available.

Part D: Aircraft Maintenance

Aircraft Maintenance: Continuous Airworthiness Maintenance Program (CAMP)

The basic FARs require commercial aircraft to be maintained according to 100 hour inspection. In most airline environments this is very impractical as the aircraft would be set down for extended times on a regular basis. Continuous airworthiness allows the maintenance tasks to be broken into much smaller pieces and performed a bit at a time at each layover or overnight stay. This may be authorized by ops specs.

Short-Term Escalation Authorization

Even with the continuous airworthiness inspections described above, the carrier may face a problem where a check is due but the aircraft is needed for operations. In this case the carrier is permitted to exceed a "weekly" check by 1 day and an "A" check by 50 flight hours.

Short-Term Escalation Authorization for Borrowed Parts Subject to Overhaul Requirements

In the world of airline maintenance, aircraft are often found in remote locations with inoperative equipment that must be fixed prior to further flight. If the carrier doesn't have the spare part, in many cases it may borrow the part or equipment from another carrier. Different carriers sometimes have different intervals for overhauling various parts, so it is possible that your carrier borrows a part from another carrier that is within the other carrier's overhaul interval but beyond your carrier's overhaul interval. In that case you may be permitted to use the borrowed part for a period of time pursuant to this provision.

Special Flight Permit with Continuous Authorization to Conduct Ferry Flights

In Part 91 operations if an aircraft is unairworthy but still safe to fly, it is possible to obtain a special flight permit (ferry permit) that allows the operator to ferry the aircraft to a facility where repairs may be made or maintenance performed. To do this, the operator needs to secure the permit from a Designated Engineering Representative or FAA Maintenance Inspector. This ops specs provision is sort of an open ended ferry permit that doesn't require individual application for each permit, but rather allows the carrier to make the determination that it is permissible to fly.

Aircraft Listing

Typically, this section will incorporate by reference a list containing the specific airplanes (N numbers) to be used. That way, if the list changes, all copies of the op specs do not have to be amended. Instead, only this referenced list needs to be changes.

Maintenance Time Limitations Section

The carrier is required to specify the time intervals for its maintenance. The time intervals (or limitations) will be addressed in the maintenance manual(s).

Coordinating Agencies for Suppliers Evaluation

This provision allows the carrier to use CASE (Coordinating Agencies for Suppliers Evaluation) as a means of qualifying a vendor for services, parts, and materials to satisfy the requirements of FAR 121.373. As discussed in chapter 14, the carrier may not delegate its responsibility for complying with the quality control requirements, but it may use the services of another agency to perform the work.

Arrangements with Other Organizations to Perform Substantial Maintenance

As with training, the carrier may utilize the services of another carrier or air agency to perform certain of its maintenance tasks. These maintenance providers must be identified and approved in the ops specs along with the limitations placed on the use of these firms.

Minimum Equipment List (MEL) Authorization

The basic rule is that an airplane with *any* inoperative equipment is unairworthy. This would be impossible to deal with in the real world of airline flying as things break all the time. With all the redundancy of equipment, broken equipment doesn't necessarily mean unsafe aircraft. A carrier is permitted to establish a program where the aircraft manufacturer and carrier develop a document called a minimum equipment list. This document must be approved in the ops specs and allows the carrier to operate with certain items or (combinations of items) inoperative.

Part E: Weight and Balance Control Procedures

Weight and Balance Control Procedures
This provision sets the company's procedures for determining passenger weights, aircraft weight, baggage weights, and so forth, for the purpose of calculating weight and balance prior to flight.

All of the above material will be contained (in detail) in the op specs once the FAA issues them. How do the op specs get produced in the first place? For some time now the FAA has used an automated process of producing op specs. At the Part 135 on-demand air carrier level, the carrier's first point of contact is with the local FSDO (flight standards district office). Their handbook provides guidance for the FSDO personnel to assist the carrier in getting op specs prepared. This process begins with a series of discussions with the FSDO operations inspector assigned the case, wherein the proposed operation is outlined in detail. In these discussions issues such as reduced minimums, waivers, limitations, and operational control are addressed. As a result of that meeting and follow-up meetings, computer generated op specs are produced by the FAA.

If the start-up carrier is going to be a Part 121 domestic, flag, or commuter carrier, the process is similar to that of Part 135 except that the initial meeting is with a representative of the FAA national certification team. They will meet with you, evaluate the needs of the carrier, and set limitations on the operations. Again, computer generated op specs are produced and become the guiding document for the company's operations.

Maintenance of Operations Specifications

Once op specs have been approved and the carrier begins operations, it must maintain the document at its principal base of operations [FAR 119.43(a)]. This is the formal or official copy that is available to any FAA operations inspector. In addition the carrier must insert pertinent sections of its op specs into its manual(s). It must clearly identify the sections as coming from the op specs and indicate that, therefore, compliance is mandatory. The carrier has the further obligation to assure that each employee that is affected by the op specs shall be kept informed as to his or her responsibility under the op specs.

Duration of Operations Specifications

FAR 119.61 says that generally speaking, once the op specs are issued they remain effective until surrendered by the holder or until they are suspended or revoked in an action by the FAA. Other things can also affect the validity of the op specs. For example, if the holder does not conduct the kind of operations approved for a period of 30 days (for domestic, flag, and commuter carriers) and fails to follow the procedures of FAR 119.63 upon resumption of service, the ops specs are no longer valid. Amending the op specs renders the amended sections invalid.

Before we leave this section, there are a few odds and ends to pick up in Part 119.

Obtaining the Air Carrier Certificate

We earlier mentioned the air carrier certificate in passing. A carrier must have an air carrier certificate to operate. Prior to deregulation of the airline industry in 1979, this certificate was issued primarily in the sense of an economic "franchise" to conduct business and then a safety evaluation as to fitness to conduct air operations. It required approval of the Civil Aeronautics Board prior to the carrier going to the FAA for the operating certificate. Since deregulation, this step is no longer required for domestic flights. (International flights/routes are a different matter and are subject to treaty agreements and approvals by the affected governments.) Today, holding an operating certificate shows that the carrier has been found "fit" by the FAA to conduct air carrier operations. It's a safety thing, no longer an economic issue for domestic operations.

FAR 119.37 spells out the contents of the air carrier certificate and FAR 119.39 provides the criteria the FAA will use to determine whether or not to issue an air carrier certificate. To be issued the certificate, the carrier must be in compliance with the requirements of FAR Part 119 and must have shown that it is properly and adequately equipped and able to conduct safe operations under Part 121 or Part 135. Application for the certificate may be denied if the FAA finds that the carrier is not so equipped or that it held a previous air carrier certificate that was revoked. Additionally, if the carrier attempts to employ a person in a key management position that held a similar position in a carrier whose certificate was revoked or if the owners are found to be previous owners of a revoked certificate holder, FAA may deny the certificate.

Deviation Authority

In some cases, it is desirable to conduct a certain operation although compliance with parts 119, 121, or 135 would preclude such operations. The FARs provide some relief in this event. FAR 119.55 provides that in some cases the carrier may obtain permission to operate while not in compliance with the FARs in order to perform operations under a military contract. FAR 119.57 likewise provides that in some cases the carrier may obtain permission to operate while not in compliance with the FARs in order to perform operations during an emergency. This permission is called *deviation authority* and is obtained upon application to the FAA and compliance with 119.55 or 119.57.

Summary

In this chapter we have examined the regulatory framework imposed on the carrier that assures compliance with the Federal Aviation Regulations. This includes the preparation and approval of operations specifications. In the next chapter we will explore the organizational and managerial structure of an air carrier.

Notes

1. *Direct Air Carrier* is defined in FAR 119.3 as a person who provides or offers to provide air transportation and who has operational control over the operational functions performed in providing that transportation.

Important Terms from this Chapter

Air carrier certificate

Derived alternate minimums

Deviation authority

Direct air carriers

Operations specifications (op specs)

Standard alternate minimums

Chapter 2 Exam

1. The purpose of operations specifications (or ops specs) is to
   a. Identify to FAA and itself how it will specifically comply with various provisions of the FARs.
   b. Identify to the employees how the company will accomplish certain operations.
   c. Identify for operational management how it is to manage the carrier.
   d. None of the above.

2. Ops specs must contain
   a. Authorizations.
   b. Limitations.
   c. Certain procedures.
   d. All of the above.

3. Operating under 14 CFR Part 121
   a. Eliminates the carrier's requirement to comply with Part 91.
   b. Requires only that the carrier comply with parts 119 and 121.
   c. Requires the carrier to comply with Part 91 as well as Part 121 unless the requirements under Part 121 are more stringent than the Part 91 requirements.
   d. None of the above.

4. Which of the following is *not required* to be in a domestic carrier's ops specs?
   a. Names and addresses of the five largest shareholders.
   b. Registration markings of each aircraft.
   c. Other business names under which the carrier may be operating.
   d. Any authorized deviations or exemptions granted by FAA.

5. Production of ops specs are now automated by FAA using what amounts to a punch card system. By doing this, the FAA intends that the ops specs of each carrier be
   a. Identical to other carriers of the same size.
   b. Tailored to suit the individual, specific needs of each carrier.
   c. Completely up to the carrier what procedures it wants to include.
   d. None of the above.

6. The starting point for a new Part 121 domestic carrier in setting up ops specs is to
   a. First contact a representative of the national certification team.
   b. First contact a representative of the regional certification team.
   c. First contact a representative of the local FSDO certification team.
   d. First contact the principal operations inspector assigned to that carrier.

7. A copy of the ops specs must be maintained by the carrier at
    a. All locations where it conducts business.
    b. All locations where crew bases are located.
    c. Its general counsel's office.
    d. Its principal base of operations.

8. A domestic carrier's ops specs are valid
    a. For 1 year from date of issue.
    b. For 2 years from date of issue.
    c. Until the carrier fails to conduct the kind of approved operation for 30 days and doesn't give FAA 5 days notice before resuming operations.
    d. Permanently, once issued.

9. A domestic carrier must get an air carrier certificate prior to operations. This is
    a. An economic approval required by the Civil Aeronautics Board.
    b. An economic approval required by DOT.
    c. A safety issue required by international treaty.
    d. A safety issue required by the FAA.

10. If you were a ramp service supervisor for Aeromech Airlines, where would you look to find the loading instructions (procedures) for how to load a particular A-320-232 aircraft? (Refer to Aeromech Ops Specs E096.)
    a. Aeromech's ops specs.
    b. Volume 2 of the flight crew operations manual (FCOM).
    c. Volume 3 of the flight crew operations manual (FCOM).
    d. Aeromech Weight and Balance Manual revision 00.

Airline Organization: Required Management Positions

This is a nasty, rotten business.

—Robert Crandell
CEO and President of American Airlines

In this chapter the organizational structure of FAR parts 121 and 135 air carriers is examined in detail. Obviously, airlines come in all sizes and shapes. There are 121 carriers operating a single turbojet aircraft and 135 carriers operating dozens of airplanes. Likewise, 121 carriers may have hundreds of aircraft in their fleets and a 135 operation may consist of a single Cessna Skyhawk. With this wide variation in size and complexity, the airline needs the flexibility to organize in pretty much whatever manner suits its operations. However, having said that, it is important to understand that the FAA is quite concerned with the issue of establishing specific responsibility with specific people at the airline. For that reason, FAR 119.65 and the sections following it provide specific guidance as to *required management positions.*

First, the FAA specifies the minimum management positions a carrier must have in order to obtain and maintain a certificate. These requirements are spelled out separately for Part 121 and Part 135 air carriers.

Required Management Positions under FAR Part 121

Part 121 requirements are found in FAR 119.65. The regulations mandate five specific management positions for a Part 121 air carrier. They are

- Director of safety,
- Director of operations,
- Chief pilot,
- Director of maintenance, and
- Chief inspector.

These positions are the only required positions in a Part 121 air carrier. Of course an airline probably couldn't function with just these positions, but the FAA leaves the non–safety related positions to the discretion of the individual airline. Larger airlines may have hundreds of management positions ranging from president and chief executive officer (CEO) through positions such as marketing, finance, accounting, planning, sales, and ramp service. All of these positions may be used or not as the airline sees fit. The five positions listed above must be filled however. Note that 119.65(b) does allow the carrier to use a different number or title for the positions if the carrier can show that it can perform the operation with the *highest degree of safety* (note the old common law carryover). FAR 119.65(c) requires that the titles (or approved equivalent titles) must be set forth in the operation specifications.

(b)   *The Administrator may approve positions or numbers of positions other than those listed in paragraph (a) of this section for a particular operation if the certificate holder shows that it can perform the operation with the highest degree of safety under the direction of fewer or different categories of management personnel due to (1) the kind of operation involved; (2) the number and type of airplanes used; and (3) the area of operations.*

(c)   *The title of the positions required under paragraph (a) of this section or the title and number of equivalent positions approved under paragraph (b) of this section shall be set forth in the certificate holder's operations specifications.*

FAR 119.65

The next question that must be addressed is what training, background, or experience the people that fill these positions must have. The answer to this question is actually found in two different sections of the FARs. First, there are generalized requirements found in FAR 119.65(d)(1) through (3). This sets forth requirements such as

(1)   *Be qualified through training, experience and expertise*
(2)   *To the extent of their responsibilities, have a full understanding of the following materials with respect to the certificate holder's operation*
   (i)   *Aviation safety standards and safe operating practices*
   (ii)   *Definitions found in FAR 1*
   (iii)   *The company's Op Specs*
   (iv)   *All appropriate maintenance and airworthiness requirements of 14 CFR*
   (v)   *The manual required under FAR 121.133*
(3)   *Discharge their duties to meet applicable legal requirements and to maintain safe operations.*

FAR 119.65(d)

Further, the carrier must state in the operations manual required by 121.133 the duties, responsibilities, and authority of the required management personnel. The names of the specific individuals assigned to these positions as well as their business addresses must be listed. If there are changes (or vacancies) in the personnel, the FAA must be notified within 10 days.

Beyond these general requirements, the regulations go on to require specific background and experience for these positions. These requirements are found in 119.67.

Director of Operations (DO)

The position of **director of operations** must be filled by a pilot experienced in the type of operations the carrier conducts. He or she must be an airline transport (ATP) rated pilot who has had 3 or more years of experience in a supervisory or managerial position within the last 6 years. This experience must include managing or supervising a function that exercised operational control over operations conducted with large airplanes (unless the carrier uses only small airplanes in which case the experience may be in either large or small airplanes).

If this is the first time this person has held the position of director of operations with any company, then he or she must have at least 3 years experience within the last 6 years as pilot in command of a large airplane (unless the carrier uses only small airplanes in which case the experience may be in either large or small airplanes). If the person has previously served in the capacity of director of operations, then the 3 years pilot-in-command experience may have been obtained at any time in the past. The typical duties and responsibilities of the director of operations are

- Provides operational control of all flight operations,
- Directs and supervises chief pilot, director of inflight, and flight operations staff personnel,
- Develops the budget for flight operations,
- Ensures proper training of all required personnel and is responsible for the quality of training output,
- Reviews contract services quality and performance and ensures proper ground handling services,
- Supervises the collection and storage of flight/load manifest and weight and balance data, and
- Has authority to employ, discipline, reward, or terminate air carrier employees.

Chief Pilot

To serve in the position of *chief pilot* the person must hold an ATP certificate with type ratings for at least one of the aircraft operated by the certificate holder. He or she must have had at least 3 years of experience as pilot in command of large airplanes (unless the carrier uses only small airplanes in which case the experience may be in either large or small airplanes). As with the DO position, this experience must have been obtained within the previous 6 years if this is the first chief pilot position held by that person. If the person has held other chief pilot positions, the experience may have been obtained at any time. The typical duties and responsibilities of the chief pilot are

- Supervises all of the air carrier's pilots,
- Directs and supervises all pilot recruitment, interviewing, testing, and final selection of pilots. Also responsible for arranging FAA required pre-employment pilot background check,
- Supervises the director of training, director of flight standards, and check airman staff and is responsible for the training and checking of all pilots,
- Directs and coordinates crew scheduling, crew tracking, and crew reroute departments in setting pilot scheduling policy, and
- Participates in continual flight operations budget process.

Director of Maintenance (DM)

The candidate for *director of maintenance* must be a certificated mechanic with both airframe and power plant ratings. He or she must have at least 1 year of experience in returning aircraft to service. This means making the determination that the aircraft is airworthy and complies with all applicable regulations after maintenance or repairs. He or she must have had at least 1 year of experience in a supervisory capacity under either 119.67(c)(4)(i) or (ii) and 3 years total experience within the previous 6 years maintaining large aircraft (10 or more seats) or repairing airplanes in a certificated airframe repair station that is rated to maintain airplanes in the same category and class of airplane as the certificate holder is using. The typical duties and responsibilities of the director of maintenance are

- Manages all company maintenance activities,
- Establishes and supervises maintenance control department,
- Directs maintenance planning, scheduling, and aircraft routing to meet maintenance requirements,
- Oversees any contract maintenance activities,
- Sets standards of performance for maintenance technicians and other personnel assigned to the maintenance department, and
- Responsible for dictating work rules, job standards, and job description for all maintenance personnel.

Chief Inspector

The *chief inspector* must have held a mechanic certificate with airframe and power plant ratings for at least 3 years. In addition he or she must have had at least 3 years of maintenance experience on different types of large airplanes (10 or more seats), 1 year of which was as a maintenance inspector, and have 1 year experience in a supervisory capacity maintaining the same category and class of aircraft as is to be used by the certificate holder. The typical chief inspector duties and responsibilities are

- Conducts internal and external maintenance audits and maintains a record of all audits in accordance with standard policies and procedures,
- Evaluates and recommends approval or rejection of contract overhaul/repair facilities,
- Supervises the scheduling and conduct of all maintenance training,
- Oversees fueling, de-icing, and general aircraft familiarization training and inspections prior to any new station opening,
- Supervises all company inspectors and auditors in the performance of their duties, and
- Assures all work performed on company aircraft conforms with approved company maintenance manual and all applicable federal regulations.

Director of Safety

Note that FAR 119.67 does not have any specific experience requirements for this position. Therefore, only the general requirements of FAR 119.65(d) are applicable to the *director of safety.* The typical duties and responsibilities of the director of safety are as follows:

- Conducts safety reviews of all functions including public safety, security, maintenance, and flight operation,
- Accomplishes annual internal safety audits and investigations in accordance with company policies and procedures,
- Attends National Transportation Safety Board (NTSB), FAA, Air Transport Association, and other industry safety meetings and seminars as authorized or directed by the CEO,

- Oversees communications between the company and the FAA regarding inspection results, safety reviews, and enforcement actions,
- Participates in the use of flight data recorder/engine monitoring information to develop safety programs or recommend safety improvement actions,
- Conducts routine surveillance and inspections throughout the company's route system, and
- Conducts regulatory and safety training for company managers and maintenance and flight operations supervisors.

In the event the carrier wishes to propose a candidate for one of these positions who does not have the requisite experience, there is a relief provision contained in FAR 119.67(e). This provision allows a request for a deviation to be made to the Manager of the Air Transportation Division (AFS-200) in the case of the DO or chief pilot or to the Manager of the Aircraft Maintenance Division in the case of the DM or chief inspector position.

Required Management Positions under FAR Part 135

Part 135 requirements are found in FAR 119.69. These regulations mandate only three specific management positions for a 135 air carrier. They are

- Director of operations,
- Chief pilot, and
- Director of maintenance.

The generalized requirements for a Part 135 required management position are very similar to those required under Part 121. FAR 119.69 requires that the manager must

(1)   *Be qualified through training, experience and expertise*
(2)   *To the extent of their responsibilities, have a full understanding of the following materials with respect to the certificate holder's operation:*
  (i)   *Aviation safety standards and safe operating practices*
  (ii)   *Definitions found in FAR 1*
  (iii) *The company's op specs*
  (iv)   *All appropriate maintenance and airworthiness requirements of 14 CFR*
  (v)   *The manual required under FAR 135.21*
(3)   *Discharge their duties to meet applicable legal requirements and to maintain safe operations.*

FAR 119.69(d)

The specific requirements for these three positions are found in FAR 119.71.

Director of Operations

If the pilots in command on this operation are required to have an airline transport pilot certificate, the DO must hold an ATP certificate. If the operation only requires a commercial pilot certificate, the DO must hold a commercial pilot certificate. If the operation requires an instrument rating, the DO must hold an instrument rating. Further, he or she must have at least 3 years supervisory or managerial experience within the last 6 years in a position that exercised operational control over either Part 121 or Part 135 operations. If this is the first time appointment to a DO position, he or she must have 3 years experience in the last 6 years as pilot in command of an aircraft operated under Part 121 or Part 135. If the person has previously held a DO position, the pilot-in-command experience may have been obtained at any time previous. The director of operations typically has the following duties and responsibilities:

- Supervises the chief pilot and other employees as directed by the president,
- Ensures that all flight operations are conducted safely and in compliance with all Federal Aviation Regulations, operations specifications, and company policies,
- Has authority to act for the certificate holder, including the signing of FAA correspondence and operations specifications,
- Communicates with the FAA Flight Standards District Office and the National Transportation Safety Board. Files all required reports and documents,
- Devises revisions to this manual as needed, submits the proposed revisions to the FSDO, receives confirmation from the FSDO that the revisions are acceptable, and then distributes those revisions to all manual holders,
- Schedules aircraft availability, including scheduling the aircraft for required inspections,
- Coordinates with the director of maintenance the timely correction of mechanical irregularities and discrepancies,
- Hires and fires flight personnel, and
- Manages the minimum equipment list (MEL) program.

Chief Pilot

If the pilots in command on this operation are required to have an airline transport pilot certificate, the chief pilot must hold an ATP certificate. If the operation only requires a commercial pilot certificate, he or she must hold a commercial pilot certificate. If the operation requires an instrument rating, he or she must hold an instrument rating. Further, the chief pilot must have 3 years experience as pilot in command under either Part 121 or Part 135 within the last 6 years or, if he or she has previous experience as a chief pilot the experience may have been obtained at any previous time. The chief pilot typically has the following duties and responsibilities:

- Reports to the director of operations,
- Supervises flight crew personnel,
- Conducts or supervises all training activities of flight crew personnel,
- Advises the director of operations regarding the training of flight crew personnel,
- Assists the director of operations in formulating operations policies, coordinates those policies, and coordinates operations and training,
- Ensures that all aircraft are properly equipped for applicable operations,
- Disseminates information to all crewmembers pertaining to routes, airports, Notices to Airmen (NOTAMs), navigation aids (NAVAIDS), company policies, and regulations,
- Maintains proficiency as pilot in command,
- Supervises scheduling of flight crewmembers, including assigning pilot-in-command duties,
- Prepares and maintains proficiency records, pilot files, flight schedules, duty time records, reports, and correspondence pertaining to flight operations activities,

- Submits all reports regarding flight personnel to the director of operations,
- Keeps the aircraft copies of the air carrier's operations manual current, and
- Ensures that all flight crew personnel are certified and supervised according to the requirements specified in the Federal Aviation Regulations.

Director of Maintenance

The director of maintenance must hold a mechanic certificate with airframe and power plant ratings. In addition he or she must have either 3 years experience within the past 3 years maintaining aircraft as a certificated mechanic including experience in the same category and class as the certificate holder or 3 years experience within the last 3 years repairing aircraft in a certificated repair station including 1 year returning aircraft to service. The director of maintenance typically has the following duties and responsibilities:

- Is responsible for all maintenance and inspection personnel and signing of Part D (Aircraft Maintenance section) of the operation specifications,
- Ensures that company aircraft are maintained in an airworthy condition,
- Ensures that all inspections, repairs, and component changes are accomplished in accordance with manufacturers' or FAA approved procedures,
- Ensures compliance with maintenance procedures, airworthiness directives, service bulletins, service letters, and applicable Federal Aviation Regulations,
- Ensures all maintenance technicians are trained and current on the types of aircraft for which approved,
- Ensures that all maintenance technicians are certified and supervised according to the requirements specified in the Federal Aviation Regulations,
- Coordinates with maintenance contracting agencies when maintenance activities are being performed on company aircraft,
- Provides the director of operations with the current airworthiness status of the aircraft and the forecast down times to facilitate maintenance scheduling and ensure timely deferral or correction of aircraft discrepancies,
- Maintains a close liaison with manufacturer's representatives, parts supply houses, repair facilities and the FAA,
- Makes available to maintenance personnel the necessary overhaul manuals, service bulletins, service letters, airworthiness directives, applicable sections of this manual, and any other required technical data,
- Maintains all necessary work records and logbooks, including certification in the aircraft permanent maintenance records that the aircraft is approved for return to service,
- Maintains the weight and balance records for all aircraft, and
- Completes the required MRR (maintenance reliability report) and MIS (maintenance irregularity summary) reports and submits them to the director of operations for forwarding to the FAA.

Operational Control

In reviewing the requirements for several of the positions, the FAA wants to see that the person has had experience in exercising operational control of the air carrier. What is this concept of operational control? FAR 1.1 defines *operational control* as "the exercise of authority over initiating, conducting, and terminating a flight." Operational control is exercised through both active and passive means. *Passive control* consists of developing and publishing policies and procedures for operational control personnel and flight crew to follow in the performance of their duties and assuring adequate information and facilities are available to conduct the planned operation. Active control consists of making those decisions and performing those actions necessary to operate a specific flight such as crew scheduling, accepting charter flights from the public, reviewing weather and NOTAMs, and flight planning.

This concept of operational control is a crucial one in air carrier operations. It is one of the key distinctions of the difference between air carrier operations and private carriage under Part 91. Operational control means that someone other than the pilot in command is involved in the decision making as to whether a flight starts, how it is conducted, and how and where it terminates. The pilot in command retains emergency authority to act independently, but under routine operations, the flight is conducted under control and through consensus with the appropriate authority within the company. The required management positions of chief pilot and director of operations require previous exercise and experience in the application of the concept of operational control.

The scope of operational control varies with the type of operation authorized. In accordance with company policy, the major responsibility for operational control is with the director of operations. When operating as an air carrier, the director of operations may delegate the active control of flight to the pilot in command (PIC) or other persons but always retains full responsibility. The persons delegated to exercise active operational control are usually termed flight dispatchers (Part 121) and flight followers (Part 121 or 135).

Within a flight dispatching system the air carrier is required to be able to establish direct radio contact with a flight while en route (FAR 121.99).

Each domestic and flag air carrier must show that a two way radio communication system is available at points that will ensure reliable and rapid communications, under normal operating conditions over the entire route between each airplane and the appropriate dispatch office.

FAR 121.99

The flight following system may be divided into two distinct categories: the flight release system (used by 121 supplemental air carriers and commercial operators) and the flight locating system (used by Part 135 operators). Within the flight following system, the carrier is not required to be able to establish direct radio contact with a flight while en route. However, if a carrier uses the flight release system, it is required to maintain a suitable means of communication between the flight follower and the PIC at each point of departure.

Operational control includes, but is not limited to, the performance of the following:

- Ensuring that only those operations authorized by the operations specifications are conducted,
- Ensuring that only crewmembers trained and qualified in accordance with the applicable regulations are assigned to conduct a flight,
- Ensuring that crewmembers are in compliance with flight, duty, and rest requirements when departing on a flight,
- Designating a pilot in command (PIC) for each flight,
- Providing the PIC and flight control personnel access to the information necessary for the safe conduct of the flight (such as weather, NOTAMs, airport information),
- Specifying conditions under which flights may be released (weather minimums, flight planning, aircraft airworthiness, aircraft loading, and fuel requirements),

- Ensuring that each flight has complied with the conditions specified for release before it is allowed to depart,
- Ensuring that when the conditions specified for release cannot be met, the flight is cancelled, delayed, or rerouted, and
- Monitoring the progress of each flight and initiating timely actions when the flight cannot be completed as planned, including diverting or terminating a flight.

Other Management Positions

This chapter is concerned with the *required* managerial positions within an air carrier. However, in order to put them into perspective, it might help to look at typical organizational arrangements in a variety of carriers. The first example (fig. 3.1) is that of a major international (flag) airline, and the second (fig. 3.2) is that of a small regional airline.

There are many more positions than those required by the FARs. For a smoothly functioning airline, all of these positions must integrate and work well together. That is the role of the chief operating officer (COO). Typically, this person will hold the title of President. In a large company this position will usually be separate from that of *chief executive officer (CEO). The chief operating officer (COO)* is responsible to the chairman of the board and the board of directors for the company. The CEO's primary duties are maintaining the relationship between the air carrier and the board of directors of the company and overseeing senior financial matters such as lender relations, shareholder concerns, and representation with senior regulatory agencies. This position is responsible for the operation of all aspects of the company, not just the airline operations.

Below this level in the organization, there are as many variations in management structure as there are airlines. Each one has its own unique way of organizing and managing its affairs. Some trends that have been seen over the years include placing all operational departments such as flight operations, maintenance, operational control, and in-flight service under a single department. The idea is that one strong operational leader can force the departments to work together smoothly. Unfortunately, many times this position has been filled by a flight related person (usually a pilot) who was too often insensitive to the nonflight issues.

A sometimes solution to this dilemma is to break off maintenance and in-flight services into separate organizational reporting, ultimately to the COO. There are numerous organizational strategies, and it is not uncommon for a carrier to reorganize these functions every few years in an effort to keep them from becoming bogged down or mired in tradition. However, whenever these organizational changes take place, the carrier must be sensitive to the required managerial positions and make certain that the requirements of FARs are complied with at all times.

An important department within the airline is the dispatch center, which may also be called the flight control or flight following department. This department serves to specifically implement the concept of operational control. *Dispatch* has the responsibility to plan the details of each specific flight and maintain communications with the flight at all times to keep it apprised of things such as weather, NOTAMs, and operational limitations. The dispatchers hold, along with the pilots and mechanics, a certificated position. Even though there is not a required position of head dispatcher, the FAA does mandate the presence of the dispatch function.

The *flight control* department (used in 121 operations) or the *flight following* department (common in 135 operations) can be thought of as being the nerve center of the tactical operation of the airline. This is where aircraft routings and scheduling, equipment substitutions, and cancellations are all brought together to come up with the minute-by-minute plan for running the airline. This department responds to the real world assaults

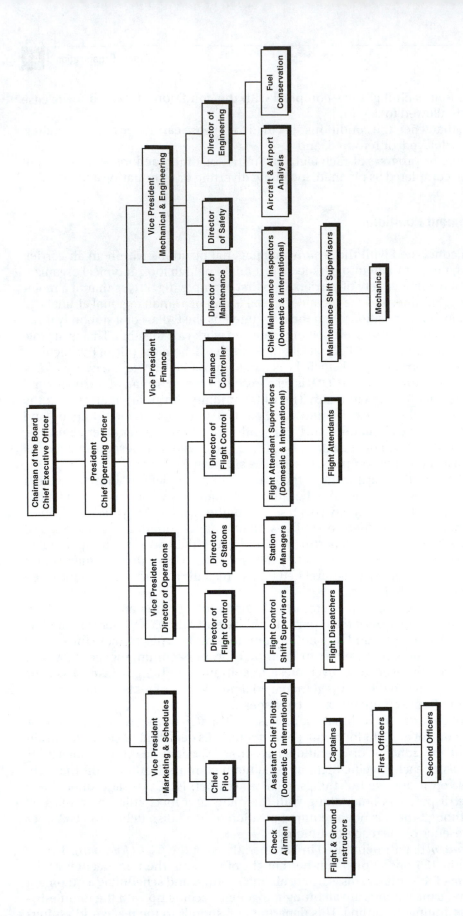

Figure 3.1 Typical organizational arrangement for a major international (flag) airline.

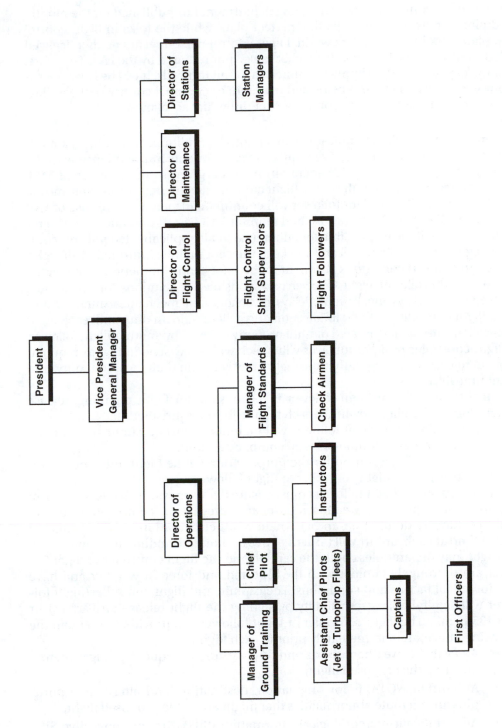

Figure 3.2 Typical organizational arrangement for a small regional airline.

on the nice neat schedules that the scheduling department has published for the month. The scheduling department develops the "perfect plan" while the folks in flight control make that plan work in an imperfect world. Flight control personnel are neither licensed (although they often come from the dispatcher ranks) nor required by the FAA. Therefore, the company may organize this important function to suit its needs. It will be closely scrutinized, however, in its ability to provide and maintain operational control of the airline. Typical flight control/flight following or dispatcher duties are as follows:

- No aircraft will be released unless it is in airworthy condition. However, an aircraft may be released with inoperative or missing components in accordance with the minimum equipment list. Consideration must be given to the number of MEL items in effect on any aircraft so that flight crew management is not compromised.
- The flight controller or flight follower will coordinate dispatch and release of FAR Part 121 or FAR Part 135 operations and monitor FAR Part 91 operations (e.g., ferry flights). They will be responsible for adherence to all applicable federal and company regulations and policies and will keep the captain fully informed of all flight, traffic, and airport conditions pertinent to the safety and completion of the flight.
- The flight controller or flight follower is responsible for solutions for operational problems, caused by cancellations, delays, diversions, and mechanical interruptions.
- Each flight controller or flight follower on duty will remain on duty until each flight released by him has terminated or until properly relieved by another flight follower.
- A flight controller or flight follower will check with crew scheduling, as required prior to releasing any flight, that the flight crew is within their legal rest, duty, and flight time limitations.
- The flight controller or flight follower is responsible for flight planning, release generation, and flight following of each flight within his jurisdiction.
- The flight controller or flight follower will maintain a current summary list of all inoperative or missing components on company aircraft.
- All aircraft departing a station for the purpose of revenue flight, must be authorized by an approved flight controller or flight follower.
- Flight controllers or flight followers must ensure flights may only be released to an airport if the appropriate weather reports and forecasts or combination thereof indicate that the destination and alternate weather conditions at the estimated arrival time at each airport will be at or above authorized landing minimums.
- No flight may depart unless both the captain and the flight controller or flight follower are thoroughly familiar with the reported and forecast weather and have considered all factors and conditions. The captain and flight controller/flight follower will signify their responsibility by signing the flight release for Part 121 or Part 135 flights. The flight controller or flight follower will provide the captain the following information immediately prior to each flight:
  - ➢ All available weather reports and forecasts or subsequent changes thereto affecting the proposed flight,
  - ➢ All current NOTAMs for origination, destination, and alternate airports, plus any en route abnormalities that might affect the proposed flight,
  - ➢ All significant meteorological information (SIGMETs) or convective SIGMETs affecting the proposed route of flight,
  - ➢ Advisories of all anticipated adverse changes in the weather phenomena affecting the proposed flight,
  - ➢ All inoperative or missing components on the aircraft to be flown and any restrictions that may apply. Any irregularities of facilities and services, even though a NOTAM has not been issued,

> Anticipated or known traffic delays,
> Field condition reports and braking action reports that might adversely affect the operation,
> Forecasts or reported icing conditions that exist, including the intensity thereof, and
> Any information not discussed above, but having an adverse effect on a safe operation.

Summary

In this chapter the organizational structure of FAR parts 121 and 135 air carriers has been examined. We've discussed the minimum management positions the FAA requires in order to obtain and maintain a certificate and the experience requirement of personnel filling those positions. In the next chapter we will see the FAA requires a description of the air carrier's operational structure to be contained in the operations manual or the general operating manual.

Important Terms from this Chapter

Active control

Chief executive officer (CEO)

Chief inspector

Chief operating officer (COO)

Chief pilot

Director of maintenance (DM)

Director of operations (DO)

Director of safety

Dispatch

Flight control

Flight following

Operational control

Passive control

Chapter Exam

1. As per the Part 121 requirements found in FAR 119.65, what five specific management positions are required for a Part 121 air carrier?
   a. Director of maintenance, director of quality assurance, chief pilot, director of operations and chief counsel.
   b. Director of safety, director of operations, director of maintenance, chief pilot and chief inspector.
   c. Director of operations, chairman of the board of directors, director of inflight, chief pilot, chief inspector.
   d. Chief pilot, chief inspector, director of maintenance, director of safety and director of inflight.

2. As per the Part 135 requirements found in FAR 119.69, what three specific management positions are required for a Part 135 air carrier?
   a. Director of safety, director of maintenance and chief pilot.
   b. Director of operations, director of safety and director of maintenance.
   c. Director of inspections, chief pilot and director of maintenance.
   d. Director of operations, chief pilot and director of maintenance.

3. What two required management positions, for both Part 121 and Part 135 air carriers,
   must be filled by a pilot holding an air transport pilot certificate (ATP)?
   a. Chief pilot and the chief inspector.
   b. Chief pilot and the director of safety.
   c. Director of operations and the chief pilot.
   d. Chief director and chief pilot.

4. What minimum required management positions must be filled by a mechanic holding an airframe and power plant certificate (A&P)?
   a. Director of maintenance and the chief inspector.
   b. Chief inspector, director of safety and the director of maintenance.
   c. Director of maintenance, director of operations and the chief inspector.
   d. Director of maintenance and the director of safety.

5. What required management position is responsible for the overall *operational control* of an air carrier's flight?
   a. Chief pilot.
   b. Director of operations.
   c. Pilot in command.
   d. Director of inflight.

6. Which department serves to specifically implement the concept of operational
   control?
   a. The dispatch center.
   b. The in-flight center.
   c. The maintenance control center.
   d. The director of operations office.

7. The director of safety is required to hold which FAA certificates?
   a. Air transport pilot certificate (ATP) and airframe and power plant certificate
      (A&P).
   b. ATP only.
   c. A&P only.
   d. None.

8. FAR Part 1 defines *operational control* as?
   a. Ensuring only crewmembers trained and qualified in accordance with the
      applicable regulations are assigned to conduct a flight.
   b. Ensuring each flight has complied with the conditions specified for release
      before it is allowed to depart.
   c. The exercise of authority over initiating, conducting, and terminating a flight.
   d. Designating a pilot in command.

Operating Manuals: Requirement for and Development of

Everything in the company manual—policy, warnings, instructions, the works—can be summed up to read, "Captain, it's your baby."

—Anon.

The FAR seeks to assure that everyone involved in a safety critical function has a detailed description or explanation of how that function is to be performed. That requirement starts with the requirements for the specific management positions, as we discussed previously in chapter 3. Those positions set specific responsibilities upon specific people within the carrier. By doing this, the FAA knows exactly who is accountable for the operational areas of the carrier. The next issue is that of "getting the word out"; this is done by requiring specific manuals to be prepared, distributed, and updated continually. The carrier must do this to comply with both its ops specs and the FARs.

The manual requirements of FAR Part 121 are set forth in Subpart G. The manual requirements of FAR 135 are set forth in FAR 135.21 and FAR 135.23.

Approval of Manuals

The required manuals must be reviewed and approved by the operator's FAA principal operations inspector (POI) or other FAA inspector assigned to the air carrier. The inspector reviews the manuals to determine whether they comply with all current Federal Air Regulations. The inspector also ensures the manuals contain safe operating policies and procedures in enough detail that the operator's personnel can properly carry out the policy or procedure for which he or she is responsible with the *highest degree of safety*.

Manual Requirements: FAR Part 121

FAR 121.131 makes the requirements to prepare and maintain manuals applicable to all Part 121 air carriers. FAR 121.133 sets forth the specific form the manuals must take. First, they must contain, as a minimum, the following major provisions:

- *Flight operations* for flight personnel,
- *Ground operations* for ground service personnel, and
- *Management policy and procedures* for management personnel.

Except for the portion of the manual pertaining to maintenance, these must be in a paper "manual" format. Maintenance manuals *upon specific approval* of the FAA may be in other formats such as microfilm, microfiche or computer. Whether on paper, microfilm, or computer the system used must be approved by the certificate holding FSDO.

FAR 121.135 sets forth items required to be in the manual. 121.135(a)(1) says it all:

Each manual required by 121.133 must
(1)   Include instructions and information necessary to allow the personnel concerned to perform their duties and responsibilities with a high degree of safety.

To do this the FAA reviews the air carrier's operations manual to ensure these instructions contain clear descriptions of the duties and responsibilities for each type of employee group (i.e., mechanic, flight crew, management personnel, etc.).

The FAR also requires the manual be in a form easy to revise, have a date of revision printed on each page, and be consistent with the regulations and the carrier's ops specs. In order for the employee or FAA representative to quickly determine whether the manual is current, each manual should contain a revision control page (fig. 4.1) or similar section. Each revision is numbered, dated, and logged in the revision control page.

The manual must also contain a description of the types and kinds of operations the air carrier is authorized to conduct. In addition, the operations manual must contain information on the authorized areas of en route operations in which the air carrier is approved to operate. This must include the types of aircraft authorized, required flight crew staffing, and specific en route and instrument approach procedures authorizations and requirements.

While the FARs only require the air carrier to produce a single manual, the carrier is permitted to break the manual down into "submanuals." That is, the required information doesn't have to be all in one volume or publication. That would yield an unwieldy publication and work against its general usage. 121.135 (b) sets forth the exact information which must be in each manual or manual part. This includes

(1)   General policies;
(2)   Duties and responsibilities of crewmembers, ground personnel and management;
(3)   Reference to appropriate regulations where applicable;
(4)   Flight dispatching and operational control;
(5)   En route flight, navigation and communications procedures;
(6)   For domestic and flag operations information from the appropriate ops specs;
(7)   For supplemental operations, appropriate information from operations specifications, including area of operations authorized, types of airplanes authorized, type of operation such as VFR, IFR, day, night, etc. authorized;
(8)   Appropriate information from the airport operations specifications which includes
       Airport location,
       Designation as a regular, alternate, or provisional airport,
       Types of airplanes authorized for use,
       Instrument approach procedures,
       Landing and takeoff minimums, and
       Other pertinent information;

Revision Number	Revision Date	Revision Number	Revision Date	Revision Number	Revision Date
1	10 Feb 97				
2	20 Apr 97				
3	3 Sept 97				
4	29 Jan 98				
5	11 May 98				
6	22 DEC 98				
7	1 FEB 99				
8	8 Jun 99				
9	17 Oct 99				
10	7 Mar 00				
11	15 Mar 00				
12	30 Aug 00				
13	9 SEPT 00				
14	1 JAN 01				
15	9 Jan 01				
16	12 Feb 01				
17	15 FEB 01				
18	3 Mar 01				
19					
20					
21					
22					
23					
24					
25					

Sample Revision Control Log

Figure 4.1   Sample revision control log.

(9)   *Takeoff, en route, and landing weight limitations;*
(10) *Procedures for familiarizing passengers with safety equipment in flight;*
(11) *Emergency equipment and procedures;*
(12) *Method for designating succession of command in the event of in flight dis-ability of the captain or other crewmembers;*
(13) *Procedures for determining usability of landing and takeoff areas and for disseminating this information;*
(14) *Procedures for operating in periods of ice, hail, thunderstorms, turbulence, or other potentially hazardous meteorological conditions;*
(15) *Each required training program (see FAR 121.403);*
(16) *Instructions and procedures for maintenance, preventative maintenance, and service;*
(17) *Time limits on aircraft, engines, parts, etc.;*
(18) *Refueling procedures and procedures for assuring a noncontaminated supply of fuel and fire protection during fueling;*
(19) *Airworthiness inspections of the aircraft including responsibilities for performing the inspections;*
(20) *Methods and procedures for determining the weight and balance of each aircraft;*
(21) *Pilot and dispatcher route qualifications (where applicable);*
(22) *Accident notification procedures;*
(23) *Hazardous material (HAZMAT) procedures; and*
(24) *Other information or procedures relating to safety.*

FAR 121.135

An air carrier will typically develop a series of manuals tailored to its particular needs covering this information and more. The FAA allows wide latitude in the organization of an air carrier's manuals. Some common manual titles in use at many air carriers are described below.

The Airplane Flight Manual

The ***airplane flight manual*** (AFM) is prepared by the manufacturer and approved by the FAA Aircraft Certification Office. FAR 121.141 requires an AFM to be carried aboard the aircraft at all times. The AFM is designed to give the crew all of the operational and performance information it needs in order to operate the aircraft. Note that this manual requirement is separate and distinct from the operations manual required in FAR 121.133, although FAR 121.141 does allow for all of the information to be placed in one book. It is, as we've discussed, far more common for carriers to give the flight crews two separate manuals along with approach and en route procedure charts. These two manuals would be the flight operations manual (FOM) required in FAR 121.133 and the airplane flight manual (AFM) required in FAR 121.141. The AFM includes the necessary information on aircraft systems, aircraft limitations, specific procedures (e.g., normal and abnormal checklists), techniques, and operating methods by which a specific aircraft should be operated.

The Company Flight Manual

An air carrier may choose to develop an FAA approved ***company flight manual*** (CFM). This is simply an AFM developed by, or for, a specific operator. An air carrier may carry an approved CFM in place of an AFM. The CFM must, however, contain at a minimum all of the procedures required by the AFM and must include enough procedural details to allow a flight crew to operate the aircraft to the highest level of safety.

General Operations Manual

The general operations manual (GOM) is prepared by the air carrier and includes flight operations material not related specifically to a particular aircraft's operation. FAR 121.135 specifies topics that must be addressed in the air carrier's GOM. The GOM contains clear descriptions of the types of operations the air carrier is authorized to conduct. The GOM includes information such as policies, procedures, and guidance necessary for flight operations personnel to perform their duties with the highest degree of safety. The information in this manual is not aircraft or fleet specific but covers the entire airline operation. Information and policies pertaining to passenger handling, the carriage of dangerous goods, safety training, and general company "housekeeping" information (i.e., employee appearance standards, jumpseat policy, and important company phone numbers) can all be found in the GOM. When the air carrier operates a wide variety of aircraft types the FAA prefers the flight operations procedures common to all of the air carrier's aircraft be published in the GOM as opposed to a particular aircraft's company flight manual.

General Maintenance Manual

The general *maintenance manual* (GMM) is prepared by the air carrier or aircraft manufacturer and covers the airworthiness information for a particular model of aircraft. The GMM contains policies and procedures for an air carrier's technical operations organization (i.e., mechanics, inspectors, and engineering support personnel) so they may provide safe and reliable aircraft, power plants, and other components for daily flight operations.

Access and Distribution of Manuals

In order to facilitate the FAA's ability to inspect an air carrier, each carrier must keep at least one complete copy of the manual(s) at its principal base of operations [121.135(c)]. These manuals must be complete and current at all times. The manuals are to be used by the FAA to review any procedures or incidents at the carrier. In addition to these copies, the carrier must set up a publication and distribution system that assures each employee who may require the information in the manual either has a manual or has access to the manual. This distribution system must be spelled out, indicating exactly who has to physically possess a manual (pilots, for example, must have a flight operations manual, while mechanics must have a maintenance manual available to them while performing their work).

FAR 121.137(a) states that the carrier must distribute the manual and its updates to appropriate ground operations and maintenance personnel and flight crewmembers. The carrier must also furnish a complete manual (or collection of manuals) to the specific representatives of the FAA assigned to that carrier.

FAR 121.137(b) then further requires each person assigned to hold a manual must keep it up to date with the changes and additions and have it accessible while performing his or her assigned duties.

In the case of the maintenance manuals, these are very often kept in some type of storage retrieval system such as microfilm, microfiche, or computer files. Given the detail of the maintenance diagrams and instructions, this is really the only feasible way to do this. FAR 121.137(c) provides specific relief to the carrier to develop an alternative means of distributing the maintenance manual. It only requires approval of the Administrator (which, practically speaking, means the principal maintenance inspector (PMI) or MI assigned to the carrier).

In the case of supplemental carriers, since by the nature of their operations they don't operate to the same locations on a repetitive basis, FAR 121.139 requires them to have a copy of the entire manual aboard the aircraft for use by the contract personnel at those locations. Further, if the carrier maintains the maintenance manual in a form other than a paper manual, it must carry an appropriate reading device with the aircraft. This assures that the personnel at remote locations will have the ability to read all parts of the manuals when performing their tasks.

Manual Requirements: FAR Part 135

FAR 135.21 makes the requirements to prepare and maintain manuals applicable to all Part 135 air carriers *except those employing only one pilot*. FAR 135.23 sets forth the specific form the manuals must take. First, they must contain, as a minimum, the following major provisions:

- *Flight operations* for flight personnel,
- *Ground operations* for ground service personnel, and
- *Maintenance procedures* for maintenance personnel.

The requirements for preparing and distributing the manual are very similar to those required by FAR 121 except that the regulations recognize that the size of the operation may be so limited that safety may be met by allowing some other method of distributing the manuals. By and large, the manual design and preparation will be the same for the 121 and 135 manuals.

FAR 135.23 also spells out the specific contents of the manual. While these requirements are similar to those in FAR 121, there are some differences. Most significant is the reliance on the pilot in command to perform many different functions. The small size of many Part 135 air carriers dictates the pilot in command must wear many different "hats" (e.g., flight attendant, flight dispatcher, maintenance coordinator, etc.). The manual must contain

(a) *The name, address, and responsibilities of each required management employee,*
(b) *Procedures for ensuring compliance with weight and balance limitations,*
(c) *Copies of the ops specs or appropriate extracted information,*
(d) *Procedures for complying with accident notification requirements,*
(e) *Procedures ensuring the pilot can ascertain that the aircraft airworthiness inspections have been complied with and the aircraft has been returned to service,*
(f) *Procedures for reporting and recording mechanical irregularities,*
(g) *Procedures for the pilot in command to determine that the mechanical irregularities have been corrected or deferred,*

(h)   Procedures for the pilot in command to secure maintenance or service at a place where no prior arrangements have been made,

(i)   Procedures under FAR 135.179 for the release for or continuation of a flight in the case of inoperable equipment,

(j)   Procedures for refueling and assuring noncontamination of fuel,

(k)   Procedures for the pilot in command to follow for the passenger in flight briefing,

(l)   Flight locating procedures,

(m)   Procedures for ensuring compliance with emergency procedures,

(n)   En route qualification procedures,

(o)   The approved aircraft inspection program (if any),

(p)   HAZMAT procedures,

(q)   Emergency evacuation procedures for those who may need assistance, and

(r)   Other procedures as issued by the certificate holder.

FAR 135.23

Operational Control

In reviewing the requirements for an air carrier's operating manual, the FAA wants to see that a carrier's operational control procedures are included. Remember FAR 1.1 defines *operational control* as "the exercise of authority over initiating, conducting, and terminating a flight." The FAA requires the air carrier's operating manual to make certain the procedures, duties, and responsibilities of pilots and operational control personnel are thoroughly described. The FAA also requires the general operating manual to include flight dispatching or flight-following procedures as discussed in chapter 3. Specifically, the FAA requires policies for handling late flights, adverse weather conditions, and procedures for discontinuing a flight when confronted with unsafe conditions to be clearly described in the air carrier's general operating manual. Finally, the operations manual must describe the relationship between flight dispatchers, maintenance coordinators, crew schedulers, and flight crew.

Summary

In this chapter we've discussed the manual requirements set forth in 121.133 and 135.21. That is, the FAA requirement that each operator prepare and keep current a general operations manual or series of manuals containing guidance for use by ground and flight personnel during the conduct of the air carrier's operations. These manuals must be in a form easy to revise and be consistent with the regulations and the carrier's ops specs. Finally, each carrier must keep at least one complete copy of the manual(s) at its principal base of operations.

Important Terms from this Chapter

Airplane flight manual	Maintenance manual
Company flight manual	Management policy and procedures
Flight operations	Operational control
Ground operations	

Chapter 4 Exam

1. What manuals are required to be carried aboard an air carrier aircraft operated under Part 121?

2. What manuals are required to be carried aboard a Part 121 air carrier aircraft in supplemental operations?

3. What manuals are required to be carried aboard an air carrier aircraft operated under Part 135?

4. What parts of the manual are required to be in a paper format?

5. When is a Part 121 or Part 135 air carrier required to carry a maintenance manual onboard the aircraft?

6. When is a Part 121 supplemental air carrier required to carry a maintenance manual onboard the aircraft?

FAR 121 Subpart M: Airman and Crewmember Requirements

You can always tell when a man has lost his soul to flying. The poor bastard is hopelessly committed to stopping whatever he is doing long enough to look up and make sure the aircraft purring overhead continues on course and does not suddenly fall out of the sky. It is his bound duty to watch every aircraft within view take off and land.

—Ernest Gann
Fate Is the Hunter

We now turn our attention to the requirements FAA places on Part 121 carriers in regard to mandatory staffing for certain safety critical functions. These provisions are primarily intended to ensure standardization in company operations as they relate to the various activities of operating complex, transport aircraft.

FAR 121.381 covers applicability and is really quite simple: this subpart applies to all Part 121 carriers, no exceptions.

Next, in 121.383 the FAA sets forth common sense rules that provide that if a position requires that the person filling it have a particular certificate then the carrier is responsible for assuring that the person actually has the required certificate and that it is current for performing the tasks required of that crewmember or airman. What positions require an airman certificate?

- Cockpit crewmembers,
- Dispatchers, and
- Mechanics.

A certificated airman must fill each of these positions. Note that flight attendants are not certificated, although as we will later see, they do require training.

The airman or crewmember must also carry these certificates on his or her person while engaged in operations (performing the tasks) that require the certificate [121.383(a.2)]. In addition, he or she must be qualified for the operation for which he or she is to be used. What does this mean? Simply that all required training, qualification, and recentness of experience requirements have been met. The FAA has the right to assure that all personnel are properly certificated, so 121.383(b) requires the airman to present any required certificate(s) to representatives of the Administrator.

While we are here, let's take a look at the ***age 60 rule.*** Probably one of the most contentious provisions in all of the FARs is found in 121.383(c). This rule, quite simply, prohibits the use of pilots in Part 121 operations after they reach the age of 60 years old. Depending on where you are in your career, this is either the greatest thing since sliced bread or the most onerous rule on the books. Airline management and younger pilots are typically in favor of the age 60 rule. Management likes the rule in part because it ensures pilot seats are filled by more junior (read *lower paid*) pilots. Younger pilots tend to like it because it creates movement in the seniority list. Older pilots, on the other hand, see themselves being forced out of their profession right at their peak. They see other professionals just hitting their stride at age 60 and being allowed, as required by federal law, to work to at least age 70. Pilots, however, are gone upon reaching their sixtieth birthday. Invest wisely!

Prior to March 20, 1997, the age 60 rule only affected pilots for 121 air carriers. Pilots flying for 135 operators were allowed to fly until they could no longer pass an FAA medical exam. Some retiring pilots for 121 carriers decided to continue flying for a 135 airline, with a few flying till nearly 70 years of age. Then the 1990s saw explosive growth of large regional Part 135 scheduled air carriers. As an ever increasing percentage of airline passengers began flying these 135 carriers it exposed what was seen by many as a large gap in the level of safety offered by the 135 operators and that offered by Part 121 carriers. Following an intense lobbying effort by pilot unions and consumer protection associations, the FAA mandated "one level of safety" regulations, forcing a large number of 135 operators to comply with 121 regulations. The 135 operators affected were those who conduct scheduled passenger-carrying operation with

- Nontransport category turboprop aircraft with 10-19 seats,
- Transport category turboprop aircraft with 20-40 seats, and/or turbojet aircraft with 30 seats or less, and/or
- Turbojet powered aircraft having a seating configuration of less than 30 seats.

This forced just about all scheduled regional or commuter airlines to transition from 135 to 121 regulations. With the transition to 121 regulations came the phased implementation of the age 60 rule for these carriers; by December 20, 1999, compliance with 121.383(c) became mandatory.

It is still possible to be a Part 121 cockpit crewmember because 121.383(c) only applies to the pilot positions. Flight engineers are allowed to continue past their sixtieth birthday. Many airlines allow pilots who have reached 60 years of age to bid the flight engineer's position. These pilots are affectionately known as "double-down bidders" or ROPs (pronounced ropes), for *R*etired *O*n the *P*anel. Many pilots have taken advantage of this opportunity to continue working, although typically for a large reduction in salary. Unfortunately for these pilots, the next decade will see the retirement of virtually all aircraft requiring a flight engineer, and this will end the ability of over-60 pilots to be a cockpit crewmember for a 121 carrier.

Composition of Flight Crews Part 121

To really understand the rules in Subpart M regarding **composition of flight crews,** you need to know a little of the historical background of why we staff airplanes as we do. In the early days of commercial aviation (1920s and early 1930s), airline equipment was flown single pilot (often out in the rain, but that's another story). With the advent of the first generation all metal airliners (DC-3) in the mid 1930s, designers built the cockpits around two **pilots.** Tradition held that the captain was a virtual god on the airplane and the copilot not much more than a flunky to assist with unpleasant tasks like loading bags and assisting boarding. It was a number of years before operators of this class of equipment really incorporated their copilots into the operation in any meaningful way.

With the development of more complex transport equipment (e.g., the Douglas DC-4 and DC-6 and the Lockheed Constellations), the copilot became more integral in the operations. These aircraft were much more complicated, and the designs pretty much required the involvement of both crewmembers in the successful and safe operations of the airplanes. By the end of the World War II period, two pilot operations were pretty well accepted on the world's airlines. Then tragedy struck.

The DC-6s were originally built for two pilot crews. However, a series of accidents in the immediate postwar period highlighted a fact that later would be part of the concept of crew resource management philosophy. The review of these accidents revealed that when mechanical problems occurred on flight decks of two-member-crew airliners of the DC-6's complexity, the crew quickly became involved in trying to solve the mechanical/systems problems and that seriously distracted the pilots from their primary tasks of flying the airplane safely. The response to this was to require *flight engineers* for the DC-6 series of aircraft and later certificated aircraft of a similar size, weight, and complexity. Beginning in the late 1940s all four-engine aircraft and larger aircraft were required to have flight engineers during "overwater" operations and when the gross weight of an aircraft exceeded 80,000 pounds.

The early jets (Boeing 707, Douglas DC-8, Convair 880, Boeing 727) all were certificated with three person crews—two pilots and one flight engineer. This was taken as standard until Douglas sought to certificate its DC-9-10 aircraft. During development of this *light jet* Douglas sought to deliberately keep the gross weight under that (80,000 lb.) which had been placed as the threshold for requiring flight engineers to be part of the crew. Initially the ramp weight of the DC-9-10 was to be 78,500 pounds; however, during the final development of the DC-9-10 the ramp weight topped out at well over 80,000 pounds. Douglas successfully lobbied the government to discard the 80,000 pound, three pilot limit during certification of the DC-9-10. The DC-9 was then successfully certificated for only two pilots in 1965. This began a long period of discussion and fighting between the airlines and their pilot unions over the acceptability of a very complex aircraft being flown with two pilot crews. Many unions simply refused to fly it. Delta Air Lines was one of the first companies to get its union (ALPA) to accept the two pilot concept. The DC-9-10 began service with Delta in February of 1965. Once that wall came down in 1965 Boeing also sought certification of a two pilot jet. Their model, the Boeing 737, was based on the overall fuselage of the B-707/727 series of aircraft but included substantially improved flight controls and automation. Boeing argued that the weight of the aircraft was irrelevant as to whether two or three crewmembers operated the aircraft. Rather, Boeing argued, the determining factor should be the complexity of operations and whether two or three crewmembers were required for safe operations. After a protracted period of hostility between the union and the companies (some B-737s were actually delivered with a "Flight Engineer" position, although there was little for the flight engineer to do!), the 737s were certificated with a two member crew. At least one airline had a catchy name for the third 737 crewmember; he was called a "GIB" or *Guy in Back*.

Since the late 1960s, each aircraft has been certificated on its own merit, not by an arbitrary weight limitation. The last three member crew aircraft certificated in the United States were the three widebodies delivered in the early 1970s. These include the B-747 Classic (100/200 models), the Lockheed L-1011, and the Douglas DC-10. All aircraft certificated in the United States since then have been with a two pilot (no flight engineer) crew.

Now, with that backdrop, 121.385–121.389 make sense. 121.385 says for all Part 121 operations the operations must be conducted with two pilots. Further, the company must designate one pilot as pilot in command and the other as second in command. If the aircraft certification requires a flight engineer, you can't use one person as both a pilot and the flight engineer. If a FE is required, the crew is then at least three people. Finally, 121.385(d) spells out the requirements for backup positions. If the airplane certificate requires a flight engineer, then one of the other crewmembers must be trained to perform the emergency functions of the flight engineer. This provision specifically does not require the other person to be qualified in the position, merely trained in performing the functions of the position.

Composition of Flight Crews Part 135

The composition of flight crew for 135 operators is covered in 135.99(a) and states the minimum required flight crew component is ultimately determined by the approved aircraft operating limitations or aircraft flight manual. However, a two pilot minimum flight crew requirement for all aircraft with 10 or more passenger seats is mandated by 135.99(b). In other words, for aircraft with 10 or more passenger seats you must have a pilot in command and a pilot who is second in command. For aircraft with less than 10 passenger seats it is legal under certain circumstances to fly with only one pilot. An aircraft equipped with less than 10 passenger seats may be flown under Part 135 without a second in command under the following conditions:

- The aircraft is equipped with an operative approved autopilot system and the use of that system is authorized by the appropriate operations specifications [135.105(a)].
- The pilot in command must have at least 100 hours PIC time in the make and model of aircraft to be flown and have met all other applicable requirements of this part[135.105(a)].
- The certificate holder must apply for an amendment of its operation specifications to authorize the use of an autopilot system in place of a second in command [135.105(b.1)].
- The certificate holder demonstrates, to the satisfaction of the Administrator, that operations using the autopilot system can be conducted safely and in compliance with this part [135.105(b.2)].
- The aircraft is not operated in a Category II operation (135.111).

Flight Navigator

Forget about it. *Flight navigators* haven't been used on U.S. commercial airliners in years. As far back as the mid 1970s TWA was down to one navigator who worked in management. 121.389 provides two alternatives for operating. A company may use a navigator or *specialized navigation equipment*. This is the provision under which virtually all aircraft are operated. The cost considerations make it much more efficient to invest several million dollars per aircraft in specialized navigation equipment and not have the recurring costs of labor of real, live navigators. Interestingly, some pilot contracts still pay "navigation pay" to the pilots. When the navigators came off airliners beginning in the late 1950s, some pilot unions were able to negotiate that since the pilots were doing the navigation (using the specialized navigation equipment), they should be paid extra for performing the task.

Flight Attendants

FAA wants *flight attendants* aboard the aircraft primarily to assist passengers in emergencies. Their presence is particularly important in helping with emergency evacuation of the aircraft. Since they are aboard the flight the whole time, the airlines have developed the position into one that is perceived as primarily customer service. 121.391 provides minimum staffing levels of flight attendants for 121 carriers. Part 135 staffing levels are briefly addressed in 135.107 and state simply that aircraft having seating configurations of more than 19 seats must have a flight attendant crewmember on board the aircraft. These minimums have nothing to do with customer service. They are there to assure safety standards can be met in emergency situations.

The formula for *flight attendant minimum staffing levels* is quite simple:

From 9 seats to 19 seats	
(less or equal to 7,500 lb. payload capacity)	0 flight attendants
(more than 7,500 lb. payload capacity)	1 flight attendant
From 20 to 50 seats	1 flight attendant
From 51 to 100	2 flight attendants
Over 100 seats	1 additional flight attendant for each unit (or part of a unit) of 50 seats

Note that 121.391 covers *seating capacity*, not passengers. So if an aircraft is certificated with 127 seats, but only 43 passengers are aboard this flight, how many flight attendants are required? Three are required for the 127 seating capacity.

When a manufacturer designs and certificates a new model of aircraft with more than 44 seats, it must demonstrate to the FAA that it can do an emergency evacuation of the airplane in 90 seconds. This is demonstrated with a "generic" airplane. However, FAR 121.291 also requires that *each airline* must do an *emergency evacuation demonstration* as well. This is to prove that the airline can evacuate its aircraft as configured by that airline in 90 seconds or less. Installed equipment, seating configurations, and so forth may hinder the evacuation, so the airline must demonstrate its ability. 121.391(b) states that if the carrier had to put on flight attendants in excess of the formula discussed above in order to meet the evacuation tests, then the increased number becomes the minimum number of flight attendants required for that airline. This is so important that 121.391(c) requires that the number of extra flight attendants required must be set forth in the carrier's ops specs.

We'll see in chapter 7 that the flight attendant duty period limitations also affect required staffing. For example, a flight attendant's duty period is normally limited to a scheduled duty day of 14 hours. This, however, may be extended to between 14 and 16 hours if the carrier assigns an extra flight attendant to the flight; 16 to 18 hours if the carrier assigns two extra flight attendants to the flight; and 18 to 20 hours if three extra flight attendants are assigned to the flight.

121.391(d) sets forth the requirements that flight attendants be located near the emergency exits and that during taxi flight attendants must be in their seats with belts and harnesses fastened except as necessary to carry out duties related to the safety of the aircraft and its occupants.

Passengers on Board: Through Stops

FAA is concerned about the safety of passengers on the aircraft at any time, not just the time the aircraft is under way. For this reason, when passengers remain aboard the aircraft at through stations someone must be nearby and available to assist the passengers in an emergency evacuation, if required. Normally, this will be a flight attendant. If the full complement (minimum number required for dispatch) of flight attendants remains aboard, then passengers may be boarded or deplaned with the engine running. What if the stopover is also a crew change station? That is, the passengers are continuing on to another destination and are not deplaning but the flight attendants are laying over, completing a trip, or are assigned to another flight. In this case, during boarding and deplaning of through flights, either the full complement of flight attendants must remain onboard or, alternatively and with limitations, one-half the FAA minimum number of flight attendants (rounded down, minimum one) required for dispatch must be onboard the aircraft (see table 5.1).

Also, 121.393 allows that instead of a flight attendant, a non–flight attendant may be available on board to assist in emergencies. If the aircraft does not require flight attendants [as a result of 121.391(a)], or the carrier chooses, it may substitute a non–flight attendant (e.g., station gate agent) to perform these evacuation duties. That person must be qualified (trained) in emergency evacuation procedures, must be identified to the passengers, and must be on or nearby the aircraft. In addition, the engines must be shut down and at least one floor level door must remain open to provide a route for deplaning.

Note that the responsibility of each person who is assigned a task in the emergency evacuation plan must be spelled out in the manual provided to the crews. This assignment of tasks must consider issues such as what happens if a crewmember is incapacitated or can't reach a portion of the cabin.

Table 5.1. Flight attendant staffing requirements
(information courtesy of Delta Air Lines)

Aircraft Type (Seat Capacity)	Number of Flight Attendants Required For	
	Minimum Dispatch	En Route Stopovers
B-727 (138)	3	1
B-737-200/300/700 (109-128)	3	1
B737-800 (Shuttle 156)	4	2
B-737-800 (154)	4	2
B-757 (183)	4	2
B-767-200 (204)	5	2
B-767-300 (252)	6	2
B-767-300ER (195)	5	2
B-767-400 (289)	8	3
B-777 (279)	8	4
MD-11 (268)	8	3
MD-88/90 (142/150)	3	1
B-737 (Delta Express 119)	3	1

Dispatchers

As discussed in chapter 3, an aircraft dispatcher is an individual holding an FAA aircraft dispatcher certificate. Part 121 flag and domestic operators must employ aircraft *dispatchers* who exercise certain operational control functions over an air carrier's flight.

These functions include the flight planning of each specific flight and maintaining communications with the flight at all times to keep its flight crew apprised of things such as weather, NOTAMs, operational limitations, and so on. Air carriers must ensure these aircraft dispatchers are supplied with the necessary information to plan, conduct, and control flight operations. 121 supplemental and 135 operators are not required to use FAA certified aircraft dispatchers. Each Part 121 carrier conducting either domestic or flag operations must provide enough qualified aircraft dispatchers to ensure proper operational control over each flight (121.395).

Emergency Evacuation Duties

To complete 121 Subpart M, we'll visit emergency evacuation duties covered in 121.397. Simply put, an air carrier must, for each type and model of airplane, make sure every required crewmember is assigned specific duties to be performed in an emergency or a situation requiring emergency evacuation. These FAA approved duties must be described in the air carrier's operations specifications and approved by the FAA. Finally the air carrier must demonstrate that these duties are *realistic, can be practically accomplished, and will meet any reasonably anticipated emergency including the possible incapacitation of individual crewmembers or their inability to reach the passenger cabin because of shifting cargo in combination cargo-passenger airplanes.*

Summary

In this chapter we have seen what airmen and crewmembers are required for FAR 121 operations. We must have certificated airmen including pilots, copilots, and if required by the aircraft type certificate, flight engineers aboard the aircraft. Flight attendants are required to be aboard the aircraft in minimum numbers, but they are not certificated airmen. The number required to evacuate all occupants of the aircraft in 90 seconds or less determines the minimum staffing level of flight attendants. Additionally, certificated airmen are required to fill positions of dispatchers (except for supplemental carriers) and mechanics. Pilots are limited by regulation to working only until their sixtieth birthday, while there is no limit on other airman certificates including flight engineers.

Important Terms from this Chapter

Age 60 rule

Composition of flight crews

Dispatchers

Emergency evacuation demonstration

Flight attendant minimum staffing levels

Flight attendants

Flight engineers

Flight navigators

Pilots

Specialized navigation equipment

Chapter 5 Exam

1. What positions in an air carrier require an FAA airman's certificate?
   a. Captain, first officer and flight follower.
   b. Flight crew, flight attendants, mechanics.
   c. Cockpit crewmembers, dispatchers, mechanics.
   d. Captain, chief executive officer, dispatchers.

2. Which air carrier personnel are required to carry a FAA Airman's Certificate on his/her person when performing the tasks which require the certificate?
   a. Cockpit crewmembers, flight attendants, and mechanics.
   b. Mechanics, captains, first officers, head flight attendant, and dispatchers.
   c. Cockpit crewmembers, mechanics, and dispatchers.
   d. Cockpit crewmembers, dispatchers, and chief operating officer.

3. The mandatory retirement age for all required cockpit crewmembers is?
   a. No person may serve as a cockpit crewmember on an airplane engaged in operations under Part 121 if that person has reached his/her sixtieth birthday.
   b. No person may serve as a pilot on an airplane engaged in operation under Part 121 if that person has reached his/her sixty-second birthday.
   c. No person may serve as a pilot on an airplane engaged in operations under Part 121 if that person has reached his/her sixtieth birthday.
   d. No person may serve as a flight engineer on an airplane engaged in operations under Part 121 if that person has reached his/her sixtieth birthday.

4. What is the minimum pilot crew operating under Part 121?
   a. 1
   b. 2
   c. 3
   d. 4

5. What is the minimum pilot crew operating under Part 135 in a Category II operation?
   a. 1
   b. 2
   c. 3
   d. 4

6. Which is an untrue statement?
   a. An aircraft, equipped with less than 10 passenger seats, may be flown under Part 135 without a second in command if the aircraft is equipped with an operative and approved autopilot system and the use of that system is authorized by the appropriate operations specifications.
   b. An aircraft, equipped with less than 10 passenger seats, may be flown under Part 135 without a second in command if the certificate holder applies for an amendment of its operation specifications authorizing the use of an autopilot system in place of a second in command.
   c. An aircraft, equipped with less than 10 passenger seats, may be flown under Part 135 without a second in command if the certificate holder can supply proof of insurance for such 135 operations.
   d. An aircraft, equipped with less than 10 passenger seats, may be flown under Part 135 without a second in command if the pilot in command has at least 100 hours PIC time in the make and model of aircraft to be flown and has met all other applicable 135 requirements.

7. If an aircraft is certificated with 149 seats, but only 99 passengers are aboard for a particular flight, how many flight attendants are required?
    a. 2
    b. 3
    c. 4
    d. 5

8. If an aircraft is certificated with 275 seats, but only 249 passengers are aboard for a particular flight, how many flight attendants are required?
    a. 7
    b. 6
    c. 5
    d. 4

9. How many flight attendants are required for an aircraft that has a payload capacity of less than 7,500 pounds and is equipped with 19 passenger seats?
    a. 3
    b. 2
    c. 1
    d. 0

10. During boarding and deplaning of originating and terminating flights, the FAA requires how many flight attendants be onboard the aircraft?
    a. Two less flight attendants than the minimum number of flight attendants required for dispatch.
    b. One less flight attendant than the minimum number of flight attendants required for dispatch.
    c. The FAA minimum number of flight attendants required for dispatch must be onboard the aircraft during boarding and deplaning.
    d. The FAA minimum number of flight attendants required for a stopover must be onboard during boarding and deplaning.

chapter

6

FAR 121 Subpart N: Training Programs and FAR 121 Subpart O: Crewmember Qualifications

What can you conceive more silly and extravagant than to suppose a man racking his brains, and studying night and day how to fly?

—William Law
A Serious Call to a Devout and Holy Life XI, 1728

The FARs impose very stringent regulations in order to assure the highest duty to care by air carriers on the training airmen, crewmembers, and others must receive. In addition, a complex set of proficiency checking and recurrent training requirements are imposed on air carriers. We now turn our attention to what these two subparts of the FAR require of air carriers.

121 Subpart N: Training Programs

FAR 121 Subpart N defines the type of training programs that are required of 121 carriers, the requirements for the instructors and check airmen to be used in the program, and program specific syllabi for the various types of training that are required. 121.400 makes the training program requirements applicable to all Part 121 air carriers and defines a number of terms which are used in the training regulations. Some of these important terms are covered below.

For the purpose of the training regulations, airplanes are broken down into three categories. These categories are reciprocating powered (piston propeller driven) airplanes, turbopropeller airplanes, and pure jet airplanes. The first two categories *(piston and turboprop)* are *Group I airplanes,* and the last category *(jet aircraft)* are *Group II airplanes.* These definitions will be important in determining what specific training is required and the minimum (or programmed) hours of instruction required for various types of required training.

121.400 goes on to define some of the different types of training found in Part 121. These include

- *Initial training* is the training required for crewmembers and dispatchers who have not qualified and served in the same capacity on another airplane of the same group.
- *Transition training* is the training required for crewmembers and dispatchers who have qualified and served in the same capacity on another airplane in the same group.

- *Upgrade training* is the training required for crewmembers who have qualified and served as second in command or flight engineer on a particular airplane type, before they serve as pilot in command or second in command, respectively, on that airplane.
- *Differences training* is the training required for crewmembers and dispatchers who have qualified and served on a particular type airplane when the FAA determines that additional training is necessary before a crewmember serves in the same capacity on a particular variation of that airplane.
- *Requalification training* is the training required for crewmembers previously trained and qualified, but who have become unqualified due to not having had the recurrent training required under FAR 121.427 or not having taken the proficiency check required by FAR 121.441.

Carriers are required by FAR 121.401 to establish training programs that provide all of the training and checking required by *FAR 121 appendices E and F*. These appendices are quite interesting, especially to the pilot or flight engineer, in that they lay out exactly what material must be trained, how it is to be trained (e.g., simulator, flight training device, or airplane) and who must receive what training. Any pilot that is embarking on 121 training (especially initial training) should review appendix E to see what will be required in the training program. Other types of training required include

- *Flight attendant training.* FAR 121.401 doesn't just apply to pilots and flight engineers. Dispatchers are specifically named here in 121.401. Flight attendants are included by use of the term "crewmembers" as opposed to "flight crewmembers," and their training is spelled out in FAR 121.421 and 121.427.
- *HAZMAT training.* In addition, anyone who is assigned duties for the carriage of hazardous or magnetic materials must be trained in *HAZMAT* procedures {see FAR 121.433a [be careful, 121.433a is not the same reference as 121.433(a). This is an odd FAR reference that is nonstandard!]}. This training is included as part of other training courses so as to assure that all applicable employees have received training in marking, identifying, handling, and storing hazardous materials.
- *Recurrent training* ensures each crewmember or dispatcher is adequately trained and currently proficient with respect to the type of airplane s/he is crewing or dispatching (FAR 121.427).
- *Crew resource management (CRM) training/dispatcher resource management (DRM) training.* FAR 121.404 requires that each crewmember or dispatcher receive crew or dispatcher resource management training. CRM/DRM training focuses on the interrelationships between crewmembers, dispatch, maintenance, FAA, and other agencies. It is especially designed to help crewmembers learn to communicate effectively and to use all available resources when dealing with in flight problems or emergencies.

The training programs are required to keep meticulous records to show that all required persons have been trained in accord with the training program. These records are used for many purposes. First, they are used to show compliance with required training program content. That is, they show that the syllabus of training was followed. Next they show that the crewmember, dispatcher, or other required person has actually received the training in the required time frame.

On that point, by the way, notice that FAR 121.401(b) allows the actual recurrent training or proficiency check accomplishment date to be a month early or a month late and still count as having been accomplished as required. For example, if you (a second-in-command pilot) completed your initial training on a piece of equipment last July, you would be due recurrent training, by virtue of 121.433(c), this July. The FAR recognizes that this may be highly impractical or impossible. Due to scheduling problems, operating requirements, simulator availability, and so forth, the carrier simply may not be able to schedule you for recurrent training this July. July is referred to as your *base month*. FAR 121.401 (b) allows the training to be accomplished a month before the base month, during the base month, or in the month after the base month. These months are sometimes called *base month early* or *grace month late*.

Note well: There is a big trap waiting for you here! What happens if you were due in July, but for the reasons given above, the carrier assigns you to an August recurrent training class (say, August 28 and 29) and you continue flying your August schedule, which is allowed by operation of 121.401(b)? Come August 27 you become quite ill with flu and can't leave your house for a week. At the end of that week (early September) are you legal to fly? Clearly you are not because you have not completed your recurrent training during your base month or *grace month*. That is the easy part. Now, what about your August flying? Was it legal? Well, it was while you were doing it in the month of August. By operation of FAR 121.401(b) you could continue to fly. However, and this is a *big* however, once August passed without your having completed the required recurrent training, any flying you did in August has become illegal. If flying takes you into the grace month, it is imperative that you and the carrier assure that the training is completed in that grace month.

Conduct of Training

Part 121 training can only be conducted by one of two entities. To conduct required training, the company must either be a certificate holder or hold a FAR 142 Flight Training Certificate. If either another certificate holder or a FAR 142 certificate holder is to conduct the training, the FAA must authorize this. FAR 121.402 allows this training to be contracted out as described.

Curriculum

FAA requires that the training program be well structured and approved. FAR 121.403 sets forth the requirements for the certificate holder to prepare and keep current a training *curriculum* for each type of airplane and each crewmember or dispatcher. This curriculum must specify things such as the content of the course, the training devices and pictorials to be used, the maneuvers to be taught, and the number of *programmed hours* (or *reduced programmed hours*) [see 121.400(c)(5)] which are approved.

Approval of the training program is required and the requirements for that are set forth in FAR 121.405. Each program must receive initial approval from the FAA before it may be used in a certificate holder's operation. After the program has been implemented and is being executed, the FAA reviews it and notes any deficiencies in the program. These deficiencies must then be corrected once they are brought to the carrier's attention.

Training Facilities

Carriers are required to have adequate ground and flight training facilities for the conduct of training. There must be enough flight and simulator instructors and check airmen to do the required work [FAR 121.401(a)(2)]. Any training devices or simulators that are used as part of the course of training by virtue of 121.409 or are allowed in checking/training activities found in Subpart O or appendices E or F must be specifically approved both as to the device and as to the course (FAR 121.407).

Furthermore, note that 121.407(c) allows an approved simulator to be used to meet the *in flight* training requirements for both the airplane recency of experience requirements of 121.439 and the proficiency check requirements of 121.441. In other words, with an approved simulator these elements of training need not be performed in the aircraft. But 121.407 goes even further. In 121.407(d) the FAA *requires* that the **low altitude windshear flight training program** be conducted in a simulator and not in an aircraft. This is not only because it is virtually impossible to simulate these conditions but also because to do so would be extremely dangerous in an airplane.

A carrier may have a training course for performing the proficiency checks under 121.144. This course may utilize flight simulators or flight training devices. The carrier must design the course so that it includes at least 4 hours of training at the pilot controls of the airplane simulator as well as proper preflight and postflight briefings. The course may be designed either to perform the training required by Appendix F or may be used to provide **line oriented flight training (LOFT)**. The requirements for these programs are listed in 121.409. Notice that 121.409(c) allows for the reduction of programmed hours of flight training for certain pilot and flight engineer training programs.

Training Requirements for Check Airman

Part 121 defines two different types of check airman. Check airmen are the carrier or training center employees that actually perform the required checks at the conclusion of a course of training. The are two types of check airman, *airplane* and *simulator*. As the name suggests, a simulator check airman is only authorized to conduct training or flight checks in a simulator, while an airplane check airman may conduct training or checks in an airplane, a simulator, or a flight training device [121.411(a)].

In order to perform as a check airman (airplane), the person must hold the certificates required to serve as either pilot in command or flight engineer (as appropriate) on the airplane on which he or she is instructing. Furthermore, s/he must be qualified on the operation for that carrier. That would include such things initial and recurrent training, proficiency checks, recency of experience, and so on. S/he would also have had to complete the check airman training specified in 121.413. Since this person is authorized to serve aboard an aircraft, s/he must hold a medical certificate. If s/he were not serving as a required flight crewmember, s/he would only need to hold a third class medical certificate. If the check airman is serving as either second in command or pilot in command, s/he must hold either a second class or a first class medical certificate, as appropriate.

The requirements to perform duties as a check airman (simulator) are very similar to the check airman (airplane) *except* there is no requirement to hold a medical certificate or to have met the recency of experience requirements of 121.439 (three landings and takeoffs in 90 days). Since this person will not be performing functions in an airplane, there is no requirement to actually be current on the operation.

Training Requirements for Flight Instructors

As with the check airmen, Part 121 specifies the required training for the two types of flight instructors, namely airplane and simulator flight instructors. 121.412 allows a flight instructor (airplane) to instruct in airplanes, simulators, or flight training devices, while a flight instructor (simulator), may only instruct in simulators or flight training devices. 121.412(b) establishes requirements for the flight instructor (airplane) that are very similar to those for the check airman. The only substantial difference is that s/he doesn't need to be approved by the FAA. Rather, s/he only needs to be trained by the carrier. 121.414 sets out the training requirements for flight instructor, airplane and simulator.

Training Flow

Beginning with 121.415, the regulations spell out exactly what training is required for a pilot during any phase of his or her career. The first training a new crewmember or dispatcher receives is *basic indoctrination ground training (or Indoc).* This training must consist of at least 40 programmed hours (unless reduced) and includes things such as duties and responsibilities of crewmembers or dispatchers, FARs, ops specs, and company manuals. At the conclusion of indoctrination, the crewmember would move on to initial training.

Initial training is the portion of the training which is spelled out in 121.419 for ground training for pilots and flight engineers, 121.424 for flight training for pilots and flight engineers, 121.421 for flight attendants, and 121.422 for dispatchers. For pilots and flight engineers this training must include general topics such as dispatch or release procedures; weight and balance; runway limitations for takeoff or landing; meteorology; ATC systems, procedures, and phraseology; navigation systems and procedures; communications procedures; visual cues used in instrument approaches; crew resource management (CRM) initial training; and other instruction as necessary to ensure competence [121.419(a)(1)].

Pilots and flight engineers then go on to the second half of initial ground training, commonly called "systems" training. Here, the pilots are assigned classes based upon the specific make and model of airplane to be flown. Topics required by 121.419(a)(2) include a general description of the airplane, performance characteristics, engines and propellers, major components, major airplane systems, severe weather training, operating limitations, fuel consumption and cruise control, flight planning, normal and emergency procedures, and approved airplane flight manual. 121.419(b) sets the programmed hours of instruction for initial ground training as follows:

Group I piston airplanes	64 programmed hours
Group I turboprop airplanes	80 programmed hours
Group II airplanes (jets)	120 programmed hours

At the successful conclusion of initial ground training, pilots and flight engineers proceed to flight training under the provisions of 121.424. This training is governed by the training program outline found in appendix E of Part 121. It also must include the certificate holder's low altitude windshear flight training program. Note that 121.424(b) appears to say that this training must all be performed in an airplane in flight. However, the reference in 121.424(b)(2) to "other maneuvers" directs you to appendix E, where a table presents a layout of what maneuvers may be performed in simulators or training devices.

Flight attendant initial training is specified in 121.421 and includes topics such as authority of the pilot in command, passenger handling, and CRM. Airplane specific flight attendant training includes a general description of the airplane, especially as it relates to emergency procedure, evacuation, or ditching; communications with passengers and crew; and proper use of galley equipment and environmental controls such as cabin heat and ventilation. 121.421(c) sets the programmed hours of instruction for initial ground training of flight attendants as follows:

Group I piston airplanes	8 programmed hours
Group I turboprop airplanes	8 programmed hours
Group II airplanes (jets)	16 programmed hours

Dispatcher initial training is specified in 121.422 and includes topics such as use of communications systems; meteorology; NOTAMs, NAVAIDS, and publications; joint dispatcher and pilot responsibilities; airport characteristics; prevailing weather and sources of weather information; ATC and instrument approach procedures; and DRM initial training. Then, like pilots and flight engineers, dispatchers receive airplane specific training. 121.422(a)(2) requires training in topics such as general airplane description, which emphasizes operating and performance characteristics; navigation equipment; instrument approach and communication equipment; emergency equipment and procedures; flight operation procedures including severe weather avoidance and escape procedures; weight and balance; basic airplane performance dispatch requirements and procedures; flight planning and fuel requirements; and emergency procedures including government notification. 121.422(c) sets the programmed hours of instruction for aircraft dispatchers as follows:

Group I piston airplanes	30 programmed hours
Group I turboprop airplanes	40 programmed hours
Group II airplanes (jets)	40 programmed hours

Other required training that is typically accomplished during initial training includes the HAZMAT training of 121.433a, the crewmember emergency training of 121.417, and the CRM/DRM training required in 121.404.

All of the above training requires a competency check at the end of the course of training. That is, there is a comprehensive "final exam." It often is broken into a series of exams during the course of training. For pilots and flight engineers it will include a check ride in the simulator and, in many cases, in the aircraft as well. For pilots and flight engineers, at the conclusion of initial training and the check ride, the next step is to move on to the *initial operating experience (IOE)* required by 121.434.

Initial Operating Experience

Once the pilot or flight engineer has been trained on the aircraft, the regulations (121.434) require a period of supervised flying for the purpose of *consolidation of knowledge*. This is a period of time that the new crewmember (new to the operation, not necessarily the company) flies while under the direct supervision of a qualified check pilot.

In the case of a new captain (pilot in command) s/he will legally be second in command of the aircraft since s/he is fully qualified in that position. The check pilot will legally be pilot in command and ultimately responsible for the conduct of the flights. During a captain's IOE, the new captain will sit in the left seat and make all of the decisions for the operation of the flight. Only in the event the new captain is about to make a serious error of judgment or violate the FARs will the check airman (pilot in command) exert his or her authority over the flight. In the case of a captain's initial or upgrade training, an FAA operations inspector, not just a company check airman, must observe at least one leg of the IOE, including one takeoff and one landing.

In the case of a new second in command (copilot), the copilot is legal to fly as second in command. He or she will sit in the right seat and perform all of the duties of a second in command under the watchful eye of the check captain (pilot in command). The check captain is performing the evaluation of the second in command in this case.

In the case of a flight engineer, a check engineer will be aboard the airplane and is the legal flight engineer. The IOE engineer will sit at the panel and operate the flight under the supervision of the check engineer.

121.434 requires minimum experience hours and cycles (takeoffs and landings). The pilot operating experience minimum requirements for *initial training* are as follows:

Group I piston airplanes	15 hours of operating experience
Group I turboprop airplanes	20 hours of operating experience
Group II airplanes (jets)	25 hours of operating experience

In each case, the experience must include at least four cycles, with at least two cycles actually being flown by the person being checked. These times may be reduced by 1 hour for each takeoff and landing above the minimum of four required. The times may be reduced a maximum of 50 percent. In other words the minimum *reduced* hours for a Group I propeller airplane would be 7.5 hours and 12 takeoffs and landings, Group I turboprop minimum *reduced* hours would be 10 hours and 14 takeoffs and landings, and Group II minimum *reduced* hours would be 12.5 hours and 17 takeoffs and landings (121.434(f)).

Line Operating Flight Time

Our new pilot or copilot is almost finished. At the conclusion of IOE s/he may fly with a "regular" pilot, (i.e., not a check airman). However, the FAA wants to see that the new pilot gets substantial experience in a relatively short period of time. This is also for the purpose of consolidation of knowledge. 121.434(g) requires that each pilot that is new to the equipment obtain 100 hours of flight time on that equipment within 120 days of completing the type rating check ride or final proficiency check on the aircraft during training. If this experience is not met, 121.434(h)(4) allows the time to be extended to 150 days if the pilot completes refresher training. If this isn't done or the time period exceeds 150 days, the pilot must undergo a new proficiency check.

Flight attendants must also undergo IOE. 121.434(e) requires a 5 hour period of IOE under the supervision of an authorized supervisor.

Other Training and Checking

Once a new copilot completes the 100 hours of consolidation of knowledge, s/he may perform as a regular crewmember. The next training/checking event in his or her career is likely to be annual *recurrent training*. 121.433(c) requires annual recurrent ground and flight training. (Note that dispatchers and flight attendants also require annual recurrent ground training and a competence check.) The content of recurrent training programs for pilots, flight engineers, and flight attendants is spelled out in FAR 121.427. It also specifies the minimum program times for the recurrent training (see table 6.1). The training is essentially a "refresher course" of the material that was covered in the initial training program, and the objective is to ensure that crewmembers continue to be knowledgeable of, and proficient in, their specific aircraft type and crew position.

Recurrent training also offers air carriers the opportunity to introduce crewmembers to changes in company operating procedures and to emphasize new developments in training that reflect changes in the operating environment (e.g., fatigue issues, LAHSO operations, precision monitored approaches, etc.).

The next most likely event in our flight engineer or copilot's career is likely to be a move (in the same capacity) to another (bigger) airplane. That is because at most companies that means an increase in pay because of the larger airplane. When that happens, what training is required of the pilot? Referring to 121.400(c)(2) and assuming that the airplane group is the same, the pilot would need transition training.

Transition Training

As stated in 121.400(c)(2), transition training is the training that is provided to a crewmember that is changing airplanes to serve in the same capacity on another airplane of the same group. So, a MD-80 copilot who is moving on to the 757 as a copilot would require transition training. The contents of the ground training course are defined in 121.419 and are the same as for initial training. The flight training portion of transition training is spelled out in 121.424. At the conclusion of this training, the pilot would have to go through IOE and 100 hours of consolidation of knowledge for this aircraft.

The next step in the career would be for the flight engineer to become a copilot or a copilot to become a captain. If the crewmember has never served on this airplane before, s/he would require initial training for that status for that aircraft. On the other hand, if the crewmember had served on that particular airplane, s/he would require upgrade training.

Upgrade Training

Once again, 121.419 and 121.424 are the applicable regulations for ground and flight training. Each course the carrier develops would have to meet these minimum standards as far as content and, if specified, programmed hours.

Table 6.1. Recurrent ground training programmed hours

	Pilots and Flight Engineers	Flight Attendants	Aircraft Dispatchers
Group I piston airplanes	16 hours	4 hours	8 hours
Group I turboprop airplanes	20 hours	5 hours	10 hours
Group II airplanes (jets)	25 hours	12 hours	20 hours

Proficiency Checks

Once a pilot or flight engineer is qualified on an operation and continues to fly, the regulations require that s/he be monitored fairly frequently as to training and proficiency. 121.441 requires that all captains receive a proficiency check every 12 months and an intermediate proficiency check or course of simulator training within the last 6 months. These are commonly referred to as "PCs" or "6 checks." Second-in-command pilots and flight engineers need to undergo either a proficiency check or line oriented simulator training every 24 months and a proficiency check and any other simulator course within 12 months. The content of the proficiency check is spelled out in Part 121 Appendix F.

Line Checks

In addition to all of the "school house" training and checking that the pilot in command is subjected to, s/he must also undergo routine evaluation of his or her flying skills while operating live line flights. These check rides are conducted in the normal course of business by company check airmen and consist of observations of one or more legs. 121.440 requires that captains receive these check rides at least once every 12 months; they are therefore referred to as *annual line checks.*

Recency of Experience

While not technically a training or checking requirement, FAR 121.439 specifies that a pilot must have performed at least three takeoffs and landings as a pilot within the last 90 days. If this *recency of experience* requirement is not met, the pilot may requalify either in an airplane *(although not in line operations)* or in a simulator. If the recency has expired, the pilot must meet the specific requirements of 121.439(b) and (c). These provisions require that the takeoffs and landings meet certain criteria such as the failure of the most critical engine and ILS approaches to minimums. Further, to use the visual simulator for currency, the pilot must have had at least 100 hours in the airplane.

A flight engineer has a recency of experience requirement imposed by FAR 121.453 that requires that the flight engineer have met the *50 in 6* requirements. This means that s/he has at least 50 hours of flight engineer time in the same make/model aircraft within the preceding 6 months.

An aircraft dispatcher must complete a type of recency of experience too. 121.463 requires a dispatcher to have observed, within the preceding 12 calendar months, flight operations from the flight deck for at least 5 hours in one of the types of aircraft in each group to be dispatched.

Route and Airport Qualifications

Route and airport qualifications require that the carrier establish a system for disseminating information to each pilot concerning the routes and airports to be served by that pilot. 121.443 requires that the captain must be *route qualified* and *airport qualified*. This entails having provided the following information to each crewmember: weather characteristics appropriate to the season; navigation facilities; communications procedures including visual aids; kinds of terrain and obstructions; minimum safe flight levels; en route, terminal area, departure, holding, and authorized instrument approach procedures; congested areas and physical layout of the terminal areas in which the pilot will operate; and NOTAMs.

Special Airport Qualifications

In addition to these general requirements, there are *special airport qualifications* for those airports designated by the FAA as *special airports*. 121.445 requires that each pilot in command operating IFR in conditions where visibility is less than 3 statute miles and the ceiling is less than 1,000 feet below the minimum en route altitude or minimum obstruction clearance altitude into a special airport must have made an actual entry into that airport within the last 12 months or have qualified using *pictorial means* to train for the unusual circumstances affecting that airport. Pictorial means is simply a group of pictures and instructional pages describing the peculiarities of operations to and from a particular airport. The most common reasons for the FAA to designate an airport as a *special airport* are precipitous terrain, congested or unusual airspace, obstructions or complex arrival or departure procedures, or a combination or any of these.

Pairing Limitations

As a result of several serious accidents where one or more of the flight crewmembers had limited experience in the type of aircraft, FAA has implemented rules which limit who can fly with who and under what conditions. 121.437 first looks at the experience of the second in command.

If the second in command has less than 100 hours in type (and under Part 121) and the pilot in command is not a check airman, the pilot in command must make all take-offs and landings (1) at special airports (see above); (2) if visibility is less than 3/4 statute mile; (3) if runway visual range (RVR) is less than 4,000 feet; (4) if runways are contaminated (snow, slush, water, etc.); (5) if braking action is reported as less than good; (6) if the reported crosswind component is in excess of 15 knots; (7) if windshear is reported in the vicinity of the airport; (8) in any other condition where the PIC determines it is prudent to exercise his or her prerogative.

Secondly, 121.438(b) limits pairing a low time captain with a low time first officer. One of the two must have over 75 hours in type under Part 121. Some minor exemptions are available that recognize a new piece of equipment or a domicile where the airplane has never been operated.

Advanced Qualification Program (AQP)

Another type of training program is currently revolutionizing the airline industry. The *advanced qualification program (AQP)* is a type of voluntary training program that offers air carriers an alternative to the traditional Part 121 and Part 135 crewmember training and checking requirements. The development of the AQP was the result of a cooperative relationship between the FAA and U.S. air carriers and had its beginnings back in 1987. The FAA and U.S. air carriers sought to develop an improved training program that recognized the dramatic changes in the capabilities of simulators and other computer-based training devices in the training and qualification of flight crews. This working relationship between the FAA and U.S. carriers led to a list of recommendations that eventually became the framework for Special Federal Aviation Regulation 58 (SFAR 58) and Advisory Circular AC 120.54. These documents authorized the use of advanced qualification programs. AC 120.54 describes AQP this way, *"AQPs are systematically developed, continuously maintained, and empirically validated proficiency-based training systems."* The AQP is, in a nutshell, a redesign of traditional air carrier training and checking programs to better suit the requirements of new aircraft and the capabilities of modern training methods.

SFAR 58 and AC 120.54 contain the requirements which air carriers must fulfill to gain approval of an AQP for qualifying, training, certifying, and checking the competency of pilots, flight attendants, and aircraft dispatchers as well as instructors and evaluators who are required to be trained or qualified under parts 121 and 135 of the FARs. AQP is founded on the principle that the content of training and checking requirements should be directly driven by the requirements of the job. Under the AQP each air carrier develops its own ***proficiency objectives*** and submits them to the FAA for approval. A proficiency objective is a statement describing the behavior a crewmember must demonstrate to be able to successfully perform a task. Once approved by the FAA, these proficiency objectives become regulatory requirements for that particular carrier. An obvious advantage is that this allows air carriers to develop a training program that better suits its needs.

Another advantage of the AQP is the FAA is authorized to approve significant differences from traditional training requirements if it can be shown these differences will achieve an equivalent or better level of safety. For instance, the FAA allows development of a ***single visit training program.*** A single visit training program allows air carriers to place all flight crewmembers in the same recurrent training cycle (i.e., annual check). Traditionally the pilot in command received flight training and/or proficiency checks every 6 months; under AQP single visit training programs this is done on an annual basis.

In general an AQP differs from traditional regulatory requirements in terms of the characteristics shown in table 6.2.

Table 6.2. Traditional Part 121/135 program vs. AQP training and checking

Traditional FAR Part 121 Training and Checking	(AQP Training and Checking)
Mandatory compliance by air carriers governed by the appropriate provisions of Parts 121 and 135.	Participation is *voluntary*.
Training and checking of each crewmember on an individual basis.	Training and checking performed on a crew-oriented basis.
LOFT and CRM are "nonjeopardy" training events.	LOFT training is evaluated; CRM evaluation factors are used.
Carriers maintain training records of final results only.	Carriers submit de-identified data on each evaluation point for each trainee.
Evaluation period is fixed at 12 months	Evaluation period can be adjusted as crew performance warrants.
Simulator training is not required.	Simulator training must be utilized.

Flight Operations Quality Assurance (FOQA)

While *flight operations quality assurance (FOQA)* is not technically a training or checking requirement, it does provide a means for measuring the effects of flight crew training directly on line operations. FOQA is a new program air carriers use to collect and analyze digital flight data of actual line aircraft operations. The capability to monitor physical aircraft performance in extensive detail was made possible with the arrival of digital flight data computers. Air carrier FOQA programs actually began with European air carriers, primarily British Airways and SAS. Over a 10 year period, the FAA and U.S. air carriers had been monitoring the European carriers' successful digital flight data recording and analysis programs in the hope of developing a similar program in the United States. Many major airlines are now implementing FOQA programs with their newer aircraft fleets. The primary goal of these FOQA programs is to identify significant performance trends before they become accidents.

Most of the FOQA programs are concerned with the detection and reporting of exceedances and other identifiable special events (e.g., in flight engine shutdown, flap overspeed, engine temperature, etc.). This data is collected and analyzed for trends. After years of research on the relationship between collected flight data and specific crew qualification standards, the FAA and participating air carriers have been able to develop distinct measurements of crew performance that are thought to be more objective than those applied in traditional training programs.

FOQA data collection is now being used in conjunction with the AQP and will eventually revolutionize air carrier training. Separately, FOQA and AQPs are valuable, but when combined they provide complementary approaches to ensuring training effectiveness. FOQA provides a means for measuring the effects of flight crew training directly on line operations through the collection and analysis of digital flight data. FOQA also affords air carriers the capability to measure the effectiveness of their training programs in directly improving line operations.

Unfortunately, FOQA data collection programs have become a somewhat contentious issue for flight crews, airline management, and the FAA over the last few years. Flight crews and air carriers, for obvious reasons, would like to make certain FOQA data is not used for detection of FAR violations. The FAA to its credit has agreed for now to use only "de-identified" data to monitor for safety trends.

Summary

The air transport industry has probably the most extensive and demanding training and retraining requirements of any field of endeavor. Training programs for pilots, flight attendants, dispatchers, and mechanics are mandated in minute detail by FAA and must be strictly adhered to by the carriers and their employees. A pilot should be familiar with all of the required training because he or she shares joint responsibility with the carrier to assure that the training has been performed. The same holds true for the other certificated airmen. The specific equipment and procedures training required for cockpit crewmembers is spelled out in appendices E and F of Part 121, and crewmembers should familiarize themselves with these requirements prior to initiating training.

Important Terms from this Chapter

50 in 6

Advanced qualification program (AQP)	Initial operating experience (IOE)
Annual line checks	Initial training
Base month	Line oriented flight training (LOFT)
Basic indoctrination ground training (Indoc)	Low altitude windshear flight training
Crew resource management (CRM) training	Proficiency objectives
Curriculum	Programmed hours
Differences training	Recency of experience
Dispatcher resource management (DRM) training	Recurrent training
FAR 121 Appendices E and F	Reduced programmed hours
Flight attendant training	Requalification training
Flight operations quality assurance (FOQA)	Route and airport qualifications
Grace month	Single visit training
Group I airplanes	Special airport qualifications
Group II airplanes	Transition training
HAZMAT training	Upgrade training

Chapter 6 Exam

1. For the purpose of the training regulations, airplanes are broken down into three categories of aircraft called?
    a. Group I, Group II and Group III.
    b. Piston aircraft, turbofan aircraft and turbojet aircraft.
    c. Piston aircraft, turboprop aircraft and turbojet aircraft.
    d. Group A, Group B, Group C.

2. What type of training would be required for crewmembers that have qualified and served in the same capacity on another airplane in the same group?
    a. Programmed training.
    b. Differences training.
    c. Initial operating training.
    d. Transition training.

3. What type of training ensures each crewmember or dispatcher is adequately trained and currently proficient with respect to the type of airplane s/he is crewing or dispatching?
    a. Requalification training.
    b. Remedial training.
    c. Recurrent training.
    d. Initial training.

4. If a pilot completes initial training as a second in command (first officer) on a piece of equipment in March, when would be the latest this pilot could complete recurrent training?

    a. Recurrent must be completed by the end of March of the next year.
    b. Recurrent must be completed before the 1st March of the next year.
    c. Recurrent must be completed before the end of April of the next year.
    d. Recurrent must be completed before the end of September of the same year.

5. Who may conduct the required Part 121 training?
    a. Any authorized Part 141 flight school or the Part 121 training center.
    b. Either the 121 certificate holder or a company holding a FAR 142 flight training certificate may conduct the required training.
    c. Either a Part 141 flight school or Part 142 flight training center may conduct the required training.
    d. Only a company holding a FAR 142 flight training certificate.

6. What is the recency of experience requirement for a flight engineer?
    a. A flight engineer must have at least 50 hours of flight engineer time in the same make/model aircraft within the preceding 6 months.
    b. A flight engineer must have at least 50 hours of flight engineer (turbojet) time in Group II aircraft within the preceding 6 months.
    c. A flight engineer must have at least 50 hours of flight engineer time in the same make/model aircraft within the preceding 120 days.
    d. A flight engineer must have at least 100 hours of flight engineer time in the same make/model aircraft within the preceding 6 months.

7. No person may serve as a pilot in command unless that pilot has received a line check within?
    a. The preceding 6 calendar months.
    b. The preceding 24 calendar months.
    c. The preceding 120 days.
    d. The preceding 12 calendar months.

8. When the visibility is below what value must the pilot in command make all takeoffs and landings when flying with a second in command who has less than 100 hours in the type of airplane to be flown?
    a. When the visibility is below the standard takeoff minimums of 1 statute mile or 5,000 RVR.
    b. When the visibility is below 3/4 statute mile or 4,000 RVR for the runway to be used.
    c. When the visibility is below 1/2 statute mile or 1,800 RVR for the runway to be used.
    d. When the visibility is below published Category I landing minimums.

9. How many hours is an aircraft dispatcher required to observe flight operations from the flight deck within the preceding 12 calendar months? May observing simulator training satisfy this requirement?
    a. 5 hours, yes.
    b. 12 hours, no.
    c. 10 hours, no.
    d. 5 hours, no.

10. How often must a pilot serving as pilot in command satisfactorily complete a proficiency check?
    a. Within the preceding 24 calendar months.
    b. Within the preceding 6 calendar months, also must complete a special airport qualification.
    c. Must complete a proficiency check every 12 calendar months.
    d. Within the preceding 12 calendar months, must also complete either simulator training or a proficiency check within the preceding 6 calendar months.

Air Carrier Flight and Duty Time Limitations

I want to die like my grandfather did, peacefully in his sleep. Not screaming in terror like his passengers.

—Anon.

In this chapter we'll discuss one of the more contentious areas of the Federal Air Regulations, that is, the issue of what constitutes an appropriate and safe working day and an appropriate and safe rest period. Through ***flight and duty time limitations*** the FAA attempts to balance the rest needs of pilots with the cost and scheduling needs of the companies that employ them.

In this chapter we will discuss the FAR Part 121 subparts covering the most common flight and duty time limitations. FAR Part 121 Subpart Q covers limitations for pilots in ***domestic operations*** while Subpart R covers limitations for pilots in ***flag operations***. FAR Part 121 Subpart S covers limitations for pilots in ***supplemental*** (nonscheduled) ***operations***. Duty and rest times for dispatchers and flight attendants for both domestic and flag are covered in Subpart P.

There are a couple of important points to remember when discussing ***flight time*** limitations. First, these limitations are based primarily on ***scheduled*** amounts of flight time not ***actual flight time***. We will illustrate this important difference in this chapter by presenting a few examples. The FAA chooses to use scheduled flight time as opposed to writing regulations based on actual time in an effort to offer some schedule flexibility to the air carrier. This schedule flexibility allows air carriers to continue to operate a flight even though events beyond the control of the air carrier cause a pilot's flight time to exceed the scheduled limitations. The FAA allows this in order to avoid "stranding" passengers, aircraft, and pilots at some intermediate location.

Secondly, while the FAA allows air carriers to use scheduled flight time as opposed to actual flight time during a pilot's workday, it does require the scheduled flight time to be reasonable. For example if a flight between two city pairs consistently takes 2:30 hours, then the air carrier is expected to use the historic block time for that particular type of aircraft. FAR 121.541 covers both domestic and international (flag) operations:

In establishing flight operations schedules, each certificate holder conducting domestic or flag operations shall allow enough time for the proper servicing of aircraft at intermediate stops, and shall consider the prevailing winds en route and the cruising speed of the type of aircraft used. This cruising speed may not be more than that resulting from the specified cruising output of the engines.

Finally, compliance with these flight and duty time limitations carries a dual responsibility from the company *and* the pilot. Notice the wording in FAR 121.471 Flight Time Limitations and Rest Requirements:

(a) *No* certificate holder *conducting domestic operations may schedule any flight crewmember* and no flight crewmember may accept *an assignment for flight time in scheduled air transportation or in other commercial flying if that crewmember's total flight time in all commercial flying will exceed those limitations set down in this regulation.*

The FAA imposes this dual responsibility of compliance on the air carrier and the pilot as a check and balance mechanism. Also, there may be instances when a pilot has performed some other **commercial flying** without the knowledge of the air carrier (i.e., charter flying, banner towing, etc.). In basic terms a pilot may not fly any commercial flying if that commercial flying plus any flying in air transportation will exceed any flight time limitation set forth in domestic, flag or supplemental regulations (FAR 121.489, FAR 121.517).

Let's look at the calendar year, monthly, weekly, and hourly flight and duty limitations.

Subpart Q: Flight Time Limitations and Rest Requirements: Domestic Operations

This subpart applies to all domestic operations except for two exceptions carved out in FAR 121.470. The most significant exception is granted for 121 operators of smaller aircraft (30 seats or less) who are permitted to choose to comply with Subpart Q or the slightly less restrictive provisions of Part 135. The other exception applies to operations conducted entirely within the states of Alaska or Hawaii with aircraft having more than 30 seats. These operators are permitted to operate under the flag rules found in FAR 121 Subpart R.

Domestic flight crew flight time limitations are set out in FAR 121.471. The first limitations are self-explanatory and limit the pilot's flying on an annual, monthly, weekly, and daily basis. These limits are

Calendar year	1,000 flight hours maximum
Calendar month	100 flight hours maximum
7 consecutive calendar days	30 flight hours maximum
Between rest periods	8 flight hours maximum

The annual, monthly, and weekly (called **30 in 7**) limits are pretty self-explanatory as all use a calendar day basis for determining compliance with the regulations. The 8 hours between required rest periods is a lot trickier in application and raise a number of basic questions.

First of all, what does the FAA define as "rest"? FAR 121.471(e) clarifies the term **rest period**. The FAA has determined rest to mean a continuous period of time a flight crewmember is free from *all* duty requirements. These duty requirements include answering the phone, pager, or email or in any way remaining in contact with the company for the reason of being available for assignment if the need arises. Also, time spent deadheading to or from a duty assignment may not be considered a rest period [FAR 121.471(f) Domestic Operations, 121.491 Flag Operations, and 121.519 Supplemental Operations].

Most air carriers operate flights between different time zones. With regard to flight and duty limitations, what time zone is used in this case? Nowhere in the FARs is this specifically addressed; however, the FAA flight and duty limitations are absolute, that is, the air carrier may not use "creative time zone scheduling" to work around the duty time limitations. For this reason, the FAA allows the company to choose the time zone, but whatever time zone the company decides to use for the crewmember must be used throughout the computation of the entire duty period. This could be the time zone of the pilot's base, or Universal Coordinated Time without regard to what time zone the pilot actually operates in.

How does the FAA define flight time for the purposes of flight limitations? The FAA defines flight time as the moment the aircraft begins to move under its own power for the purposes of flight until the moment the aircraft comes to a complete stop at a gate, ramp area, or elsewhere at the landing airport (FAR Part 1 Definitions).

Finally, what does the FAA define as a **duty period**? FAR 121.471(b) explains that a duty period begins from the first flight duty assignment and continues until that duty period is broken by a minimum rest period. Until that duty period is broken by a rest period, the pilot may not be *scheduled* for more than 8 hours flight time. That is, the rule is a **"look-back"** rule. The rest periods required to break the duty period are

- 9 consecutive hours of rest for less than 8 hours scheduled flight time within the last 24 hours,
- 10 consecutive hours of rest for 8 or more hours and less than 9 hours scheduled flight time within the last 24 hours, and
- 11 consecutive hours of rest for 9 or more hours of scheduled flight time within the last 24 hours. [FAR 121.471(b)(1,2,3)]

The way these rules are applied is by looking at the end of *each* flight segment and then looking back 24 hours. A crewmember must be able to determine that a legally scheduled rest period *began* within the last 24 hours. For example, assume the schedule shown below:

Report time		
(beginning of the		
pilot's duty period):	0700Z	
Departure time:	0800Z	
Arrival time:	1150Z	Flight time = 3:50 hours
Departure time:	1545Z	
Arrival time:	1900Z	Flight time = 3:15 hours
Release time:	1915Z	

What is the longest flight this pilot may be assigned? Total flight time since 0800Z = 7:05. Therefore, he may only be assigned for an additional 0:55 minutes of flight time before receiving a required rest period. What rest period would be required? If the pilot's last assignment was 0:54 minutes or less, then he would have flown less than 8 hours and that would then require rest period of 9 consecutive hours. Remember, by saying the carrier may not assign the pilot *any duty* during the rest period, it means that the required preflight *report times* and postflight *release times* may not be counted as part of the rest period.

These report and release times are the time periods, before and after the actual flight time, that the pilot spends briefing for the flight and completing required company paperwork such as payroll sheets, and chart and manual revisions. While the FAA hasn't defined what length these periods of time are, preferring to leave that to the collective bargaining process (union contract), it has taken action to declare as insufficient report (preflight) times of only 30 minutes and release times of only 10 minutes. The test will be one of reasonableness. That is, is the time allotted reasonable for the tasks being required of the pilot. The minimum required preflight tasks are spelled out in FAR 91.103 *Preflight Action*. The generally accepted times are 1 hour for preflight duties and 15 minutes for postflight duties.

The contentiousness on this issue comes from the pilot perspective of wanting rest time to be "pillow time," that is, time actually spent in a hotel room, in bed. Frequently the crew bus ride to the hotel, check-in, dinner, early morning preparation, and breakfast can reduce the amount of sleep actually possible to only 5 or 6 hours. The companies on the other hand have a real concern in terms of schedules and costs. The FAA to date has largely stayed out of the debate, by only stating that rest time runs from release (after the last flight) until report (before the next flight). Notice that while a crew bus ride to the local hotel *may be included in the rest period*, the deadhead time of a crew transported by airplane or surface transportation to a point that is *not local in nature may not be counted in the rest period*.

Now, let's look at an example that uses 121.471(b)(2). Assume the pilot has done no other flying for several days and then encounters this schedule:

Report time:	0700Z	
Departure time:	0800Z	
Arrival time:	1150Z	Flight time = 3:50 hours
Departure time:	1215Z	
Arrival time:	1530Z	Flight time = 3:15 hours
Release time:	1545Z	

What is the earliest clock time that the pilot may be assigned to a flight of 1:25? 1:25 when added to the previous flight time will give a total of 8:30 for this pairing. That falls into the provision of subparagraph (b)(2) in that it is 8 or more hours but less than 9 hours scheduled flight time so it requires 10 consecutive hours of rest. Allowing for report/release time this could result in the following schedule:

Report time:	0700Z	
Departure time:	0800Z	
Arrival time:	1150Z	Flight time = 3:50 hours
Departure time:	1215Z	
Arrival time:	1530Z	Flight time = 3:15 hours
Release time:	1545Z	
Rest		*Rest* = 10:00 hours
Report time:	0145Z	
Departure time:	0245Z	
Arrival time:	0410Z	Flight time = 1:25 hours

What if instead of wanting to add a flight of 1:25 we had wanted to assign a flight of 2:00 to the original schedule. Now, the scheduled time of 2:00 when added to the previous flight time will give a total of 9:05 for this pairing. That falls into the provision of subparagraph (b)(3) in that it is more than 9 hours scheduled flight time so it requires 11 consecutive hours of rest. Allowing for report/release time this could result in the following schedule:

Report time:	0700Z	
Departure time:	0800Z	
Arrival time:	1150Z	Flight time = 3:50 hours
Departure time:	1215Z	
Arrival time:	1530Z	Flight time = 3:15 hours
Release time:	1545Z	
Rest		*Rest* = 11:00 hours
Report time:	0245Z	
Departure time:	0345Z	
Arrival time:	0545Z	Flight time = 2:00 hours

These examples cover the circumstances where a single minimum rest period is given. Typically, in airline operations, the schedules or *trip pairings,* as they are known, go on for 3 or 4 days. In this circumstance, the required minimum rest periods may be reduced if at a later time a longer rest period is granted. FAR 121.471(c) covers these contingencies.

121.471(c)(1) says a minimum 9 hour rest period may be reduced to 8 hours if no later than 24 hours after the commencement of the reduced rest period the pilot is given a 10 hour rest period. So, going back to our original example, normally this schedule would require a 9 hour minimum rest:

Report time:	0700Z	
Departure time:	0800Z	
Arrival time:	1150Z	Flight time = 3:50 hours
Departure time:	1545Z	
Arrival time:	1900Z	Flight time = 3:15 hours
Release time:	1915Z	

9 hour minimum rest would mean report no earlier than 0415Z.

However, this could be reduced to 8 hours (with a 0315Z report) if, no later than 1915Z on the second day the pilot is given a 10 hour minimum rest:

Report time:	0700Z	
Departure time:	0800Z	
Arrival time:	1150Z	Flight time = 3:50 hours
Departure time:	1545Z	
Arrival time:	1900Z	Flight time = 3:15 hours
Release time:	1915Z	

8 hour reduced rest commencing at 1915Z—Pilot may return to duty (report) at 0315Z earliest.

Report time:	0315Z	
Departure time:	0415Z	
Arrival time:	0615Z	Flight time = 2:00 hours
Departure time:	1230Z	
Arrival time:	1400Z	Flight time = 1:30 hours
Departure time:	1600Z	
Arrival time:	?	Flight time = ?

What is the longest flight that this crew may be assigned? That is, What is the latest possible scheduled arrival time? First, we see that since the last assigned break, the pilot has flown 3:30. 121.471(a)(4) says a pilot may not be scheduled for more than 8:00 since the last required rest period. Using this rule, the pilot could be scheduled for an additional 4:30 hours, which would bring his total hours up to 8:00.

However, since the pilot had a reduced rest period at the last required rest and that was reduced using 121.471(c)(1), we must start a 10 hour rest period no later than 24 hours after the last rest period began. The last rest period began at 1915Z, so our pilot must be released no later than 1915Z. Given our release period of 0:15, the arrival time must be scheduled no later than 1900Z. Therefore the longest flight we may schedule the pilot for is 3:00 hours, which results in an arrival time of 1900Z and a release time of 1915Z. The earliest next *report time* would then be 10 hours later at 0515Z.

121.471(c)(2) and (c)(3) work exactly the same way except that (c)(2) allows a 10 hour rest period to be reduced to 8 hours if an 11 hour rest period is scheduled to commence no later than 24 hours after the start of the reduced rest period. (c)(3) allows an 11 hour rest period to be reduced to a minimum of 9 hours (note the time difference) if a 12 hour rest period is scheduled to commence no later than 24 hours after the start of the reduced rest period.

Finally, the question arises: What happens if the schedule goes "nonroutine"? 121.471(g) covers this by saying if a flight normally terminates at its scheduled time but, because of weather or other delays, goes nonroutine, then the pilot is not considered to be in violation of the minimum rest period if it was otherwise scheduled legally. In other words, if the crewmember was legal to start a trip segment, then he is legal to finish regardless of how long the flights take. Neither the carrier nor the crewmember will be penalized with a violation if a normally scheduled flight goes longer than planned. The pilot simply gets more fatigued!

Let's look at an example of a scheduled flight day that becomes nonroutine: A crewmember is scheduled to fly four 1 hour 59 minute flight segments totaling 7 hours 56 minutes. Due to air traffic control and flight delays the first three segments have totaled 7 hours. Is the crewmember legal to fly the last leg of the day even though the total flying time between rest periods will be more than 8 hours? Yes, the pilot is legal to fly the last segment because FAA flight time limitations are placed on *scheduled* flight time only, not *actual* flight time. The crewmember was legal to begin the trip assigned that day; that crewmember is therefore legal to finish the trip as long as duty day limitations are not exceeded.

Now let's look at an example of a scheduled flight day that becomes nonroutine and the company decides to alter the pilot's schedule midday: A crewmember is scheduled to fly four 1 hour 59 minute flight segments totaling 7 hours and 56 minutes. Due to air traffic control and weather delays the actual flight time for the first three segments has totaled 7 hours. At the completion of the third segment the crew scheduling department advises the crewmember that he or she has been rerouted or *rescheduled* to fly a shorter 1 1/2 hour flight. Surprisingly, this would not be a legal trip even though the flight time in this example is less the originally scheduled day. This is because any time a trip is *rescheduled* you must examine the *actual* flight time since the last rest period. Because the crewmember had already flown 7 hours, that pilot may only be rescheduled to fly an additional 1 hour flight segment.

Maximum Time "On Duty"

Now that we've taken a look at maximum flight time regulations let's look at what limitations are placed on a pilot's **duty day.** As we mentioned earlier, a pilot must always be able to "look back" 24 hours and find at least an 8 hour rest period. For this reason, the maximum duty day can never exceed 16 *actual* duty hours in a 24 hour period. (See fig. 7.1.) This means that a pilot must be certain when departing on each flight segment that he will be able to be released from duty before the 16 hour duty limit. A pilot must look at weather, ATC delays such as ground stops, or any known holding which may be anticipated. If any of these factors may cause a crewmember to exceed the 16 hour duty day then the aircraft must not leave the gate. If you have already left the gate but because of an unanticipated ground stop you have been delayed and now calculate you will exceed the 16 hour duty day limitation before reaching your destination, you will not be legal to finish the trip and must return to the gate.

Before we leave the domestic rules, look at 121.471(d). This is sometimes referred to as the **1 in 7 rule.** It requires the carrier give the pilot 1 day (24 consecutive hours) free from all duty in each 7 day period. Recently, the FAA has changed its view on how this rule is to be interpreted. The issue is reserve pilots who are on call each day.

Previous to 1999, the view was that at any time the company could look backwards and find a 24 hour period where the pilot had not flown, it could count that as the 24 hour period free from all duty. A reserve pilot could therefore "sit" reserve for more than 6 calendar days at a stretch. [Note carefully the wording of 121.471(d)]. In the summer of 1999 FAA issued a policy statement that beginning in December 1999, it would apply an interpretation of this rule that says the 24 hour period must be planned into the pilot's schedule—*looking forward*. That is, if a reserve pilot was required to be available to answer the telephone, then he was not free from all duty; therefore, a break from flying, *per se*, did not constitute a period free from all duty. This meant the air carrier was required to place 24 hour rest periods on a reserve pilot's future weekly or, as is most common, monthly schedule.

This was a major change of the way scheduling had been performed and it soon became evident many more pilots would be needed to "sit" reserve. This meant air carriers would have to hire more pilots. The carriers were given until December 1999 to work out with their pilot unions how it would be applied. By November 1999 all major domestic carriers had applied for and been granted a waiver from this provision until some time in 2000 to work out a mutually acceptable method of compliance. This was done without public comment (i.e., from the pilot unions). As you can imagine, since they were not consulted on this issue, the pilot unions were not happy with the FAA's handling of the exemption applications of the airlines.

Eventually the "new" reserve system was implemented. Most pilots appear to like the new reserve rest requirements. However there were some complaints. The most common complaint by some pilots is that the new reserve rest requirement does not allow the flexibility of scheduling large blocks of reserve days in a row. Some pilots, i.e., pilots who commuted from another city to "sit" reserve in their domicile, preferred to schedule large blocks of reserve days together so they could spend larger blocks of time at home and keep the number of days spent commuting to and from work to a minimum.

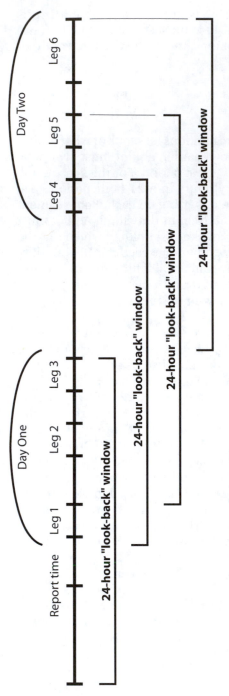

To determine required rest periods, take into account all of your scheduled flying in a 24-hour "look-back" window surrounding the rest period you are about to start. Check to see if you are scheduled to fly more than 8 hours of flying in the 24-hour window before the completion of any flight leg.

Scheduled Flight time within 24 hours	Normal Rest	Minimum Reduced Rest	Minimum Required Compensatory Rest (to begin no later than 24 hours after the commencement of the reduced rest period)
less than 8:00 hours	9:00 hours	8:00 hours	10:00 hours
8:00 hours to 8:59	10:00 hours	8:00 hours	11:00 hours
9:00 hours or more	11:00 hours	9:00 hours	12:00 hours

Figure 7.1   Required rest periods.

Subpart R: Flight Time Limitations: Flag Operations

Flag or international flight operations are flights flown to destinations outside the 48 contiguous states, including to or from Alaska and Hawaii. Like domestic flight time limitations flag flight time limitations are for *scheduled* flight time while rest requirements are based on *actual hours flown*. Flag flight time limitations and regulations, because of the long routes flown in international operations, are considerably different for Part 121 flag operators. FAR 121.480 makes the section applicable to flag operators operating with more than 30 seats. Those with fewer seats have the option to operate under Part 121 or the slightly less restrictive rules of Part 135.

Two Pilot Crews

Flight time limitations for flag operations flight crews are set out in FAR 121.481. The first flag limitations are self-explanatory and limit the pilot's flying on an annual, monthly, weekly, and daily basis. Notice however, that there are a few differences in the wording of some of the flight time limitations; for instance, the domestic 1,000 flight hours in any calendar year limitation has been changed to 1,000 flight hours in any *12 calendar month* period.

The flag operation limits are

12 calendar months	1,000 flight hours maximum
1 calendar month	100 flight hours maximum
7 consecutive calendar days	32 flight hours maximum
24 consecutive hours	8 flight hours maximum
	(without a rest period)

When a two pilot crew is operating the flight, it may be scheduled for up to 8 hours in a 24 hour period [FAR 121.481(a)]. If this crew is scheduled to fly more than 8 hours in a 24 consecutive hour period, then it must be given a rest period prior to exceeding 8 hours. This rest period must be of at least twice the scheduled flight time, but no less than 8 hours rest. That is, it takes a minimum rest period of 8 hours to break a duty period. At the conclusion of the flying in excess of 8 hours in a 24 hour period, FAR 121.481(c) requires the pilot to receive a rest period of at least 18 hours free from all duty.

Would the following schedule be legal for a flag crew?

Report time:	1900Z	
Departure time:	2000Z	
Arrival time:	0100Z	Flight time = 5:00 hours
Release time:	0115Z	
Rest		*Rest* = 8:00 hours
Report time:	0915Z	
Departure time:	1015Z	
Arrival time:	1530Z	Flight time = 5:15 hours
Release time:	1545Z	

This would *not* be a legal pairing because while the crew gets 8:00 hours rest (which exceeds the basic minimum) it must also equal or exceed twice the number of hours flown since the last rest. In this case, the first leg was a 5 hour flight, so the rest period must be at least 10 hours. The earliest the crew could be required to report would be 1115Z. Their maximum legal schedule would then be

Report time:	1900Z	
Departure time:	2000Z	
Arrival time:	0100Z	Flight time = 5:00 hours
Release time:	0115Z	

| *Rest* | | *Rest* = 10:00 hours |

Report time:	1115Z	
Departure time:	1215Z	
Arrival time:	2015Z	Flight time = 8:00 hours
Release time:	2030Z	

How long does the next rest period have to be? At the end of his trip at 2015Z the pilot has flown 12:45 during the period 2015Z on day one and 2015Z on day two. On day one he flew from 2015Z until 0100Z (4:45 hours) and on day two he flew from 1215Z to 2015Z (8:00 hours) or a total of 12:45. Therefore, according to 121.481(c) he must receive a minimum of 18 hours rest. Therefore, the minimum rest period would result in a pairing on the third day of:

Release Time:	2030Z	

| *Rest* | | *Rest* = 18:00 hours |

Report Time:	1430Z	
Departure Time:	1530Z	
Arrival Time:	2330Z	Flight time = 8:00 hours
Release Time:	2345Z	

Flight time limitations and rest requirements for a two pilot crew are summarized in table 7.1.

Two Pilots Plus One Additional Flight Crewmember

Recognizing that the long international flights have unique needs, FAR 121.483 provides a relief valve for operating flights in excess of 8 hours and up to 12 hours duration. In order to avail the carrier of the use of this provision, the carrier must put on a relief pilot in the form of "an additional crewmember." In this case the limiting factors are 12 hours flight time in a 24 hour period, 20 flight hours in a 48 hour period, and 24 flight hours in a 72 hour period. At the end of these duty periods he must be given at least 18 hours free from all duty. The total flight hour limitations for two pilots plus one relief crewmember are

12 calendar months	1,000 flight hours
90 consecutive days	300 flight hours
30 consecutive days	120 flight hours

Notice that with the additional crewmember and, as we'll see below, with three pilots plus one additional flight crewmember, the 30 in 7 (domestic) or 32 in 7 (flag) limitation is removed.

Table 7.1. Flag flight time limitations and rest requirements (two pilot crew)

Time Period	Flight-Time Aloft	Duty-Time Limitation	Rest Requirement
12 calendar months	1,000 hours		
1 calendar month	100 hours		
7 consecutive days			24 consecutive hours of rest
24 consecutive hours	Maximum of 8 hours *scheduled* without an intervening rest period	Maximum total time on duty is 16 hours in any 24 hour period	
	More than 8 hours	Maximum total time on duty is 16 hours	A rest period twice the number of flight hours since the preceding rest period. *8 hours minimum rest*
	More than 8 hours—*Actual*	Maximum total time on duty is 16 hours	18 hours of rest

Three (or More) Pilots Plus One Additional Flight Crewmember

FAR 121.485 provides relief for the really long haul flights such as the transpacific flights operating from the United States to China and Japan or Australia. It is available for flights in excess of 12 hours. In this case, the airplane must be crewed with at least three pilots and one additional flight crewmember. First the carrier has to schedule its flights so as to provide "adequate rest periods on the ground for each pilot who is away from his base." Next, the airplane must have adequate sleeping quarters in the form of bunks or an isolated set of first class seats that are somewhat removed from the cabin commotion. Then, upon the pilot's return to his or her base, the carrier must give a rest period that is at least twice the number of hours flown since the pilot's last rest period *at his or her base.*

These crews are limited in terms of total hours of service as follows:

12 calendar months	1,000 flight hours
90 consecutive days	350 flight hours

FAR 121.487(b) covers the pilot who is not regularly assigned to one of these types of crews for the entire month. That is, he may fly part of the month as a two pilot plus one crewmember crew and part of the month as part of a two pilot crew, for example. In that case, the monthly maximums are those of FAR 121.481(e), namely 100 hours in the calendar month. The quarterly and annual limitations of a pilot who is scheduled for more than 20 hours in augmented crews will be found in 121.483(c)(2) and (3), namely 300 hours in 90 days and 1,000 hours in 12 calendar months.

FAR 121.489 provides that in calculating a pilot's flight time limits a carrier must include not only the flying done for it but also *any other commercial flying*. In other words, if the pilot has any other flying job (civilian), that flight time must be considered in determining the flight limitations under FAR 121.483 and FAR 121.485. Military reserve or guard flying *is not counted toward the flight time limits*.

FAR 121.491 further spells out that deadhead time (time spent traveling on an airplane as a passenger) does not count as rest time.

Flight Engineers and Navigators

Flight and duty limitations for flight engineers and navigators are briefly mentioned in FAR 121.493. If only *one* flight engineer or *one* navigator is required then the air carrier must use the flight time limitations for *two pilots and one additional flight crewmember* (FAR 121.483). For any flight operation requiring more than one flight engineer or more than one navigator the air carrier must use the flight time limitations for *three or more pilots and additional flight crewmembers* (FAR 121.485).

Subpart S: Flight Time Limitations: Supplemental Operations Pilots

This subpart applies to *nonscheduled* or *supplemental domestic* and *supplemental overseas and international* flight operations for aircraft having a seating capacity of more than 30 passengers and a payload capacity of greater than 7,500 pounds. Flight time limitations for **supplemental operations** are covered in FAR 121.503 and are similar to flag flight time limitations with some interesting differences.

Calendar year	1,000 flight hours maximum
30 consecutive days	100 flight hours maximum
Between rest periods	8 flight hours maximum

Notice the standard calendar month limitation, used in domestic and flag operations, has been changed to read *in any 30 consecutive days*. Also, flight time limitations have been relaxed to allow an air carrier to exceed the 8 flight hour maximum between rest periods by up to 2 hours. To be allowed to exceed the 8 hour maximum the flight must be a transcontinental nonstop flight (not overseas). The aircraft must have an operative pressurization system at the beginning of the flight, and the flight crew consists of at least two pilots *and* a flight engineer [FAR 121.503(f)(1)&(2)].

Two Pilot Crews

When a two pilot crew is operating the flight, it may be scheduled to fly more than 8 hours in a 24 hour period [FAR 121.505(a)]. If this crew is scheduled to fly more than 8 hours in a 24 consecutive hour period, then it must be given a rest period prior to exceeding 8 hours. This rest period must be at least twice the scheduled flight time, but no less than 8 hours. Therefore, as we mentioned in the previous FAR subparts, it takes a minimum rest period of 8 hours to break a duty period.

The duty day limitation for a two pilot crew is similar to the domestic duty day limitation. A pilot may not be on duty more than 16 hours in any consecutive 24 hour period

[FAR 121.505(b)]. Flight time limitations and rest requirements for a two pilot crew are summarized in table 7.2.

Let's take a look at a 3 day trip scheduled to the maximum allowable flight and duty time limitations for a two pilot crew under supplemental operations.

Report time:	0700Z	
Departure time:	0800Z	
Arrival time:	1300Z	Flight time = 5:00 hours
Release time:	1315Z	
Rest		*Rest* = 10:00 hours
Report time:	2315Z	
Departure time:	0015Z	
Arrival time:	0815Z	Flight time = 8:00 hours
Release time:	0830Z	

In this case how long does this rest period have to be? At the end of his trip at 0815Z the pilot has flown 12:45 during the period 0815Z on day one and 0815Z on day two. On day one he flew from 0815Z until 1300Z (4:45 hours) and on day two he flew from 0015Z to 0815Z (8:00 hours) or a total of 12:45. Therefore, according to 121.503(b) he must receive a minimum of 16 hours rest. For this reason, the minimum rest period would result in a pairing on the third day of

Table 7.2. Supplemental flight time limitations and rest requirements (two pilot crew)

Time Period	Duty-Time Aloft	Duty-Time Limitation	Rest Requirement
Calendar year	1,000 hours		
30 consecutive days	100 hours		
7 consecutive days			24 consecutive hours of rest
24 consecutive hours	Maximum of 8 hours—*Scheduled*	Maximum total time on duty is 16 hours in any 24 hour period	
	More than 8 hours	Maximum total time on duty is 16 hours	A rest period twice the number of flight hours since the preceding rest period. *8 hours minimum rest*
	More than 8 hours—*Actual*	Maximum total time on duty is 16 hours	16 hours of rest

Release time:	0830Z		
Rest		*Rest* = 16:00 hours	
Report time:	0030Z		
Departure time:	0130Z		
Arrival time:	0930Z	Flight time = 8:00 hours	
Release time:	0945Z		

Three Pilot Crews

For three pilot crews in supplemental operations we begin to see the FAA distinguish between *flight deck duty* time and *aloft duty* time. No pilot may be scheduled for more than 8 hours *flight deck duty time* or 12 hours *aloft* in any 24 consecutive hours [FAR 121.507(a)]. Also, when a three pilot crew is flying in supplemental operations the maximum duty day has been extended 2 hours for a maximum of 18 hours in any 24 hour period [FAR 121.507(b)].

Four Pilot Crews

For a crew of four pilots the maximum flight and duty time limitations have been extended still more. No pilot may be scheduled for more than 8 hours *flight deck duty time* or 16 hours *aloft* in any 24 consecutive hours [FAR 121.509(a)]. Also, when a four pilot crew is flying in supplemental operations the maximum duty day has been extended another 2 hours for a maximum of 20 hours in any 24 hour period [FAR 121.509(b)].

Flight Engineers and Navigators

Supplemental flight and duty limitations for flight engineers and navigators are covered in FAR 121.511. If only *one* flight engineer or *one* navigator is required then the air carrier must use the flight time limitations for *two pilots and one additional flight crewmember* (FAR 121.503 and 121.505). For any flight operation requiring more than one flight engineer or more than one navigator the air carrier must use *flight time limitations: four pilot crews* (FAR 121.509).

Flight Time Limitation for Supplemental Overseas and International Operations

For overseas and international supplemental operations an air carrier may choose to comply with the more restrictive domestic supplemental regulations (121.503-121.511) or may use the following flight and duty time limitations:

12 calendar month period   1,000 hours aloft

Notice the 1,000 hours in a calendar year limitation found in the supplemental domestic limitations has been changed to read in any 12 calendar month period. Also, the limitation is based on 1,000 hours *aloft,* not just the time the pilot spends up front in the pilot seat.

Two Pilots and One Additional Crewmember

With a crew of two pilots and one additional crewmember (e.g., flight engineer or navigator), the supplemental limitations are covered in 121.521 and are

24 hour period	12 hours aloft
30 consecutive days	120 hours aloft
90 consecutive days	90 hours aloft

Additionally, an air carrier is required to give a pilot 18 hours of rest for the following times aloft:

20 or more hours in a 48 consecutive hour period
24 or more hours in a 72 consecutive hour period

Three (or More) Pilots and Additional Crewmembers as Required

FAR 121.523 covers ultra long haul flight and duty limitations and contains some interesting additional limitations. For ultra long haul flying, or flights in excess of 12 hours, another pilot is required. Adding the third pilot, with the additional crewmembers, allows the air carrier to fly routes in excess of 12 flight hours. Instead of limiting the flight time aloft to 12 hours as in the two pilot limitation, the FAA limits the *flight deck duty time*. Just as we've seen with flag ultra long haul operations, supplemental ultra long haul operations require the air carrier to schedule its flights so as to provide "adequate rest periods on the ground for each pilot who is away from his base." Next, the airplane must have adequate sleeping quarters in the form of bunks or an isolated set of first class seats that are somewhat removed from the cabin commotion. Then, upon the pilot's return to his or her base, the carrier must give a rest period that is at least twice the number of hours flown since the pilot's last rest period *at his or her base*. The 121.523 limitation is

90 consecutive days	350 hours aloft

With a flight crew consisting of three or more pilots, the maximum continuous duty is extended to 30 hours! The FAA defines continuous duty as the time from report time to the time the pilot is released for at least a 10 hour rest *on the ground*. If the flight crew is on continuous duty for more than 24 hours they must be given 16 or more hours of rest on the ground, after the last flight scheduled for that duty period [121.523(c)].

Deadhead time aloft in excess of 4 hours requires at least one-half of that time aloft be considered duty time if the flight crew is required to deadhead before the start of any flight duty [121.523(d)]. This limitation is waived if the flight crew is given at least 10 hours of rest on the ground before beginning any flight duty.

Once a pilot has returned to his or her domicile the air carrier is required to give the pilot a rest period of at least twice the total number of hours the pilot was aloft during the entire previous trip since first reporting at that domicile [121.523(e)].

Subpart P: Flight Attendant Duty Period Limitations and Rest Requirements: Domestic, Flag, and Supplemental Operations; Aircraft Dispatcher Qualifications and Duty Time Limitations: Domestic and Flag Operations

Flight Attendant Duty Time Limitations

Flight duty time limitations for flight attendants (both domestic and flag) are found in FAR 121.467. The concept of the flight attendant duty time is a little different than for that of the flight crews. Their duty time is not flight duty (measured from block out to block in) as for pilots, but rather is the total time spent "at work" between reporting for duty involving flight time and being released from duty. Therefore, the ground layovers are included in the calculation of flight attendant duty time [FAR 121.467(a)]. The basic flight attendant duty period limitation is 14 hours. If given 14 hours or less duty time, the carrier need only provide at least 9 consecutive hours of rest [FAR 121.487(b)(1) and (2)]. This rest period may be reduced like that of a pilot to a minimum of 8 hours if a compensatory rest period of 10 hours is provided.

The duty period limitation may be extended to between 14 and 16 hours if the carrier assigns an extra flight attendant to the flight, 16 to 18 hours if the carrier assigns two extra flight attendants to the flight, and from 18 to a whopping 20 hours if three extra flight atten-

Table 7.3. Flight attendant duty limitations and rest requirements

Number of FAs	Scheduled Duty Period	Rest	Reduced Rest	Compensatory Rest**
FAA minimum staffing (refer to 121.391)	14 hours maximum	9 hours	8 hours	10 hours
Minimum staffing plus one extra FA	14–16 hours maximum	12 hours	10 hours	14 hours
Minimum staffing plus two extra FAs	16–18 hours maximum	12 hours	10 hours	14 hours
Minimum staffing plus three extra FAs	18–20 hours maximum*	12 hours	10 hours	14 hours

*Scheduled duty period includes one or more flights that land or take off outside the 48 contiguous states and the District of Columbia.

**Compensatory rest must begin within 24 hours after the beginning of the reduced rest period.

dants are assigned to the flight. To schedule for 18 to 20 hours, the flight must take off or land at a point outside the 48 contiguous United States and the District of Columbia. If these extended duty periods are used, the rest requirements are increased accordingly. A flight attendant must receive at least 24 consecutive hours free from all duty in each 7 consecutive day period. Table 7.3 summarizes flight attendant duty limitations and rest requirements.

As an alternative to these provisions, the carrier may apply to flight attendants the same rules as are applied to the flight crew. To do this, the carrier must state the procedures in its general operations manual.

Aircraft Dispatcher Duty Time Limitations

Dispatcher duty time limitations are found in FAR 121.465. These apply to domestic or flag operations. First off, the dispatcher must begin his or her shift so as to allow time to become thoroughly familiar with the existing and anticipated weather conditions along the route of flight for all aircraft he is dispatching. He must remain on duty until each airplane he has dispatched has completed its flight or gone beyond his jurisdiction or until he is relieved by another qualified dispatcher. Except for emergency situations, the carrier may not schedule the dispatcher for duty in excess of 10 consecutive hours. If a dispatcher is scheduled for duty in excess of 10 consecutive hours in a 24 consecutive hour period, he or she must be given a rest period of at least 8 hours at or before the end of the 10 hours on duty. Further, the dispatcher must be relieved of all duty with the carrier for at least 24 consecutive hours in any 7 consecutive day period. Table 7.4 summarizes dispatcher duty time limitations.

Table 7.4. Aircraft dispatcher duty time limitations

Scheduled Duty Period	Rest
Less than or equal to 10 hours in a 24 hour period	Normal rest equals remainder of the 24 hour period
More than 10 hours in a 24 hour period	8 hours rest commencing at or before the end of 10 hours of duty

No certificate holder conducting domestic or flag operations may schedule a dispatcher for more than 10 consecutive hours of duty. [FAR 121.465 (b)].

Summary

Air carriers and their pilots, flight attendants, and flight dispatchers share the responsibility for conducting flight operations at the highest level of safety. Both flight crews and air carriers are responsible for ensuring that flight and duty time limitations are not exceeded. Pilots have the responsibility to take advantage of the opportunity for rest and report for their assignments well rested and ready for duty. Air carriers have the responsibility to conduct their operations at the highest level of safety. That includes establishing the appropriate scheduling practices that provide pilots with adequate rest. Preventing the degradation of alertness and performance caused by fatigue is a shared responsibility that brings shared benefits in terms of increased safety, better working conditions, and greater overall operational efficiencies.

Important Terms from this Chapter

30 in 7 rule

1 in 7 rule

Commercial flying

Domestic operations

Duty aloft vs. flight deck duty

Duty day

Duty period

Flag operations

Flight and duty time limitations

Flight time

Rest "look-back" requirement

Rest period

Scheduled vs. actual flight time

Supplemental operations

Chapter 7 Exam

1. A pilot is scheduled to fly for 6 consecutive days. May that pilot be scheduled to dead-head on the seventh day? Furthermore, may the pilot additionally be assigned a training period on the seventh day? Could the pilot then be required to ferry an aircraft to some destination in order to position the aircraft for some future revenue service?

2. A pilot is scheduled to deadhead on the first day of a trip. May the pilot be scheduled to fly for the next 6 days? Is the time a pilot spends en route deadheading considered rest?

3. A pilot is originally scheduled for a minimum rest period of 8 hours; because of weather delays this pilot's flight has been delayed. In this circumstance would an air carrier be allowed to schedule a pilot for less than an 8 hour rest period?

4. A flight crew is scheduled for a 7:45 flight. Prior to departure the company adjusts the flight time to 8:10 to compensate for headwinds. Is this flight a legal assignment?

5. A pilot is given the minimum reduced rest the first night of a 3 day trip. How soon must the pilot be given the required compensatory rest?

6. A flight crew, because of a prior reduced rest period, is scheduled to receive compensatory rest beginning at 2130 hours. The flight crew is scheduled to complete the last leg of the day at 2115 hours; because of a ground stop ATC delay the flight crew will arrive at the final destination at 2145 hours. Can the flight crew legally depart on this last leg?

7. Is it legal for a company to require a normally scheduled pilot to be available to answer a phone call or pager during designated rest period? What if the pilot is "sitting reserve" for the month but in a designated rest period?

8. If during a pilot's designated rest period, the company calls to notify the pilot of an adjustment to the departure time, does this require the pilot to "reset" the clock and begin a new rest period?

9. A pilot is scheduled to fly 97 hours for this month (at fifteen 6.5 hour flight days). Due to circumstances beyond the control of the company, the pilot has accumulated 96 hours prior to the last scheduled duty day of the month. Is it legal for the pilot to fly the last 6.5 hour assignment?

10. A domestically assigned pilot is scheduled to fly 97 hours for this month (at fifteen 6.5 hour flight days). Due to circumstances beyond the control of the company, the pilot has accumulated 96 hours prior to the last scheduled duty day of the month. Is it legal for the pilot to be assigned to deadhead home on a 6.5 hour flight?

11. What is the maximum flight time allowable for a two pilot crew for the following time periods in domestic, flag, or supplemental operations? 12 calendar months? Calendar month or 30 consecutive days? 7 consecutive days? Between rest periods?

12. What is the maximum duty day for a pilot in a two pilot crew flying in supplemental operations?

13. Can a pilot in a two pilot crew flying in domestic operations exceed more than 8 hours of flying in a 24 hour period?

14. Is a rest period required for a pilot given a domestic reserve assignment? How about an international pilot sitting reserve?

15. What is the maximum duty day for a pilot in a domestic operation?

16. What is the maximum amount of duty an aircraft dispatcher may be scheduled for?

17. What is the maximum number of hours a pilot in supplemental operations, on a three pilot crew, may be scheduled in a 24 consecutive hour period?

18. What is the maximum number of hours a pilot assigned flying in supplemental operations may be aloft in any 30 consecutive day period, as a member of a flight crew consisting of two pilots and one additional flight crewmember?

19. What is the maximum number of hours an air carrier may schedule a pilot to fly in flag operations, having two pilots and one additional flight crewmember?

20. What type of flying counts towards a pilot's annual, monthly, and weekly flight time limitations?

8 Airplanes Used in Part 121 Operations

Scientific investigation into the possibilities [of jet propulsion] has given no indication that this method can be a serious competitor to the airscrew-engine combination.

—British Undersecretary of State for Air, 1934

Most of us are familiar with the operational provisions of FAR Part 91 that prescribe general operating rules to be applied to non–air carrier operations. They are focused on basic operation of the aircraft in the national airspace system and are not very restrictive in regards to the airplanes to be used. These airplanes may be a wide variety of aircraft from homebuilt, experimental aircraft to aircraft licensed in a number of different categories such as normal, limited and so forth. For noncarriage operations, these rules serve well to provide an adequate level of safety balanced against operational usage. In Part 121 operations, we have a whole different ball game. In the same way that air carriers have the highest standards imposed on them when it comes to operating rules, the aircraft used in air carrier operations also are required to meet the highest standards in terms of design, certification, and performance. In this chapter we take a look at some of the unique aspects of air carrier aircraft operated under FAR Part 121.

General Aircraft Requirements

Subpart H of Part 121 sets forth the requirements for the aircraft to be used in Part 121 operations. The first of these requirements is found in FAR 121.153. This requires either that the aircraft be registered as a civil aircraft in the United States or that it be a complying foreign registered civil aircraft. To be a complying foreign registered aircraft, it must be registered in a country that is a party to the Convention on International Civil Aviation and be leased, without crew (*dry lease*), to a U.S. carrier. In addition it must be of a type design which is approved under a U.S. type certificate and complies with all airworthiness standards that would apply to it were it a U.S. registered aircraft. FAR 121.159 limits the aircraft used in Part 121 operations to multi-engine aircraft.

Any aircraft used in a Part 121 operation must meet appropriate certification standards. FAR 121.157 serves to grandfather a number of aircraft certificated under previous versions of the FARs and the old Civil Aeronautical Rules (CARs). If a company is involved in flying older aircraft (typically cargo and commuter operators), it should pay close attention to FAR 121.157 and the exceptions the grandfather clauses create. If we ignore those exceptions, the most important requirements for Part 121 aircraft are found in FAR 121.157(b), which requires that aircraft type certificated after June 30, 1942, be *transport category aircraft* and meet certain performance standards found in FAR 121.173(b),(d),(e). Transport category aircraft are certificated under *FAR Part 25 (14 CFR Part 25)* to the highest possible standards to assure that the performance and safety levels required by Part 121 are achieved.

Proving Tests

Prior to being used in air carrier operations, air carrier aircraft must be shown to be suitable for the kind of operations proposed by the carrier. This is done by performing *proving tests*. These are dry runs operated by the carrier to show the suitability of the aircraft for the operations it contemplates performing. FAR 121.163 requires that for a new type of aircraft that has not been previously proven for Part 121 operations, the aircraft must be operated for at least 100 hours that include a number of representative flights into airports. The FAA may reduce the 100 hours of flight time if an equivalent level of safety is shown. In addition, a minimum of 10 hours of the proving tests must be made at night. If the aircraft type has been previously proven by a carrier, then FAR 121.163 allows for a minimum of 50 hours of proving tests for the kinds of operations to be conducted by the carrier. Finally, if the carrier desires to operate an aircraft that is materially altered in design, the carrier must also conduct 50 hours of proving tests for each kind of operation it proposes to conduct. Generally, a carrier may not carry passengers during proving test flights.

Airplane Performance and Operating Limitations

The major distinction between aircraft operated under Part 121 and those under Part 91 is the level of operational performance required of the aircraft. Part 121 Subpart I contains numerous considerations as to the performance of the aircraft to be used in air carrier operations. It is important to keep in mind that these rules for *operating* the aircraft work hand in hand with the rules found in FAR Part 25 for *certificating* transport category aircraft. Part 25 certification standards assure that the aircraft is *capable* of the performance while Part 121 assures that it is *operated so as to comply with* or *achieve* the requisite performance standards required by the aircraft certification rules. Let's now examine the performance requirements for aircraft flown under Part 121.

As you study this subpart of the FAR, you may find the frequent reference to dates confusing. The reason for these dates is to recognize that over the years performance standards have been updated and refined. As this happens, older aircraft that were not certificated under the more stringent standard are frequently "grandfathered" to allow them to continue to operate for a period of time so as to allow the owners and operators to secure the economic life from their expensive assets. In our discussions we will mostly refer to modern, turbine aircraft that meet current design standards so the dates will not be so important. This includes virtually all turbine aircraft and most (but not all) turboprop aircraft operated by Part 121 carriers. We will not discuss any reciprocating (piston) aircraft rules. If you find yourself flying these museum pieces, be sure to revisit Subpart I of Part 121 on your own and pay close attention in your initial training. In the discussions below, we will examine only aircraft certificated after August 29, 1959.

We will now turn our attention to the specific performance requirements of these modern turbine (and turboprop) transport category aircraft operated under Part 121. There is a major conceptual difference between air carrier aircraft (transport category aircraft) and other airplanes used in Part 91 operations. In air carrier operations FAA insists on certain minimum performance requirements that assure safe operation of the aircraft is possible even with loss of thrust at critical points in the flight envelope. These limitations include the following:

- *Takeoff limitations,*
- *En route limitations: one engine inoperative,*
- *En route limitations: two engines inoperative,*
- *Landing limitations: destination airports, and*
- *Landing limitations: alternate airports.*

Before going into the specifics of these limitations, let's establish some definitions used in parts 1, 25, and 121 or commonly used in the industry.

Definitions

V_1

V_1 is the maximum speed in the takeoff at which the pilot must take first action (e.g., apply brakes, reduce thrust, deploy speed brakes) to stop the airplane within the accelerate-stop distance. V_1 also means the minimum speed in the takeoff, following a failure of the critical engine at V_{EF}, at which the pilot can continue the takeoff and achieve the required height above the takeoff surface within the takeoff distance.

Although it is not quite accurate, this speed, V_1, is often referred to as the ***takeoff decision speed***. This term is not quite accurate because it implies that we can make the decision to continue or abort at this speed. In reality, allowing for the reaction time of the pilot, he or she must have made the decision to stop prior to attaining this speed and first take action to execute the abort no later than this speed.

In summary, if during the takeoff roll, we have a problem with the aircraft below V_1 we reject the takeoff and stop on the remaining runway. At or above V_1 we are committed to flight even in the event of an engine failure, fire, or other problem. It is safer to go than to stop because we cannot stop on the remaining runway and stopway if we are above V_1.

V_R

V_R is the ***rotation speed*** or the speed at which the nose may be raised to initial climb attitude. This is not a safety speed, *per se*, but rather is the speed to which the aircraft should be accelerated prior to establishing the takeoff/climb pitch attitude for liftoff. It is an aerodynamic consideration to achieve proper performance from the aircraft for the liftoff and climb.

V_2

V_2 is the single engine ***takeoff safety speed***. In the event of an engine failure on takeoff, this is the minimum speed to be maintained to at least 400 feet above the takeoff surface. Maintaining V_2 will guarantee that a twin engine aircraft is capable of a 2.4 percent (or 24 feet per 1,000 feet) single engine climb gradient (2.7 percent for three engine aircraft and 3.0 percent for four engine aircraft). V_2 is analogous to the best single engine rate of climb (V_{YSE}) for a light twin engine aircraft.

V_{EF}

V_{EF} (**engine failure speed**) is the airspeed at which the critical engine is assumed to fail. V_{EF} may not be less than V_{MCG}. This is a "reference" airspeed used in certification of the aircraft, not one which will bear on our operation of the aircraft.

V_{MC}

V_{MC} [**minimum controllable airspeed (airborne)**] is the airspeed at which when the critical engine is suddenly made inoperative, it is possible to maintain control of the airplane with that engine still inoperative and maintain straight flight with an angle of bank of not more than 5 degrees. Additional requirements for V_{MC} may be found in FAR 25.149.

V_{MCG}

V_{MCG} (**minimum control speed on the ground**) is the airspeed during the takeoff run at which when the critical engine is suddenly made inoperative, it is possible to maintain control of the airplane using the rudder control alone (without the use of nose-wheel steering). Additional requirements for V_{MCG} may be found in FAR 25.149.

Accelerate/Stop Distance

Accelerate/stop distance is the amount of runway required to accelerate the aircraft to just below V_1, lose an engine, take the first action to stop the airplane, and come to a complete stop on the remaining runway and stopway.

Balanced Field Length

Balanced field length is the amount of runway and stopway that allows us either to accelerate to just below V_1, lose an engine, and then stop on the remaining runway or to accelerate to at or above V_1 and continue with guaranteed obstacle clearance.

Clearway

Clearway (for turbine aircraft certificated after August 29, 1959) is an area beyond the runway, not less than 500 feet wide, centrally located about the extended centerline of the runway and under the control of the airport authorities. It is expressed in terms of a *clearway plane* with an upward slope not exceeding 1.25 percent, above which no object nor any terrain protrudes. (Threshold lights may protrude if they are 26 inches or less above the end of the runway and are located to the side of the runway.) In other words, it is an obstacle free area at least 250 feet either side of the runway centerline and inclining or rising no more than 12 1/2 feet per 1,000 feet from the runway end. The only obstacles that are permitted in this area are the runway threshold lights.

Net Takeoff Flight Path

Net takeoff flight path is the actual flight path of the aircraft as determined during design and certification trials reduced by a factor specified in FAR 25.111. That reduction factor is 0.8 percent or 8 feet per 1,000 feet traveled for twin engine aircraft. (For three engine aircraft it is 0.9 percent or 9 feet per 1,000 feet traveled, and for four engine airplanes it is 1.0 percent or 10 feet per 1,000 feet traveled.) This is done to create a "fudge factor" so that the actual performance a flight crew obtains from the aircraft will be at least equal to and probably better than that required. Net takeoff flight path will be compared to the climb gradients required by Part 121 to determine compliance with Part 121. (See fig. 8.1.)

Takeoff Path

The *takeoff path* extends from brake release on the runway to point in the takeoff at which the airplane is 1,500 feet above the takeoff surface, *or* a point at which the transition from the takeoff to the cruise climb configuration is completed and a speed is reached at which compliance with Section 25.1211(c) is shown (a specified climb gradient and air speed at least 1.25 V_S), whichever point is higher. In addition,

- The takeoff path must be based on the procedures prescribed in Section 25.101(f),
- The airplane must be accelerated on the ground to the engine failure speed (V_{EF}), *at which point the critical engine must be made inoperative and remain inoperative* for the rest of the takeoff, and
- After reaching V_{EF}, the airplane must be accelerated to V_2;
- The slope of the airborne part of the takeoff path must be positive at each point;
- The airplane must reach V_2 before it is 35 feet above the surface and then continue at a speed as close as practical to V_2 (but not less than V_2) until it is 400 feet above the surface;
- At each point along the takeoff path, starting 400 feet above the takeoff surface, the available climb gradient may not be less than

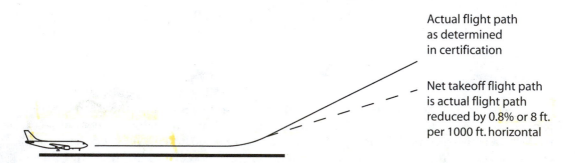

Actual flight path
as determined
in certification

Net takeoff flight path
is actual flight path
reduced by 0.8% or 8 ft.
per 1000 ft. horizontal

Figure 8.1 Twin engine net takeoff flight path.

> ➤ 1.2 per cent for two engine airplanes,
> ➤ 1.5 per cent for three engine airplanes, or
> ➤ 1.7 per cent for four engine airplanes; and

- No pilot action except to raise the landing gear or feather propellers may be required until the airplane is 400 feet above the takeoff surface. Other than automatic power adjustments, no change in configuration is permitted

In other words, the takeoff path is designed to allow us to lose an engine at or above V_1. We then accelerate to V_R, rotate the aircraft, accelerate to V_{LOF}, and liftoff. After liftoff at V_{LOF}, we retract the landing gear and climb to 400 feet (sometimes called **acceleration altitude**), run emergency checklists and clean up the aircraft for climb, then climb to at least 1,500 feet (or higher) above the takeoff surface while maintaining the specified obstacle clearance. The takeoff path provides obstacle clearance for the entire **four segment climb** (discussed below) so that the takeoff and departure is obstacle protected all the way from the surface to 1,500 feet (or sometimes higher altitude).

Takeoff Run

If the *takeoff distance* calculation does not include use of a clearway, the **takeoff run** is equal to the **takeoff distance** (see below).

If the *takeoff distance* includes a clearway, the *takeoff run* (on a dry runway) is the greater of the horizontal distance along the takeoff path to a point halfway between the point at which V_{LOF} (**liftoff airspeed**) is reached and the point at which the airplane is 35 feet above the takeoff surface (as determined by FAR 25.111 for a dry runway) or 115 percent of the horizontal distance along the takeoff path, with all engines operating from the start of the takeoff to a point halfway between the point at which V_{LOF} is reached and the point at which the airplane is 35 feet above the takeoff surface.

If the takeoff distance includes a clearway, the takeoff run (on a wet runway) is the greater of the horizontal distance along the takeoff path from the start of the takeoff to the point at which the airplane is 15 feet above the takeoff surface, achieved in a manner consistent with the achievement of V_2 before reaching 35 feet above the takeoff surface (as determined by FAR 25.111 for a wet runway) or 115 percent of the horizontal distance along the takeoff path, with all engines operating from the start of the takeoff to a point halfway between the point at which V_{LOF} is reached and the point at which the airplane is 35 feet above the takeoff surface.

Perhaps at the risk of oversimplifying, the *takeoff run* is the distance that allows us to

- Release brakes,
- Accelerate to V_1,
- Lose the critical engine,
- Accelerate to V_R,
- Accelerate to V_{LOF}, and
- Proceed horizontally to a point that is halfway between the point where liftoff speed was attained and the point where we reached an altitude of 35 feet above the takeoff surface.

It is somewhat analogous to the *ground roll* of a light aircraft. Alternatively, it is 115 percent of the horizontal distance (with all engines operating) from brake release to a point that is halfway between the point where liftoff speed was attained and the point where we reached an altitude of 35 feet above the takeoff surface.

Takeoff Distance

Takeoff distance on a *dry runway* is the greater of

- The horizontal distance along the takeoff path from the start of the takeoff to the point at which the airplane is 35 feet above the takeoff surface, determined under Section 25.111 for a dry runway or
- 115 percent of the horizontal distance along the takeoff path, with all engines operating, from the start of the takeoff to the point at which the airplane is 35 feet above the takeoff surface, as determined by a procedure consistent with Section 25.111.

Takeoff distance on a *wet runway* is the greater of

- The takeoff distance on a dry runway determined in accordance with the dry runway procedures, above, or
- The horizontal distance along the takeoff path from the start of the takeoff to the point at which the airplane is 15 feet above the takeoff surface, achieved in a manner consistent with the achievement of V_2 before reaching 35 feet above the takeoff surface, determined under Section 25.111 for a wet runway.

Again, perhaps at the risk of oversimplifying, the *takeoff distance* is the distance that allows us to

- Release brakes,
- Accelerate to V_1,
- Lose the critical engine,
- Accelerate to V_R,
- Accelerate to V_{LOF}, and
- Proceed horizontally to a point 35 feet above the takeoff surface (by which V_2 must be achieved).

Takeoff distance is somewhat analogous to the total distance to clear a 50 foot obstacle given for light aircraft. There are two alternative ways of computing the takeoff distance. On a dry runway it is 115 percent of the horizontal distance (with all engines operating) from brake release to a point where the aircraft reaches an altitude of 35 feet above the takeoff surface. (See fig. 8.2.) On a wet runway, it is the horizontal distance (with all engines operating) from brake release to a point where we reached an altitude of 15 feet above the takeoff surface.

The foregoing has all considered the certification requirements of the aircraft used in Part 121 operations. Now, let's look at the operating limitations of Part 121.

Takeoff Limitations (FAR 121.189)

The first requirement of FAR 121.189(a) is quite straightforward. It simply requires that no one operating a turbine-powered airplane may take off at a weight that exceeds the maximum allowable weight allowed by the airplane flight manual considering the altitude (airport elevation) and temperature existing at the time of departure. This requirement is satisfied by referring to the *WAT limit* charts—weight-altitude-temperature limit charts. The WAT limit charts will be prepared for use for each aircraft type for each runway used by the carrier. Several limiting weights will appear on these charts.

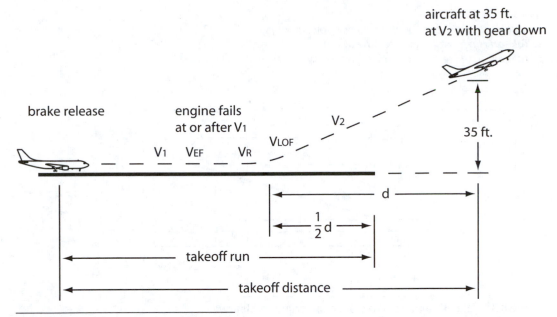

Figure 8.2 Takeoff run/takeoff distance.

The first such limit is the ***runway limit weight***. The runway limit weight is the maximum weight, at existing conditions, that will guarantee that the aircraft meets the balanced field length requirements. In other words, it is the maximum weight at which we can experience a so-called V_1 failure and still stop on the remaining runway or continue to a point 35 feet above the runway within the runway/clearway distance limits. The runway limit weight is the most restrictive weight limit.

FAR 121.189(c) requires that several conditions be met (see fig. 8.3):

- We may not take off at a weight so great that the *accelerate/stop distance* would exceed the length of the *runway and any **stopway***. That is, the weight must allow us to accelerate to engine failure speed and still be able to stop on the concrete (or improved) surface.
- The *takeoff run* must not be greater than the length of the *runway.*
- Further, the weight may not be so great that the *takeoff distance* exceeds the *length of the runway plus any clearway*. If we are using any clearway to compute the takeoff distance, we may only use clearway less than or equal to one-half the length of the runway surface.

The second limiting weight is the so-called ***climb limit weight***. The climb limit weight guarantees that we can proceed from the point 35 feet above the runway to 1,500 feet above the runway surface (or specified higher altitude) while maintaining required climb gradients in order to achieve adequate obstacle clearance.

Another weight limiting factor to control is V_{MC}. The V_{MC} *limit* is used in aircraft where reduced power takeoffs are used. Reduced power takeoff techniques might be used for economy, noise abatement, or other reasons. However, in the event of an engine failure, we would probably increase the power on the operating engine(s). Remember that this is permitted if it occurs automatically. V_2 protects against loss of control due to V_{MC}, but only to the original reduced power setting. When the higher power is automatically applied, that could cause loss of control due to the speed at the existing weight

Notes:

1. ***Accelerate/stop*** must occur on runway plus stopway.
2. ***Takeoff run*** must occur over runway only.
3. ***Takeoff distance*** must occur within runway and allowable clearway.

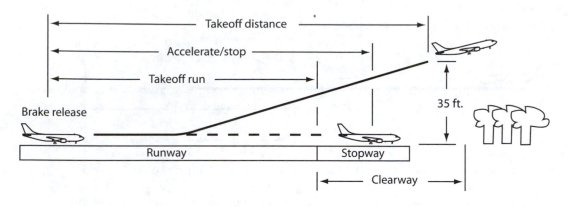

Figure 8.3 Takeoff run/takeoff distance over runway/clearway.

being below the new V_{MC} that results from the higher power setting. V_{MC} is higher at lower weights; therefore, the V_{MC} weight limit is a *minimum weight* whereas the runway limit weight and the climb limit weight are *maximum weights.*

FAR 121.189(d) looks at the net takeoff flight path after takeoff to assure that we have increasing separation from obstacles and terrain as we work our way out of the immediate airport/runway environment. Our weight must allow a *net takeoff flight path* that clears all obstacles either by a height of 35 feet vertically, or by at least 200 feet horizontally within the airport boundaries (300 feet after passing the airport boundaries).

In performing our maximum weight calculations for FAR 121.189 flight paths we must consider (correct for)

- The runway to be used,
- The airport elevation,
- The effective runway gradient,
- The ambient temperature (normally gotten from ATIS),
- Wind component at the time of takeoff, and
- Runway surface condition (wet/dry) if the airplane flight manual adjusts for this. (Note the manual may allow a correction for grooving or porous friction courses. You may only use this correction if the runway actually has this surface.)

Therefore, as we mentioned earlier, the takeoff performance charts used by the flight crew and dispatch in calculating this information must be for each runway to be used, for any reasonable weight likely to be encountered, and for the wind and temperature conditions existing at the time of departure. That is, takeoff charts (and landing charts) are runway and condition specific.

Finally, FAR 121.189 makes some assumptions about maneuvering the aircraft immediately after departure as banking would reduce performance. First, the aircraft *may not be banked* prior to reaching a height of 50 feet as shown by the flight path or net flight path data. Second, after attaining 50 feet in height, the aircraft *may not be banked more than 15 degrees* in any additional maneuvering.

Let's see if we can now summarize the takeoff limitations in a way that simplifies and explains more clearly what they actually accomplish. To do this we will examine the *four segment climb performance.* (See fig. 8.4.) Four segment climb performance requirements take all of the requirements previously discussed and relate them in such a way as to ensure adequate terrain/obstacle clearance all the way from the runway up to the en route environment.

First segment climb begins at brake release and ends at a point after takeoff where the speed is V_2 and the landing gear has finished retracting. This will be at an altitude of more than 35 feet above the runway surface and at an airspeed of V_2. During first segment climb (starting from V_{LOF}) the aircraft is only required to demonstrate a *positive rate of climb* after liftoff. During this portion of the departure, the crew is neither expected nor required to do anything except fly the airplane and raise the landing gear.

Second segment climb begins at the point where the aircraft achieves gear retraction at a speed of V_2 and ends at *acceleration altitude* (normally 400 feet). During this segment of the departure, in the event of an engine failure the crew is only expected to do the immediate items required to fly the airplane. This would include feathering an inoperative turboprop propeller. The aircraft must maintain a *minimum climb gradient of 2.4 percent or 24 feet per 1,000 feet traveled.* No turning or banking of the aircraft is permitted prior to 50 feet above the runway surface. A maximum 15 degree bank is permitted after that.

Third segment climb begins at acceleration altitude and continues until the aircraft is cleaned up and established in the cruise climb configuration at the cruise climb airspeed. During this segment of departure the aircraft is accelerated, flaps are retracted, any emergency checklists are run, and maximum continuous or cruise climb power is set. The aircraft must maintain a net takeoff flight path *minimum climb gradient of 1.2 percent or 12 feet per 1,000 feet traveled.* The minimum gradient is 1.5 percent for three engine aircraft (15 feet per 1,000 feet traveled) and 1.7 percent for four engine aircraft (17 feet per 1,000 feet traveled).

Fourth segment climb begins with the climb configuration and airspeed set and ends (normally) at 1,500 feet above the surface. During fourth segment climb a twin engine aircraft must also be able to maintain a net takeoff flight path *minimum climb gradient of 1.2 percent or 12 feet per 1,000 feet traveled.* The minimum gradient is 1.5 percent for three engine aircraft (15 feet per 1,000 feet traveled) and 1.7 percent for four engine aircraft (17 feet per 1,000 feet traveled).

En Route Limitations: One Engine Inoperative (FAR 121.191)

Our takeoff limitations of FAR 121.189 protected us in the event of an engine failure on departure from anywhere on the runway to a point nominally 1,500 feet above the surface. It did this by assuring that the aircraft is operated so that it is able to climb out and provide an increasing separation between the aircraft and the terrain/obstacles. Our en route limitations are similarly concerned about assuring that should we lose an engine (or engines) en route the aircraft has sufficient performance to clear all terrain on our way back into an airport terminal area.

The first requirement is found in FAR 121.161(a). This says that a two- or three-engine turbine-powered airplane may not be operated over a route that contains a point farther than 1 hour of flying time (in still air at normal cruising speed with one engine inoperative) from an adequate airport. We will see later that there are exceptions to this rule in an area known as ETOPS or extended range twin engine operations.

FAR 121.191(a) requires that the aircraft be operated at a such a weight that for one engine inoperative (OEI) performance, if we should we lose an engine, we have the ability

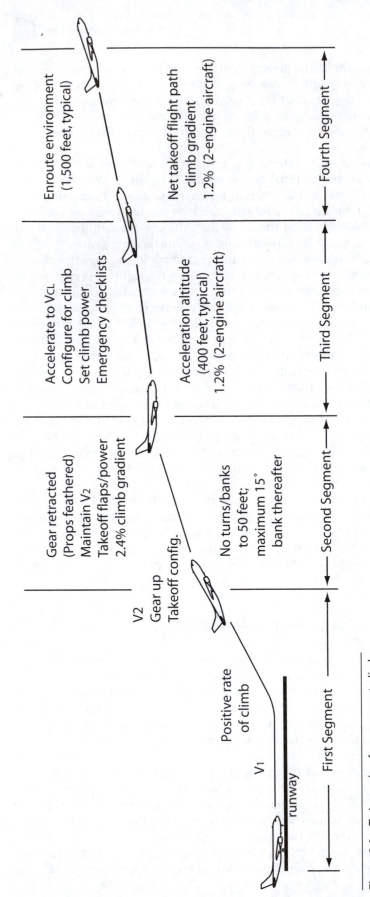

Figure 8.4 Twin engine four segment climb.

to operate the aircraft safely to an alternate airport (en route alternate). This can be demonstrated in either of two ways. First, FAR 121.191(a)(1) requires that the net flight path exhibit a positive slope (meaning that we are climbing faster than the terrain is rising or the terrain is falling away at a rate greater than our descent rate) from cruise altitude all the way down to within 1,000 feet of the ground. This is measured within 5 statute miles on either side of the flight track of the aircraft. In addition, we require a positive slope at 1,500 feet above the airport of intended emergency landing after the engine failure. The other way we can comply with this en route limitation is by using the so-called ***driftdown*** technique.

FAR 121.191(a)(2) recognizes that we may be operating the aircraft at a high altitude where the OEI performance would result in a descent rate that was not a positive slope net flight path. That is, we are descending at a faster rate than the ground is falling away. This is not necessarily dangerous. For example, we may be descending at a descent gradient of 300 feet per nautical mile while the terrain is only lowering at an average of 100 feet per nautical mile. This would be a negative slope of 200 feet per nautical mile. If we were only a couple of thousand feet above the terrain, this might be a problem. On the other hand, we may have begun the OEI operation at flight level 390 over terrain that is only 3,000 feet MSL. Clearly, there is no immediate hazard even though we are descending at a rate greater than the terrain is lowering. In fact, our maximum service ceiling—OEI may only be 12,000 feet MSL. FAR 121.191(a)(2) says we may operate in this situation so long as the net flight path allows the aircraft to clear all terrain and obstructions within 5 statute miles by at least 2,000 feet vertically and with a positive slope at 1,500 feet above the airport. The lowest altitude where we could lose an engine and still comply with this provision is sometimes referred to as the ***driftdown altitude*** (see fig. 8.5).

In calculating our ability to comply with FAR 121.191 we must make several assumptions:

- The engine fails at the most critical point en route,
- The airplane passes over the critical obstruction after engine failure at a point that is no closer to the obstruction than the nearest approved radio navigation fix (although alternatives to this may be approved),

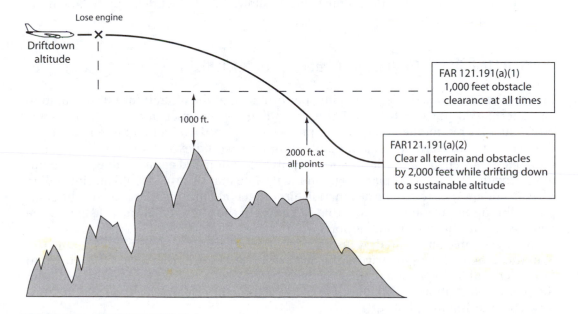

Figure 8.5 Driftdown altitude.

- An approved method for considering adverse winds is employed,
- The crew may jettison fuel if the crew is trained and precautions are taken to assure jettisoning may be performed safely,
- The alternate airport to be used must be specified in the dispatch or flight release and must meet alternate weather minimums, and
- Fuel consumption is based on approved values in the approved net flight path data in the airplane flight manual (AFM).

En Route Limitations: Two Engines Inoperative (FAR 121.193)

This provision is designed to provide that reasonable options exist to successfully complete a flight for aircraft having three or more engines in the event of a dual engine failure. The operator is given two alternatives. The first, found in FAR 121.193(c)(1), is quite simple. It says simply that the operator can comply so long as there is no point on the route structure where the flight is more than 90 minutes flying time (all engines operating) from an approved alternate airport. If the operator cannot comply with this provision, then it may use a concept similar in nature to what we saw earlier for OEI operations.

FAR 121.193(c)(2) says if the aircraft can be operated at a weight that allows it to fly from a point where the two engines failed simultaneously to an authorized alternate airport and clear all terrain and obstructions within 5 statute miles of the intended track by at least 2,000 feet vertically then it is good to go. This performance is achieved under the following assumptions:

- The two engines fail simultaneously at the most critical point en route;
- The net flight path has a positive slope at 1,500 feet above the alternate airport;
- The crew may jettison fuel if the crew is trained and precautions are taken to assure this may be performed safely;
- The weight at the point of engine failure includes enough fuel to continue to the airport, arrive at an altitude of 1,500 feet directly over the airport, and fly for 15 additional minutes at cruise thrust; and
- Fuel and oil consumption is the same as allowed in the net flight path data in the airplane flight manual.

Landing Limitations: Destination Airports (FAR 121.195)

The next area to consider is the landing performance of the aircraft for our destination and alternate airports. FAR 121.195 covers landing performance at the destination airport. The first requirement is quite simple: we cannot *take off* an airplane at a weight that, allowing for normal fuel and oil consumption, would exceed the approved maximum landing weight (at the destination airport's elevation and actual ambient temperature) provided for in the airplane flight manual. Note that this rule would be violated on *takeoff,* not upon arrival at the destination airport. It is a *planning rule* and must be complied with upon takeoff. Also, note that it applies to the alternate airports listed for the flight as well as the destination airports.

Next, we consider the landing distance requirements. FAR 121.195(b) says that an aircraft must take off so as to arrive at the destination at a weight that allows the aircraft to be landed within 60 percent of the effective length of the runway. This is measured from the point 50 feet above the intersection of the obstruction clearance plane and the runway. The rule assumes that

- In still air the operator may select the most favorable runway and the most favorable direction and
- If there is forecast to be winds upon arrival, the airplane is landed on the most suitable runway considering the probable wind velocity and direction, ground handling characteristics of the aircraft, and other conditions such as landing aids and terrain.

FAR 121.195(c) provides some relief from the above rule for aircraft that can't comply with FAR 121.195(b)(2). If a turbine aircraft can't comply with this rule, it may take off if an alternate airport is filed that meets the requirements of paragraph (b). A turboprop aircraft may take off if we file an alternate airport where the aircraft can be landed within 70 percent of the effective length of the runway.

Wet runways require a further consideration. FAR 121.195(d) says that unless there are approved landing distances/techniques in the AFM, if the runways are forecast to be wet or slippery at the estimated time of arrival, the available runway at the destination must be at least 115 percent of the length calculated above.

Let's put all of this together. If our aircraft required a landing distance of 4,900 feet to land, we would require $(4,900)/(0.60) = 8,316$ feet effective runway length. If it were forecast to be wet or slippery, we would require $(8,316) \times 1.15 = 9,563$ feet.

Landing Limitations: Alternate Airports (FAR 121.197)

This rule is similar to the landing limitations for destination airports. It says that the operator may not list an airport as an alternate airport if [based on the same assumptions as used in FAR 121.195(b)] at the anticipated weight at the anticipated time of arrival the aircraft cannot be brought to a stop in 60 percent of the effective runway length for turbine aircraft or 70 percent of the effective runway length for turboprop aircraft. In the case of a departure airport alternate, the rule allows fuel to be jettisoned (dumped) in addition to normal consumption.

Summary

In this chapter we have looked at the performance required of transport category aircraft used in Part 121 operations. We have seen that the requirements are there to assure that in the event of readily anticipated equipment failures we will still have adequate performance to operate the aircraft safely. In the next chapter we look in detail at the wide variety of special airworthiness standards that apply to Part 121 aircraft.

Important Terms from this Chapter

Accelerate/stop distance	Driftdown altitude
Acceleration altitude	Dry lease
Balanced field length	En route limitations: one engine inoperative
Clearway	En route limitations: two engines inoperative
Climb limit weight	FAR Part 25 (14 CFR Part 25)
Driftdown	First segment climb

Four segment climb performance

Fourth segment climb

Landing limitations: alternate airports

Landing limitations: destination airports

Net takeoff flight path

Proving tests

Runway limit weight

Second segment climb

Stopway

Takeoff decision speed

Takeoff distance

Takeoff distance, dry runway

Takeoff distance, wet runway

Takeoff limitations

Takeoff path

Takeoff run

Third segment climb

Transport category aircraft

V_1

V_2: takeoff safety speed

V_{CL}: minimum climb speed

V_{EF}: engine failure speed

V_{LOF}: liftoff speed

V_{MC}: minimum controllable airspeed (airborne)

V_{MC} limit

V_{MCG}: minimum control speed on the ground

V_R: rotation speed

V_S

WAT limit charts

Chapter 8 Exam

1. All aircraft operated by FAR 121 carriers must either be U.S. registered aircraft or
    a. Foreign aircraft operated under wet lease to the U.S. carrier.
    b. Foreign aircraft, approved under U.S. type design and operated under dry lease to the U.S. carrier.
    c. Foreign aircraft, approved under ICAO type design and operated under dry lease to the U.S. carrier.
    d. Foreign aircraft may not be operated by U.S. carriers.

2. Proving tests are required of new type designs. If the design has never been proved under Part 121, it must be operated for
    a. 25 hours including 10 at night.
    b. 50 hours including 10 at night.
    c. 100 hours including 10 at night.
    d. 200 hours including 10 at night.

3. V_1, or takeoff decision speed, is the
    a. Maximum speed in the takeoff at which the pilot must first take action to stop.
    b. Maximum speed in the takeoff at which the pilot must decide to take action to stop.
    c. Maximum speed in the takeoff where a takeoff may still be initiated.
    d. Minimum speed in the takeoff where it is possible to get airborne.

4. In the event of an engine failure at or above V_1, the pilot should achieve and maintain V_2, until
    a. 35 feet above the runway surface.
    b. The landing gear is retracted.
    c. Acceleration altitude.
    d. The airplane is established (configured) for en route climb.

5. Net takeoff flight path is used in computing takeoff/climb performance capability of the aircraft. What is net takeoff flight path?
    a. The climb performance of the aircraft as determined in certification testing.
    b. The climb performance of the aircraft as determined in certification testing reduced by 8 feet per 1,000 feet traveled.
    c. The climb performance of the aircraft as determined in certification testing reduced by the loss of performance in the event of an engine failure.
    d. All of the above.

6. Takeoff run must be accomplished
    a. Within the length of the runway.
    b. Within the length of the runway plus stopway.
    c. Within the length of the runway plus stopway plus clearway.
    d. Within the length of the runway plus clearway (except clearway may only be counted up to one-half the length of the runway).

7. Takeoff distance must be accomplished
    a. Within the length of the runway.
    b. Within the length of the runway plus stopway.
    c. Within the length of the runway plus stopway plus clearway.
    d. Within the length of the runway plus clearway (except clearway may only be counted up to one-half the length of the runway).

8. Runway limit weight guarantees that an aircraft may
    a. Accelerate to V_1, lose an engine, and stop on the remaining runway.
    b. Accelerate to V_1, lose an engine, and stop on the remaining runway plus stopway.
    c. Accelerate to V_1, lose an engine, and continue the flight.
    d. None of the above.

9. The maximum weight at which an air carrier aircraft may depart is limited to
    a. The maximum weight that will assure compliance with engine out climb limits.
    b. The maximum weight that will guarantee en route OEI terrain clearance.
    c. The maximum weight that will assure landing below maximum landing weight.
    d. All of the above.

10. A turbine aircraft is scheduled into a runway that is 8,600 feet in length. May our aircraft (which will require 5,100 feet to land) land there on a wet day?
    a. Yes.
    b. No.
    c. Insufficient information to determine.

Airworthiness Requirements

A commercial aircraft is a vehicle capable of supporting itself aerodynamically and economically at the same time.

—William Stout
Designer of the Ford Tri-Motor

In this chapter we will examine the airworthiness standards applicable to air carrier transport category aircraft. We will begin our study with the *special* airworthiness requirements of Subpart J of Part 121 but will expand that to include some of the certification requirements under FAR Part 25 as well.

Subpart J to Part 121

Subpart J to Part 121: Special Airworthiness Standards is a good example of why it is important to read the applicability section of each subpart of Part 121 closely. Upon close reading of FAR 121.211 we see that most of Subpart J is applicable only to older aircraft certificated under the CAR (Civil Aeronautics Regulations of the CAA) prior to November 1, 1946. The intent of those rules (FAR 121.215 through FAR 121.283) is to bring the safety standards of older aircraft up to approximately the standards of more modern aircraft. These things are now required as part of the certification of newer aircraft (and in some cases current standards are more stringent than those found in Subpart J). Later in this chapter we will look at the current standards for many of these issues. All certificate holders must comply with FAR 121.285 through FAR 121.291. Therefore, let's start with a look at those rules.

Carrying Cargo

The first two rules in this area relate to carrying cargo aboard the aircraft either in the passenger cabin or the cargo compartment. FAR 121.285 begins with the basic premise that, subject to exceptions, a carrier may not carry cargo in a passenger compartment of the aircraft. This rule is imposed in consideration of the reaction of the cargo and its containers in the event of an accident. The exceptions that allow cargo to be carried in the passenger compartment fall into two general areas. The first exception is if the cargo is carried in properly designed bins and the second is if the cargo is carried behind a bulkhead and is properly restrained. Let's look at the specifics.

Cargo Bins

FAR 121.285(b) says that cargo may be carried anywhere in the passenger compartment so long as it is in an approved cargo bin that can withstand "G" forces equal to 1.15 times the load factors applicable to emergency landing conditions. The maximum weight that can be carried must be conspicuously marked on the bin along with any instructions necessary to ensure proper loading and weight distribution of the cargo. The bin must be securely anchored to either the floor or seat tracks in the aircraft. Installation of the bin cannot in any way interfere with or restrict the access to or use of any required emergency exit or aisle in the passenger compartment and it may not block the view of the "no smoking" and "fasten seat belt" signs. The bin itself must be made of material that is at least flame resistant. The bin must be designed to prevent the cargo from shifting in the bin.

Bulkheads

FAR 121.285(c) permits a carrier to install a bulkhead to separate the passenger and cargo compartments on the main deck of the aircraft. The cargo must be carried behind the bulkhead and must be properly secured by a safety belt or tie-down that is strong enough to eliminate the possibility of cargo shifting in all normally anticipated conditions. The cargo must be packaged or covered so as to prevent injury to the passengers. The cargo must comply with the load limitations that are imposed on the floor and seat tracks (if used). Location of the main deck cargo compartment cannot restrict or limit access to any required emergency or regular exit or the aisle in the passenger compartment. The cargo compartment cannot restrict the passenger's view of the "fasten seat belt" and "no smoking" signs unless alternative signs are installed.

Access to Cargo Compartments

If the cargo compartment is designed to require crewmembers to enter the compartment to extinguish fires in flight then FAR 121.287 requires that the cargo must be loaded in such a manner as to allow the crewmember to effectively reach all parts of the compartment with the contents of a hand fire extinguisher.

Landing Gear Aural Warning Device

Current Part 25 regulations require a ***landing gear aural warning device:*** *The flight crew must be given an aural warning that functions continuously, or is periodically repeated, if a landing is attempted when the landing gear is not locked down.* Older regulations required only that the warning system test the throttle position. FAR 121.289 therefore applies to aircraft certificated prior to January 6, 1992, that only tested the throttle position. Now, those aircraft systems must also test the flap position. If the system detects the flaps in a position normally used for landing and the landing gear is not down, the warning must sound.

Evacuation Demonstrations

FAR 121.291 requires operators of aircraft with 44 or more seats to conduct ***evacuation demonstrations*** prior to placing the aircraft in service. This demonstration requires that the carrier be able to evacuate the entire aircraft in 90 seconds or less. If the manufacturer has demonstrated this in certification under Part 25 since December 1, 1978, then the carrier may dispense with the full evacuation demonstration. In that case, the carrier may perform the partial evacuation demonstration required by FAR 121.291(b). This partial evacuation demonstration is required when the carrier initially places the aircraft in service. Note that the carrier must also perform partial evacuation tests any time it alters the aircraft by changing the number, location, type of exits, or type of opening mechanism on emergency exits available for evacuation.

Part 25 Airworthiness Requirements

Part 25 airworthiness requirements impose a large number of airworthiness standards on transport category aircraft. For the balance of this chapter we will explore some of these requirements that make air carrier aircraft quite different from the light, general aviation aircraft with which you may be familiar.

Flight Control Systems

FAR 25.671 pertains to flight controls and contains some interesting requirements. First, each control and control system must operate with the ease, smoothness, and positiveness appropriate to its function. Each element of each ***flight control system*** must be designed, or distinctively and permanently marked, to minimize the probability of incorrect assembly that could result in the malfunctioning of the system. The airplane must be shown to be capable of continued safe flight and landing after any of the following failures or jamming in the flight control system and surfaces (including trim, lift, drag, and feel systems), within the normal flight envelope, without requiring exceptional piloting skill or strength:

(1) *Any single failure, excluding jamming (for example, disconnection or failure of mechanical elements, or structural failure of hydraulic components, such as actuators, control spool housing, and valves).*

(2) *Any combination of failures not shown to be extremely improbable, excluding jamming (for example, dual electrical or hydraulic system failures, or any single failure in combination with any probable hydraulic or electrical failure).*

(3) *Any jam in a control position normally encountered during takeoff, climb, cruise, normal turns, descent, and landing unless the jam is shown to be extremely improbable, or can be alleviated. A runaway of a flight control to an adverse position and jam must be accounted for if such runaway and subsequent jamming is not extremely improbable.*

FAR 25.671

Probable malfunctions can have only minor effects on control system operation and must be capable of being readily counteracted by the pilot. The requirement that the aircraft be able to be flown in the event of a control jam leads to a major difference between many air carrier aircraft and light general aviation aircraft. Since the aircraft must be controllable even in the event of a control jam, many transport category aircraft have split controls. That means that one side (left ailerons for example) is controlled by the pilot's control yoke and the other side (right ailerons in this example) is controlled by the copilot's control yoke. In normal operations the two systems are interconnected and flown as a single unit as on light aircraft. In the event of a jam the crew can disconnect the two sets of controls, identify the jammed side (or *circuit*), and continue control of the aircraft using the operating control system.

Control Systems Gust Locks

While some light aircraft have *control systems gust locks*, which are installed or operated by the pilot, many others do not. In transport category aircraft this is not an option. There must be a device to prevent damage to the control surfaces (including tabs) and the control system from gusts striking the airplane while it is on the ground. If the device, when engaged, prevents normal operation of the control surfaces by the pilot, it must

> *(1)   Automatically disengage when the pilot operates the primary flight controls in a normal manner; or*
> *(2)   Limit the operation of the airplane so that the pilot receives unmistakable warning at the start of takeoff.*

FAR 25.679

Further, the device must have means to preclude the possibility of it becoming engaged inadvertently in flight.

Takeoff Warning System

Transport category aircraft must have a *takeoff warning system* installed that meets the following requirements:

The system must provide an aural warning that is automatically activated during the initial portion of the takeoff roll if the airplane is in a configuration that would not allow a safe takeoff. That includes the following erroneous configurations:

> *(1)   The wing flaps or leading edge devices are not set within the approved range for takeoff.*
> *(2)   Wing spoilers (except lateral control spoilers, speed brakes, or longitudinal trim devices) are in a position that would not allow a safe takeoff.*

FAR 25.703

Once the takeoff warning is given, it must continue to sound until

> *(1)   The configuration is changed to allow a safe takeoff,*
> *(2)   Action is taken by the pilot to terminate the takeoff roll,*
> *(3)   The airplane is rotated for takeoff, or*
> *(4)   The warning is manually deactivated by the pilot.*

FAR 25.703

Flight Crew Emergency Exits

All airplanes having a passenger seating capacity greater than 20 seats require that *flight crew emergency exits* be located in the flight crew area. These exits must be of sufficient size and located so as to permit rapid evacuation by the crew. One exit shall be provided on each side of the airplane; or, alternatively, a top hatch shall be provided. Each exit must encompass an unobstructed rectangular opening of at least 19 by 20 inches unless satisfactory exit utility can be demonstrated by a typical crewmember.

Emergency Lighting

An *emergency lighting* system that is independent of the main lighting system must be installed in transport category airplanes. The sources of general cabin illumination may be common to both the emergency and the main lighting systems if the power supply to the emergency lighting system is independent of the power supply to the main lighting system. The emergency lighting system must include illuminated emergency exit marking and locating signs, sources of general cabin illumination, interior lighting in emergency exit areas, and floor proximity escape path marking. It must also include exterior emergency lighting.

Emergency Exit Signs

Each passenger *emergency exit* locator *sign* required and each passenger *emergency exit marking sign* required must have red letters on an illuminated white background. These signs must be internally electrically illuminated. The floor of the passageway leading to each floor-level passenger emergency exit, between the main aisles and the exit openings, must be provided with illumination centered on the passenger evacuation path. *Floor proximity emergency escape path marking* must provide emergency evacuation guidance for passengers when all sources of illumination more than 4 feet above the cabin aisle floor are totally obscured. At night, the floor proximity emergency escape path marking must enable each passenger to

(1) *After leaving the passenger seat, visually identify the emergency escape path along the cabin aisle floor to the first exits or pair of exits forward and aft of the seat; and*

(2) *Readily identify each exit from the emergency escape path by reference only to markings and visual features not more than 4 feet above the cabin floor.*

FAR 25.812(e)

Emergency Lighting Controls

Generally, but not always, the lights must be operable manually from the flight crew station and from a point in the passenger compartment that is readily accessible to a normal flight attendant seat. There must be a flight crew warning light, which illuminates when power is on in the airplane and the emergency lighting control device is not armed. The cockpit control device must have an "on," "off," and "armed" position so that when armed in the cockpit or turned on at either the cockpit or flight attendant station the lights will either light or remain lighted upon interruption of the airplane's normal electric power. There must be a means to safeguard against inadvertent operation of the control device from the "armed" or "on" positions. The energy supply to each emergency lighting unit must provide the required level of illumination for at least 10 minutes at the critical ambient conditions after emergency landing.

Emergency Lighting Energy Supply

If storage batteries are used as the energy supply for the emergency lighting system, they may be recharged from the airplane's main electric power system, provided that the charging circuit is designed to preclude inadvertent battery discharge into charging circuit faults. Components of the emergency lighting system, including batteries, wiring relays, lamps, and switches, must be capable of normal operation after being subjected to the inertia forces typical of a crash landing. The emergency lighting system must be designed so that after any single transverse vertical separation of the fuselage during crash landing, not more than 25 percent of all electrically illuminated emergency lights (in addition to the lights that are directly damaged by the separation) are rendered inoperative. In addition, each required electrically illuminated exit sign must remain operative (again, exclusive of those that are directly damaged by the separation) and at least one exterior emergency light for each side of the airplane must remain operative.

Pressurized Cabins

Pressurized cabins and compartments must be equipped to provide a cabin pressure altitude of not more than 8,000 feet at the maximum operating altitude of the airplane under normal operating conditions. If certification for operation above 25,000 feet is requested, the airplane must be designed so that occupants will not be exposed to cabin pressure altitudes in excess of 15,000 feet after any probable failure condition in the pressurization system. Further, the airplane must be designed so that occupants will not be exposed to a cabin pressure altitude that exceeds the following after decompression from any failure condition not shown to be extremely improbable:

- 25,000 feet for more than 2 minutes or
- 40,000 feet for any duration.

Interior Fire Protection and Flammability Standards

Part 25 sets rigorous *interior fire protection and flammability standards* for everything that goes into a transport category airplane interior. For each interior compartment occupied by the crew or passengers, the following apply:

(1)   *Materials (including finishes or decorative surfaces applied to the materials) must meet the applicable test criteria prescribed in Part I of Appendix F of Part 25 (or other approved equivalent methods).*

(2)   *In addition to meeting the requirements of paragraph (a), seat cushions, except those on flight crewmember seats, must meet the test requirements of Part II of Appendix F of Part 21 (or other approved equivalent methods).*

(3)   *Except for certain crew and public spaces, the following interior components of airplanes with passenger capacities of 20 or more must also meet the test requirements of parts IV and V of Appendix F of Part 25 in addition to the flammability requirements prescribed in paragraph (1):*

    (a)   *Interior ceiling and wall panels, other than lighting lenses and windows;*

    (b)   *Partitions, other than transparent panels needed to enhance cabin safety;*

    (c)   *Galley structure, including exposed surfaces of stowed carts and standard containers and the cavity walls that are exposed when a full complement of such carts or containers is not carried; and*

    (d)   *Large cabinets and cabin stowage compartments, other than underseat stowage compartments for stowing small items such as magazines and maps.*

FAR 25.853

Smoking Regulations

Smoking is not allowed in lavatories. If smoking is to be allowed in any other compartment occupied by the crew or passengers, an adequate number of self-contained removable ashtrays must be provided for all seated occupants. Smoking is currently prohibited on all U.S. air carrier aircraft. Regardless of whether smoking is allowed in any other part of the airplane, lavatories must have self-contained removable ashtrays located conspicuously on or near the entry side of each lavatory door, except that one ashtray may serve more than one lavatory door if the ashtray can be seen readily from the cabin side of each lavatory served.

Lavatory Fire Protection

Because the United States has banned smoking on all U.S. air carrier aircraft, **lavatory fire protection** receives special attention: There is a real concern that nicotine addicts will adjourn to the rest rooms and smoke. A major problem with this is that the trash bins (full of lightweight paper) become the most likely place to dispose of cigarette butts. To protect against the possibility of a serious fire in the lavatories each lavatory must be equipped with a smoke detector system or equivalent that provides either a warning light in the cockpit or a warning light or audible warning in the passenger cabin that would be readily detected by a flight attendant. In addition, each lavatory must be equipped with a built-in fire extinguisher for each disposal receptacle for towels, paper, or waste located within the lavatory. The extinguisher must be designed to discharge automatically into each disposal receptacle upon occurrence of a fire in that receptacle.

Cargo Compartment Classification

The FAA has classified the cargo and baggage spaces aboard aircraft into four classes: A, B, C, and E (a Class D compartment is no longer permitted by the FAA). This is done to provide distinctions for these spaces as related to fire detection and protection. Class A, B, and C compartments are found on passenger and cargo aircraft while Class E compartments are found only on all-cargo aircraft. The following definitions apply:

Class A

A **Class A cargo or baggage compartment** is one in which

(1)   *The presence of a fire would be easily discovered by a crewmember while at his station; and*
(2)   *Each part of the compartment is easily accessible in flight.*

FAR 25.857

Class B

A **Class B cargo or baggage compartment** is one in which

(1)   *There is sufficient access in flight to enable a crewmember to effectively reach any part of the compartment with the contents of a hand fire extinguisher;*
(2)   *When the access provisions are being used, no hazardous quantity of smoke, flames, or extinguishing agent will enter any compartment occupied by the crew or passengers;*
(3)   *There is a separate approved smoke detector or fire detector system to give warning at the pilot or flight engineer station.*

FAR 25.857

Class C

A **Class C cargo or baggage compartment** is one not meeting the requirements for either a Class A or B compartment but in which

(1)   *There is a separate approved smoke detector or fire detector system to give warning at the pilot or flight engineer station;*

(2)   *There is an approved built-in fire extinguishing or suppression system controllable from the cockpit;*

(3)   *There are means to exclude hazardous quantities of smoke, flames, or extinguishing agent from any compartment occupied by the crew or passengers;*

(4)   *There are means to control ventilation and drafts within the compartment so that the extinguishing agent used can control any fire that may start within the compartment.*

FAR 25.857

Class D

Class D cargo or baggage compartments are not currently defined by the FAA. In older aircraft, Class D cargo compartments were those that were not accessible during flight and were designed to choke out fires due to lack of oxygen rather than detect or extinguish the fire. These were eliminated after the ValueJet Flight 592 accident in 1996.

Class E

A **Class E cargo compartment** is one on airplanes used only for the carriage of cargo and in which

(1)   *There is a separate approved smoke or fire detector system to give warning at the pilot or flight engineer station;*

(2)   *There are means to shut off the ventilating airflow to, or within, the compartment, and the controls for these means are accessible to the flight crew in the crew compartment;*

(3)   *There are means to exclude hazardous quantities of smoke, flames, or noxious gases from the flight crew compartment; and*

(4)   *The required crew emergency exits are accessible under any cargo loading condition.*

FAR 25.857

Cargo or Baggage Stowage Compartments

Each compartment for the stowage of cargo, baggage, carry-on articles, and equipment (such as life rafts) must be designed for its placarded maximum weight of contents considering the maximum load factors corresponding to flight and ground load conditions and to the emergency landing conditions. The loads applied in the emergency landing conditions need not be applied to compartments located below or forward of all occupants in the airplane. Except for underseat and overhead passenger convenience compartments, each stowage compartment in the passenger cabin must be completely enclosed.

There must be a means to prevent the contents in the compartments from becoming a hazard by shifting under load. For stowage compartments in the passenger and crew cabin, if the means used to prevent shifting is a latched door, the design must take into consideration the wear and deterioration expected in service. If cargo compartment lamps are installed, each lamp must be installed so as to prevent contact between lamp bulb and cargo.

We have seen the definitions of the various classes of cargo compartments. Now let's turn our attention to some specific requirements for the construction of these compartments. First, any compartment classified as Class B through Class E cargo or baggage compartments must have a liner, and the liner must be separate from (but may be attached to) the airplane structure. The ceiling and sidewall liner panels and other materials used in the construction of the compartments must meet the flammability test requirements of Part 25. Class C compartments have to meet the higher standards found in a separate section of the flammability test standards.

> *No compartment may contain any controls, wiring, lines, equipment, or accessories whose damage or failure would affect safe operation, unless those items are protected so that (1) They cannot be damaged by the movement of cargo in the compartment, and (2) Their breakage or failure will not create a fire hazard.*

FAR 25.855

In designing the compartments there must be means to prevent cargo or baggage from interfering with the functioning of the fire protective features of the compartment. Sources of heat within the compartment must be shielded and insulated to prevent igniting the cargo or baggage. Flight tests must be conducted to show compliance with the provisions concerning

- Compartment accessibility,
- The entries of hazardous quantities of smoke or extinguishing agent into compartments occupied by the crew or passengers, and
- The dissipation of the extinguishing agent in Class C compartments.

In these tests, it must be shown that no inadvertent operation of smoke or fire detectors in any compartment would occur as a result of fire contained in any other compartment, either during or after extinction, unless the extinguishing system floods each such compartment simultaneously. In other words, any alarms have to be limited only to the protected area unless all areas are subject to extinguishing actions.

Cargo or Baggage Compartment Smoke or Fire Detection Systems

If the aircraft is certificated with ***cargo or baggage compartment smoke or fire detection equipment***, the following must be met for each cargo or baggage compartment:

(a) *The detection system must provide a visual indication to the flight crew within one minute after the start of a fire.*

(b) *The system must be capable of detecting a fire at a temperature significantly below that at which the structural integrity of the airplane is substantially decreased.*

(c) *There must be means to allow the crew to check, in flight, the functioning of each fire detector circuit.*

(d)   The effectiveness of the detection system must be shown for all approved operating configurations and conditions.

FAR 25.858

Fire Extinguishers

Each airplane must have the following minimum number of hand *fire extinguishers* conveniently located and evenly distributed in passenger compartments:

Passenger Capacity	No. of Extinguishers
7 through 30	1
31 through 60	2
61 through 200	3
201 through 300	4
301 through 400	5
401 through 500	6
501 through 600	7
601 through 700	8

These extinguishers must be distributed around the airplane so that at least one hand fire extinguisher is conveniently located in the pilot compartment and one is readily accessible for use in each Class A or Class B cargo or baggage compartment. One must be available to use in each Class E cargo or baggage compartment that is accessible to crewmembers in flight. At least one hand fire extinguisher must be located in, or readily accessible for use in, each galley located above or below the passenger compartment. All hand fire extinguishers must be approved.

The quantity of extinguishing agent used in each extinguisher required must be appropriate for the kinds of fires likely to occur where used. Each extinguisher intended for use in a personnel compartment must be designed to minimize the hazard of toxic gas concentration.

If a built-in fire extinguisher is provided it must be installed so that no extinguishing agent likely to enter personnel compartments is hazardous to the occupants and discharge of the agent cannot cause structural damage. The capacity of each required built-in fire extinguishing system must be adequate for any fire likely to occur in the compartment where used, considering the volume of the compartment and the ventilation rate.

Designated Fire Zones

Designated fire zones are

(1)   The engine power section;
(2)   The engine accessory section;

   (3)   Any complete power plant compartment in which no isolation is provided between the engine power section and the engine accessory section;

   (4)   Any auxiliary power unit compartment;

   (5)   The compressor and accessory sections of turbine engines; and

   (6)   Combustor, turbine, and tailpipe sections of turbine engine installations that contain lines or components carrying flammable fluids or gases.

FAR 25.1181

Fire Protection: Flight Controls, Engine Mounts, and Other Flight Structures

Fire protection for essential *flight controls, engine mounts, and other flight structures* located in designated fire zones or in adjacent areas which would be subjected to the effects of fire in the fire zone requires that these items be constructed of fireproof material or shielded so that they are capable of withstanding the effects of fire.

Fire Protection: Other Components

Fire protection for *other components* (other than tail surfaces to the rear of the nacelles that could not be readily affected by heat, flames, or sparks coming from a designated fire zone or engine compartment of any nacelle): surfaces to the rear of the nacelles, within one nacelle diameter of the nacelle centerline, require that those components be at least fire resistant.

Fire Extinguishing Systems

Except for combustor, turbine, and tail pipe sections of turbine engine installations that contain lines or components carrying flammable fluids or gases for which it is shown that a fire originating in these sections can be controlled, there must be a fire extinguisher system serving each designated fire zone. The *fire extinguishing system*, the quantity of the extinguishing agent, the rate of discharge, and the discharge distribution must be adequate to extinguish fires. It must be shown by either actual or simulated flights tests that under critical airflow conditions in flight the discharge of the extinguishing agent in each designated fire zone will provide an agent concentration capable of extinguishing fires in that zone and of minimizing the probability of reignition.

    An individual "one-shot" system may be used for auxiliary power and other combustion equipment. For each other designated fire zone, two discharges must be provided, each of which produces adequate agent concentration. The fire extinguishing system for a nacelle must be able to simultaneously protect each zone of the nacelle for which protection is provided.

Fire Detector Systems

For *fire detector systems*, each aircraft must have approved, quick acting fire or overheat detectors in each designated fire zone and in the combustion, turbine, and tailpipe sections of turbine engine installations, in sufficient numbers and in locations that will ensure prompt detection of fire in those zones. The fire detector system must be constructed and installed so that it will withstand the vibration, inertia, and other loads to which it may be subjected in operation.

There must be a means to warn the crew in the event that the sensor or associated wiring within a designated fire zone is severed unless the system continues to function as a satisfactory detection system after the severing. The fire detection system must also warn the crew in the event of a short circuit in the sensor or associated wiring within a designated fire zone unless the system continues to function as a satisfactory detection system after the short circuit. The fire or overheat detector may not be affected by any oil, water, other fluids, or fumes that might be present. The crew must be able to check, in flight, the functioning of each fire or overheat detector electric circuit.

The wiring and other components of each fire or overheat detector system in a fire zone must be at least fire resistant. No fire or overheat detector system component for any fire zone may pass through another fire zone, unless it is protected against the possibility of false warnings resulting from fires in zones through which it passes or else each zone involved is simultaneously protected by the same detector and extinguishing system. Each fire detector system must be constructed so that when it is in the configuration for installation it will not exceed the alarm activation time approved for the detectors using the response time criteria specified in the appropriate standards for the fire detector.

PBE: Protective Breathing Equipment

If there is a Class A, B, or E cargo compartment on the airplane, *protective breathing equipment (PBE)* must be installed for the use of appropriate crewmembers. In addition, protective breathing equipment must be installed in each isolated separate compartment in the airplane, including the upper and lower lobe galleys, in which crewmember occupancy is permitted during flight for the maximum number of crewmembers expected to be in the area during any operation.

For required protective breathing equipment, the following apply:

(1)   *The equipment must be designed to protect the flight crew from smoke, carbon dioxide, and other harmful gases while on flight deck duty and while combating fires in cargo compartments.*

(2)   *The equipment must include:*
    (a)   *Masks covering the eyes, nose, and mouth; or*
    (b)   *Masks covering the nose and mouth, plus accessory equipment to cover the eyes.*

(3)   *The equipment, while in use, must allow the flight crew to use the radio equipment and to communicate with each other while at their assigned duty stations.*

(4)   *The part of the equipment protecting the eyes may not cause any appreciable adverse effect on vision and must allow corrective glasses to be worn.*

(5)   *The equipment must supply protective oxygen of 15 minutes duration per crewmember at a pressure altitude of 8,000 feet with a respiratory minute volume of 30 liters per minute.*

FAR 25.1439

Warning, Caution, and Advisory Lights

If warning, caution or advisory lights are installed in the cockpit, they must, unless otherwise approved by the Administrator, be *red* for warning lights (lights indicating a hazard which may require immediate corrective action); *amber* for caution lights (lights indicating the possible need for future corrective action); *green* for safe operation lights; and any other color, including white, for lights not described above. These other colors must differ sufficiently from the colors above to avoid possible confusion.

Cockpit Voice Recorders

Air carrier, transport category aircraft must have ***cockpit voice recorders (CVRs)***. These are the recorders that record the cockpit communications and noises from the airplane. They must be approved and must be installed so that it will record the following:

(1) *Voice communications transmitted from or received in the airplane by radio.*
(2) *Voice communications of flight crewmembers on the flight deck.*
(3) *Voice communications of flight crewmembers on the flight deck, using the airplane's interphone system.*
(4) *Voice or audio signals identifying navigation or approach aids introduced into a headset or speaker.*
(5) *Voice communications of flight crewmembers using the passenger loud-speaker system, if there is such a system and if the fourth channel is available.*

FAR 25.1457

Each cockpit voice recorder must be installed so that it receives its electric power from the bus that provides the maximum reliability for operation of the cockpit voice recorder without jeopardizing service to essential or emergency loads. There must be an automatic means to simultaneously stop the recorder and prevent each erasure feature from functioning, within 10 minutes after crash impact; and there must be an aural or visual means for preflight checking of the recorder for proper operation.

The CVR typically records on a continuous loop of magnetic tape for 30 minutes. By union/management agreement, in most cases the CVR tape may only be used for accident/incident investigation by the National Transportation Safety Board (NTSB). Most cockpit voice recorders, therefore, have the ability to bulk erase the tape. This erasure feature is provided so that the crew may, upon termination of a "routine" flight, erase the cockpit voice recording. If the CVR has this erasure device, the installation must be designed to minimize the probability of inadvertent operation and actuation of the device during crash impact.

Flight Data Recorders (FDRs) or Digital Flight Data Recorders (DFDRs)

Air carrier transport category aircraft also must carry ***flight data recorders (FDRs)***. The flight data recorder records a wide variety of parameters concerning the ongoing operation of the aircraft. They record items such as airspeed, attitude, control inputs, switch positions, and so on. Many union/management agreements limit the use of the flight data recorder information to either accident/incident investigation by the NTSB or analytical purposes, where the data is de-identified as to flight number or crew and used to develop statistical models of aircraft operations.

Summary

In this chapter we have examined a number of airworthiness issues that affect the certification of transport category airplanes. In the next chapter we will look at the Part 121 rules relating to the use of the equipment and instruments that must be aboard the airplane due to Part 25.

Important Terms from this Chapter

Cargo compartment classification

Cargo or baggage compartment smoke or fire detection systems

Class A cargo or baggage compartment

Class B cargo or baggage compartment

Class C cargo or baggage compartment

Class E cargo or baggage compartment

Cockpit voice recorder (CVR)

Control systems gust locks

Designated fire zones

Emergency exit signs

Emergency lighting

Evacuation demonstrations

Fire detector systems

Fire extinguishers

Fire extinguishing systems

Fire protection: flight controls, engine mounts, and other flight structures

Fire protection: other components

Flight control systems

Flight crew emergency exits

Flight data recorders (FDRs)

Interior fire protection and flammability standards

Landing gear aural warning device

Lavatory fire protection

Part 25 airworthiness requirements

Pressurized cabins

Protective breathing equipment (PBE)

Subpart J to Part 121: Special Airworthiness Standards

Takeoff warning system

Warning, caution, and advisory lights

Chapter 9 Exam

1. In order to carry cargo on the passenger level in a passenger aircraft, the cargo
    a. Must be approved by the ramp services agent responsible for the flight.
    b. Must be on pallets that are securely strapped to the flooring of the aircraft.
    c. Must be secured in bins that can withstand 1.15 times the emergency landing g loads.
    d. Must be smaller than 15 pounds.

2. Landing gear aural warning devices must sound a warning if
    a. A landing is attempted with the gear not locked down.
    b. Throttles are reduced for landing with the gear not locked down (only).
    c. Flaps are set for landing with the gear not locked down (only).
    d. None of the above.

3. To be used in Part 121 operations, aircraft with more than 44 seats must be shown to be able to conduct an evacuation in
   a. 60 seconds or less.
   b. 90 seconds or less.
   c. 120 seconds or less.
   d. No time is specified for conducting evacuations.

4. Transport category aircraft elevators typically
   a. Are interconnected but may be operated separately in an emergency.
   b. Are rigidly interconnected and operate together as a unit.
   c. Are only connected to the control columns by electrical circuits.
   d. Are a single unit that may be operated from either the pilot or copilot seat.

5. The takeoff warning system of a transport category aircraft must operate from the initial portion of the takeoff (application of takeoff power) until
   a. The aircraft passes the takeoff decision speed.
   b. The aircraft passes through 500 feet on the takeoff.
   c. The aircraft is rotated for takeoff.
   d. The warning system must operate until the aircraft is properly configured.

6. Under normal operating conditions the pressurized cabin of a Part 121 aircraft must maintain a maximum cabin pressure altitude of
   a. 8,000 feet
   b. 10,000 feet
   c. 12,500 feet
   d. 15,000 feet

7. Which cargo compartment on a passenger airplane has fire extinguishing equipment built into the compartment that is controllable from the cockpit?
   a. Class A.
   b. Class B.
   c. Class C.
   d. Class D.

8. An aircraft with 254 passenger seats would require
   a. 1 fire extinguisher.
   b. 2 fire extinguishers.
   c. 3 fire extinguishers.
   d. 4 fire extinguishers.

9. A blue cockpit annunciator light would indicate
   a. Warning.
   b. Caution.
   c. Status.
   d. Exit.

10. Cockpit voice recorders are required to continuously record the
    a. Last 15 minutes of each flight.
    b. Last 30 minutes of each flight.
    c. Last 45 minutes of each flight.
    d. Last 1 hour of each flight.

Instrument and Equipment Requirements

First, by the figurations of art there be made instruments of navigation without men to row them, as great ships to brooke the sea, only with one man to steer them, and they shall sail far more swiftly than if they were full of men.

—Roger Bacon
Thirteenth century Franciscan Friar

In the last chapter we explored some of the equipment required for certification of aircraft in the transport category. Those rules assure that the airplane is designed and built to the much more exacting standards demanded of aircraft to be used in public transportation. In this chapter we will look at the interaction between the certification rules found in Part 25 and the operational rules found in Part 121. Most of the rules we will be discussing are contained in Part 121 Subpart K.

Section 121.303 Airplane Instruments and Equipment

The instrument and equipment requirements of this subpart apply to all operations under Part 121. Any of the instruments and equipment required by sections 121.305 through 121.359 must be approved and installed in accordance with the Part 25 airworthiness requirements that are applicable to them. Airspeed indicators must be calibrated in knots, and each airspeed limitation and item of related information in the airplane flight manual and pertinent placards must be expressed in knots.

No person may take off any airplane unless the following instruments and equipment are in operable condition:

- Instruments and equipment required to comply with airworthiness requirements under which the airplane is type certificated. (Slightly different rules are applicable to the older aircraft—remember, we are limiting our discussions to aircraft certificated since August 29, 1959.)
- Instruments and equipment specified in sections 121.305 through 121.321, 121.359, and 121.360 for all operations and the instruments and equipment specified in sections 121.323 through 121.351 for the kind of operation indicated. These latter rules apply to issues such as night operations, operations over the top or in IFR (IMC) conditions, overwater operations, and flight in icing conditions.

Notice that this rule is violated on *takeoff.* If any of the specified equipment is inoperative and the carrier hasn't complied with the relief provision discussed below, it is in violation as soon as the airplane leaves the ground. On the other hand, if the equipment breaks in flight, different rules will apply. The relief provisions mentioned above are found in FARs 121.627 and 121.628. 121.627 covers en route failures and 121.628 covers equipment failure prior to departure. This last provision is commonly referred to as the minimum equipment list provisions or, simply, MELs. This is discussed in more detail in chapter 11.

Section 121.305 Flight and Navigational Equipment

The following *flight and navigational equipment* and instruments are required to be installed and operational:

(a)   *An airspeed indicating system with heated pitot tube or equivalent means for preventing malfunctioning due to icing.*

(b)   *A sensitive altimeter. (That means adjustable for variable pressure.)*

(c)   *A sweep–second hand clock (or approved equivalent such as a digital clock).*

(d)   *A free-air temperature indicator.*

(e)   *Two gyroscopic bank and pitch indicators (artificial horizon or ADI).*

(f)   *A gyroscopic rate-of-turn indicator combined with an integral slip-skid indicator (turn-and-bank indicator) except that only a slip-skid indicator is required when a third attitude instrument system usable through flight attitudes of 360 degrees of pitch and roll is installed.*

(g)   *A gyroscopic direction indicator (heading indicator or equivalent).*

(h)   *A magnetic compass.*

(i)   *A vertical speed indicator (rate-of-climb indicator).*

(j)   *In addition to two gyroscopic bank and pitch indicators (artificial horizons), a standby (third) artificial horizon. This third artificial horizon must be powered from a source independent of the electrical generating system and continue reliable operation for a minimum of 30 minutes after total failure of the electrical generating system. It must operate independently of any other attitude indicating system. Its use can't require any crew selection after total failure of the electrical generating system. It must be lighted and plainly visible to and usable by each pilot at his or her station.*

FAR 121.305

Section 121.306 Portable Electronic Devices

With the advent of all sorts of *portable electronic devices* such as computers, cell phones, and game devices, etc., the FAA has become concerned that internal signals generated by these devices may interfere with the aircraft's complex electronic navigation and communications systems. Therefore, with the exception of portable voice recorders, hearing aids, heart pacemakers, electric shavers, and devices that the Part 119 certificate holder has determined will not cause interference with the navigation or communication system of the aircraft on which it is to be used, no one may operate any portable electronic device on any U.S. registered civil aircraft operating under Part 121. This provision also makes the pilot in command responsible if a passenger operates a forbidden appliance.

Section 121.309 Emergency Equipment

Air carriers must be equipped to deal with a number of different emergency situations. For this reason, the carrier must equip the aircraft with the ***emergency equipment*** listed below:

(c)   *Hand fire extinguishers for crew, passenger, cargo, and galley compartments including*
    (1)   *At least one hand fire extinguisher conveniently located for use in each Class E cargo compartment that is accessible to crewmembers during flight.*
    (2)   *Cargo compartments.*
    (3)   *Galley compartments. At least one hand fire extinguisher must be conveniently located for use in each galley located in a compartment other than a passenger, cargo, or crew compartment.*
    (4)   *Flight crew compartment. At least one hand fire extinguisher must be conveniently located on the flight deck for use by the flight crew.*
    (5)   *Passenger compartments. Hand fire extinguishers for use in passenger compartments must be conveniently located and, when two or more are required, uniformly distributed throughout each compartment. Hand fire extinguishers shall be provided in numbers as required by Part 25. [See chapter 9.] At least two of the required hand fire extinguishers installed in passenger-carrying airplanes must contain Halon 1211 or its equivalent as the extinguishing agent. At least one hand fire extinguisher in the passenger compartment must contain Halon 1211 or its equivalent.*
(d)   *First aid and emergency medical equipment and protective gloves.*
    (1)   *In airplanes for which a flight attendant is required, an emergency medical kit.*
(e)   *Crash ax.*
(f)   *Portable battery-powered megaphone or megaphones. There must be one megaphone on each airplane with a seating capacity of more than 60 and less than 100 passengers and two megaphones in the passenger cabin on each airplane with a seating capacity of more than 99 passengers.*

FAR 121.309

Of course it would make no sense to require a carrier to have this emergency equipment unless it was "current," that is, inspected according to the required schedules. Therefore, each item of emergency and flotation equipment listed must be inspected regularly in accordance with inspection periods established in the operations specifications to ensure its condition for continued serviceability and immediate readiness to perform its intended emergency purposes. When carried in a compartment or container, the compartment or container must be marked as to contents and the compartment or container must be marked as to the date of last inspection.

Section 121.310 Additional Emergency Equipment

We saw in chapter 9 some of the certification requirements in regard to emergency escape and lighting equipment required for aircraft certification. Here we apply requirements specifically to Part 121 carriers. First, if the airplane's emergency exit (other than over the wing) is more than 6 feet from the ground with the airplane on the ground and the landing gear extended, it must have an approved ***means to assist the occupants in descending to the ground***. An assisting means that deploys automatically must be armed during taxiing, takeoffs, and landings. If the FAA finds that the design of the exit makes compliance impractical, it may grant a deviation from the requirement of automatic deployment if the assisting means automatically erects upon deployment.

Next, the airplane must have ***interior emergency exit markings***. For passenger airplanes, each passenger emergency exit, its means of access, and its means of opening must be conspicuously marked. The identity and location of each passenger emergency exit must be recognizable from a distance equal to the width of the cabin. A sign visible to occupants must indicate the location of each passenger emergency exit approaching along the main passenger aisle. There must be locating signs

(b) (1) (i) *Above the aisle near each over-the-wing passenger emergency exit or at another ceiling location if it is more practical because of low headroom;*

(ii) *Next to each floor level passenger emergency exit, except that one sign may serve two such exits if they both can be seen readily from that sign; and*

(iii) *On each bulkhead or divider that prevents fore and aft vision along the passenger cabin, to indicate emergency exits beyond and obscured by it, except that if this is not possible the sign may be placed at another appropriate location.*

FAR 121.310

No passenger emergency exit shall be more than 60 feet from any adjacent passenger emergency exit on the same side of the same deck of the fuselage, as measured parallel to the airplane's longitudinal axis between the nearest exit edges.

Each passenger-carrying airplane (except for nontransport category airplanes type certificated after December 31, 1964) must have an ***emergency lighting system,*** *for interior emergency exit markings*. This system must be independent of the main lighting system. The sources of general cabin illumination may be common to both the emergency and the main lighting systems if the power supply to the emergency lighting system is independent of the power supply to the main lighting system.

The emergency lighting system must

- Illuminate each passenger exit marking and locating sign,
- Provide a specified level of general lighting in the passenger cabin, and
- Include floor proximity emergency escape path marking which meets the requirements of Section 25.812(e).

Except for lights forming part of emergency lighting subsystems provided in compliance with Section 25.812(n).

Emergency light operation. Each emergency light required for interior exit lights or exterior exit lighting must comply with the following:

(i) *Be operable manually both from the flight crew station and from a point in the passenger compartment that is readily accessible to a normal flight attendant seat,*

(ii) *Have a means to prevent inadvertent operation of the manual controls, and*

(iii) *When armed or turned on at either station, remain lighted or become lighted upon interruption of the airplane's normal electric power.*

FAR 121.310(d)(1)

These lights must be armed or turned on during taxiing, takeoff, and landing. Each light must provide the required level of illumination for at least 10 minutes at the critical ambient conditions after emergency landing. These lights must have a cockpit control device that has an "on," "off," and "armed" position.

Emergency exit operating handles. For a passenger-carrying airplane for which the application for the type certificate was filed on or after May 1, 1972, the location of each passenger emergency exit operating handle and instructions for opening the exit must be shown in accordance with the requirements under which the airplane was type certificated. On these airplanes, no operating handle or operating handle cover may continue to be used if its luminescence (brightness) decreases to below 100 microlamberts.

Emergency exit access must be provided as follows for each passenger-carrying transport category airplane:

(1) *Each passageway passing between individual passenger areas or leading to a Type I or Type II emergency exit must be unobstructed and at least 20 inches wide.*

(2) *There must be enough space next to each Type I or Type II emergency exit to allow a crewmember to assist in the evacuation of passengers without reducing the unobstructed width of the passageway below that required.*

(3) *There must be access from the main aisle to each Type III and Type IV exit. The access from the aisle to these exits must not be obstructed by seats, berths, or other protrusions in a manner that would reduce the effectiveness of the exit.*

(4) *If it is necessary to pass through a passageway between passenger compartments to reach any required emergency exit from any seat in the passenger cabin, the passageway must not be obstructed. Curtains may be used if they allow free entry through the passageway.*

(5) *No door may be installed in any partition between passenger compartments.*

(6) *If it is necessary to pass through a doorway separating the passenger cabin from other areas to reach a required emergency exit from any passenger seat, the door must have a means to latch it in open position, and the door must be latched open during each takeoff and landing.*

FAR 121.310(f)

Exterior exit markings. Each passenger emergency exit and the means of opening that exit from the outside must be marked on the outside of the airplane. There must be a 2 inch colored band outlining each passenger emergency exit on the side of the fuselage. Each outside marking, including the band, must be readily distinguishable from the surrounding fuselage area by contrast in color. Exits that are not in the side of the fuselage must have external means of opening and applicable instructions marked conspicuously in red (or, if red is inconspicuous against the background color, in bright chrome yellow) and, when the opening means for such an exit is located on only one side of the fuselage, a conspicuous marking to that effect must be provided on the other side.

Exterior emergency lighting. Each passenger-carrying airplane must be equipped with exterior emergency lighting.

Slip resistant escape route. Each passenger-carrying airplane must be equipped with a slip resistant escape route that meets the requirements of Part 25.

Floor level exits. Each floor level door or exit in the side of the fuselage (other than those leading into a cargo or baggage compartment that is not accessible from the passenger cabin) that is 44 or more inches high and 20 or more inches wide, but not wider than 46 inches, each passenger ventral exit, and each tail cone exit must meet the requirements of this section for floor level emergency exits.

Additional emergency exits. Approved emergency exits in the passenger compartments in excess of the minimum number of required emergency exits must meet all of the applicable provisions of this section except for the minimum access-way requirements and must be readily accessible.

Ventral exits and tailcone exits. On each large passenger-carrying turbojet-powered airplane, each ventral exit and tailcone exit must be

- Designed and constructed so that it cannot be opened during flight and
- Marked with a placard readable from a distance of 30 inches and installed at a conspicuous location near the means of opening the exit, stating that the exit has been designed and constructed so that it cannot be opened during flight.

Portable lights. No person may operate a passenger-carrying airplane unless it is equipped with flashlight stowage provisions accessible from each flight attendant seat.

Section 121.311 Seats, Safety Belts, and Shoulder Harnesses

Seats, safety belts, and shoulder harnesses. No person may operate an airplane unless there are available during the takeoff, en route flight, and landing phases of flight an approved seat or berth for each person (over the age of two) on board the airplane. Each person (over the age of two) on board the airplane must have an approved safety belt for his or her separate use. Two people occupying a berth may share one approved safety belt, and two persons occupying a multiple lounge or divan seat may share one approved safety belt during the en route phase of flight only.

Each person on board an air carrier airplane must occupy an approved seat or berth with a separate safety belt properly secured about him or her during movement on the surface, takeoff, and landing. A safety belt provided for the occupant of a seat may not be used by more than one person (over the age of two).

Carriage of infants and children under 2 years of age. A child (under two) may be held by an adult who is occupying an approved seat or berth provided the child does not occupy or use any restraining device. A child under 2 years of age may occupy an approved child restraint system furnished by the certificate holder, a parent, guardian, or attendant designated by the child's parent or guardian to attend to the safety of the child during the flight. The child must be accompanied by a parent, guardian, or attendant designated by the child's parent or guardian. The restraint system must be approved and bear one or more of the following labels:

(A)   *Seats manufactured to U.S. standards between January 1, 1981, and February 25, 1985, must bear the label: "This child restraint system conforms to all applicable Federal motor vehicle safety standards."*

(B)   *Seats manufactured to U.S. standards on or after February 26, 1985, must bear two labels:*
"This child restraint system conforms to all applicable Federal motor vehicle safety standards"; and
"THIS RESTRAINT IS CERTIFIED FOR USE IN MOTOR VEHICLES AND AIRCRAFT" in red lettering.

(C)   *Seats that do not qualify as above must bear either a label showing approval of a foreign government or a label showing that the seat was manufactured under the standards of the United Nations.*

FAR 121.311(b)(2)(ii)

The restraint system must be properly secured to an approved forward-facing seat or berth, the child must be properly secured in the restraint system and must not exceed the specified weight limit for the restraint system, and the restraint system must bear the appropriate label(s). A certificate holder may not allow a child in an aircraft to occupy a booster type child restraint system, a vest type child restraint system, a harness type child restraint system, or a lap held child restraint system during takeoff, landing, or movement on the surface.

Sideward facing seats. Each sideward facing seat must comply with the applicable requirements of Part 25.

No certificate holder may take off or land an airplane unless each passenger seat back is in the upright position. Each passenger shall comply with instructions given by a crewmember in compliance with this paragraph. An exception is made for persons who are unable to sit erect for a medical reason and are carried in accordance with procedures in the certificate holder's manual if the seat back does not obstruct any passenger's access to the aisle or to any emergency exit. In aircraft that don't require a flight attendant, the certificate holder may take off or land as long as the flight crew instructs each passenger to place his or her seat back in the upright position for takeoff and landing.

Crew seat belts/shoulder harnesses. Part 121 aircraft flight crew seats must be equipped with a combined safety belt and shoulder harness. This harness must meet the applicable requirements specified in Part 25 (except that shoulder harnesses and combined safety belt and shoulder harnesses that were approved and installed before March 6, 1980, may continue to be used).

Flight attendant seats. Each flight attendant that is a required part of the crew must have a seat for takeoff and landing in the passenger compartment that meets the requirements of Part 25. Nonrequired flight attendants placed aboard the aircraft for customer service may occupy a passenger seat.

Each crewmember with a shoulder harness or with a combined safety belt and shoulder harness must have the shoulder harness or combined safety belt and shoulder harness properly secured during takeoff and landing. If a shoulder harness is not combined with a safety belt, it may be unfastened if the occupant cannot perform the required duties with the shoulder harness fastened.

At each unoccupied seat, the safety belt and shoulder harness, if installed, must be secured so as not to interfere with crewmembers in the performance of their duties or with the rapid egress of occupants in an emergency.

Section 121.313 Miscellaneous Equipment

As the name suggests, various items of miscellaneous equipment are required by Part 121.

(a)   *If protective fuses are installed on an airplane, there must be the number of spare fuses approved for that airplane and appropriately described in the certificate holder's manual.*

(b)   *There must be a windshield wiper or equivalent for each pilot station.*

(c)   The electrical system must have a power supply and distribution system that meets the requirements of Part 25 in regards to normal and emergency operations.

(d)   Engine-driven sources of energy, when used, must be on separate engines.

(e)   There must be a means for indicating the adequacy of the power being supplied to required flight instruments.

(f)   Two independent static pressure systems vented to the outside atmospheric pressure so that they will be least affected by air flow variation or moisture or other foreign matter, and installed so as to be airtight except for the vent.

(g)   When a means is provided for transferring an instrument from its primary operating system to an alternate system, the means must include a positive positioning control and must be marked to indicate clearly which system is being used.

(h)   A door between the passenger and pilot compartments, with a locking means to prevent passengers from opening it without the pilot's permission.

(i)   A key for each door that separates a passenger compartment from another compartment that has emergency exit provisions. The key must be readily available for each crewmember.

(j)   A placard on each door that is the means of access to a required passenger emergency exit, to indicate that it must be open during takeoff and landing.

(k)   A means for the crew, in an emergency, to unlock each door that leads to a compartment that is normally accessible to passengers and that can be locked by passengers.

FAR 121.313

Section 121.315 Cockpit Check Procedure

Each certificate holder must provide flight crews with an approved *cockpit check procedure* for each type of aircraft that it operates. The approved procedures must include each item necessary for flight crewmembers to check for safety before starting engines, taking off, or landing, and in engine and systems emergencies. The procedures must be designed so that a flight crewmember will not need to rely upon his or her memory for items to be checked. (Remember this rule when you go for your initial equipment training!) The approved procedures must be readily usable in the cockpit of each aircraft and the flight crew shall follow them when operating the aircraft.

Section 121.317 Passenger Information

Each carrier must equip its aircraft with *passenger information* signs regarding no smoking and fastening seat belts. The "Fasten Seat Belt" sign shall be turned on during any movement on the surface, for each takeoff, for each landing, and at any other time considered necessary by the pilot in command. Additionally, a "Fasten Seat Belt While Seated" sign must be visible at each passenger seat. If smoking is prohibited, the "No Smoking" passenger information signs must be lighted during the entire flight segment or one or more "No Smoking" placards must be posted during the entire flight segment. If both the lighted signs and the placards are used, the signs must remain lighted during the entire flight segment. Smoking is prohibited on scheduled flight segments:

(1)   *Between any two points within Puerto Rico, the United States Virgin Islands, the District of Columbia, or any state of the United States (other than Alaska or Hawaii) or between any two points in any one of the above-mentioned jurisdictions (other than Alaska or Hawaii);*

(2)   *Within the state of Alaska or within the state of Hawaii; or*

(3)   *Scheduled in the current Worldwide or North American Edition of the Official Airline Guide for 6 hours or less in duration and between any point listed in paragraph 1 (above) and any point in Alaska or Hawaii, or between any point in Alaska and any point in Hawaii.*

FAR 121.317(c)

A sign must be placed in each lavatory that reads: "Federal law provides for a penalty of up to $2,000 for tampering with the smoke detector installed in this lavatory." Not surprisingly, no person may smoke in any airplane lavatory nor may any person tamper with, disable, or destroy any smoke detector installed in any airplane lavatory.

Section 121.318 Public Address System

Airplanes with more than 19 passengers must be equipped with a ***public address system*** (PA) that is capable of operation independent of the required crewmember interphone system (except for handsets, headsets, microphones, selector switches, and signaling devices). The PA system must be accessible for immediate use from each of two flight crewmember stations in the pilot compartment. For each required floor level passenger emergency exit that has an adjacent flight attendant seat, there must be a microphone that is readily accessible to the seated flight attendant. One microphone may serve more than one exit, provided the proximity of the exits allows unassisted verbal communication between seated flight attendants. The PA must be capable of being operated within 10 seconds by a flight attendant at each position in the passenger compartment where it is accessible.

Section 121.319 Crewmember Interphone System

Aircraft with more than 19 passenger seats must be equipped with a ***crewmember interphone system*** that is capable of operation independent of the public address system. The interphone system must provide a means of two-way communication between the pilot compartment and each passenger compartment and between the pilot compartment and each galley located on other than the main passenger deck level. It must be accessible for immediate use by flight crewmembers and from at least one normal flight attendant station in each passenger compartment. Like the PA system, it must be capable of operation within 10 seconds by a flight attendant at those positions from which its use is accessible

Large turbojet powered airplanes have additional interphone requirements. The interphone system must be accessible for use at enough flight attendant stations so that all floor level emergency exits (or entryways to those exits in the case of exits located within galleys) in each passenger compartment are observable from one or more of the positions equipped with an interphone. It must have an alerting system incorporating aural or visual signals for use by flight crewmembers to alert flight attendants and for use by flight attendants to alert flight crewmembers. The alerting system must have a means for the recipient of a call to determine whether it is a normal call or an emergency call, and when the airplane is on the ground, it must provide a means of two-way communication between ground personnel and either of at least two flight crewmembers in the pilot compartment. The interphone system station for use by ground personnel must be located so that personnel using the system may avoid visible detection from within the airplane.

Section 121.323 Instruments and Equipment for Operations at Night

Operations at night. To operate at night under Part 121, an airplane must be equipped with the following additional *instruments and equipment:*

  (a) *Position lights.*
  (b) *An anticollision light.*
  (c) *Two landing lights.*
  (d) *Instrument lights providing enough light to make each required instrument, switch, or similar instrument, easily readable and installed so that the direct rays are shielded from the flight crewmembers' eyes and so that no objectionable reflections are visible to them.*
  (e) *An airspeed indicating system with a heated pitot tube or equivalent means for preventing malfunctioning due to icing.*

FAR 121.323

Section 121.325 Instruments and Equipment for Operations under IFR or Over-the-Top.

Operations under IFR. For IFR operations, the aircraft must be equipped with the following *instruments and equipment* in addition to all previously mentioned equipment except the required night operations equipment:

  (a) *An airspeed indicating system with heated pitot tube or equivalent means for preventing malfunctioning due to icing.*
  (b) *A sensitive altimeter.*
  (c) *Instrument lights providing enough light to make each required instrument, switch, or similar instrument, easily readable.*

FAR 121.325

Section 121.329 Supplemental Oxygen for Sustenance: Turbine Engine Powered Airplanes

This section on *supplemental oxygen for sustenance* covers the oxygen requirements for continuing operations in an unpressurized or partially pressurized airplane. Turbine engine powered airplanes must be equipped with oxygen and dispensing equipment. The amount of oxygen to be provided depends on the person, the altitude, and the time spent at that altitude.

Crewmember Oxygen

Above 10,000 feet, flight deck crewmembers must be provided with and use oxygen. At cabin pressure altitudes from 10,000 feet and up to and including 12,000 feet, oxygen must be provided for other crewmembers for the portion of the flight at those altitudes in excess of 30 minutes duration. At cabin pressure altitudes above 12,000 feet, oxygen must be provided for and used by each member of the flight crew on flight deck duty, and must be provided for other crewmembers during the entire flight at those altitudes. When a flight crewmember is required to use oxygen, he must use it continuously except when necessary to remove the oxygen mask or other dispenser in connection with his regular duties. Standby crewmembers that are on call or are definitely going to have flight deck duty before completing the flight must be provided with an amount of supplemental oxygen equal to that provided for crewmembers on duty other than on flight duty. If a standby crewmember is not on call and will not be on flight deck duty during the remainder of the flight, he is considered to be a passenger for the purposes of supplemental oxygen requirements.

Passenger Oxygen

From 10,001 feet and up to and including 14,000 feet, 10 percent of the passengers must be supplied oxygen for that part of the flight that exceeds 30 minutes duration (at those altitudes). For flights at cabin pressure altitudes between from 14,001 feet and up to and including 15,000 feet, enough oxygen must be supplied for that part of the flight at those altitudes for 30 percent of the passengers. For flights at cabin pressure altitudes above 15,000 feet, enough oxygen must be provided for each passenger carried during the entire flight at those altitudes.

Other Considerations

In determining how much sustaining and first aid oxygen is required for a particular operation, the cabin pressure altitudes, the flight duration, and the operating procedures of the carrier will be considered. In pressurized airplanes the assumption is made that a cabin pressurization failure will occur at the altitude or point of flight that is most critical from the standpoint of oxygen need. After the failure the airplane will descend in accordance with the emergency procedures specified in the airplane flight manual without exceeding its operating limitations. It will descend to a flight altitude that will allow successful termination of the flight. Following the failure, the cabin pressure altitude is considered to be the same as the flight altitude unless it is shown that no probable failure of the cabin or pressurization equipment will result in a cabin pressure altitude equal to the flight altitude. Under those circumstances, the maximum cabin pressure altitude attained may be used as a basis for certification or determination of oxygen supply or both.

Section 121.333 Supplemental Oxygen for Emergency Descent and for First Aid; Turbine Engine Powered Airplanes with Pressurized Cabins.

This rule on ***supplemental oxygen for emergency descent and first aid*** provides for the emergency descent after a loss of pressurization.

Crewmember Oxygen

In the event of a cabin pressurization failure at flight altitudes above 10,000 feet, crewmembers must be supplied enough oxygen to comply with Section 121.329, but not less than a 2 hour supply for each flight crewmember on flight deck duty. The required 2 hour supply is that quantity of oxygen necessary for a constant rate of descent from the airplane's maximum certificated operating altitude to 10,000 feet in 10 minutes followed by 110 minutes at 10,000 feet. The oxygen required for protective breathing equipment (PBE) may be included in determining the supply required for flight crewmembers on flight deck duty.

When operating at flight altitudes above flight level 250, each flight crewmember on flight deck duty must be provided with an oxygen mask that can be rapidly placed on his face from its ready position, properly secured, sealed, and supplying oxygen upon demand. It must be designed so that after being placed on the face it does not prevent immediate communication between the flight crewmember and other crewmembers over the airplane intercommunication system. When it is not being used at flight altitudes above flight level 250, the oxygen mask must be kept ready for use and located so as to be within the immediate reach of the flight crewmember while at his duty station.

Unless each flight crewmember on flight deck duty has a quick donning type of oxygen mask, when operating at flight altitudes above flight level 250, one pilot at the controls of the airplane must wear and use an oxygen mask at all times. It must be secured, sealed, and supplying oxygen. If both pilots have quick donning type masks, neither pilot needs to wear an oxygen mask at or below the following flight levels:

- For airplanes having a passenger seat configuration of more than 30 seats, excluding any required crewmember seat, or a payload capacity of more than 7,500 pounds, at or below flight level 410.
- For airplanes having a passenger seat configuration of less than 31 seats, excluding any required crewmember seat, and a payload capacity of 7,500 pounds or less, at or below flight level 350.

Whenever a quick donning type of oxygen mask is to be used the carrier must show that the mask can be put on without disturbing eyeglasses and without delaying the flight crewmember from proceeding with his assigned emergency duties. The oxygen mask after being put on must not prevent immediate communication between the flight crewmember and other crewmembers over the airplane intercommunication system.

If for any reason at any time it is necessary for one pilot to leave his station at the controls of the airplane when operating at flight altitudes above flight level 250, the remaining pilot at the controls shall put on and use his oxygen mask until the other pilot has returned to his duty station.

Before the takeoff of a flight, each flight crewmember must personally preflight his oxygen equipment to ensure that the oxygen mask is functioning, fitted properly, and connected to appropriate supply terminals and that the oxygen supply and pressure are adequate for use.

Each flight attendant shall, during flight above flight level 250 flight altitude, carry portable oxygen equipment with at least a 15 minute supply of oxygen. This is not required if it is shown that enough portable oxygen units with masks or spare outlets and masks are distributed throughout the cabin to insure immediate availability of oxygen to each flight attendant, regardless of his location at the time of cabin depressurization.

Passenger Oxygen

When the airplane is operating at flight altitudes above 10,000 feet, emergency oxygen must be provided for the use of passenger cabin occupants. First consider airplanes certificated to operate at flight altitudes up to and including flight level 250. If it can (at any point along the route to be flown), descend safely to a flight altitude of 14,000 feet or less within 4 minutes, oxygen must be available for a 30 minute period for at least 10 percent of the passenger cabin occupants. If an airplane is operated at flight altitudes up to and including flight level 250 and cannot descend safely to a flight altitude of 14,000 feet within 4 minutes, or when an airplane is operated at flight altitudes above flight level 250, oxygen must be available for at least 10 percent of the passenger cabin occupants for the entire flight after cabin depressurization, at cabin pressure altitudes above 10,000 feet up to and including 14,000 feet and, as applicable, to allow compliance with 121.329. There must be not less than a 10 minute supply for the passenger cabin occupants.

A supply of oxygen for first aid treatment of occupants who, for physiological reasons, might require undiluted oxygen following descent from cabin pressure altitudes above flight level 250 must be provided for 2 percent of the occupants for the entire flight after depressurization. An appropriate number of acceptable dispensing units, but in no case less than two, must be provided, with a means for the cabin attendants to use this supply.

Before a flight is operated above flight level 250, a crewmember must instruct the passengers on the necessity of using oxygen in the event of cabin depressurization and shall point out to them the location and demonstrate the use of the oxygen dispensing equipment.

Section 121.335 Equipment Standards (Oxygen Equipment)

With minor exceptions, operators of turbine engine powered airplanes must show that the oxygen apparatus, the minimum rate of oxygen flow, and the supply of oxygen necessary to comply with sections 121.329 and 121.333 must meet the standards established in Section 4b.651 of the Civil Air Regulations as in effect on September 1, 1958.

Section 121.337 Protective Breathing Equipment

Operators of air carrier aircraft must furnish approved *protective breathing equipment (PBE)* to their flight crews. Protective breathing equipment with a fixed or portable breathing gas supply must be conveniently located on the flight deck and be easily accessible for immediate use by each required flight crewmember at his or her assigned duty station. In addition, PBE will be located at other points in the cabin. This equipment protects crewmembers from the effects of smoke, carbon dioxide, or other harmful gases or an oxygen deficient environment caused by something other than an airplane depressurization. It must protect crewmembers from these effects while they combat fires on board the airplane.

Typically this equipment is in the form of a "smoke hood" or a device that covers the entire head and shoulders of the crewmember. That part of the equipment protecting the eyes can't impair the wearer's vision to the extent that a crewmember's duties cannot be performed. The hood must allow corrective glasses to be worn without impairment of vision or loss of protection. In addition to protecting the crew from smoke and other gasses, the hood must allow at least two flight crewmembers to communicate using the airplane radio equipment and to communicate by interphone with each other and at least one flight attendant station while at their assigned duty stations. The PBE or smoke hood may also be used to meet the supplemental oxygen requirements for the flight crew. Protective breathing gas duration and supply system equipment requirements are as follows:

(i) *The equipment must supply breathing gas for 15 minutes at a pressure altitude of 8,000 feet for the following:*
Flight crewmembers while performing flight deck duties; and
Crewmembers while combating an in flight fire.

(ii) *The breathing gas system must be free from hazards in itself, in its method of operation, and in its effect upon other components.*

(iii) *For breathing gas systems other than chemical oxygen generators, there must be a means to allow the crew to readily determine, during the equipment preflight, that the gas supply is fully charged.*

(iv) *For each chemical oxygen generator, the supply system equipment must deliver the required oxygen flow and contain cautions regarding excess heat generation.*

FAR 121.337(b)(7)

One PBE is required for each hand fire extinguisher located for use in a galley other than a galley located in a passenger, cargo, or crew compartment. One PBE must be located on the flight deck, except that the Administrator may authorize another location for this PBE if special circumstances exist that make compliance impractical. There must be a PBE in each passenger compartment, one for each hand fire extinguisher required by Section 121.309 of this part, to be located within 3 feet of each required hand fire extinguisher (or other location as allowed by the FAA).

Flight crewmembers must perform a preflight inspection of their PBE. In addition, each item of PBE located at other than a flight crewmember duty station must be checked by a designated crewmember to ensure that each is properly stowed and serviceable, and, for other than chemical oxygen generator systems, the breathing gas supply is fully charged. Each certificate holder, in its operations manual, must designate at least one crewmember to perform those checks before he or she takes off in that airplane for his or her first flight of the day.

Section 121.339 Emergency Equipment for Extended Overwater Operations

Unless otherwise authorized by the FAA, a carrier may not operate an airplane in *extended overwater operations* without having on the airplane the following *emergency equipment*:

(1) *A life preserver equipped with an approved survivor locator light, for each occupant of the airplane.*

(2) *Enough life rafts (each equipped with an approved survivor locator light) of a rated capacity and buoyancy to accommodate the occupants of the airplane. Unless excess rafts of enough capacity are provided, the buoyancy and seating capacity beyond the rated capacity of the rafts must accommodate all occupants of the airplane in the event of a loss of one raft of the largest rated capacity.*

(3) *A survival kit, appropriately equipped for the route to be flown, must be attached to each required life raft.*
(4) *At least one pyrotechnic signaling device for each life raft.*
(5) *An approved survival type emergency locator transmitter.*

FAR 121.339(a)

Batteries used in the emergency locator transmitter must be replaced (or recharged, if the battery is rechargeable) when the transmitter has been in use for more than 1 cumulative hour or when 50 percent of their useful life (or for rechargeable batteries, 50 percent of their useful life of charge) has expired, as established by the transmitter manufacturer under its approval. The new expiration date for replacing (or recharging) the battery must be legibly marked on the outside of the transmitter. The battery useful life (or useful life of charge) requirements of this paragraph do not apply to batteries (such as water-activated batteries) that are essentially unaffected during probable storage intervals.

The required life rafts, life preservers, and survival type emergency locator transmitter must be easily accessible in the event of a ditching without appreciable time for preparation. This equipment must be installed in conspicuously marked, approved locations.

Section 121.340 Emergency Flotation Means

Unless FAA approves the operation of an airplane over water without life preservers or **emergency flotation means**, a carrier may not operate an airplane in any overwater operation unless it is equipped with a life preserver for each occupant. This life preserver must be within easy reach of each seated occupant and must be readily removable from the airplane.

Section 121.341 Equipment for Operations in Icing Conditions

Unless an airplane is type certificated under the transport category airworthiness requirements relating to ice protection, a carrier may not operate an airplane in icing conditions without appropriate **equipment for operations in icing conditions.** This equipment must provide means for the prevention or removal of ice on windshields, wings, empennage, propellers, and other parts of the airplane where ice formation will adversely affect the safety of the airplane. At night means must be provided for illuminating or otherwise determining the formation of ice on the parts of the wings that are critical from the standpoint of ice accumulation. Any illumination device that is used must be of a type that will not cause glare or reflection that would handicap crewmembers in the performance of their duties.

Section 121.342 Pitot Heat Indication Systems

A carrier may not operate a transport category airplane or, after December 20, 1999, a nontransport category airplane type certificated after December 31, 1964, that is equipped with a flight instrument **pitot heating system** unless the airplane is also equipped with an operable pitot heat indication system.

Sections 121.343; 121.344; 121.344(a) Flight Recorders

Aircraft certificated for operations above 25,000 feet altitude or turbine engine powered aircraft must be equipped with one or more approved *flight recorders (FDR and DFDR)*. As we saw earlier, these are required to assist the NTSB in performing accident/incident investigations of air carrier aircraft. Over the years the flight data recorders have been developed and expanded from recorders that record perhaps as few as six variables in an analogue medium to modern recorders that digitally record several hundred parameters. Modern air carrier aircraft (manufactured since May 1989) must have digital flight data recorders (DFDR) and record as many as 88 parameters.

The flight data recorder must be operated continuously from the instant the airplane begins its takeoff roll until it has completed the landing roll at an airport. The recorded data must be kept until the airplane has been operated for at least 25 hours of operating time. Each flight recorder must have an approved device to assist in locating that recorder under water. A total of 1 hour of recorded data may be erased for the purpose of testing the flight recorder or the flight recorder system. Any erasure made in accordance with this paragraph must be of the oldest recorded data accumulated at the time of testing. In the event of an accident or occurrence that requires immediate notification of the National Transportation Safety Board and that results in termination of the flight, the carrier shall remove the recording media from the airplane and keep the recorded data for at least 60 days (or for a longer period upon the request of the NTSB or the FAA).

Section 121.345 Radio Equipment

Air carrier aircraft must be equipped with *radio equipment* required for the kind of operation being conducted. Where two independent (separate and complete) radio systems are required, each system must have an independent antenna installation except that, where rigidly supported nonwire antennas or other antenna installations of equivalent reliability are used, only one antenna is required.

Section 121.347 Radio Equipment for Operations under VFR over Routes Navigated by Pilotage

Operations under VFR. The minimum radio equipment requirements for aircraft flown under VFR are

(1) *Communications equipment to communicate with at least one ground station from any point on the route,*
(2) *Communications equipment to communicate with appropriate traffic control facilities from any point within Class B, C, D, or E airspace, and*
(3) *Communications equipment to receive meteorological information from any point en route by either of two independent systems.*

FAR 121.347(a)

If the airplane is to be flown under VFR at night, then it requires the radio equipment necessary to receive navigational signals applicable to the route to be flown. A marker or ILS receiver is not required.

Section 121.349 Radio Equipment for Operations under VFR over Routes Not Navigated by Pilotage or for Operations under IFR or over the Top

Operations under IFR. For IFR operations, air carrier aircraft must be equipped with the radio equipment necessary to fulfill the functions required for VFR operations and to receive satisfactorily by either of two independent systems radio navigational signals from all primary en route and approach navigational facilities intended to be used. Only one marker beacon receiver providing visual and aural signals and one ILS receiver need be provided. Equipment provided to receive signals en route may be used to receive signals on approach, if it is capable of receiving both signals.

Where the airplane is to be operated over routes on which navigation is based on low frequency radio range or automatic direction finding, only one low frequency radio range or ADF receiver need be installed if the airplane is equipped with two VOR receivers and if VOR navigational aids are so located and the airplane is so fueled that in the case of failure of the low frequency radio range receiver or ADF receiver the flight may proceed safely to a suitable airport using VOR equipment and complete an instrument approach using the remaining radio system. If VOR receivers are required, at least one distance measuring equipment (DME) unit capable of receiving and indicating distance information from VORTAC facilities must be installed when operating in the 50 states and the District of Columbia. If the DME becomes inoperative en route, the pilot shall notify ATC of that failure as soon as it occurs.

Carriers operating airplanes having a configuration of 10 to 30 passenger seats and a payload of 7,500 pounds or less in IFR or in extended overwater operations must have, in addition to any other required radio communications and navigational equipment, facilities to communicate with at least one ground facility. There must be both two microphones and two headsets or one headset and one speaker available on the aircraft.

Section 121.351 Radio Equipment for Extended Overwater Operations and for Certain Other Operations

When the aircraft is used for *extended overwater operations,* it must be equipped with the radio navigation and communications required for IFR operations. In addition, it must have an independent (backup) system that meets the requirements for VFR operations and two long-range navigation systems when VOR or ADF radio navigation equipment is unusable along a portion of the route. The FAA may also require that this same combination of equipment be installed for flag or supplemental operations or a domestic operation within the state of Alaska. This would be required if the FAA finds that equipment is necessary for search and rescue operations because of the nature of the terrain to be flown over.

If the carrier has installed and uses a single long-range navigation system (LRNS) and a single long-range communications system (LRCS), it may be authorized by the FAA to use this equipment in lieu of the dual long-range systems mentioned above. This relief provision will apply to operations and routes in certain geographic areas. The following are among the operational factors the FAA may consider in granting this relief authorization:

(1)   *The ability of the flight crew to reliably fix the position of the airplane within the degree of accuracy required by ATC,*

(2)   *The length of the route being flown, and*

(3)   *The duration of the very high frequency communications gap.*

FAR 121.351(c)

Section 121.353 Emergency Equipment for Operations over Uninhabited Terrain Areas: Flag, Supplemental, and Certain Domestic Operations

Operations over uninhabited terrain. Flag or supplemental operations and domestic operations within the states of Alaska or Hawaii over an uninhabited area or any other area that the FAA specifies in the op specs must use aircraft that have the following required equipment for search and rescue in case of an emergency:

  (a) *Suitable pyrotechnic signaling devices (flares).*
  (b) *An approved survival type emergency locator transmitter. Batteries used in this transmitter must be replaced (or recharged, if the battery is rechargeable) when the transmitter has been in use for more than 1 cumulative hour. Alternatively they must be recharged or replaced when 50 percent of their useful life (or for rechargeable batteries, 50 percent of their useful life of charge) has expired, as established by the transmitter manufacturer under its approval.*
  (c) *Enough survival kits, appropriately equipped for the route to be flown for the number of occupants of the airplane.*

FAR 121.353

Section 121.355 Equipment for Operations on Which Specialized Means of Navigation Are Used

Equipment required when specialized means of navigation are used. Many aircraft operating over oceans or large unsettled areas where ground based navigation signals are not available rely on specialized navigation systems such as inertial navigation, or in some older aircraft, Doppler navigation. The carrier can't conduct these operations using Doppler radar or an inertial navigation system outside the 48 contiguous states and the District of Columbia unless such systems have been approved. For use of these systems within the 48 contiguous states and the District of Columbia, any specialized means of navigation must be shown to be an adequate airborne system for the specialized navigation authorized for the particular operation.

Section 121.356 Traffic Alert and Collision Avoidance System

All air carrier aircraft that have a passenger seating configuration of more than 30 seats must be equipped with an approved ***traffic alert and collision avoidance system (TCAS II)*** and the appropriate class of Mode S transponder. This equipment provides traffic alerts (TAs) of conflicting traffic. In case of a collision threat, it also issues resolution advisories (RAs) that give the crew specific guidance as to the maneuvers required to avoid collision.

In addition, no one may operate a passenger or combination cargo/passenger (combi) airplane that has a passenger seat configuration of 10 to 30 seats unless it is equipped with an approved traffic alert and collision avoidance system.

Section 121.357 Airborne Weather Radar Equipment Requirements

Air carrier aircraft (other than those operating solely within Alaska, Hawaii, and parts of Canada) must have an approved ***airborne weather radar*** unit installed in the aircraft. When using the radar it must comply with the following:

(1)   The carrier may not dispatch an airplane under IFR or night VFR conditions when current weather reports indicate that thunderstorms or other potentially hazardous weather conditions that can be detected with airborne weather radar may reasonably be expected along the route to be flown, unless the airborne weather radar is working.

(2)   If the airborne weather radar becomes inoperative en route, the airplane must be operated in accordance with the company's approved operations manual.

FAR 121.357(c)

Section 121.358 Low Altitude Windshear System Equipment Requirements

Low altitude windshear system. There have been a number of serious, fatal air carrier accidents resulting from wind shear. Technology has become available to allow the hazardous conditions to be detected and for warnings of windshear danger to be issued. Newer aircraft (airplanes manufactured after January 2, 1991) and specific models of older airplanes (those manufactured before January 3, 1991) must be equipped with either an approved airborne windshear warning and flight guidance system, an approved airborne detection and avoidance system, or an approved combination of these systems. As a minimum requirement, all other turbine powered (excluding turboprop) airplanes that are not specifically listed must be equipped with an approved airborne windshear warning system. These airplanes may be equipped with an approved airborne windshear detection and avoidance system, or an approved combination of these systems.

Section 121.359 Cockpit Voice Recorders

The FAA has for many years required air carrier and turbine aircraft to be equipped with **cockpit voice recorders (CVRs)**. These devices record the words of each flight crewmember, the radio communications, and the general ambient cockpit noise and speech. They have been invaluable in assisting in accident investigations. Their appearance in the commercial airline cockpits was not without debate however. There was a widespread resentment among pilots of the "spying" or monitoring of all communications, and as a result, the use of the cockpit voice recorder has been limited by union contracts. In most airlines the recorders may only be "read out" in the event of a reportable accident or incident. The CVR must be operated continuously from the start of the use of the checklist (before starting engines for the purpose of flight) to completion of the final checklist at the termination of the flight. At the conclusion of a "routine" flight, the crew usually has the right to erase the recording. Like the FDR, the CVR must be either bright orange or bright yellow and have reflective tape affixed to the external surface to facilitate its location under water. It must have an approved underwater locating device on or adjacent to the container that is secured in such a manner that they are not likely to be separated during crash impact. The recorder must record information for at least 30 minutes. Earlier information may be erased or otherwise obliterated.

Section 121.360 Ground Proximity Warning: Glide Slope Deviation Alerting System

Air carrier aircraft must be equipped with a **ground proximity warning system (GPWS)**. The GPWS is a device that can detect certain hazardous conditions and warn the crew.

Conditions such as too rapid closure to the ground (sink rate), being too close to the ground (terrain), or going below the approach flight path (glide slope) will be called to the crew's attention through a verbal annunciator.

Summary

Transport category aircraft used in Part 121 air carrier operations have extensive requirements for the equipment and instruments that must be installed. We have not covered many of these that are familiar to the reader from previous training. This list would include items such as attitude indicators, heading indicators, and airspeed indicators. Rather, we have gone through the list unique to Part 121 and provided an indication of the specialized equipment that must be carried by Part 121 carriers.

Important Terms from this Chapter

Additional emergency exits

Airborne weather radar

Carriage of infants and children under 2 years of age

Cockpit check procedure

Cockpit voice recorders (CVRs)

Crew seat belts/shoulder harnesses

Crewmember interphone system

Emergency equipment

Emergency equipment: extended overwater operations

Emergency equipment: operations over uninhabited terrain

Emergency exit access

Emergency exit operating handles

Emergency flotation means

Emergency light operations

Emergency lighting system

Equipment for operations in icing conditions

Equipment required when specialized means of navigation are used

Exterior emergency lighting

Exterior exit markings

Flight and navigational equipment

Flight attendant seats

Flight recorders (FDR and DFDR)

Floor level exits

Ground proximity warning system (GPWS)

Instruments and equipment: operations at night

Instruments and equipment: operations under IFR

Interior emergency exit markings

Low altitude windshear system

Means to assist the occupants in descending to the ground

Passenger information

Pitot heating system

Portable electronic devices

Portable lights

Protective breathing equipment (PBE)

Public address system

Radio equipment

Radio equipment: extended overwater operations

Radio equipment: operations under IFR

Radio equipment: operations under VFR

Seats, safety belts, and shoulder harnesses

Sideward facing seats

Slip resistant escape route

Supplemental oxygen for emergency descent and first aid

Supplemental oxygen for sustenance

Traffic alert and collision avoidance system (TCAS II)

Ventral exits and tailcone exits

Chapter 10 Exam

1. The rule requiring all required, installed equipment to be operative is violated when
   a. The aircraft is started.
   b. The aircraft is taxied.
   c. The aircraft takes off.
   d. The aircraft lands.

2. In passenger-carrying airplanes, at least two of the fire extinguishers must
   a. Be of the Halon 1211 (or equivalent) type.
   b. Be of the CO_2 type.
   c. Be of the water/pressure type.
   d. Be of the dry chemical type.

3. In considering the need for escape slides or similar evacuation means, the aircraft is assumed to be
   a. On the ground with collapsed landing gear.
   b. On the ground with a single collapsed landing gear.
   c. On the ground with the nose gear collapsed.
   d. On the ground with all landing gear extended.

4. Emergency lighting for interior or exterior use must be able to be controlled at the
   a. Flight crew's station in the cockpit.
   b. A position in the passenger compartment.
   c. Both of the above.
   d. Neither of the above.

5. During ground operations, it is
   a. Suggested, but not required, that each passenger be seated with his seat belt fastened.
   b. Required that each passenger be seated and belts fastened only when taking the runway.
   c. Required that each passenger be seated and belts fastened only when taking off.
   d. Required that each passenger be seated and belts fastened during all movement on the surface.

6. The crew uses checklist procedures that are provided by the
   a. FAA.
   b. Manufacturer of the aircraft.
   c. Operator of the aircraft.
   d. Pilot's union.

7. Flight crewmembers must be provided and use oxygen when
   a. The cabin pressure altitude exceeds 10,000 feet.
   b. The cabin pressure altitude exceeds 12,500 feet.
   c. The cabin pressure altitude exceeds 14,000 feet.
   d. The cabin pressure altitude exceeds 15,000 feet.

8. If one pilot leaves his station at the controls, it is necessary for the other pilot to don his or her oxygen mask if the aircraft is above

    a. 12,500 feet.
    b. Flight level 250.
    c. Flight level 350.
    d. Flight level 410.

9. In the event of cabin pressurization failure, the crew must be provided with oxygen that allows for a total of
    a. 10 minutes operation allowing descent to 10,000 feet altitude.
    b. 110 minutes total operation.
    c. 120 minutes total operation.
    d. None of the above.

10. The flight recorder must continuously record
    a. 30 minutes of continuous data.
    b. 1 hour of continuous data.
    c. 24 hours of continuous data.
    d. 25 hours of continuous data.

11. Traffic Alert and Collision Avoidance System—II (TCAS II) equipment is required for
    a. All Part 121 carrier aircraft.
    b. All large Part 121 aircraft.
    c. Part 121 aircraft with more than 10 seats.
    d. Part 121 aircraft with more than 30 seats.

12. The cockpit voice recorder (CVR) is required to operate starting at
    a. Engine start.
    b. Application of ground or aircraft power to the aircraft.
    c. First use of a checklist.
    d. From the time the crew is seated in the cockpit.

Dispatching and Flight Release Rules

Where am I?

—Charles Lindbergh,
upon his arrival in Paris

In this chapter we'll look at the air carrier dispatching and release requirements that must be considered prior to a flight's departure. FAR 121 Subpart U contains the rules applicable to **dispatching** domestic and flag operations and **releasing** supplemental operations. The requirements to dispatch domestic, flag, and supplemental operations are found in FAR 121.593, 121.595, and 121.597, respectively. These rules are very clear and unambiguous.

A *domestic or flag* flight must be authorized by a dispatcher or *dispatch released*. In the case of domestic flights *each* flight must be dispatched, unless the flight was originally included in the dispatch of a multi-leg flight and the aircraft doesn't spend more than 1 hour on the ground. In that case, the dispatch may cover multiple legs. In the case of flag operations, the rule is similar in concept, but the times are different. In this case, each flight must be dispatched except that a flight involving a stop (layover) may be conducted on a single dispatch so long as the aircraft doesn't remain on the ground for over 6 hours.

The **flight release** of *supplemental* operations is addressed in 121.597 and contains a couple of interesting allowances not offered to domestic and flag operators. The first allowance is that there exists no requirement to have an aircraft dispatcher release each flight, hence there's no requirement to employ a certified aircraft dispatcher. The only requirement under 121.597(a) is that a flight may not depart under a flight following system without specific authority from the person authorized by the operator to exercise operational control over the flight. Secondly, the pilot in command or the person authorized by the operator to exercise operational control over the flight is allowed to execute a flight release for the flights to be conducted. The pilot in command may sign the flight release only when he and the person authorized by the operator to exercise operational control believe that the flight can be made safely. Also, as in the flag operators' multi-leg dispatch provision, no person operating under a supplemental flight release may continue a flight from an intermediate airport without a new flight release if the aircraft has been on the ground more than 6 hours.

Dispatch Release (Domestic and Flag) and Flight Release Document (Supplemental)

A *dispatch release document* is required to be prepared by the dispatcher by 121.663. Both the pilot in command and the dispatcher must sign this document, although the dispatcher may delegate his authority to sign the document. Notice 121.663 makes it clear that he is only delegating his authority to *sign* the dispatch release, not his authority to dispatch the flight.

Contents of the dispatch release document are spelled out in 121.687 for domestic and flag operations. (See sample release, fig. 11.1.) The release must include

- Identification number of the aircraft;
- Flight number (trip number);
- Departure airport, intermediate stops, destination airport and alternate(s);
- Type of operation (IFR/VFR);
- Minimum required fuel supply; and
- Latest weather reports and forecasts at time of departure.

FAR 121.599(a) requires that both domestic and flag dispatchers be familiar with the weather reports and forecasts along the route(s) to be flown. Since there may not be an aircraft dispatcher assigned to a supplemental operator's flight, 121.599(b) assigns the responsibility for becoming familiar with reported and forecast weather conditions on the route to be flown to the pilot in command.

FAR 121.601 addresses what information the dispatcher must provide to the pilot in command for both domestic and flag operations. The dispatcher must also provide current information on the airports' conditions and the navigation facilities to be used. The dispatcher must also provide the pilot in command with all available weather reports and forecasts that may affect the safety of the flight such as clear air turbulence, thunderstorms, and wind shear for each airport to be used and route to be flown. During the conduct of the flight, the dispatcher must update the pilot in command on any changes to any of this information as changes occur.

A *flight release document* rather than a dispatch release is used by supplemental operators. Instead of an aircraft dispatcher, supplemental operators are allowed by 121.603 to assign the pilot in command the duty of obtaining all available current reports or information on airport conditions and irregularities of navigation facilities that may affect the safety of the flight. Like the aircraft dispatcher in domestic and flag operations, the pilot in command in supplemental operations is required to obtain any additional available information of meteorological conditions and irregularities of facilities and services that may affect the safety of the flight.

Finally, in order for a flight to be either dispatched or flight released, 121.605 requires the aircraft to be airworthy and equipped as prescribed in *Subpart K: Instrument and Equipment Requirements* (see chapter 10).

Load Manifest

Another document that must be prepared is the *load manifest*. 121.693 requires both domestic and flag operators to prepare a load manifest (see sample, fig. 11.2) containing the following information:

```
***************************************************************************
*Flight 580/02JUL          Aircraft N0222DL          CAE-ATL          Release #1 *
***************************************************************************
Flight Dispatch Release-Captain Copy
Dispatcher: Higgins #73   ph#999-715-4473


Delta Flt. 580/02JUL     Release #1 CAE-ATL    Alternate: CAE
Aircraft:N0222DL    Type of Flt.:IFR    Block Fuel:15,800 lbs
Minimum Fuel for Takeoff:14,630 lbs

By signing the attached flight release document I consider all factors including my own
physical condition satisfactory for this flight.


Delta 580/02 RLS 1 CAE/ATL ALTN CAE

              Scheduled            Planned            Actual
KCAE      2030z/1630L           2030z               ....
Taxi                            0012                ....
OFF                             2042z               ....
ETE                             0037                ....
ON                              2119z               ....
Taxi                            0010                ....
KATL      2140z/1740z           2129z               ....

DOT On-time arvl limit is sked plus 14 minutes or 2154z/1754z-applies only to flight
within 50 states/Puerto Rico/U.S. Virgin Isles

Ship 222 T/Boeing737-300/F  DMCS  Type:ECON    Filed Alt:260 Company Route: 2    Miles: 188
Elev. KCAE: 236 Ft.   KATL: 1026 Ft.


Route: KCAE..CAE.J4.IRQ.SINCA3.KATL      ETE: 37 min.


Ramp Wt.: 103,519 LWT: 099,290  Payload 066/013,753
MPTW: 109,135  Flight Plan includes cargo  000,421
Target Arrival Fuel: 11,300 lbs. Gate: B14 Ramp#2 (128.87)

Trip Time/Burn CAE ATL      37/004230-Taxi 12/00380
IFR/ALTN   CAE   FL230      33/003470
PLND Contingency Fuel       45/003310 see remarks
UNPLND CNTNGNCY Fuel        10/000790
Reserve Fuel                   004000
Block Fuel                     015800
Minimum Fuel for T/O           014630


Dispatcher and Maintenance Remarks:
-Dispatcher-
Fuel Added for:
01 Anticipated Weather
02 Traffic
Smooth rides reported at 260
-Maintenance-
-MEL/CDL:
M22-00-04  Autothrottle System
    MEL Expiration Date-06JUL01 at 0400z
M49-00-01B Auxiliary Power Unit
    MEL Expiration Date-11JUL01 at 0400z
Aircraft Remarks: 222 Please note cost indexes-15OCT98**ECON 62/LRC 00/OTA 183

Descent LNDG Rnwy 27 Cross CANUK at 12,000 ft. 250 KIAS
Descent LNDG Rnway 09 Cross HUSKY at 14,000 ft.


Computed En Route winds
Fix    TROP SAT  CRZ FL
TOC    -47  -26  280/018
IRQ    -47  -26  280/022
TOD    -45  -26  280/017


Airport/Notams/Navigational Remarks
CAE/Caution Terminal construction...at night ramp area not well lit.
CAE/11 ALS OTS
ATL/TACAN OTs
```

Figure 11.1   Sample flight plan. Dispatch release.

a.   *Weight of the loaded aircraft*
b.   *Maximum allowable weight that must not exceed the least of:*
    (1)   *Max takeoff weight for runway to be used*
    (2)   *Max takeoff weight that allows compliance with en route limitations*
    (3)   *Max takeoff weight (considering fuel/oil consumption) that allows compliance with the max landing weight limitations*
    (4)   *Max takeoff weight (considering fuel/oil consumption) that allows compliance with landing distance limitations on arrival at destination/alternate airports*
c.   *Total weight computed under approved procedures*
d.   *Evidence the aircraft is loaded within center of gravity limits*
e.   *Names of passengers unless that list is maintained by the carrier* (e.g., in a reservations systems).

FAR 121.693

121.695 requires the pilot in command of a domestic or flag flight to carry aboard the aircraft copies of:

a.   *Completed load manifest,*
b.   *Copy of the dispatch release, and*
c.   *Copy of the flight plan.*

FAR 121.695

Supplemental carriers, on the other hand, may carry the original or a copy of the load manifest, flight release, and flight plan and are additionally required by 121.697 to carry the

• Pilot route certification and the
• Aircraft's airworthiness release certificate.

IFR Dispatching Rules

Next we see that FAR 121.613 says that we can't dispatch an airplane under Part 121 unless the weather reports and forecasts indicate that at the time of arrival at the destination airport it is forecast to be at or above the authorized **landing minimums**. This provision is much more restrictive than the rules of Part 91 where you may depart for a destination that is forecast below landing minimums so long as a suitable alternate airport is available. There is a commonly granted exemption to this provision called the "People's Express Exemption," which we'll discuss a little bit later in this chapter.

The next set of rules of concern to the dispatcher are those that help assure that no matter what situations are encountered, there will always be an "out" available to the flight to assure that the trip can be completed safely. In chapter 8, we briefly mentioned the requirements to have en route alternate airports. These requirements were part of the single engine inoperative and two engine inoperative rules discussed earlier. Now we will introduce two additional situations that may require filing alternate airports in the flight plan. These additional alternate airport requirements are the **departure airport alternate airport** and the **destination airport alternate airport**.

```
*******************************************************************************
*Flight 580/02JUL          Aircraft N0222DL        CAE-ATL          Release #1 *
*******************************************************************************
FLT 0580/02 CAE-ATL                              Load Planner M-EVANS  A69c789
Final   Weight Data Record                       Date/Time 02JUL  2023z
Flight Plan Release Number 01


Passenger Configuration: 8 FC/114 YC

074025  OEW 737-300 A/C 222 Includes 3 Flight Attendants W/Bags
 1000   ADD 4 PAX/260lbs -or- SUB 2 PAX


 1440   8 FC
10440   58 YC


    0   Bin 1 Cargo
  175   Bin 2 Cargo
 1500   Bin 3 Cargo
  110   Bin 4 Cargo


88690   Zero Fuel Weight   MAX 105000
          88719.0  Adjusted ZFW        CG 18.8 pct MAC
15670   Fuel/1- 7580/2- 7440/C-650
 -380   Less Taxi Fuel

103980  Actual Takeoff Weight    Aft Index 45  16.6 pct MAC
*******************************************************************************
104017.0 Adjusted Takeoff Weight                 CAE Takeoff Weather/ NWS
                                                 Temp 93 F  Alt 30.07
                                                 Wind 006/005 kts


109135  Max Takeoff WT this flight limited by flight planning restrictions

Max Takeoff Wt.   Ldg. ATL   Max Ldg. Wt.   Burnoff     Forcast Temp
117850            Flap 30    114000         3850         85

130000 Maximum Structural Takeoff Weight
*******************************************************************************
CAE RWY 29                            / 8602 ft.     93F/34C      1 HW/5 XW
Standard Profile
Rwy Condition   Thrust/Flap   Climb Limit   RATOW   STAB Trim    V1    VR    V2

Dry             AT50/05       105793        123965    4.9        127   128   134
Dry             AT45/05       110698        127280    4.9        127   127   134
Dry             AT40/05       115418        130474    4.9        126   126   134
Dry             AT35/05       120048        133349    4.9        126   126   135
Dry             Norm/05       120965        134091    4.9        126   126   135
SLWET           Norm/05       120965        132893    4.9        126   126   135
ICY             Norm/05       120965        125354    4.9        122   126   135
*******************************************************************************
CAE RWY 11                            / 8602 ft.     93F/34C      1 HW/5 XW
Standard Profile
Rwy Condition   Thrust/Flap   Climb Limit   RATOW   STAB Trim    V1    VR    V2

Dry             AT50/05       105793        104464    4.9        127   128   134
Dry             AT45/05       110698        107250    4.9        127   127   134
Dry             AT40/05       115418        111680    4.9        126   126   134
Dry             AT35/05       120048        115670    4.9        126   126   135
Dry             Norm/05       120965        116552    4.9        125   126   135
SLWET           Norm/05       120965        114614    4.9        124   126   135
ICY             Norm/05       120965        107652    4.9        122   126   135
*******************************************************************************
Performance Notes:
Tailwind: -1000 lbs/knot from RATOW
Temp Inc: -495 lbs/deg F-up to 94 F From Climb Limit and RATOW
Headwind - ADD 100 lbs/knot to RATOW

Bleed Air Corrections - Engine Anti-ice
  Subtract 500 lbs. from climb limit and RATOW
Cutback Correction - Normal Power Required
  Subtract 10 lb/ft from RATOW
```

Figure 11.2 Sample load manifest.

Departure Airport Alternate Airport

The requirement for a departure airport alternate airport is found in 121.617 and is addressed in Part C: IFR Takeoff Minimums of an air carrier's op specs. This provision protects the operator when weather conditions are such that an aircraft departs an airport with takeoff minimums below the departure airport's landing minimums. But how can that happen? How can the takeoff be at less than landing minimums when FAR 91.175(f) prescribes takeoff minimums in excess of most landing minimums? Standard takeoff minimums are 1/2 statute mile visibility or 2,400 feet RVR (runway visual range) for three or more engine airplanes and 1 statute mile visibility or 5,000 feet RVR for twin engine aircraft.

The answer is found in 121.651 (takeoff minimums). The certificate holder may be authorized to use lower than standard takeoff minimums in its ops specs. These lower than standard takeoff minimums may be much lower than the required landing minimums. Let's take a look at a large air carrier's lower than standard takeoff minimums as authorized in its ops specs Paragraph C.078.

| U.S. Department of Transportation Federal Aviation Administration | Operation Specifications

Paragraph C.078 |

Delta Air Lines Ops Specs   **Paragraph C.078**

IFR Lower Than Standard Takeoff Minimums, 14 CFR Part 121
Airplane Operations: All Airports

The certificate holder is authorized to use lower than standard takeoff minimums in accordance with the limitations and provisions of this operations specification as follows.

   a. Runway visual range (RVR) reports, when available for a particular runway, shall be used for all takeoff operations on that runway. All takeoff operations, based on RVR, must use RVR reports from the locations along the runway specified in this paragraph.
   b. When takeoff minimums are equal to or less than the applicable standard takeoff minimum, the certificate holder is authorized to use the lower than standard takeoff minimums described below:
      (1) Visibility or runway visual value (RVV) 1/4 statute mile or touchdown zone RVR 1,600, provided at least one of the following visual aids is available. The touchdown zone RVR report, if available, is controlling. The mid-RVR report may be substituted for the touchdown zone RVR report if the touchdown zone RVR report is not available.
         (a)   Operative high intensity runway lights (HIRL).
         (b)   Operative runway centerline lights (CL).
         (c)   Serviceable runway centerline marking (RCLM).
         (d)   In circumstances when none of the above visual aids are available, visibility or RVV 1/4 statute mile may still be used, provided other runway markings or runway lighting provide pilots with adequate visual reference to continuously identify the takeoff surface and maintain directional control throughout the takeoff run.
      (2) Touchdown zone RVR 1,000 (beginning of takeoff run) and rollout RVR 1,000, provided all of the following visual aids and RVR equipment are available.

(a) Operative runway centerline lights (CL).

(b) Two operative RVR reporting systems serving the runway to be used, both of which are required and controlling. A mid-RVR report may be substituted for either a touchdown zone RVR report if a touchdown zone report is not available or a rollout RVR report if a rollout RVR report is not available.

(3) Touchdown zone RVR 500 (beginning of takeoff run), mid-RVR 500, and rollout RVR 500, provided all of the following visual aids and RVR equipment are available.

(a) Operative runway centerline lights (CL).

(b) Runway centerline markings (RCLM).

(c) Operative touchdown zone and rollout RVR reporting systems serving the runway to be used, both of which are controlling, or three RVR reporting systems serving the runway to be used, all of which are controlling. However, if one of the three RVR reporting systems has failed, a takeoff is authorized, provided the remaining two RVR values are at or above the appropriate takeoff minimum as listed in this subparagraph.

Lower than standard takeoff minimums utilizing Heads-up Guidance Systems (HGS) omitted for the sake of brevity.

1. The Certificate Holder applies for the Operations in this paragraph.
2. Support information reference: JAR-OPS changes.
3. These Operations Specifications are approved by direction of the Administrator.

ORIGINAL SIGNED BY:
Ms. F. Faye Phisdo
Principal Operations Inspector

4. Date Approval is effective: 01/17/2000 Amendment Number: 0
5. I hereby accept and receive the Operations Specifications in this paragraph.

ORIGINAL SIGNED BY:
Al B. Phlying
System Manager Quality Assurance & Compliance Date: 01/17/2000

This air carrier is authorized in it's ops specs to perform takeoffs when the visibility in the touchdown zone (beginning of takeoff run) RVR is as low as 500 feet, mid-portion of the runway as low as 500 feet RVR, and rollout (departure end of runway) as low as 500 feet RVR, provided all of the stated visual aids and RVR equipment are available. This is less than the standard Category I landing minimums of 1/2 statute mile or 1,800 feet RVR. What would happen if the aircraft took off then suffered an emergency of some sort and couldn't return to the airport of departure because the weather was below that field's *landing minimums?*

FAR 121.617 specifies that if the conditions at the takeoff airport are below the landing minimums, a *departure airport alternate airport* must be specified in the dispatch release. For two engine aircraft, that airport must be no more than 1 hour (at normal cruising speed with one engine inoperative) away from the departure airport (e.g., the takeoff alternate must be within 300 nm of the departure airport for a Boeing 737-300). For three or more engine airplanes the departure alternate must be no more than 2 hours from the departure airport at normal cruising speed with one engine inoperative. Keep in mind, even though an aircraft might be certified for Category II and/or Category III landings, a departure airport alternate airport is still required in many cases when the weather at the departure airport is below Category I landing minimums. The reason is that many aircraft, though certificated for all-engine Category II or Category III landing minima are only certified to Category I landing minimums with one engine inoperative!

Destination Alternate

This third type of alternate airport required by the FAA is called a ***destination alternate airport***. This type of alternate airport comes into play when the forecast for the destination airport is less than "perfect" weather. In that case, as we will see, the rules require us to have a "contingency plan" in the form of a destination alternate airport. FAR 121.619 covers this for domestic operations while 121.621 contains the destination alternate airport rules for flag operations.

In domestic operations the rule is as simple as 1-2-3. That is:

From *1 hour* before scheduled arrival
until *1 hour* after, we require:

2,000 foot ceiling and *3 statute miles visibility.*

If the weather is not forecast to be at least this good then we must file a destination alternate airport. In other words, this ***1-2-3 rule*** answers the question: Do I need a destination alternate airport?

Do I Need a Destination Alternate Airport?

If an alternate is needed, then you again look to 121.625 to find what weather conditions the alternate airport must be forecasting. Furthermore, an additional alternate may also be required. When weather conditions at the destination airport and the first alternate airport are marginal, 121.619(a) requires at least one additional alternate airport be designated.

In flag operations, the rules for determining the need for an alternate airport are similar in concept but differ in the numbers involved. First, if the flight is over 6 hours, an alternate must be filed, period. If the flight is 6 hours or less in duration, then in order not to file an alternate airport, the weather must be better than 1,500 feet above the lowest circling minimum descent altitude (MDA) if a circling approach is required, or at least 1,500 feet higher than the lowest published instrument minimums or 2,000 feet above airport elevations, whichever is greater. The visibility must be at least 3 miles or 2 miles added to the lowest published minimum visibility, whichever is greater.

Supplemental operators must list a destination alternate airport on the flight release unless the air carrier meets FAA fuel load stipulations covered in 121.645. A flight may not depart (flight released) unless, considering wind and other weather conditions expected, it has enough fuel

(1) *To fly to and land at the airport to which it is released,*
(2) *After that, to fly for a period of 10 percent of the total time required to fly from the airport of departure to, and land at, the airport to which it was released,*
(3) *After that, to fly to and land at the most distant alternate airport specified in the flight release, if an alternate is required,*

(4)   After that, to fly for 30 minutes at holding speed at 1,500 feet above the alternate airport (or the destination airport if no alternate is required) under standard temperature conditions.

FAR 121.645(b)

At a minimum, a turbojet powered airplane in flag operations may not depart for an airport for which an alternate is *not* specified in the flight release unless it has enough fuel, considering wind and other weather conditions expected, to fly to the destination airport and thereafter fly for at least 2 hours at normal cruising fuel consumption. The FAA reserves the right to require more fuel than any of the *fuel minimums* stated in 121.645 if they find that additional fuel is necessary on a particular route in the interest of safety. This additional fuel requirement will appear in that air carrier's ops specs.

The destination and en route alternate airport rules are intended to assure that no matter what situations are encountered, there will always be sufficient fuel aboard the aircraft to complete the trip safely. Let's see how that works. To begin with, 121.647 contains all of the factors for computing fuel required by the FAA. Each person computing fuel required must consider the following:

(a)   Wind and other weather conditions forecast.
(b)   Anticipated traffic delays.
(c)   One instrument approach and possible missed approach at destination.
(d)   Any other conditions that may delay landing of the aircraft.

Also included in 121.647 is a brief definition of *required fuel*. Required fuel is in addition to unusable fuel.

Alternate Airport Weather Minimums

FAR 121.625 specifies what weather conditions must exist at the alternate airport in order to file it as an alternate. *Alternate airport weather conditions* must meet or exceed whatever weather conditions are specified in the carrier's ops specs. The *standard alternate (weather) minimums* are found in Part 91.169 and are *600-2* for *precision (ILS)* approaches and *800-2* for *nonprecision (VOR, NDB, GPS, etc.)* approaches. This means the forecast ceiling must be at least 600 feet or 800 feet while the forecast visibility must be in excess of 2 miles to use this airport as an alternate *of any kind.*

It is common, however, for a carrier to have approval of an alternative method of computing the alternate weather minimums required. This method will often result in lower than standard alternate airport minimums. Let's take a look at typical lower than standard alternate airport minimums [often called *derived alternate (weather) minimums*], which are permitted by approval in an air carrier's op specs.

U.S. Department of Transportation Federal Aviation Administration	Operation Specifications
	Paragraph C.055

JetBlue Airways Ops Specs   **Paragraph C.055**

Alternate Airport IFR Weather Minimums

a. The certificate holder is authorized to derive alternate airport weather minimums from the "Alternate Airport IFR Weather Minimums" table listed below.

b. Special limitations and provisions.

   (1) In no case shall the certificate holder use an alternate airport weather minimum other than any applicable minimum derived from this table.

   (2) In determining alternate airport weather minimums, the certificate holder shall not use any published instrument approach procedure which specifies that alternate airport weather minimums are not authorized.

   (3) Credit for alternate minima based on CAT II or CAT III capability is predicated on authorization for engine inoperative CAT III operations for the certificate holder, aircraft type, and qualification of flightcrew for the respective CAT II or CAT III minima applicable to the alternate airport.

Alternate Airport IFR Weather Minimums
(sm = statute mile)

Approach Facility Configuration	Ceiling	Visibility
For airports with at least one operational navigational facility providing a straight-in nonprecision approach procedure, or a straight-in precision approach procedure, or when applicable, a circling maneuver from an instrument approach procedure.	A ceiling derived by adding 400 ft to the authorized Category I HAT or, when applicable, the authorized HAA.	A visibility derived by adding 1 sm to the authorized Category I landing minimum.
For airports with at least two operational navigational facilities, each providing a straight-in nonprecision approach procedure or a straight-in precision approach procedure to different, suitable runways. (However, when an airport is designated as an ER-OPS En Route Alternate Airport in these operations specifications, the approach procedures used must be to separate, suitable runways.)	A ceiling derived by adding 200 ft to the higher Category I HAT of the two approaches used.	A visibility derived by adding 1/2 sm to the higher authorized Category I landing minimum of the two approaches used.

—continued

Alternate Airport IFR Weather Minimums (continued)
(sm = statute mile)

Approach Facility Configuration	Ceiling	Visibility
For airports with a published CAT II or CAT III approach, and at least two operational navigational facilities, each providing a straight-in precision approach procedure to different, suitable runways.	CAT II procedures, a ceiling of at least 300 ft HAT, or for CAT III procedures, a ceiling of at least 200 ft HAT.	CAT II procedures, a visibility of at least RVR 4,000, or for CAT III procedures, a visibility of at least RVR 1,800.

1. The Certificate Holder applies for the Operations in this paragraph.
2. Support information reference: JAR-OPS changes.
3. These Operations Specifications are approved by direction of the Administrator.

ORIGINAL SIGNED BY
Mr. Turner A. Rench
Principal Operations Inspector

4. Date Approval is effective: 01/17/2000 Amendment Number: 0
5. I hereby accept and receive the Operations Specifications in this paragraph.

ORIGINAL SIGNED BY
Mr. I. L. Phly
System Manager Quality Assurance & Compliance Date: 01/17/2000

The purpose of paragraph C.055 of an air carrier's ops specs is to specify what minimum weather conditions must exist at a particular airport in order for its dispatchers to file it as an alternate. The dispatcher must check the ceiling and visibility information in the weather report and compare that information to the approaches available at the desired airport. Let's look at an example.

A dispatcher desires to use XYZ airport for an alternate. First, the dispatcher will look up the navigational charts for that field. XYZ airport is located near sea level with a field elevation of 80 feet. Let's say XYZ has two different suitable runways; one offers a straight-in VOR approach with a minimum descent altitude (MDA) of 800 feet with a height above touchdown (HAT) of 720 feet; the other runway offers a straight-in ILS approach with a decision altitude (DA) of 280 feet and a HAT of 200 feet.

Next, the dispatcher will refer to the *Alternate Airport IFR Weather Minimums* table to determine what minimum required ceiling and visibility is allowed for filing XYZ as an alternate airport. Since XYZ has two different straight-in instrument approaches to two different suitable runways, the ceiling and visibility minimums are derived by adding 200 feet to the HAT for the VOR approach and adding 1/2 statute mile (sm) to VOR's minimum visibility requirement. Note, in this example the VOR approach has the highest HAT *and* the higher visibility requirement of the two approaches. *This might not always be the case*; in some cases you might use the HAT from one approach and the visibility from another.

Table 11.1. Published approach minimums for XYZ airport

Straight-in ILS Precision Approach	Straight-in VOR Nonprecision Approach
DA(H) 280 ft (200 ft)	MDA(H) 800ft (720 ft)
A	
B	
C RVR 1800 or 1/2 sm	RVR 4000 or 3/4 sm
D	

The ceiling is derived by adding 200 feet to the higher Category I approach HAT of the two approaches. Since the VOR approach has a higher HAT, then we are required to add 200 feet to the HAT of 720 feet, for a required ceiling of at least 920 feet. To derive the visibility we again look at both the VOR and ILS approaches (see table 11.1). The VOR has the higher visibility requirement of 3/4 statute mile, so we are required to add 1/2 statute mile to the published visibility requirement of 3/4 statute mile for a total required visibility of 1 1/4 statute miles. If the ceiling is higher than 920 feet and the visibility is better than 1 1/4 statute miles, then XYZ may be filed as an alternate.

Intuitively, one might think since an airport offering two straight-in approaches offers a lower alternate minimum additive (+200 feet and +1/2 statute mile), it might also offer the lowest derived alternate minimum. However, it is possible to have higher alternate minimums when using two operational navigational facilities than when using an airport with only one navigational facility. For instance, an airport with one straight-in nonprecision approach with a HAT of 400 feet and 1 statute mile visibility would have alternate minimums of 800 feet and 2 statute miles visibility. That is, minimums derived by added 400 feet + 400 feet and 1 statute mile + 1 statute mile. Now if an airport with two straight-in approaches, one precision ILS with HAT of 280 feet and 1/2 statute mile visibility and the other a nonprecision VOR approach with an HAT of 800 feet and 1 statute mile visibility, we would have alternate minimums of 1,000 feet and 1 1/2 statute mile visibility. That is, 200 feet + 800 feet = 1,000 feet and 1/2 statute mile + 1 statute mile = 1 1/2 statute miles. Since the air carrier's op specs will require that the higher ceiling and visibility be used, the minimums for the airport with two straight-in approaches are higher than for the airport with only one straight-in approach. In this case the dispatcher may elect to file an alternate to an airport offering only one straight-in approach. So even though it requires that higher alternate additives be used, it provides the dispatcher with the lowest possible ceiling and visibility requirements.

This seems like a lot of work for the aircraft dispatcher to go through every time a flight is dispatched. In the real world the dispatch department figures out in advance what the minimum ceiling and visibility requirements are for every airport the air carrier may ever desire to use as an alternate. These figures are then placed in a reference manual and on computer. The dispatcher simply refers to the manual for the minimum weather requirements and then compares that information with the weather reports for that airport.

People's Express Exemption 3585

FAA exemption 3585 was a petition People's Express Airlines filed in 1982 with the FAA to gain some relief from the restrictive requirements of 121.613 and 121.625. Because People's Express Airlines was a "low cost" start-up airline, it could not afford to maintain its own meteorology department or even contract weather reporting services. It therefore relied solely on the National Weather Service (NWS) for the weather reports needed to dispatch flights. Other major airlines employed their own licensed meteorologists to provide up-to-date weather reports and forecasts, which enabled those carriers to rely on more immediate information rather than on historic (as much as 6 hours old) NWS reports. This, many times, would allow other airlines to depart for a destination while People's Express flights would cancel due to destination weather forecasts that were below minimums.

Let's review the structure of the terminal area forecast (TAF) for a moment. The TAF can be broken down into two parts. The first is the main body that contains the prevailing weather for a specified time period. The second section is the remarks section. The remarks section contains restrictions and modifications to the NWS's weather forecast in the main body (e.g., becoming, probability of 40 percent, or temporarily).

The requested exemption from 121.619(a) allowed People's Express to dispatch, under IFR, an aircraft to a destination airport, even though weather reports or forecasts contain such conditional words as, "becoming," "temporarily," etc., so long as there is at least one alternate airport for which weather reports or forecasts indicate that weather conditions will be at or above authorized minimums.

Included in the People's Express petition was a list of what it felt were some major flaws in Part 121 dispatching regulations. They charged the FAA had informally (by nonrulemaking) interpreted the words "will be at or above" to mean that whenever a forecast or report includes such *conditional remarks* as "becoming," "temporarily," etc., at the destination airport, the flight couldn't be dispatched even though the weather reports indicated that weather conditions may be at or above minimums at the ETA. People's Express believed this interpretation ignored the reality of NWS forecasting and gave too much operational significance to terms that were, at best, vague and uncertain. People's Express concluded that because the NWS reports are too infrequently issued and the *conditional remarks* so vague and uncertain, it was inappropriate for the FAA to rely on the *conditional remarks* section of a weather forecast as a basis for permitting or not permitting an airline to dispatch flights. The FAA agreed.

The FAA granted People's Express and other qualifying air carriers an exemption to Sections 121.613, 121.619(a), and 121.625 of the FARs, to the extent necessary to permit them to dispatch an airplane, under IFR, to a destination airport when the weather forecast for that airport indicated by the use of conditional words such as "occasionally," "intermittently," "briefly," or "a chance of," in the remarks section of that report, that the weather could be below authorized weather minimums at the time of arrival. Exemption was subject to the following conditions and limitations:

1.   *Each certificate holder shall apply for and obtain approval from the FAA certificate–holding office having jurisdiction over its operations before commencing operations in accordance with this exemption.*

2.   *Each certificate holder shall list one additional alternate airport in the dispatch release whenever the weather reports or forecasts, or any combination thereof, for the destination airport and first alternate airport indicate, by the use of conditional words in the remarks section of such reports or forecasts, that the forecast weather conditions for the destination and first alternate airport might be as low as one-half the visibility value established for the lowest visibility minimum of the instrument approach procedure expected to be used for an instrument approach at the destination or first alternate. For the additional alternate to be listed in the dispatch release, the weather*

reports or forecasts, or any combination thereof, for this additional alternate, shall not contain any conditional words, including but not limited to "occasionally," "intermittently," "briefly," and "a chance of," in either the main body or the remarks section of such reports.

3. *No person may dispatch or take off an airplane, when operating under this exemption, unless it has enough fuel*
   a. *To fly to the airport to which it is dispatched;*
   b. *Thereafter, to fly to and land at the most distant alternate airport for the airport to which dispatched, taking into account the anticipated air traffic control routing; and*
   c. *Thereafter, to fly for 45 minutes at normal cruising fuel consumption.*

4. *Each certificate holder's pilot in command, while en route, shall ensure by way of air-ground voice communication with their company's Dispatch Center and other appropriate facilities, that he/she is in receipt of the most current relevant weather reports and forecasts for the destination and the alternate airport(s). This current weather information shall be used when making a decision to proceed to an alternate airport for landing.*

Exemption 3585

Most air carriers use exemption 3585 today, although the exemption must be renewed periodically (usually every 2 years). The Air Transport Association, on behalf of all the member airlines, has undertaken that task. In granting this exemption the FAA stated it believed it had preserved the safety objectives of the applicable sections of the FARs, while at the same time it allowed air carriers to avoid canceling flights on the basis of vague, speculative, and ultimately unfulfilled NWS weather forecasts. Over time this exemption has allowed many carriers to realize enormous efficiencies and economic benefits without denigrating safety to any extent (Table 11.2).

Table 11.2. Alternate restrictions under exemption 3585

	Criteria	Terminal Forecast Main Body	Terminal Forecast Remarks Section
Destination requirements	Visibility minimums only	All needed for landing on suitable runway	1/2 of ceiling and visibility needed for landing on the suitable runway
First alternate requirements	Ceiling *and* Visibility minimums required	All needed to designate as an alternate per op specs Paragraph C.055	1/2 of ceiling and visibility needed for landing on the suitable runway
Second alternate requirements	Ceiling *and* Visibility minimums required	All needed to designate as an alternate per op specs Paragraph C.055	All needed for landing on suitable runway

Domestic Fuel Requirements: All Aircraft

FAR 121.639 states that for domestic operations, the flight can't depart unless it has enough fuel

    a.   *To fly to the airport to which it is dispatched, then*
    b.   *To fly to the most distant alternate (if required), then*
    c.   *Fly for 45 minutes at normal cruising fuel consumption rates.*

    FAR 121.639

A good way to work these problems is to use this worksheet:

a. Destination fuel	_____	hours
b. Alternate fuel	_____	hours
c. Holding fuel	:45	minutes
Total	_____	hours

For example:

A Turboprop aircraft is operating in domestic service from ABC to QRS airport and requires a destination alternate of TUV. The flight times are as stated below:

ABC ⟶ QRS   (1:12 hours)

     ⟶ TUV   (:36 minutes) (alternate airport)

How much fuel is required if this turboprop aircraft burns an average of 1,500 lbs/hour?

a. Destination fuel	1:12 hours	=	1,800 lbs
b. Alternate fuel	:36 minutes	=	900 lbs
c. Holding fuel	:45 minutes	=	1,125 lbs
Total fuel	2:33 hours	=	3,825 lbs

Flag Operation Fuel Requirements: Nonturbine and Turboprop Aircraft

FARs 121.641 and 121.645 state the requirements for flag operators. Note that 121.641 covers nonturbine and turboprop flag operations and 121.645 covers turbojet powered flag operations.

    FAR 121.641 requires nonturbine and turboprop operators to assure that at time of departure the aircraft has enough fuel to

a.   Fly and land at the airport to which it is dispatched, then
b.   Fly and land at the most distant alternate airport, plus
c.   30 minutes of fuel, plus
d.   15 percent of the total required in a and b above or 90 minutes, whichever is less.

A good way to work these problems is to use this worksheet:

a. Destination fuel _____ hours
b. Alternate fuel _____ hours
c. 15% of a + b or 90 min. _____ minutes
d. 30 minutes holding fuel _____:30_____ minutes
Total _____ hours

For example:

A Turboprop aircraft is operating in flag service from ABC to XYZ airport and requires a destination alternate of MNO. The flight times are as stated below:

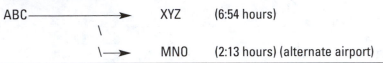

ABC ⟶ XYZ (6:54 hours)

⟶ MNO (2:13 hours) (alternate airport)

How much fuel is required if this turboprop aircraft burns an average of 1,500 lbs/hour?

a. Destination fuel	6:54 hours	=	10,350 lbs
b. Alternate fuel	2:13 hours	=	3,325 lbs
c. 15% of a + b or 90 mins.	1:22 hours	=	2,050 lbs
d. 30 minutes holding fuel	:30 minutes	=	750 lbs
Total fuel required	10:59 hours	=	16,475 lbs

Flag Operation Fuel Requirements: Turbojet Powered Aircraft

As we discussed in alternate airport requirements for supplemental operators, 121.645 covers the operation of turbine engine powered airplanes (other than turboprops). The requirements are similar in concept to the turboprop rules of 121.641, just different numbers. For jet aircraft in flag operations, the requirements are to have enough fuel to

a.　Fly to the destination airport, plus
b.　10% of the fuel required to the destination, plus
c.　Fuel to fly to the alternate airport, plus
d.　30 minutes at 1,500 feet above the alternate airport.

If there is no alternate required, then you must have enough fuel to get to the destination plus 2 hours of reserve fuel. A good worksheet for this problem would look like this:

a. Destination fuel _____ hours
b. 10% of a _____ minutes
c. Alternate fuel _____ hours
d. 30 minutes holding fuel _____:30_____ minutes
Total fuel _____ hours

If we had exactly the same problem as above, just with a turbojet powered aircraft, let's see what fuel is required:

A turboprop aircraft is operating in flag service from ABC to XYZ airport and requires a destination alternate of MNO. The flight times are as stated below:

ABC ──────────────→ XYZ   (6:54 hours)

       \
        \──→ MNO   (2:13) (alternate airport)

What fuel is required if the turbojet powered aircraft burns 12,000 lbs/hour?

a. Destination fuel	6:54 hours	=	82,800 lbs
b. 10% of a	:42 minutes	=	8,400 lbs
c. Alternate fuel	2:13 hours	=	26,600 lbs
d. 30 minutes holding fuel	:30 minutes	=	6,000 lbs
Total fuel	10:19 hours	=	123,800 lbs

Rerelease Rules

Earlier we have seen references to a flight that is released or *rereleased*. Just what is a **rerelease?** This is simply a situation where the flight was originally dispatched and released to one destination, and during the course of the flight the flight's destination was changed and the flight was sent on to a different destination. Why would we do this? Well, there are several reasons. One would be that due to extensive air traffic delays, which were not forecast, we no longer have sufficient fuel to get to our destination. In conjunction with the dispatcher, the pilot in command decides to proceed to an alternate airport to put on more fuel before continuing to the destination.

Another, more interesting, use of the rerelease occurs (particularly in international operations) where the amount of fuel required on long legs may be limiting as to our ability to perform the flight. Let's take a look at the problem first and then the solution. Suppose the following trip is being planned:

Turbojet powered aircraft with an average fuel burn of 14,500 lbs/hour:

Schedule: ATH ──→ JFK ── alternate ──→ BGR

Dep   ATH   1000Z

Arr   JFK   2113Z   ETE: ATH ──→ JFK = 11:13 hours

                            JFK ──→ BGR = 1:38 hours

Calculated Fuel Requirements:

a. Destination fuel	11:13 hours	=	162,646 lbs
b. 10% of a	1:08 hours	=	16,436 lbs
c. Alternate fuel	1:38 hours	=	23,696 lbs
d. 30 minutes holding fuel	:30 minutes	=	7,250 lbs
Total fuel	14:29 hours	=	210,028 lbs

This is all well and good if the aircraft has adequate fuel supply. But, suppose the airplane's fuel tanks only had the capacity for 200,000 lbs of fuel, which would be just about

14:00 hours of flying time. Could we still do the trip? A rerelease can often solve this problem. Instead of releasing the flight to JFK, let's try the following:

Schedule: ATH ⟶ BGR — alternate ⟶ JFK	
Dep ATH 1000Z	
Arr BGR 1935Z	ETE: ATH ⟶ BGR = 9:35 hours
	JFK ⟶ BGR = 1:38 hours

Notice, the flight time to JFK is still the same as before (11:13 hours), but the primary destination of JFK is shown as our alternate.

Fuel Requirements:

a. Destination fuel	9:35 hours	=	138,970 lbs
b. 10% of a	:58 minutes	=	14,036 lbs
c. Alternate fuel	1:38 hours	=	23,696 lbs
d. 30 minutes holding fuel	:30 minutes	=	7,250 lbs
Total fuel	12:41 hours	=	183,952 lbs

So we are legal (with 14:00 hours of fuel) to dispatch/release to BGR with a JFK alternate.

Now, as we approach BGR we perform a "How Goes It" check and find we are operating exactly on this schedule. That means we will arrive over BGR having consumed 9:35 of fuel. Lets see what a BGR to JFK flight would require. We have the choice of using domestic or flag rules here, but let's stick with the flag rules for the sake of clarity. If it helps to use domestic rules, remember that in this situation you may since the flight is entirely within the 48 contiguous United States.

The "new flight" would be a BGR to JFK with a BGR alternate. We'll assume 1:38 each way.

a. Destination fuel	1:38 hours	=	23,696 lbs
b. 10% of a	:10 minutes	=	2,420 lbs
c. Alternate fuel	1:38 hours	=	23,696 lbs
d. 30 minutes holding fuel	:30 minutes	=	7,250 lbs
Total fuel	3:56 hours	=	57,062 lbs

Now, if we have burned 9:35 of fuel getting to Bangor (BGR) and require 3:56 hours or 57,062 lbs of fuel on board to release from BGR to JFK with a BGR alternate, that means that if we left Athens with:

9:35	hours (actual ATH to BGR)
	hours (minimum dispatch fuel: BGR ⟶ JFK ⟶ BGR)
+3:56	
13:31	hours of fuel onboard at Athens.

For our example, 13:31 hours = 195,750 lbs of fuel. Since the tanks hold 14:00 hours (or 200,000 lbs) we would be legal to make this flight. The "savings," if you will, come from the reduced "10% fuel" needed if we compute the trip this way. So, as we approach BGR as long as we have 3:56 in the tanks, we're good to go. This type of *redispatch* is commonly used in extending the planned range of a long-range flight.

Landing Minimums

There are a number of locations where IFR landing minimums can be found. For example, FARs 91.175, 135.225, and 121.651 all address minimum approach and landing weather conditions. The landing minimums an air carrier is authorized to use are those specified in its ops specs and are dependent on a few criteria. First, the certificate holder is only authorized to conduct the types of instrument approach procedures contained in Paragraph C.052 of its ops specs. The air carrier may not conduct any other types of approach procedures. Let's take a look at a sample of an air carrier's basic instrument approach procedure authorizations found in its ops specs.

U.S. Department of Transportation Federal Aviation Administration	Operation Specifications Paragraph C.052

AeroMech Airlines, Inc.

Basic Instrument Approach Procedure Authorizations: All Airports

The certificate holder is authorized to conduct the following types of instrument approach procedures and shall not conduct any other types.

Instrument Approach Procedures (Other Than ILS) Nonprecision Approaches Without Vertical Guidance	Instrument Approach Procedures (Other Than ILS) Precision-like Approaches With Vertical Guidance	Precision Approach Procedures (ILS, GLS)
ASR	LDA with Glide Slope	ILS
LDA/DME		ILS/DME
LOC		PAR MD-11 only-Pacific operations
LOC/DME		
NDB		
NDB/DME		
VOR		
VOR/DME		

   b. <u>Conditions and Limitations</u>.
      (1) All the approaches approved by this Operations Specification must be published in accordance with Title 14 of the Code of Federal Regulations (14 CFR) Part 97.
      (2) Approach procedures listed in column 1 of this Operations Specification must be trained and conducted in accordance with an approved procedure that assures

(continued)

descent will not go below Minimum Descent Altitude (MDA) unless the required visual references for continuing the approach are present.

(3) Approach procedures listed in column 2 of this Operations Specification authorize the certificate holder to conduct instrument approach procedures approved with vertical guidance that provides a precision-like approach and are to be trained using an approved method that allows descent to a published decision altitude (DA).

1. The Certificate Holder applies for the Operations in this paragraph.
2. These Operations Specifications are approved by direction of the Administrator.
    Original signed by: Hantla, Becky J., Principal Operations Inspector
4. Date Approval is effective: 11/07/2000 Amendment Number: 3
5. I hereby accept and receive the Operations Specifications in this paragraph.

Original signed by: Wakning, Rudy
Senior Vice President, Flight Operations Date: 11/07/2000

This air carrier is authorized to do a number of nonprecision and precision approaches. Would an AeroMech Airlines flight crew be legal to conduct a localizer back-course (LOC/BC) approach or simplified directional finder (SDF) approach at a destination airport? The answer is no, because LOC/BC approaches or SDF approaches do not appear in the air carrier's ops specs.

Paragraph C of an air carrier's op specs contains specific ceiling and visibility minimums for each type of approach. 121.651 states that the certificate holder shall not use any IFR landing minimum lower than that prescribed by the applicable published instrument approach procedure and the carrier's ops specs. If we look at 121.651(b) we see a big difference between Part 121 and the Part 91 landing minimums. Instrument approaches conducted under Part 91 regulations are allowed to continue an approach to minimums even if the weather reports indicate the weather is below minimums. This type of approach is sometimes called a "look-see" approach. That is, the Part 91 operators may continue the approach to take a "look-see" of the actual weather conditions for themselves. Instrument approaches conducted under Part 121 regulations are prohibited by 121.651(b) from continuing an approach past the final approach fix or final approach segment or continuing an instrument procedure if an approved weather source reports the visibility to be less than the authorized visibility minimums prescribed for that procedure. These authorized landing minimums take into account the available ground-based equipment and lighting as well as operative aircraft equipment and the airspeed at which the approach will be flown (i.e., circling approaches). Table 11.3, shown below, is contained in paragraph C.074 as it appears in the Delta Air Lines ops specs.

High Minimums Captain

Now that we've covered air carrier landing weather minimums for IFR operations, let's take a look at an interesting provision contained in the FARs concerning captains with less than 100 hours as pilot in command in operations under parts 121 and 135 or in the type of airplane he or she is operating. FARs 121.652, 135.225, and Paragraph C.054 of their ops specs restrict these captains to higher landing weather minimums. These *"high minimums" captains* must add 100 feet to the minimum descent altitude (MDA) or decision altitude (DA) and 1/2 mile (or the RVR equivalent) to the visibility landing minimums in the certificate holder's ops specs. This is done to allow the captain a chance to become comfortable with the new airplane before flying approaches to the normal minimums.

Table 11.3. Precision approaches (requiring operative lateral and vertical guidance)

Approach Light Configuration	HAT	Aircraft Category A, B, C, and D	
		Visibility in Statute Miles	TDZ RVR in Feet[1]
No Lights or ODALS	200	3/4	4,000
MALS or SALS	200	5/8	3,000
MALSR, or SSALR, or ALSF-1 or ALSF-2	200	1/2	2,400
MALSR with TDZ and CL, or SSALR with TDZ and CL, or ALSF-1/ALSF-2 with TDZ and CL	200	Visibility not authorized[2]	1,800
MALS, or MALSR, or SSALR, or ALSF-1/ALSF-2, or REILS and HIRL, or RAIL, and HIRL	200	Visibility not authorized	1,800

[1]The mid-RVR and rollout RVR reports (if available) provide advisory information to pilots. The mid-RVR report may be substituted for the TDZ RVR report if the TDZ RVR report is not available.

[2]Visibility values below 1/2 statute mile are not authorized and shall not be used.

Let's look again at the published approach minimums for XYZ Airport to see how high minimums are applied to a typical ILS approach or VOR approach. (See table 11.4.)

A high minimums captain would need to increase the ILS DA to 380 feet and the visibility to 1 statute mile or an RVR of 4,500 feet. The VOR approach minimums would need to be increased to a MDA of 900 feet and a visibility of 1 1/4 statute miles.

Remember the high minimums captain we discussed in chapter 6? As you can imagine, a captain looks forward to logging the required amount of flight time to be allowed to fly to the lower published minimums. It's not much fun having to divert to your alternate because the weather conditions didn't meet your high minimums while other aircraft are successfully landing at your destination airport. Fortunately, the FAA does not require use of the higher minimums over the alternate airport published approach minimums; however, the lowest minimums allowed are 1 statute mile visibility (5,000 RVR) and a 300 foot HAT.

So far we've only discussed increased landing minimums; what about the published takeoff minimums? The FAA does allow a high minimums captain to use an airport's published takeoff minimums for departure. However, since the need for a takeoff alternate is dependent upon the landing weather minimums at the departure airport, there is a greater chance a departure airport alternate airport will be required.

Table 11.4. Published approach minimums for XYZ airport

	Straight-in ILS Precision Approach	Straight-in VOR Nonprecision Approach
	DA(H) 280 ft (200 ft)	MDA(H) 800 ft (720 ft)
A		
B		
	RVR 1800 or 1/2 sm	RVR 4000 or 3/4 sm
C		
D		

Many air carriers have been granted an exemption from the higher landing minimums provided certain weather conditions (e.g., crosswind < 15 knots) and aircraft equipment exist (e.g., autopilot/flight director with approach coupler used to DA). This, *Special Exemption 5549*, allows the authorized air carrier's high minimums captains to fly to published landing minimums.

Inoperable Instruments and Equipment

So far, we've discussed the alternate airport and fuel supply requirements covered in Subpart U. Now we'll focus on what procedures must be followed for a flight to legally depart with certain inoperable instruments and equipment. 121.628 and 135.179 both contain guidance for operating an aircraft with inoperable instruments and equipment. To begin with, unless an FAA-approved ***minimum equipment list (MEL)*** exists for that airplane *and* the certificate holder is authorized to use a minimum equipment list, no person may take off an airplane with inoperable instruments or equipment installed. Authorization for the use of a MEL is found in Paragraph D.095 of a 121 or 135 certificate holder's ops specs.

The MEL must always be on board the airplane and located so as to allow the flight crew direct access to it at all times prior to flight. Procedures and records for identifying the inoperable instruments and equipment must be listed in the air carrier's general operating manual and must be available to the pilot. The certificate holder may not use an MEL for any type of aircraft that is not specifically authorized in its ops specs Paragraph D.095. Also, the airplane must be operated under all applicable conditions and limitations contained in the MEL and the operations specifications authorizing use of the MEL (see fig. 11.3). FARs 121.628 and 135.179 both require that the approved minimum equipment list must:

(a)   (3)(ii) *Provide for the operation of the airplane with certain instruments and equipment in an inoperable condition.*

(b)   *May not include the following instruments and equipment in the Minimum Equipment List:*
   (1)   *Instruments and equipment that are either specifically or otherwise required by the airworthiness requirements under which the airplane is type certificated and which are essential for safe operations under all operating conditions.*
   (2)   *Instruments and equipment required by an airworthiness directive to be in operable condition unless the airworthiness directive provides otherwise.*
   (3)   *Instruments and equipment required for specific operations by this part.*

FAR 121.628

Take a look at a sample of a page from a L-1011 Minimum Equipment List (fig. 11.3): Reading from left to right we see the first two columns contain the *MEL number* and the *name and/or description* of the inoperative component. Notice that under the second MEL item's name and description of the Air Turbine Motor deferral, there is a note: "Dispatcher Approval Required." This notation will be added if the deferral of this item affects the performance of the aircraft. Any time an item affecting aircraft performance is deferred, the dispatcher (the person completing the performance calculations) must be

L-1011 Minimum Equipment List

MEL ITEM NO.	MEL Name/Description	Flight Crew May Placard	Number Installed	Number Required for Dispatch	Repair Category	Limitations/Procedures
29-11-71A	Air Turbine Motor (ATM) Driven Pumps (B-2)ATM		1	0	A	(M)(O): May be inoperative provided: (a) All engine driven pumps are operative (B) C-2 ATM is operative (29-11-71 B), and (C) Repairs are made within 25 flight hours. (M): Refer to M.M. 19-11-71. (O): Refer to provisos (a,b) above.
29-11-71B	Air Turbine Motor (ATM) Driven Pumps (C-2)ATM **Dispatcher Approval Required**		1	0	A	(M)(O) May be inoperative provided: (a) All engine driven pumps are operative, (b) B-2 ATM is operative (29-11-71A), (c) Operation is conducted in accordance with Landing Gear Extended Performance Calculations, and (d) Repairs are made within 25 flight hours. (M): Refer to M.M. 29-11-71. (O): Refer to proviso (a,b,c) above.
29-21-01	Ram Air Turbine (RAT) Deployment Sys. (Auto and Manual) **Dispatcher Approval Required**		2	0	B	(M)(O): May be inoperative provided: (a) Ram Air Turbine (RAT) is extended, and (b) Operations are conducted in accordance with Ops Manual Limitations Section, Hydraulics. (M): Refer to M.M 29-21-01. (O): Refer to provisos (a,b) above.
29-31-04	Hydraulic Fluid Temperature Indicator (Cockpit)	**YES**	1	0	C	
77-12-07A	N₃ RPM Indicating System	**YES**	3	2	B	(M)(O): May be inoperative provided associated EPR, N$_1$, N$_2$ and Fuel Flow Indicating Systems are operative. (M): Refer to M.M. 77-12-07. (O): Refer to proviso above.

Figure 11.3   Minimum equipment list.

notified so he/she may take the performance limitation(s) into consideration for flight planning purposes. Also, this note will be included if the item is a critical safety of flight item. If the dispatcher does not agree that flight with that item deferred can be completed with the highest level of safety then he may refuse to dispatch the flight.

The next two columns are fairly self-explanatory. The *number of installed* equipment vs. the *number required for dispatch*. Let's look at the last row of figure 11.3, the deferral for the N_3 RPM gauge. Notice that the number of installed N_3 gauges is three (the L-1011 has three engines), but the number of gauges required for dispatch is two. So according to this MEL you may depart if one N_3 gauge is inoperative, but you may not depart with more than one N_3 gauge inoperative.

Next let's look at the *Flight Crew May Placard* column. If there is a "YES" in this column it means the inoperative component does not need to be deferred by a mechanic. The flight crew may write up the item, placard it, and continue with the flight. If the word "YES" does not appear in the column, then a mechanic must be called out and the inoperative item written up and deferred by the mechanic.

When a certificate holder is authorized to use an approved minimum equipment list, Paragraph D.095 of the ops specs requires inoperative items to be repaired within the time intervals specified for the ***repair category*** of items listed below:

- Category A. Items in this category shall be repaired within the *time interval specified* in the remarks column of the certificate holder's approved MEL.
- Category B. Items in this category shall be repaired within *3 consecutive calendar days (72 hours)* excluding the calendar day the malfunction was recorded in the aircraft maintenance log and/or record.
- Category C. Items in this category shall be repaired within *10 consecutive calendar days (240 hours)* excluding the calendar day the malfunction was recorded in the aircraft maintenance log and/or record.
- Category D. Items in this category shall be repaired *within 120 consecutive calendar days (2,880 hours)* excluding the day the malfunction was recorded in the aircraft maintenance log and/or record.

Equipment with little redundancy and/or items more critical to the safety of flight will be categorized as either "A" or "B" (e.g., electric standby hydraulic pumps). Equipment that is part of highly redundant systems and not as critical to the safety of flight will be classified category "C" (e.g., auxiliary power unit). Equipment that, if inoperative, poses little hazard to flight safety is categorized as "D" (e.g., Freon air conditioner). Look again at figure 11.3. Under the repair category, the N_3 gauge is listed as a Category B item, which means the gauge must be repaired or replaced within 3 calendar days after the day the item was written up in the logbook.

The certificate holder's op specs are required to contain a program to manage the process of repairing the items listed in the approved MEL. This MEL management program is required to accomplish the following:

- Track the date and the time an item was deferred and subsequently repaired.
- Maintain a current record of the number of deferred items per aircraft and a supervisory review of each deferred item to determine the reason for any delay in repair, length of delay, and the estimated date the item will be repaired.
- Contain a plan for bringing together parts, maintenance personnel, and aircraft at a specific time and place for repair.
- Must continually review the items deferred because of the unavailability of parts to ensure that a valid back order exists with a firm delivery date.

A few important things must be kept in mind when using a minimum equipment list. All equipment not listed in the MEL and related to the aircraft's airworthiness must be operative (e.g., the aircraft's wings must be in good condition, not damaged). The aircraft may not be dispatched with any inoperative equipment not specifically listed in the MEL or items that have been deferred longer than the MEL repair category allows. The air carrier must comply with any special limitations or procedures contained in the MEL.

Summary

In this chapter we have seen the rules under which flight dispatch works. The rules are primarily centered around assuring that the dispatcher has properly planned the flight to assure that in the event of any unforeseen contingency, there is an alternative plan that guarantees the safety of the flight. This planning centers around three major issues. The first issue is the procurement of weather information and operational data on the airports and NAVAIDS and other pertinent information for the routes to be flown. The second is the assurance that sufficient fuel is available to conduct the flight. The third is that the aircraft be airworthy and have the requisite performance under the existing conditions to successfully perform the flight. In the next chapter we will move from the planning stage of dispatch to the operational rules of Part 121 Subpart T: Flight Operations.

Important Terms from this Chapter

1-2-3 rule	Flight release document
600-2	Fuel minimums
800-2	High minimums captain
Alternate airport weather minimums	Landing minimums
Departure airport alternate airport	Load manifest
Derived alternate (weather) minimums	Minimum equipment list (MEL)
Destination airport alternate airport	Redispatch/rerelease
Dispatch release document	Repair category
Flight release	Standard alternate (weather) minimums

Chapter 11 Exam

1. In the case of domestic flights *each* flight must be dispatched, unless the flight was originally included in the dispatch of a multi-leg flight and the aircraft doesn't spend more than how many hours on the ground?
   a. 4 hours
   b. 3 hours
   c. 2 hours
   d. 1 hour

2. What information is required to appear on a Part 121 domestic or flag operator's dispatch release form?
   a. Company or organization name, make and model of aircraft, aircraft VIN number, flight number, name of each flight crewmember, departure airport, destination airport and alternate airports, minimum fuel supply, and weather reports and forecasts.
   b. Identification number of the aircraft, trip number, departure airport, intermediate stops, destination airport and alternate airports, a statement about the type of operation (e.g., VFR, IFR), minimum fuel supply, and weather reports and forecasts.
   c. Aircraft VIN number, air carrier name, make and model of aircraft, trip number, name of the pilot in command, departure airport, destination airport and alternate airports, minimum fuel supply, and weather reports and forecasts.

      d. Air carrier name, trip number, departure airport, intermediate stops, destination airport and alternate airports, a statement about the type of operation (e.g., VFR, IFR), and weather reports and forecasts.

3. What is the main difference between the load manifest used in domestic and flag operations and the load manifest used in supplemental operations?
      a. Domestic, flag, and supplemental load manifests must contain identical information.
      b. Load manifests used in supplemental international operations may use metric measurements for weight and balance calculations.
      c. Load manifests used in supplemental international operations may use metric measurements for the calculation of fuel load only.
      d. None of the above.

4. FAR 121.613 says an air carrier may not dispatch an IFR flight under Part 121 unless the weather reports and forecasts indicate that at the time of arrival at the destination airport
      a. The ceiling will be at least 1,500 feet above the lowest published instrument approach minimum for at least 1 hour before and 1 hour after the estimated time of arrival at the destination airport.
      b. The visibility and RVR will be greater than the standard takeoff minimums of 1/2 statute mile visibility or 2,400 feet RVR (runway visual range) for three or more engine airplanes and 1 statute mile visibility or 5,000 feet RVR for twin engine aircraft.
      c. Conditions will be at or above the authorized landing minimums.
      d. Conditions will be at or above the authorized landing minimums for at least 1 hour before and 1 hour after the estimated time of arrival at the destination airport.

5. When is a departure airport alternate airport required prior to the departure of a flight operating under 121?
      a. When weather conditions are greater than the standard takeoff minimums of 1/2 statute mile visibility or 2,400 feet RVR (runway visual range) for three or more engine aircraft.
      b. When weather conditions are such that an aircraft departs an airport with takeoff minimums below the departure airport's landing minimums in the certificate holder's ops specs.
      c. When weather conditions are forecast to be, for at least 1 hour before and 1 hour after the estimated time of arrival at the destination airport, at or above the authorized landing minimums.
      d. When the appropriate weather reports or forecasts indicate the ceiling will be at least 1,500 feet above the lowest published instrument approach minimum or lowest circling MDA.

6. How are alternate airport weather minimums derived for an airport with *one* operational navigational facility providing a straight-in nonprecision approach procedure, or a straight-in precision approach procedure, or a circling maneuver from an instrument approach procedure?
      a. A ceiling is derived by adding 200 feet to the authorized Category I HAT or HAA, and a visibility is derived by adding 1 statute mile to the authorized Category I landing minimum.

b. A ceiling is derived by adding 400 feet to the authorized Category I HAT or HAA, and a visibility is derived by adding 1 statute mile to the authorized Category I landing minimum.
c. A ceiling is derived by adding 200 feet to the authorized Category I HAT or HAA, and a visibility is derived by adding 1/2 statute mile to the authorized Category I landing minimum.
d. A ceiling is derived by adding 400 feet to the authorized Category I HAT or HAA, and a visibility is derived by adding 1/2 statute mile to the authorized Category I landing minimum.

7. How are alternate airport weather minimums derived for an airport with at least two operational navigational facilities, each providing a straight-in nonprecision approach procedure or a straight-in precision approach procedure to different, suitable runways?
   a. A ceiling is derived by adding 200 feet to the authorized Category I HAT or HAA, and a visibility is derived by adding 1 statute mile to the authorized Category I landing minimum.
   b. A ceiling is derived by adding 400 feet to the authorized Category I HAT or HAA, and a visibility is derived by adding 1 statute mile to the authorized Category I landing minimum.
   c. A ceiling is derived by adding 200 feet to the authorized Category I HAT or HAA, and a visibility is derived by adding 1/2 statute mile to the authorized Category I landing minimum.
   d. A ceiling is derived by adding 200 feet to the higher Category I HAT of the two approaches used, and a visibility is derived by adding 1/2 statute mile to the higher authorized Category I landing minimum of the two approaches used.

8. In Part 121 domestic operations, when is a destination alternate airport required?
   a. When the destination weather is not forecast to be, from 1 hour before until 1 hour after scheduled arrival time, at least 1/2 statute mile visibility or 2,400 feet RVR (runway visual range) for three or more engine airplanes and 1 statute mile visibility or 5,000 feet RVR for twin engine aircraft.
   b. When the weather is not forecast to be better than 1,500 feet higher than the lowest published instrument minimums or 2,000 feet above airport elevations, whichever is greater. The visibility must be at least 3 miles or at least 2 miles added to the lowest published minimum visibility, whichever is greater.
   c. When the destination weather is not forecast to be, from 1 hour before scheduled arrival until 1 hour after, a ceiling of 2,000 feet and 3 statute miles visibility.
   d. When the destination weather is not forecast to be, from 1 hour before scheduled arrival until 1 hour after, a ceiling of 3,000 feet and 2 statute miles visibility.

9. What are the mandatory fuel requirements for Part 121 domestic operations?
   a. A flight may not depart unless it has enough fuel to fly to the airport to which it is dispatched, then fly to the most distant alternate (if required), then fly for 45 minutes at normal cruising fuel consumption rates.
   b. A flight may not depart unless it has enough fuel to fly to the airport to which it is dispatched, then fly to the closest alternate (if required), then fly for 30 minutes at normal cruising fuel consumption rates.
   c. A flight may not depart unless it has enough fuel to fly to and land at the airport to which it is dispatched plus an additional 15 percent of the required fuel load (from departure airport to destination airport).

     d. A flight may not depart unless it has enough fuel to fly to and land at the airport to which it is dispatched plus 90 minutes of contingency fuel, if no destination alternate is required.

10. Repair "B" on a minimum equipment list requires inoperative items to be repaired within what time interval?
     a. Repair category "B" shall be repaired within the *time interval specified* in the remarks column of the certificate holder's approved MEL.
     b. Repair category "B" inoperative items shall be repaired within *3 consecutive calendar days (72 hours)* **excluding** the calendar day the malfunction was recorded in the aircraft maintenance log and/or record.
     c. Repair category "B" inoperative items shall be repaired before midnight on the *third consecutive calendar day (72 hours)* **including** the calendar day the malfunction was recorded in the aircraft maintenance log and/or record.
     d. Repair category "B" inoperative items shall be repaired within *10 consecutive calendar days (240 hours)* **excluding** the calendar day the malfunction was recorded in the aircraft maintenance log and/or record.

12

FAR 121 Subpart T: Flight Operations

Ladies and gentlemen, this is your captain speaking. We have a small problem. All four engines have stopped. We are doing our damnedest to get them all going again. I trust you are not in too much distress.

—Capt. Eric Moody, British Airways,
after flying through volcanic
ash in a Boeing 747

In this chapter we'll discuss Subpart T, which covers the FAA requirements for flight operations for all Part 121 air carriers. These requirements are, as we'll see, broad in nature and cover many aspects of flight operations, from who controls an air carrier's flight movements to the required passenger safety briefings and carry-on bag programs. The flight operations requirements found in Subpart T are addressed throughout an air carrier's op specs and company operations manuals.

Operational Control (Domestic and Flag Operations)

A Part 121 air carrier is required by the FAA to spell out in its op specs the system and procedures for the operational control of all flight movements, including training flights, charter flights, and the ferrying of aircraft. As we've discussed previously, *operational control* means the *exercise of authority over initiating, conducting or terminating a flight*. In practice, an air carrier exercises operational control by making the necessary decisions and performing the required procedures to operate flights safely and in compliance with the FARs and the air carrier's op specs.

Operational control may be centralized in one position or delegated to many different individuals throughout the flight operations organization. Typically the authority to dispatch or release flights is held by an air carrier's director of operations (DO) or the vice president of operations. The authority to dispatch or release flights is then delegated to aircraft dispatchers (domestic and flag operations) or flight followers (supplemental operations). While operational control may be delegated, the *responsibility for operational control* may not, and it rests with the certificate holder. The system and/or procedures used to establish and maintain operational control at an air carrier must be clearly defined in Paragraph A.008 of an air carrier's op specs and the air carrier's general operations manual (GOM).

The person responsible for operational control must ensure that the air carrier's flight crews and operational control employees (aircraft dispatchers or flight followers) comply with company policies and procedures. For this reason, an air carrier's operating manuals must contain guidance on the conditions that must be met before a flight is dispatched. Let's take a look at what Paragraph A.008 looks like in the Delta Air Lines op specs.

| U.S. Department of Transportation Federal Aviation Administration | Operation Specifications

Paragraph A.008 |

Delta Air Lines Ops Specs   **Paragraph A.008**

Operational Control

A. The certificate holder provides operational control of flight operations through the use of the system described or referenced in this paragraph:

Flight Control-Flight Evaluation: *Flight Operations Manual-Chapter 33 Dispatcher Supplement*

Flight Control-Training Program: *Flight Control Training Manual*

Flight Operations-Department Organization: *Flight Operations Administrative Manual (FOAM)*

Flight Control-Duties Sabotage Threat: *Bomb Threat-Delta's Bomb Threat Procedures, Hijack-Delta Emergency Operations Manual*

Flight Control-Radio Transmissions: *Flight Operations Administrative Manual (FOAM) and Flight Operations Manual (FOM) Chapter 30*

Flight Control-Responsibility Aircraft Accident: *Emergency Operations Manual and Flight Operations Manual Chapter 10*

Flight Control-Aircraft Emergency: *Emergency Operations Manual and Flight Operations Manual Chapter 10*

1. Issued by the Federal Aviation Administration.
2. These Operations Specifications are approved by direction of the Administrator.

Principal Operations Inspector

3. Date Approval is effective: 05/24/1999 Amendment Number: 1
4. I hereby accept and receive the Operations Specifications in this paragraph.

Hantla, Becky J.
Senior Vice President, Flight Operations Date: 05/24/1999

We can see from op specs Paragraph A.008 that a major aspect of operational control consists of developing and publishing flight control policies and procedures for flight operations personnel to follow in the performance of their duties. Specific operational control duties are covered in 121.533 and 121.535. The pilot in command and the aircraft dispatcher are jointly responsible for the preflight planning, delay, and dispatch release of a flight in compliance with applicable FARs and operations specifications. This means that both the pilot in command and the aircraft dispatcher must consider all FARs and op spec rules applicable to airworthiness, crew legality, duty/flight time, and operating rules before dispatching a flight. Their respective responsibilities can be broken down by position.

The aircraft dispatcher is responsible for

- Monitoring the progress of each flight,
- Issuing necessary information for the safety of the flight, and
- Canceling or redispatching a flight if, in his opinion or the opinion of the pilot in command, the flight cannot operate or continue to operate safely as planned or released.

The pilot in command is, during a flight, responsible for

- The safety of the passengers, crewmembers, cargo, and aircraft.

Prior to flight one of a pilot in command's most important responsibilities is determining whether the aircraft is airworthy. Since the pilot in command cannot track airworthiness directives (AD) or participate in overhaul and inspection activities s/he relies upon the aircraft logbook's airworthiness release. Review of the aircraft logbook and the preflight "walk-around" inspection are the approved means by which the pilot in command determines an aircraft's airworthiness.

Finally, the pilot in command has full control and authority in the operation of the aircraft. This authority is granted by 121.533(e) and 121.535(e), without limitation, over other crewmembers and their duties during flight time, even if the pilot in command does not hold a valid certificate authorizing him to perform the duties of those crewmembers (e.g., flight engineer certificate).

Operational Control (Supplemental Operations)

For supplemental operations the responsibility for operational control differs due to the nature of supplemental operations, and as we've discussed previously, a supplemental air carrier is not required to employ an aircraft dispatcher. 121.537 places the responsibility for the operational control of supplemental carriers with the director of operations and the pilot in command. A supplemental air carrier must list in its general operations manual each person authorized to exercise operational control because there may be different individuals exercising operational control at various times (e.g., director of operations, flight follower, or even the pilot in command). Like domestic and flag operations, the system and/or procedure for establishing operational control at a supplemental carrier must be clearly defined in Paragraph A.008 of an air carrier's op specs.

121.537 gives the certificate holder the power to delegate the functions for the initiation, continuation, diversion, and termination of a flight, but like domestic and flag operations, s/he may not delegate the responsibility for those functions. The pilot in command and the director of operations are jointly responsible for the initiation, continuation, diversion, and termination of a supplemental flight in compliance with the applicable FARs and the operations specifications.

The director of operations is responsible for

- Canceling,
- Diverting, or
- Delaying a flight and
- Assuring that each flight is monitored from
  - ➢ Departure of the flight from the place of origin to arrival at the place of destination, including intermediate stops and any diversions.
  - ➢ Maintenance and mechanical delays encountered at places of origin and destination and intermediate stops.
  - ➢ Any known conditions that may adversely affect the safety of flight.

It is the responsibility of both the director of operations and the pilot in command to determine if in their opinion the supplemental flight cannot operate or continue to operate safely as planned or released. This responsibility is covered in 121.537(c). Note that because there might not be an aircraft dispatcher assigned to the flight the duties typically performed by a dispatcher are now the responsibility of the pilot in command.

The pilot in command is, during a flight, in command of the aircraft and crew and is responsible for

- The safety of the passengers, crewmembers, cargo, and aircraft.
- The preflight planning and the operation of the flight in compliance with this chapter and the operations specifications.
- Not operating an aircraft in a careless or reckless manner, so as to endanger life or property.

121.537(d) grants the pilot in command full control and authority in the operation of the aircraft, without limitation, over other crewmembers and their duties during flight time, whether or not he holds valid certificates authorizing him to perform the duties of those crewmembers.

Airplane Security

The FAA requires each air carrier to develop and maintain an ***aviation security program*** that provides for the safety of passengers and property traveling in air transportation against acts of criminal violence and air piracy. An air carrier must maintain at least one complete copy of its approved security program at its principal business office and the pertinent portions of its approved security program or appropriate implementing instructions at each airport where security screening is being conducted. The details of the required security program are spelled out in FAR Part 108 Aviation Security. All carriers conducting operations under Part 121 are required by 121.538 to comply with these security requirements. The rules contained in Part 108 also govern

- Each person aboard a Part 121 air carrier's aircraft,
- Each person on an airport at which the operations of Part 121 air carriers are being conducted, and
- Any certificate holder, if that carrier provides deplaned passengers access to an airport area where access is controlled by the inspection of persons and property in accordance with an approved security program.

A security program must provide for the following:

1. *Screening of passengers and property.*
2. *Prevention and management of hijackings and sabotage attempts.*
3. *Carriage of weapons.*
4. *Security of airplanes and facilities.*
5. *Transportation of Federal Air Marshals.*
6. *Law enforcement officers.*
7. *Use of X-ray systems.*
8. *Security Directives and Information Circulars.*
9. *Security threats and procedures.*
10. *Use of explosives detection systems.*
11. *Carriage of passengers under the control of armed law enforcement escorts.*
12. *Annual security training for ground security coordinator and crewmembers.*
13. *Approval of security programs and amendments.*
14. *Evidence of compliance.*
15. *Standards for security oversight.*
16. *Employment standards for screening personnel.*
17. *Employment history, verification and criminal history records checks.*

Part 108 FAA Aviation Security Regulations

Prior to flight the **ground security coordinator (GSC)** is responsible for airplane security. The GSC is an employee of the air carrier, typically a gate agent with additional security training, whose job it is to inform the pilot in command of any pertinent security issues that may affect the flight. The GSC brings security issues such as any irregularities or occurrences within the local community that may affect security to the attention of the pilot in command. The GSC will also brief the pilot in command about any passengers that may be boarding that may increase the security risk during routine operations (e.g., armed law enforcement officers, prisoners). Before any domestic or flag departure the GSC must signify on the dispatch release paperwork that all pertinent security issues have been brought to the attention of the pilot in command. Once airborne, the pilot in commands assumes responsibility for airplane security.

Operations Notices

All air carriers are required by 121.539 to *notify their appropriate operations personnel of each change in equipment and operating procedures.* These **operations notices** are similar in concept to Notices to Airmen (NOTAMs) or SIGMET information such as the status of navigation aids, airport facilities, special air traffic control procedures and regulations, local airport traffic control rules (e.g., Washington's Ronald Reagan National Airport), and weather reports, including icing and other potentially hazardous meteorological conditions.

The method an air carrier uses to accomplish this task must be contained in its op specs. Typically most of this information can be found in an air carrier's flight plan, flight operations bulletins, or the carrier's airway manual. To supplement this some companies publish a detailed brief of each individual airport served by the carrier. This airport brief is updated regularly and includes such information as local navigation facilities, obstacles such as terrain or towers, single engine departure procedures, noise abatement procedures, typical arrival gates, company radio frequencies, and so on.

Operations Schedules

As we discussed in chapter 7, a scheduled air carrier, that is, a domestic and flag carrier, is required by 121.541 to establish realistic operations schedules. In establishing flight operations schedules, air carriers must allow enough time for the proper servicing of aircraft at intermediate stops and must consider the prevailing winds en route and the cruising speed of the type of aircraft used. These requirements are placed on air carriers for a couple of reasons: First, to prevent them from developing "creative schedules" that would allow one carrier an unfair competitive advantage over another carrier (e.g., scheduling shorter flight times to attract more passengers). Second, to prevent an air carrier from altering a flight schedule to avoid the provisions of other FARs (e.g., flight and duty time limitations or number of required cockpit crewmembers). Normally, average or median flight times are used to determine if a schedule is realistic. If the destination is one that has never been served by the air carrier then the flight time is determined by using the planned cruising speed of the aircraft. To further clarify cruising speed, 121.541 also requires that the cruising speed used in flight planning *may not be more than that resulting from the output of the engines* (the FAA thinks of everything).

Air carriers do have an inherent desire to use realistic flight schedules because their customers demand it. For this reason, most air carriers do query flight crews for analytical help in determining the causes of repeated delays for a particular flight segment. Typically airlines ask a flight crewmember to fill out some type of a "delay report" for flights that they identify as being frequently delayed or flown over scheduled block time. The flight crew states, in the delay report, what reasons they believe cause a particular flight to be delayed. These reports are then turned in to the chief pilot, who in turn forwards them to the director of operations office for analysis.

Flight Crewmember Duties

An overwhelming majority of air carrier incidents (e.g., altitude violations, runway incursions, etc.) over the years have been attributed to the distractions caused by flight crewmembers performing duties other than those required for the safe operation of the aircraft during some critical phase of flight. For example, many altitude violations have occurred during descent into a destination when one crewmember was "off" the ATC radio and "on" the aircraft's intercom discussing passenger requirements such as connecting gate information or required wheelchairs with a flight attendant. Obviously, anytime one pilot is "out of the loop" performing other duties the chances of a mistake not being caught go up. For this reason the FAA has established, in 121.542, *critical phase of flight* periods where only duties required for the safe operation of the aircraft are allowed. This is usually referred to as the *sterile cockpit rule*.

The FAA has established *critical phases of flight* to include all ground operations involving taxi, takeoff, and landing and all other flight operations conducted below 10,000 feet, unless in level cruise flight. 121.542 states that *no certificate holder shall require, nor may any flight crewmember perform, any duties during a critical phase of flight except those duties required for the safe operation of the aircraft.* Duties such as "in-range" radio calls, company required position reports, passenger gate information, passenger special requests (e.g., wheelchairs), eating meals, and routine passenger convenience PAs (announcements) are not required for the safe operation of the aircraft and are not allowed during a critical phase of flight.

Another aspect of flight crewmember duties is the conduct of crewmembers during critical phases of flight. A good portion of crew resource management (CRM) training is devoted to instructing crewmembers how to best function during a critical phase of flight. Crewmembers are not allowed to engage in any activity during a critical phase of flight that could distract any flight crewmember from or interfere with the performance of his or her duties. Activities such as eating meals, engaging in nonessential conversations within the cockpit and nonessential communications between the cabin and cockpit crews, or reading publications not related to the proper conduct of the flight are not required for the safe operation of the aircraft and not allowed.

Flight Crewmembers at Controls

121.543 dictates that all required flight crewmembers on flight deck duty must remain at the assigned duty station with seat belt fastened while the aircraft is taking off or landing and for the duration of the flight. A required flight crewmember may leave an assigned duty station for only three reasons:

- In connection with duties in operation of the aircraft (e.g., visual check for ice on wings).
- In connection with physiological needs, including personal relief and movement to ensure mental and physical alertness.
- A required flight crewmember may also leave his assigned duty position if he or she is beginning an assigned rest period and an authorized and qualified relief pilot is provided.

Manipulation of Controls

121.545 specifies who qualifies for *manipulation of controls* of an aircraft during flight. To be authorized to manipulate an aircraft's controls you must be

(a) *A qualified pilot of the certificate holder operating that aircraft (i.e., the designated Captain or First Officer).*
(b) *An authorized pilot safety representative of the Administrator or of the National Transportation Safety Board (NTSB) who has the permission of the pilot in command, is qualified in the aircraft, and is checking flight operations.*
(c) *A pilot of another certificate holder who has the permission of the pilot in command, is qualified in the aircraft, and is authorized by the certificate holder operating the aircraft.*

FAR 121.545

Admission to Flight Deck

121.547 and air carrier policy govern admission to the flight deck. The flight deck is defined as the area forward of the cockpit-to-cabin door. Notice 121.547 does not limit the emergency authority of the pilot in command to exclude any person from the flight deck in the interests of safety. If the presence of a person on the flight deck jeopardizes the safety of flight the pilot in command may remove that person. According to 121.547(a), no person may be admitted to the flight deck unless that person is

(1)   A crewmember (flight crew or cabin crew).

(2)   An FAA air carrier inspector.

(3)   An authorized representative of the National Transportation Safety Board, who is performing official duties.

(4)   An employee of the United States, a certificate holder, or an aeronautical enterprise who has the permission of the pilot in command and whose duties are such that admission to the flight deck is necessary or advantageous for safe operations; employees of the United States who deal responsibly with matters relating to safety and employees of the certificate holder whose efficiency would be increased by familiarity with flight conditions, may be admitted by the certificate holder.

(5)   Any person who has the permission of the pilot in command and is specifically authorized by the certificate holder management and by the Administrator.

FAR 121.547(a)

According to 121.547, no person may admit any person to the flight deck *unless there is a seat available for his or her use in the passenger compartment*, **except**:

1.   An FAA air carrier inspector or an authorized representative of the Administrator or National Transportation Safety Board who is checking or observing flight operations;

Table 12.1. Admission to flight deck

Person Seeking Admission to Flight Deck of U.S. Registered Aircraft.	Required Authorization
FAA air carrier inspector on official duty.	*FAA form 110A (FAA inspector's ID card)* and FAA form 8430-13 (jumpseat form). *Reference FAR 121.548*
National Transportation Safety Board. Representative on official duty.	NTSB ID card (NTSB form 1660-2).
FAA air traffic service evaluation staff.	Air Traffic Service evaluation ID card (FAA form 7010-2) and Authorization to Flight Deck form (FAA form 7000-1).
FAA air traffic controller observing ATC procedures.	FAA ID form (DOTF 1681-1-3). Familiarization Training Authorization (FAA form 3120-28). Familiarization Training Request (FAA form 3120-31).
U.S. Secret Service agents.	U.S. Secret Service credentials. *Reference FAR 121.550*
Department of Defense personnel.	Military ID card and FAA Admission to Flight Deck form (FAA form 8430-6).
Other authorized personnel. **May require a seat in cabin for take-off and landing per FAR 121.547**	Authorization letter from FAA and FAA Admission to Flight Deck form (FAA form 8430-6). Must be approved by air carrier's director of operations or equivalent.

2. An air traffic controller who is authorized by the Administrator to observe ATC procedures;

3. A certificated airman employed by the certificate holder whose duties require an airman certificate;

4. A certificated airman employed by another certificate holder whose duties with that certificate holder require an airman certificate and who is authorized by the certificate holder operating the aircraft to make specific trips over a route;

5. An employee of the certificate holder operating the aircraft whose duty is directly related to the conduct or planning of flight operations or the in flight monitoring of aircraft equipment or operating procedures, if his presence on the flight deck is necessary to perform his duties and he has been authorized in writing by a responsible supervisor, listed in the Operations Manual as having that authority; and

6. A technical representative of the manufacturer of the aircraft or its components whose duties are directly related to the in flight monitoring of aircraft equipment or operating procedures, if his presence on the flight deck is necessary to perform his duties, and he has been authorized in writing by the Administrator and by a responsible supervisor of the operations department of the certificate holder, listed in the Operations Manual as having that authority.

FAR 121.547(b)

Observer's Seat: En Route Inspections

Now that we've discussed what credentials a person must have to gain admission to the flight deck, let's take a look at the requirement for an observer's seat on the flight deck of an air carrier's aircraft. All carriers are required by 121.581 to provide *and* make available a seat on the flight deck of each airplane for the occupancy by the Administrator (or his designee) while conducting en route inspections. The Administrator determines the location and equipment of the seat, with respect to its suitability for use in conducting en route inspections.

The only exception to this rule is for aircraft type certificated before December 20, 1995, for not more than 30 passengers. Many of these smaller aircraft were never manufactured with an observer's seat on the flight deck because prior to December 1995 these aircraft were governed by Part 135 regulations. With the implementation of Part 119, transferring the majority of these smaller aircraft to Part 121 regulations, the forward observer seat was then a requirement for all newly type certificated aircraft. For aircraft without a forward observer's seat, the air carrier must provide a forward passenger seat with headset or speaker for occupancy by the Administrator while conducting en route inspections.

Closing and Locking of Flight Crew Compartment Door

In chapter 10 we discussed 121.313(f), which required a door between the passenger and pilot compartments for aircraft certificated after 1964. This door must have a locking means to prevent passengers from opening it without the pilot's permission. 121.587 requires the pilot in command of an airplane equipped with such a door to ensure that the door separating the flight crew compartment from the passenger compartment is closed and locked during flight. There are three exceptions to this requirement; they are

- During takeoff and landing if the cockpit door is the means of access to a required passenger emergency exit or a floor level exit.
- At any time that it is necessary to provide access to the flight crew or passenger compartment, to a crewmember in the performance of his duties, or for a person authorized admission to the flight crew compartment (e.g., a relief pilot or an FAA inspector conducting an en route inspection).
- When an authorized person(s) is using a jumpseat in airplanes in which closing and locking the flight crew compartment door is impossible while the jumpseat is in use.

Personal Flying Equipment (Flight Kit)

Flight crews are required by air carrier policy and 121.549 to carry certain personal flying equipment while on duty. Typically an air carrier will require all flight crewmembers to maintain a "flight kit bag" containing company manuals, airway manuals, copies of checklists, passports, and a flashlight. As far as 121.549 is concerned the only flying equipment required of both crewmembers is an operative flashlight, which must be readily available. Additionally, the pilot in command is required to ensure the appropriate aeronautical charts containing adequate information concerning navigation aids and instrument approach procedures are aboard the aircraft for each flight. These charts are usually contained in a company airway manual issued to all flight crewmembers.

In addition to the equipment requirements discussed in 121.549, each flight crewmember must also carry

- A current airman's certificate for the pilot's position.
- A FCC radiotelephone operator permit.
- A current FAA medical certificate of the appropriate class for the pilot's position.

A current trend in the industry is for air carriers to go "paperless," that is, the carrier supplies an electronic "flight kit" in the form of a laptop computer. This computer is either supplied to each flight crewmember or is installed in a convenient location on each of the carrier's aircraft. The computer contains all required company manuals and airway manuals (including approach charts), plus a variety of other reference manuals for use by the flight crews.

Restriction or Suspension of Operation

When a certificate holder conducting domestic or flag operations knows of conditions, including airport and runway conditions, that are a hazard to safe operations, 121.551 and 121.553 require *restriction or suspension of operations* by the air carrier until those conditions are corrected. This authority to restrict or suspend air carrier operations is delegated to an air carrier's aircraft dispatchers and pilots in command. Whenever a pilot in command or the aircraft dispatcher come into knowledge that a situation exists dictating the need to restrict or suspend operations, their decision to do so is supported by the director of operations.

A good example of this is when a pilot in command and aircraft dispatcher deem weather or runway conditions are such that aircraft control and braking action might adversely affect safety; in such a case they may suspend that air carrier's service to the airport. Service will only be resumed when in the opinion of the pilot in command with the concurrence of the aircraft dispatcher weather conditions improve to a level allowing safe operations.

Compliance with Approved Routes and Limitations

As discussed in chapter 1, unlike flying under Part 91, an air carrier cannot simply fly anywhere it wishes to fly. 121.555 makes it clear that an air carrier's pilots are only authorized to conduct en route operations in the areas specified in its op specs. Specifically this is found in Paragraph B.050 of a carrier's op specs. We've seen that subparts E and F provide the basis for certificating every route or area the carrier intends to fly. This certification process looks at how the aircraft is equipped and at the adequacy of airports and other facilities and then approves those routes and airports for use. 121.93 and 121.95 set up the requirements for approving routes, and 121.97 sets the requirements for airport approvals. A small airline may only be approved to operate in the 48 contiguous states, while a large airline might be approved for the 48 contiguous states and dozens of other areas. Let's take a look at a couple of examples of a carrier's op specs Paragraph B.050 Authorized Areas of En Route Operations:

U.S. Department of Transportation Federal Aviation Administration	Operation Specifications Paragraph B.050

Delta Air Lines Ops Specs	**Paragraph B.050**

Authorized Area of En Route Operations

a. The certificate holder is authorized to conduct en route operations in the areas of en route operation specified in this paragraph. The certificate holder shall conduct all en route operations in accordance with the provisions of the paragraphs referenced for each area of en route operation. The certificate holder shall not conduct any en route operation under these operations specifications unless those operations are conducted within the areas of en route operation authorized by this paragraph.

Authorized Areas of Operation	Referenced Op Specs Paragraphs
The 48 contiguous United States and the District of Columbia	None
Africa—excluding Libya, Somalia, and Angola	B031, B032, B034, B043, B044
Asia	B031, B032, B034, B036, B043, B044
Australia	B031, B032, B044
Canada, including Canadian MNPS airspace and the Area of Magnetic Unreliability as established in the Canadian AIP	B031, B032, B034, B036, B039, B040, B042, B043, B044

—continued

Authorized Areas of Operation	Referenced Op Specs Paragraphs
Europe and the Mediterranean Sea Including Albania	B031, B032, B034, B036, B044, B046
Japan	B031, B032, B034, B044
Mexico and Central America	B031, B032, B034
Moscow-Karmanovo via direct	None
New Zealand	B031, B032, B044
Singapore	B031, B032, B034, B044
South America	B031, B032, B044
Thailand	B031, B032, B034, B044
The Atlantic Ocean and the islands of Greenland and Iceland	B031, B032, B036, B041, B042, B043, B044, B046
The Caribbean Sea and the Gulf of Mexico	B031, B032, B034, B036, B043, B044
The Indian Ocean	B031, B032, B043, B044
The State of Alaska	B031, B032, B034, B035
The State of Hawaii	B031, B032, B034, B036

1. The Certificate Holder applies for the Operations in this paragraph.
2. Support information reference: Added RVSM B046 for European operations.
3. These Operations Specifications are approved by direction of the Administrator.

Original signed by:
Gann, Ernest K.
Principal Operations Inspector

4. Date Approval is effective: 04/12/2001 Amendment Number: 2
5. I hereby accept and receive the Operations Specifications in this paragraph.

Original signed by:
Mr. Alfred Kahn II
Senior Vice President, Flight Operations Date: 04/18/2001

(Delta Air Lines paragraph B.050 has been abbreviated for simplicity.)

Now let's take a look at JetBlue Airways op specs Paragraph B.050.

| U.S. Department of Transportation Federal Aviation Administration | Operation Specifications

Paragraph B.050 |

JetBlue Airways

a. The certificate holder is authorized to conduct en route operations in the areas of en route operation specified in this paragraph. The certificate holder shall conduct all en route operations in accordance with the provisions of the paragraphs referenced for each area of en route operation. The certificate holder shall not conduct any en route operation under these operations specifications unless those operations are conducted within the areas of en route operation authorized by this paragraph.

Authorized Areas of Operation	Referenced Op Specs Paragraphs
Atlantic-The North Atlantic Ocean west of the western boundary of NAT/MNPS airspace, between 45 degrees N and 24 degrees N, but excluding Bermuda and the Caribbean Islands.	A005, B031, B032, B034, B036, B045, C077
USA-The 48 contiguous United States and the District of Columbia.	A005, B031, B032, B034, B035, C077

1. The Certificate Holder applies for the Operations in this paragraph.
2. Support information reference: Added RVSM B046 for European operations.
3. These Operations Specifications are approved by direction of the Administrator.

Original signed by:
Gann, Ernest K.
Principal Operations Inspector

4. Date Approval is effective: 02/23/2001 Amendment Number: 3
5. I hereby accept and receive the Operations Specifications in this paragraph.

Original signed by:
Tyler O'Conner
Vice President, Flight Operations Date: 02/23/01

Finally, anytime a carrier would like to provide service to a destination in an area not appearing in Paragraph B.050 of their op specs the carrier must complete the entire route approval process for that route.

Use of Certificated Land Airports

Now that we've discussed what routes an air carrier is authorized to fly, let's turn our attention to **certificated land airports** and the regulations governing the airports a Part 121 air carrier may serve. For aircraft larger than 30 seats, 121.590 prohibits operations to or from an airport unless that airport is federally certificated under Part 139; the only exception is that an air carrier may designate *and* use as a required alternate airport for departure or destination an airport that is not certificated under Part 139 of this chapter. Part 139 governs the certification and operations of land airports. Let's take a look at some of the major sections of Part 139:

> *139.5 Standards and procedures for compliance with the certification and operations requirements of this part.*
> *139.201 Airport operating certificate: Airport certification manual.*
> *139.203 Preparation of airport certification manual.*
> *139.205 Contents of airport certification manual.*
> *139.209 Limited airport operating certificate: Airport certification specifications.*
> *139.213 Contents of airport certification specifications.*
> *139.301 Inspection authority.*
> *139.303 Personnel.*
> *139.305 Paved areas.*
> *139.307 Unpaved areas.*
> *139.309 Safety areas.*
> *139.311 Marking and lighting.*
> *139.313 Snow and ice control.*
> *139.315 Aircraft rescue and firefighting: Index determination.*
> *139.317 Aircraft rescue and firefighting: Equipment and agents.*
> *139.319 Aircraft rescue and firefighting: Operational requirements.*
> *139.321 Handling and storing of hazardous substances and materials.*
> *139.323 Traffic and wind direction indicators.*
> *139.325 Airport emergency plan.*
> *139.327 Self-inspection program.*
> *139.329 Ground vehicles.*
> *139.331 Obstructions.*
> *139.333 Protection of NAVAIDS.*
> *139.335 Public protection.*
> *139.339 Airport condition reporting.*
> *139.341 Identifying, marking, and reporting construction and other unserviceable areas.*

Paragraph A.070 of an air carrier's op specs addresses the airports that carrier is authorized to use. Let's take a look at Paragraph A.070 of the Delta Air Lines op specs.

U.S. Department of Transportation Federal Aviation Administration	Operation Specifications Paragraph A.070

Delta Air Lines Ops Specs   **Paragraph A.070**

Airports Authorized for Scheduled Operations

a. The certificate holder is authorized to conduct scheduled passenger and cargo operations between the regular, refueling, and provisional airports specified in the following table. Except for alternate airports, the certificate holder shall not use any other airport in the conduct of scheduled passenger and cargo operations. The certificate holder shall maintain a list of alternate airports which can be used and shall not use any alternate airport unless it is suitable for the type of aircraft being used and the kind of operation being conducted.

b. The following definitions shall apply:

Regular Airport. An airport approved under scheduled service to a community as the regular stop to that community.

Refueling Airport. An airport approved as an airport to which flights may be dispatched only for refueling.

Provisional Airport. An airport approved for use by an air carrier for the purpose of providing scheduled service to a community when the regular airport serving that community is not available.

Alternate Airport. An airport at which an aircraft may land if a landing at the intended airport becomes inadvisable.

NOTE: Refueling and provisional airports are not applicable to Part 135 operations.
R = Regular, F = Refueling, A = Alternate, and P = Provisional

Airport	Airports Authorized for Scheduled Operations:				
Airport	**Aircraft Authorized**				
Airport Name:	Provisional Airport:	MD-88/MD90	B-737	B-757/767	B-777
Anchorage, AK	Fairbanks, AK	N/A	N/A	R	A
Albany, NY		R	R	R	A
Baltimore, MD		R	R	R	A
Paris, France		N/A	N/A	N/A	R
Shannon, Ireland		N/A	N/A	N/A	R
Cork, Ireland		N/A	N/A	N/A	A
Pasco, WA		N/A	R	A	N/A
Yuma, AZ		A	R	A	N/A

Delta Air Lines paragraph A.070 abbreviated for simplicity.

Emergencies: Domestic, Flag, and Supplemental Operations

Part 91.3(b) grants a pilot in command the authority to deviate from any FAR during an emergency situation to whatever extent necessary to meet that emergency. In 121.557(a) we see this is also the case in domestic and flag air carrier operations; however, Part 121 takes this "emergency authority" a step further. That step is to allow for the inclusion of the aircraft dispatcher. 121.557 states that a pilot in command may in an emergency *take any action that s/he considers necessary under the circumstances to the extent required in the interests of safety.* This includes deviations not only from FARs, but also from op specs limitations or company procedures. If an emergency situation arises during flight that requires immediate decision and action by an aircraft dispatcher, that person is required by 121.557(b) to advise the pilot in command of the emergency (e.g., bomb threat) and ascertain and record any decision by the captain. If the aircraft dispatcher cannot make contact with the pilot in command, *he shall declare an emergency and take any action that he considers necessary under the circumstances.* Once emergency authority has been exercised the pilot in command or dispatcher must keep the appropriate ATC facility and that air carrier's dispatch center fully informed of the progress of the flight.

Anytime emergency authority is exercised by either the pilot in command or dispatcher, the person declaring the emergency is required by 121.557(c) to send in a written report to the Administrator within 10 days after the date of the emergency (aircraft dispatcher) or within 10 days of returning to that pilot's home base (pilot in command). Typically an air carrier will require the dispatcher or the pilot in command to first send the report to the director of operations. The DO will review it and forward it to the principal operations inspector (POI) on behalf of the Administrator.

Emergency authority for supplemental operators is virtually identical to that of the domestic and flag operators. The only difference is the allowance for operations without an aircraft dispatcher. In this case the duties required of the dispatcher in domestic and flag operations are the responsibility of the appropriate management personnel under supplemental operations.

Reporting Potentially Hazardous Meteorological Conditions and Irregularities of Ground and Navigation Facilities

Whenever a pilot in command encounters a meteorological condition (e.g., wind shear, in flight icing, turbulence, etc.) or an irregularity of ground and navigation facilities (e.g., VOR outage, inoperative approach lights, etc.) the knowledge of which he considers essential to the safety of other flights, that person is required by 121.581 to notify an appropriate ground station as soon as possible. This ground station is then required to notify the agency directly responsible for the operation of that facility.

Reporting Mechanical Irregularities

Prior to flight the pilot in command is required by 121.563 to ascertain the status of any irregularity entered in the aircraft logbook at the end of the preceding flight. Either an authorized mechanic must sign off any "write-ups" or flight crews must comply with any applicable minimum equipment list provisions. Furthermore, the pilot in command must enter any maintenance mechanical irregularities occurring during flight time in the maintenance log of the airplane at the end of that flight time. Chapter 13 contains a more detailed discussion of the aircraft logbook.

Engine Inoperative: Landing and Reporting

When an aircraft engine fails or is shut down in flight as a precautionary measure to prevent possible damage, the pilot in command is required by 121.565 to do two things:

- Land the airplane at the nearest suitable airport, *in point of time*, at which a safe landing can be made (unless the airplane has three or more engines; see below).
- Notify the appropriate air traffic control (ATC) facility as soon as practicable after the engine failure or in flight shutdown.

If an aircraft has three or more engines and not more than one has failed, the FAA allows the pilot in command either to select the nearest suitable airport or to select another airport after considering the following:

1. *The nature of the malfunction and the possible mechanical difficulties that may occur if flight is continued.*
2. *The altitude, weight, and usable fuel at the time of engine stoppage.*
3. *The weather conditions en route and at possible landing points.*
4. *The air traffic congestion.*
5. *The kind of terrain.*
6. *His familiarity with the airport to be used.*

FAR 121.565(b)

If the pilot in command elects to land at an airport other than the nearest suitable airport, s/he is then required to send a written report to that carrier's director of operations (DO). The report must contain the reasons for determining that the selection of the chosen airport, other than the nearest airport, was as safe a course of action as landing at the nearest suitable airport. The director of operations is then required by 121.565(d) to forward this report with his or her comments to the certificate holding district office within 10 days after the pilot returns to his or her home base.

Instrument Approach Procedures and IFR Landing Minimums

As we discussed last chapter, you'll find an air carrier's instrument approach procedures covered in its flight operations manual (FOM), airway manual, training manuals, and op specs. A carrier's particular IFR landing minimums are covered in its op specs, specifically in Part C Terminal Instrument Procedures paragraphs C.051–.063. In Part C, the carrier lists exactly how it will conduct IFR approach procedures and what approaches its pilots are authorized to conduct (e.g., many operators do not authorize circling approaches if conditions are less than basic VFR). Air carrier pilots are only allowed to make those instrument approaches using weather minimums found in Part C of their op specs.

Equipment Interchange: Domestic and Flag Operations

Air carriers from time to time have engaged in *equipment interchange agreements* or temporary "dry leases" of aircraft from one airline to another. These agreements are commonly used to meet specific market demands and/or seasonal fluctuations. While a "wet lease" is a leasing agreement involving the aircraft *and* at least one crewmember, a dry lease is an aircraft leased without the crew. An equipment interchange agreement is a dry lease of an aircraft from one carrier to another for short periods of time.

American Airlines, during the late 1980s, entered an equipment interchange agreement with Alaska Airlines. This agreement involved a dry lease of five Alaska Airlines B-727s, painted in Alaska Airlines colors, and flown by American Airlines crewmembers on certain routes in the western United States. These five aircraft were operated from HOU-DFW-SEA-ANC-FAI and the return trip, with American crewmembers flying the HOU-DFW-SEA legs of the trip. The Alaska crewmembers would literally walk off the airplane in SEA, and the American crewmembers would board for the leg to DFW. During each exchange of crews, the aircraft was signed over and operational control responsibilities transferred to the receiving airline. American flight crews had to use a special call sign to help avoid as much confusion as possible with tower, ground control, and other aircraft expecting to see an airplane painted in American Airlines colors (e.g., American flight 71 an Alaska Airlines aircraft). Braniff International was the sole U.S. operator of the Concorde through a similar arrangement with British Airways where control was passed at Dulles Airport. Braniff operated the aircraft subsonic from Dulles to Dallas. The aircraft were painted in Braniff colors on one side and British Airways colors on the other, with two registration numbers.

121.569 governs the procedures for entering into and gaining approval for an interchange agreement between air carriers. Before a domestic or flag air carrier can gain approval to operate under an interchange agreement the carrier must show

1.   *The procedures for the interchange operation conform with the applicable FARs and with safe operating practices;*
2.   *Required crewmembers and dispatchers meet approved training requirements for the airplanes and equipment to be used and are familiar with the communications and dispatch procedures to be used;*
3.   *Maintenance personnel meet training requirements for the airplanes and equipment and are familiar with the maintenance procedures to be used;*
4.   *Flight crewmembers and dispatchers meet appropriate route and airport qualifications; and*
5.   *The airplanes to be operated are essentially similar to the airplanes of the certificate holder with whom the interchange is effected with respect to the arrangement of flight instruments and the arrangement and motion of controls that are critical to safety unless the Administrator determines that the certificate holder has adequate training programs to insure that any potentially hazardous dissimilarities are safely overcome by flight crew familiarization.*

FAR 121.569

Airplane Evacuation Capability

We discussed in chapter 10 some of the certification requirements in regard to emergency escape and lighting equipment required for Part 121 aircraft certification. Specifically we looked at 121.310, which stated, *if the airplane's emergency exit (other than over the wing) is more than 6 feet from the ground with the airplane on the ground and the landing gear extended, the airplane must have an approved means to assist the occupants in descending to the ground.* 121.570(a) requires this *automatically deployable emergency evacuation assisting means* to be ready for evacuation before an airplane carrying passengers may be moved on the ground, take off, or land.

121.570(b) requires at least one floor level exit be available that can provide for the evacuation of passengers through normal or emergency means during the time passengers are on board the aircraft prior to its movement on the surface. Note that to satisfy the requirement of 121.570(a) this floor level door must be *available* for use. This requirement may restrict certain aircraft servicing operations from being conducted while passengers are on board the aircraft. For instance, some aircraft may not fuel the left side of the aircraft while passengers are on board because the fueling operation blocks the *availability* of the one floor level exit.

Briefing Passengers Before Takeoff

Each air carrier is required by 121.571 to ensure that all passengers, prior to takeoff, are orally briefed by the appropriate crewmember on the following:

- Smoking policy,
- The location of emergency exits,
- The use of safety belts, and
- The location and use of any required emergency flotation means.

121.571(a)(2) addresses the required "after takeoff safety briefing" which states that passengers should keep their seat belts fastened, while seated, even when the seat belt sign is off.

An individual briefing is required by 121.571(a)(3) for persons who may need the assistance of another person to move expeditiously to an exit in the event of an emergency. This briefing must occur prior to every takeoff unless that person has been given a briefing before a previous leg on the same flight in the same aircraft. In the individual briefing the required crewmember shall

1. *Brief the person and his attendant, if any, on the routes to each appropriate exit and on the most appropriate time to begin moving to an exit in the event of an emergency; and*
2. *Inquire of the person and his attendant, if any, as to the most appropriate manner of assisting the person so as to prevent pain and further injury.*

FAR 121.571(a)(3)

All air carriers must carry on each passenger-carrying airplane, in convenient locations for use of each passenger, printed cards supplementing the oral briefing and containing

1. *Diagrams of, and methods of operating, the emergency exits and*
2. *Other instructions necessary for use of emergency equipment. Each card required by this paragraph must contain information that is pertinent only to the type and model airplane used for that flight.*

FAR 121.571(b)

Finally, the air carrier is required by 121.571(c) to describe in its manual the procedure to be followed in the before takeoff briefing. Usually this will be addressed in both the flight operations manual and the flight attendant's manual.

Briefing Passengers: Extended Overwater Operations

In addition to the oral briefing previously discussed in 121.571(a), 121.573 requires each air carrier operating an airplane in extended overwater operations (more than 50 nautical miles from nearest shoreline) to ensure all passengers are orally briefed by the appropriate crewmember on the location of life rafts. This includes a demonstration of the method of donning and inflating a life preserver. This briefing is not required to be given before takeoff unless the aircraft will be flying over water immediately after takeoff (e.g., departing New York's JFK airport for London Heathrow). If the aircraft does not fly over water immediately after takeoff, then the briefing is not required to be given until before entering the overwater segment of the flight (e.g., departing Dallas' DFW airport for London). 121.573(c) requires that the extended overwater briefing be described in the air carrier's operations manual. Like the before takeoff briefing, this briefing will usually be addressed in both the flight operations manual and the flight attendant's manual.

Oxygen for Medical Use by Passengers

In chapter 10 we discussed the "first aid" passenger oxygen requirements for passengers. That is, a passenger develops the need for oxygen while on a flight (e.g., chest pains, asthma, unconsciousness), not prior to boarding. 121.574 governs the carriage of *oxygen for medical use* by passengers who know of their need for oxygen in advance of the flight. 121.574(a) prohibits passengers from using their own oxygen bottles on board an air carrier's aircraft. An air carrier must provide the oxygen bottles, tubing, and mask/nasal cannula, except that a person may be allowed to use their own mask/cannula provided the equipment is shown to be compatible with the oxygen bottles supplied by the air carrier. So if any medical oxygen is to be used on a flight the bottles must be ordered from that air carrier in advance of the flight. The reason for this is simply to assure the quality control of the oxygen bottles.

121.574 allows for only two types of oxygen storage systems, gaseous oxygen bottles (compressed gas) and liquid oxygen bottles. When a gaseous oxygen system is used the equipment must have been under the air carrier's approved maintenance program since it was purchased new or since the last hydrostatic test of the storage cylinder, and the pressure in any oxygen cylinder must not exceed the rated cylinder pressure. A hydrostatic test is simply a test to see if an oxygen bottle (filled with water) can withstand a pressure that is greater than the pressure of the gas that will be carried in the bottle. Also, when using a gaseous oxygen system no air carrier may allow any person to connect or disconnect oxygen-dispensing equipment from the oxygen bottle while any passenger is aboard the airplane. When liquid oxygen bottles are used the equipment must have been under the air carrier's approved maintenance program since it was purchased new or since the storage container was last purged.

Passengers needing oxygen for medical use must order the oxygen in advance of the flight; usually this must be done at least 48 hours prior to departure time. Any person requesting oxygen is required by 121.574(a)(4) to have in their possession a licensed physician's written statement that specifies the maximum quantity of oxygen needed each hour and the maximum flow rate needed for the pressure altitude corresponding to the pressure in the cabin of the airplane under normal operating conditions. 121.574(a)(4) does allow passengers to use their own oxygen bottles during a flight if that aircraft is carrying only persons who may have a medical need for oxygen during flight (e.g., medical transport or Red Cross flight).

Whenever oxygen is used for medical reasons on board the aircraft the pilot in command must be advised of its presence on the aircraft and of when the oxygen is to be used. Oxygen equipment must be properly secured in the cabin, and the passenger must be seated in such a way as to allow access to or use of any required emergency or regular exit or of the aisle in the passenger compartment.

Alcoholic Beverages

121.575 contains a number of prohibitions (pun intended) concerning the use of alcoholic beverages on board an aircraft. They are as follows:

(a)   *No person may drink any alcoholic beverage aboard an aircraft unless the certificate holder operating the aircraft has served that beverage to him.*

(b)   *No certificate holder may serve any alcoholic beverage to any person aboard any of its aircraft who*

    (1)   *Appears to be intoxicated.*

    (2)   *Is escorting a person or being escorted in accordance with Section 108.21 (the carriage of passengers under the control of armed law enforcement officers).*

    (3)   *Has a deadly or dangerous weapon accessible to him while aboard the aircraft in accordance with Section 108.11 (carriage of weapons).*

(c)   *No certificate holder may allow any person to board any of its aircraft if that person appears to be intoxicated.*

FAR 121.575

Finally, an air carrier is required by 121.575(d) to send a report to the Administrator within 5 days after any incident involving the refusal of any person to comply with any part of 121.575, or involving any disturbance caused by a person who appears to be intoxicated aboard any of its aircraft.

Retention of Items of Mass in Passenger and Crew Compartments

When we talk of items of mass stored in the cabin or crew compartments, the first thing that comes to mind is cargo. However, considering the average fully stocked galley cart weighs more than 200 pounds, it is easy to see the need to secure these items. For this reason, 121.576 requires air carriers to provide and use means to prevent each item of galley equipment and each serving cart, when not in use, and each item of crew baggage that is carried in a passenger or crew compartment from becoming a hazard by shifting under the appropriate load factors corresponding to the emergency landing conditions under which the airplane was type certificated.

Stowage of Food, Beverage, and Passenger Service Equipment During Airplane Movement on the Surface, Takeoff, and Landing

Now that we've covered the requirement to have a means of securing galley equipment and crew baggage in the passenger cabin, let's take a look at the requirements for the stowage of food, beverage, and passenger service equipment during airplane movement. No certificate holder may move an airplane on the surface, take off, or land:

- When any food, beverage, or tableware furnished by the certificate holder is located at any passenger seat.
- Unless each food and beverage tray and seat-back tray table is secured in its stowed position.
- Unless each passenger serving cart is secured in its stowed position.
- Unless each movie screen that extends into an aisle is stowed.

To facilitate accomplishment of this task by the flight attendants, 121.577 requires all passengers to comply with instructions given by a crewmember with regard to the stowage of tray tables and food and beverage items.

Prohibition against Interference with Crewmembers

In response to an increase of air rage incidents occurring throughout the airline industry the FAA, in 1999, added a provision protecting air carrier crewmembers from interference with their duties. 121.580 governs the behavior of persons aboard an aircraft and may look familiar to you because it is identical to the language used in Part 91.11 *Prohibition Against Interference with Crewmembers*.

No person may assault, threaten, intimidate, or interfere with a crewmember in the performance of the crewmember's duties aboard an aircraft being operated under this part.

FAR 121.580

As you might imagine the most common abuse of crewmembers occurs in the cabin of an air carrier flight. Typically these air rage cases involve passengers being verbally abusive to flight attendants or other passengers. Extreme cases have involved passengers physically striking flight attendants or breaking down cockpit doors and attempting to wrestle control of the airplane from pilots.

Carriage of Persons without Compliance with the Passenger-Carrying Requirements of This Part

Throughout this text we have discussed a variety of aircraft equipment and personnel requirements necessary for 121 operations (e.g., emergency equipment, number of flight attendants, emergency exits, etc.). These requirements are all based on the passenger-carrying capacity of the aircraft. 121.583 covers the carriage of certain persons without compliance with the passenger-carrying requirements of Part 121.

The following persons may be carried aboard an airplane without complying with the passenger-carrying airplane requirements:

1. *A crewmember.*
2. *A company employee.*
3. *An FAA air carrier inspector, or an authorized representative of the National Transportation Safety Board, who is performing official duties.*
4. *A person necessary for*
   a. *The safety of the flight.*
   b. *The safe handling of animals.*

    c.   *The safe handling of hazardous materials whose carriage is governed by regulations in 49 CFR Part 175.*

    d.   *The security of valuable or confidential cargo.*

    e.   *The preservation of fragile or perishable cargo.*

    f.   *Experiments on, or testing of, cargo containers or cargo handling devices.*

    g.   *The operation of special equipment for loading or unloading cargo.*

    h.   *The loading or unloading of outsize cargo.*

5.   *A person performing duty as an honor guard accompanying a shipment made by or under the authority of the United States.*

6.   *A military courier, military route supervisor, military cargo contract coordinator, or a flight crewmember of another military cargo contract air carrier or commercial operator, carried by a military cargo contract air carrier or commercial operator in operations under a military cargo contract, if that carriage is specifically authorized by the appropriate armed forces.*

7.   *A dependent of an employee of the certificate holder when traveling with the employee on company business to or from outlying stations not served by adequate regular passenger flights.*

FAR 121.583

Even though these persons are exceptions to the Part 121 passenger-carrying requirements the FAA does require that certain safety measures be taken. For instance, all of the standard safety briefings must be accomplished before takeoff (e.g., use of oxygen, emergency exits, and seat belts). Also, there must be an approved seat with an approved safety belt for each person, and if that seat is located on the flight deck it must be in a position so that the occupant will not interfere with the flight crewmembers performing their duties. Regardless of where this person is seated he or she must have unobstructed access to a regular or emergency exit. Finally, the procedures for the safe carriage of such persons without compliance with the passenger-carrying requirements must be addressed in the air carrier's operations manual.

Exit Seating

The procedures an air carrier follows for the assignment of exit row seating must be in accordance with 121.585. As in the carry-on bag provisions, each passenger is required to comply with exit seating restrictions and/or instructions given by a crewmember or other employee of the carrier. First let's define the term exit seat. An exit seat means a seat that

- Provides access to an exit, including all the seats in a row from the fuselage to the aisle inboard of the exit.
- Has direct access to an exit (i.e., a passenger can proceed directly to the exit without entering an aisle or passing around an obstruction).

A carrier is authorized to use FAA approved selection criteria to determine the suitability of each person it permits to occupy an exit seat. These criteria must be included in its operations manual. Typically an air carrier will only allow those passengers who are able to activate an emergency exit and take whatever additional actions may be necessary to ensure the safe use of that exit in an emergency to be seated in the exit seat. 121.585(b) prohibits an air carrier from seating a person in an exit seat if

- It is likely the person would be unable to perform the required functions because of the lack of physical or mental capacity.
- The person is less than 15 years of age.
- The person is caring for small children, which might prevent them from performing the required functions.
- The person does not wish to be seated in an exit seat.

If a passenger seated in an exit row seat is deemed not suitable for exit row seating, the flight attendant is required by 121.585(l) to attempt a seat trade with a passenger who is willing and able to assume the required evacuation functions.

121.585 requires a carrier to make available for inspection by the public, at ticket counters, gates, or other passenger operations areas, written procedures used for determining a person's suitability to be seated in an exit seat. 121.585(d) requires these procedures to be included on the passenger information cards on board the aircraft and to include written procedures, in the form of passenger information cards at each exit seat. Included are the procedures for determining a passenger's suitability to be seated in an exit seat. There must also be a printed request that a passenger identify himself or herself to allow reseating if he or she cannot meet that carrier's selection criteria or does not choose to sit there. The passenger information cards must present information that a passenger may use in the event of an emergency to

1. *Locate the emergency exit;*
2. *Recognize the emergency exit opening mechanism;*
3. *Comprehend the instructions for operating the emergency exit;*
4. *Operate the emergency exit;*
5. *Assess whether opening the emergency exit will increase the hazards to which passengers may be exposed;*
6. *Follow oral directions and hand signals given by a crewmember;*
7. *Stow or secure the emergency exit door so that it will not impede use of the exit;*
8. *Assess the condition of an escape slide, activate the slide, and stabilize the slide after deployment to assist others in getting off the slide;*
9. *Pass expeditiously through the emergency exit; and*
10. *Assess, select, and follow a safe path away from the emergency exit.*

FAR 121.585(d)

Finally, no carrier may allow taxi or pushback unless at least one required crewmember has verified that no exit seat is occupied by a person the crewmember determines is likely to be unable to perform the required functions.

Authority to Refuse Transportation

121.589 addresses the issue of *if* and *when* an air carrier may refuse to transport a person with a disability. A disabled passenger is generally considered to be a person with a physical or mental impairment, disability, or condition of such nature that the individual may need the assistance of another individual to move to an exit in the event of an emergency on board the aircraft. The FAA does not allow an air carrier to refuse transportation to a disabled individual solely because that person's disability may cause him or her to need the assistance of another individual to move to an exit in the event of an emergency. An air carrier may not refuse transportation to a disabled person on the basis of safety unless

1. *The certificate holder has established procedures (including reasonable notice requirements) for the carriage of passengers who may need the assistance of another person to move expeditiously to an exit in the event of an emergency; and*
2. *At least one of the following conditions exist:*
   a. *The passenger fails to comply with the notice requirements in the certificate holder's procedures.*
   b. *The passenger cannot be carried in accordance with the certificate holder's procedures.*

FAR 121.586

Additionally, as a result of a number of legal actions, a carrier may not refuse to provide transportation to

- A disabled individual solely because the person's disability results in appearance or involuntary behavior that may offend, annoy, or inconvenience crewmembers or other passengers.
- Disabled individuals by limiting the number of such persons who are permitted to travel on a given flight.

Finally, a carrier may not require a disabled person to preboard an aircraft. It may be offered, but the disabled person may if they so choose proceed to board the aircraft at any time during the boarding process.

Carry-on Baggage

Probably one of the most contentious issues for airline passengers these days is the regulation governing carry-on bags. Nothing frustrates a passenger more than having to "gate check" a carry-on bag for the following reasons (listed in descending order of the most common occurrences):

- The passenger would like to carry on more than the allowable limit (usual limit is two bags).
- The passenger would like to carry on a bag that is larger than the allowable size (carry-on item must be of such dimensions that it may be stowed under a seat or in an overhead compartment).
- The airplane is full and there is no longer any carry-on bag space available for the last few remaining passengers to board the aircraft.

121.589 governs an air carrier's carry-on baggage program *and* requires the compliance of each passenger with instructions given by crewmembers regarding that carrier's approved carry-on bag program. This program must be approved by the FAA and will be found in Paragraph A.011 of the carrier's op specs. Normally an air carrier restricts passengers to two carry-on items, one to be stowed in an overhead compartment, and one under the seat in front of the passenger. This depends of course on the airline and the type of airplane. Regardless of the allowable amount and size of the carry-on items, 121.589 primarily addresses the stowage of carry-on items. No air carrier may allow

1.   *The boarding of carry-on baggage on an airplane unless each passenger's baggage has been scanned to control the size and amount carried on board in accordance with an approved carry-on baggage program in its operations specifications.*

2.   *A passenger to board an airplane if his/her carry-on baggage exceeds the baggage allowance prescribed in the carry-on baggage program in the certificate holder's operations specifications.*

3.   *. . . all passenger entry doors of an airplane to be closed in preparation for taxi or pushback unless at least one required crewmember has verified that each article of baggage is properly stowed.*

4.   *. . . an airplane to take off or land unless each article of baggage is stowed either in a suitable closet or stowage compartment placarded for its maximum weight and providing proper restraint for all baggage or cargo stowed within, and in a manner that does not hinder the possible use of any emergency equipment, or under a passenger seat.*

FAR 121.589

Important Terms from this Chapter

Aviation safety inspector's credentials: Form 110A

Aviation security program

Certificated land airports

Critical phase of flight

Equipment interchange agreements

Ground security coordinator (GSC)

Manipulation of controls

Operational control

Operations notices

Responsibility of operational control

Restriction or suspension of operations

Sterile cockpit rule

Chapter 12 Exam

1. Operational control may be defined as
   a. The supervision of the dispatching of flight crew by the crew scheduling department.
   b. The exercise of the FAA's inspection authority over U.S. certificated air carriers.
   c. The exercise of authority over initiating, conducting, or terminating a flight.
   d. The exercise of an air carrier's maintenance inspection authority granted under Part 145.

2. Typically the authority to dispatch or release a flight is held by which position(s)?
   a. An air carrier's director of operations (DO), aircraft dispatcher, and/or pilot in command.

    b. An air carrier's chief financial officer, chief flight instructor, or principal operations inspector (POI).

    c. The pilot in command, who may delegate this authority to the aircraft dispatcher.

    d. An air carrier's crew scheduling supervisor.

3. Prior to flight who is responsible for airplane security?

    a. The air carrier security marshal.

    b. The ground security coordinator.

    c. The airport security marshal.

    d. The ramp supervisor.

4. What is the definition of a critical phase of flight?

    a. That period during ground or flight operations anytime the cockpit-to-cabin door is closed.

    b. That period of flight involving takeoff, landing, and all flight operations conducted below 10,000 feet.

    c. That period of flight including all ground operations involving taxi, takeoff, landing, and all other flight operations conducted below 10,000 feet, unless in level cruise.

    d. That period of flight or ground operations involving taxi, takeoff, landing, and all other flight operations.

5. What credential(s) must an FAA air carrier inspector possess to gain access to the flight deck?

    a. Two forms of government photo ID, FAA form 110A (FAA inspector's ID card), and a driver's license or military ID.

    b. FAA form 121-548 jumpseat authorization letter, and a photo ID.

    c. An air carrier's standard jumpseat authorization form (DOT form 121-548).

    d. FAA form 110A (FAA inspector's ID card) and FAA form 8430-13 jumpseat form.

6. The pilot in command of a passenger-carrying airplane that has a lockable cockpit-to-cabin door must ensure the door is closed and locked during which period of aircraft operations?

    a. The cockpit-to-cabin door must be closed during taxi, takeoff, and landing.

    b. The cockpit-to-cabin door must be closed prior to aircraft pushback and for the duration of aircraft operations.

    c. The cockpit-to-cabin door must be closed and locked during flight.

    d. The cockpit-to-cabin door must be closed and locked prior to any aircraft movement.

7. What precautions must an air carrier take when transporting a passenger that requires medical oxygen?

    a. The carrier must ensure the passenger's personal oxygen canisters were manufactured in accordance with DOT 4166 oxygen safety requirements.

    b. The carrier must inspect the passenger's personal oxygen canisters to ensure they comply with the approved types authorized in the carrier's op specs.

    c. An air carrier may allow a passenger to carry and operate oxygen equipment as long as that carrier supplies the necessary equipment.

    d. The carrier must ensure the passenger's personal oxygen canisters were manufactured after December 31, 1999.

8. When a twin engine aircraft suffers engine failure or an engine is shut down in flight as a precautionary measure to prevent possible damage, the pilot in command is required to do what two things?

   a. Inform air traffic control of the engine failure or in flight shutdown and contact the person responsible for operational control for instructions.

   b. Land the airplane at the nearest suitable airport, in nautical miles, at which a safe landing can be made and notify the appropriate ATC facility as soon as practicable after the engine failure or in flight shutdown.

   c. Inform air traffic control of the engine failure or in flight shutdown and request immediate clearance to nearest airport with appropriate maintenance facilities.

   d. Land the airplane at the nearest suitable airport, *in point of time*, at which a safe landing can be made, and notify the appropriate ATC facility as soon as practicable after the engine failure or in flight shutdown.

FAR 121 Subpart V: Records and Reports and FAR 135 Subpart B: Record Keeping Requirements

Words are heavy like rocks . . . they weigh you down. If birds could talk, they wouldn't be able to fly.

—"Marilyn,"
from the TV show *Northern Exposure*

This chapter contains the air carrier regulatory requirements for record keeping under Part 121 Subpart V and Part 135 Subpart B. As a certificate holder an air carrier is subject to visits and inspections by officials of many different government agencies. These agencies include the Federal Aviation Administration (FAA), the National Transportation Safety Board (NTSB), the Department of Transportation (DOT), the Federal Communications Commission (FCC), and U.S. Customs as well as a variety of state and local government agencies. As an employer, an air carrier must also expect oversight by the Occupational Safety and Health Administration (OSHA) and, if the air carrier serves food, the Food and Drug Administration (FDA). Each of these agencies has regulatory requirements that must be followed by the air carrier. Most of these regulatory requirements begin with the need to maintain adequate documentation. The primary reason for this requirement is to allow these agencies to better verify regulatory compliance.

In this chapter we will discuss the FAA required records and reports that must be created and maintained by 121 and 135 air carriers. The FAA requires air carriers to maintain vast amounts of documentation. Some records must be kept indefinitely, while others may be discarded after 30 days. This documentation covers records kept for everything from employee training records, dispatch release forms, load manifests, flight plans, and maintenance reports to aircraft logbook entries and even en route aircraft to company communications.

FAR 121 Subpart V: Records and Reports

Crewmembers and Dispatchers Record

FAR 121.683(a) requires certificate holders conducting domestic or flag operations to maintain current records of each crewmember and each aircraft dispatcher. These ***crewmember and dispatcher records*** must show whether each crewmember or aircraft dispatcher is qualified and proficient with regard to route checks, route qualifications, airplane qualifications, currency training, and any required physical examinations. These records must also include flight, duty, and rest time records.

A record must also be kept for each action taken concerning the release from employment for professional or physical disqualification of any flight crewmember or aircraft dispatcher. This record must be maintained for a minimum of 6 months (121.683). Notice the employment records are the only records here that state a specific period of time they must be maintained. The crewmember and dispatcher qualification records are kept in a permanent file during the period that person is employed by the company. Examples of a pilot's permanent file include

- Basic indoctrination training records,
- Initial qualification training records,
- Transition and/or upgrade training records, and
- Operation experience line checks by FAA inspectors.

Air carriers involved in supplemental operations are required by 121.683(b) to maintain the records required by 121.683(a) either at its principal operations base or at another location approved by the FAA. This is different than the domestic or flag record keeping requirement. The reason is that since supplemental operations are typically transient in nature the FAA requires an established approved location for the maintenance of records.

A relatively recent advance in record keeping for 121 and 135 air carriers has been the ability for air carriers to maintain the required air carrier records on an approved computer record keeping system. Computer-based record keeping systems offer more flexible and efficient access and maintenance of records. This provides benefits for both the operator and the FAA. To gain approval to use a computer-based record keeping system an air carrier must

- Maintain manuals that fully describe the system and actions necessary to input and retrieve data stored within the system.
- Maintain a computerized record keeping system sufficient to allow verification of regulatory compliance with applicable sections of the FARs.
- Not make changes to the computerized record system without FAA approval.
- Maintain any hard copy paper files for a minimum of 30 days following completion of a flight.

For Part 121 and 135 certificate holders the approval for the use of computer-based record keeping systems can be found in the Paragraph A.025 of the carrier's ops specs. Let's again take a look at the ops specs for Delta Air Lines.

U.S. Department of
Transportation   Operation Specifications
Federal Aviation
Administration   Paragraph A.025

Delta Air Lines Ops Specs   **Paragraph A.025**

Approved Computer-based Record Keeping System

a. The certificate holder is authorized to use the approved computer-based record keeping system, described and/or referenced in this paragraph.

The Delta Air Lines computer-based record system for all crew members includes the following:
- The Aircrew Records Tracking System (ARTS) for pilot and flight engineer personnel.
- The Flight Attendant Training Records System (FATRS) for flight attendant personnel.
- The Crew Member Duty and Flight Time Record System (CDFTRS) for all crewmembers.

The continued use of this system is contingent upon adherence to the following stipulations:
- Delta Air Lines will maintain manuals which fully describe the system and the actions necessary to input and retrieve data stored within the system.
- Delta Air Lines will maintain a computerized record system which is sufficient to determine compliance with applicable sections of FAR Part 121.
- Delta Air Lines will not make changes to the computerized record system without FAA approval. Change requests will be submitted to the Certificate Management Office (CMO-27) a minimum of 60 days prior to the proposed implementation date.
- Source documents (hard copy paper files and magnetic tape records of ACARS messages) utilized for data will be maintained a minimum of 60 days following the completion of an event.

1. Issued by the Federal Aviation Administration.
2. These Operations Specifications are approved by direction of the Administrator.

ORIGINAL SIGNED BY: Mr. Drew U. Reed, Principal Operations Inspector

3. Date Approval is effective: 05/25/1999 Amendment Number: 1
4. I hereby accept and receive the Operations Specifications in this paragraph.

ORIGINAL SIGNED BY: Capt. Ima P. Ilot, Senior Vice President, Flight Operations Date: 05/25/1999

Aircraft Records

A 121 certificate holder conducting domestic or flag operations is required by 121.685 to maintain and supply the FAA's certificate-holding district office with a current list of each aircraft that it operates in scheduled air transportation. (Fig. 13.1 shows a sample *aircraft record.*)

Dispatch or Flight Release Forms

For domestic and flag operations an air carrier is required by 121.695(a) to carry a dispatch release form on every flight. As we discussed in chapter 11, 121.687(a) states that this dispatch release form may be organized in any manner but must contain at least the following information:

1. *Identification number of the aircraft.*
2. *Trip or flight number.*
3. *Departure and destination airport, also include any alternate airports and any intermediate stop if applicable.*
4. *A statement concerning the type of flight (e.g., IFR, VFR).*
5. *Minimum fuel supply.*

FAR 121.687(a)

D085. Aircraft Listing: The certificate holder is authorized to conduct operations under Part 121 using the aircraft identified on this operations specification.

Registration No.	Aircraft Manufacturer's Serial No.	Aircraft Make/Model
N001	23070	ATR-42-200
N002	23071	ATR-42-200
N003	23072	ATR-42-200
N004	23073	ATR-42-200
N005	23074	ATR-72-500
N006	23075	ATR-72-500
N007	23076	ATR-72-500
N008	23077	ATR-72-500
N009	23078	ATR-72-500
N010	23079	ATR-72-500
N011	23080	ATR-72-500
N012	23081	ATR-72-500
N1001	221	CRJ-200
N1002	222	CRJ-200
N1003	223	CRJ-200
N1004	224	CRJ-200
N1005	241	CRJ-700
N1006	242	CRJ-700
N1007	243	CRJ-700
N1008	244	CRJ-700
N1009	290	CRJ-900
N1010	291	CRJ-900
N4872	87-901	B-737-300
N4873	87-902	B-737-300
N4874	87-903	B-737-300
N4875	87-904	B-737-300
N4876	87-905	B-737-300
N4877	87-906	B-737-300
N9901	9701	B-737-800
N9902	9702	B-737-800
N9903	9703	B-737-800
N9904	9704	B-737-800
N9905	9705	B-737-800
N9910	9706	B-737-800
N9911	9707	B-737-800
N9912	9708	B-737-800
N9913	9709	B-737-800
N9922	9710	B-737-800
N9923	9711	B-737-800
N9924	9712	B-737-800

1. Issued by the Federal Aviation Administration.
2. These Operations Specifications are approved by direction of the Administrator.
3. Date Approval is effective: 4/01/01.

Figure 13.1   Sample list of aircraft currently operated by a fictional airline from the carrier's operations specifications.

The ***dispatch release*** must also contain at a minimum the latest available weather reports and forecasts for the destination airport, alternate airport, and intermediate stop, if applicable. The dispatch release must be signed by both the pilot in command and the aircraft dispatcher assigned to the flight [121.687(b)]. Additionally, the FAA requires the certificate holder to keep records of the dispatch release on file for a period of at least three months [121.695(b)].

Supplemental air carriers conducting domestic or flag operations are required by 121.689(c) to comply with the dispatch or flight release forms required for scheduled domestic or flag operations covered in 121.687. For supplemental operations *not* conducting domestic or flag operations, an air carrier is required by 121.697(a) to carry a flight release form on every flight. 121.689(a) states that this flight release form may be organized in any manner but must contain at least the following information:

1. *Company or organization name.*
2. *Make, model, and registration number of the aircraft being used.*
3. *Flight or trip number, and date of flight.*
4. *Name of each flight crewmember, flight attendant, and pilot designated as pilot in command.*
5. *Departure airport, destination airports, alternate airports, and route.*
6. *Minimum fuel supply (in gallons or pounds).*
7. *A statement of the type of operation (e.g., IFR, VFR).*

FAR 121.689(a)

The ***flight release,*** like the domestic and flag operator's dispatch release, must contain at a minimum the latest available weather reports and forecasts for the destination airport, alternate airport, and intermediate stop, if applicable. The flight release must be signed by both the pilot in command and the aircraft dispatcher assigned to the flight [121.689(b)]. Also, supplemental operators, like domestic and flag operators, are required to keep these records on file for a period of at least 3 months. These records must be kept at its principal base of operation.

Aircraft Load Manifests/Composition and Disposition

Air carriers are required by 121.693 to create a load manifest for each flight they operate. As we discussed in chapter 11, this load manifest must contain the following weight and balance and performance information at time of takeoff:

1. *The planned aircraft weight, including fuel and oil, cargo and baggage, passengers and crewmembers.*
2. *The maximum allowable weight for that flight that must not exceed the least of the following weights:*
   (a) *Maximum allowable takeoff weight for the runway intended to be used (including corrections for altitude, gradient, wind and temperature conditions existing at the takeoff time).*
   (b) *Maximum takeoff weight considering anticipated fuel and oil consumption that allows compliance with applicable en route performance limitations.*
   (c) *Maximum takeoff weight considering anticipated fuel and oil consumption that allows compliance with the maximum authorized design landing weight limitations on arrival at the destination airport.*

> (d)   Maximum takeoff weight considering anticipated fuel and oil con-
>   sumption that allows compliance with landing distance limitations on
>   arrival at the destination and alternate airports.
> 3.   The total aircraft weight computed under approved procedures.
> 4.   Evidence that the aircraft is loaded according to an approved schedule that
>   ensures that the center of gravity is within approved limits.
> 5.   Names of passengers, unless such information is maintained by other means
>   by the certificate holder.

FAR 121.693

The load manifest, like the dispatch release, is required to be carried to the aircraft's destination by the pilot in command. Domestic, flag, and supplemental operators are then required to keep the load manifest for a period of at least 3 months.

Aircraft Maintenance Logs

Not surprisingly, the FAA requires in 121.701 that each aircraft used in Part 121 domestic, flag, or supplemental operations carry aboard a FAA approved aircraft **maintenance log-book**. An aircraft logbook is used to record any maintenance difficulties or irregularities and any deferred maintenance items for an observed or reported failure or malfunction of airframe, engine, propeller, or other component critical to the safety of flight. This logbook must be kept in a location easily accessible to the flight crew and is ultimately used to record aircraft status (e.g., airworthy, nonairworthy). All maintenance items as well as any corrective action, once maintenance has been accomplished, must be written in the logbook by either a flight crewmember or a mechanic (see fig. 13.2). Verbal reports, that is, simply speaking with a mechanic about an aircraft malfunction, are not allowed. Everything must be documented because the FAA and most air carriers use these logbooks not only to verify compliance with FARs but to develop a historical record for each aircraft. This historical data is ultimately used to determine mechanical reliability, which brings us to 121.703.

Aircraft Service Difficulty Reports

In order to keep a close eye on the mechanical reliability of aircraft under the jurisdiction of the FAA, air carriers are required to report certain aircraft equipment malfunctions, failures, or structural defects to the FAA. These reports are called service difficulty reports and come in two different categories: *operational reports (mechanical equipment),* covered in 121.703, and *structural reports (aircraft structures),* addressed in 121.704. These reports help the FAA determine if an aircraft's malfunction or failure was a random occurrence or whether there is some equipment or structural defect that could be improved upon and that requires an airworthiness directive (AD) issued in the hopes of avoiding another malfunction or failure.

First, let's look at 121.703 Service Difficulty Reports (Operational). The FAA categorizes malfunctions, failures, or defects in three ways:

- Malfunctions, failures, or defects that occur *during flight.*
- Malfunctions, failures, or defects occurring or detected *on the ground.*
- Malfunction, failure, or defect in an aircraft *at any time that in the opinion of the certificate holder has endangered or may endanger the safe operation of the aircraft used by it.*

C038902			Delta							
A/C No. **222**	Serial No. C038902		0412-40205/ Log 6-01 TOPP 50-10-05					Airworthiness Release Ref. TOPP 50-10-05 By: R. J. Simpson ID No. 9195057 Sta.: ATL		
From	To	Date	Flt. No.	T/O Power	Arrival Fuel	Arrival Oil	APU Oil	Hyd. Fluid	Type Check	Mechanics Signature
ATL	MEM	08/08/01	946	Norm	11.5					
MEM	DFW	08/10/01	946	Norm	8.9					
DFW	LIT	08/10/01	302	35	7.9					
LIT	MEM	08/10/01	302	35	10.0	3.5/3.2				
MEM	CVG	08/11/01	717	45	11.1					
CVG	LEX	08/11/01	311	35	8.5					
LEX	ATL	08/11/01	311	Norm	9.1					

Item No. 1	Maintenance Code: 432-55	Irregularity: Hydraulic leak in right main wheel well

notified maintenance 1743 local time/DH

Corrective Action: Found main landing gear control valve supply line leaking. Cleared area and retorqued B-nut Pressurized hyd. system-Leak Check Good. Hyd. System Quantity O.K.

	Mechanic signature: Russell Levy	ID No. 99789411	Sta. DFW

Item No. 1	Maintenance Code: N/A	Irregularity: Max Power Takeoff ATL

Corrective Action: Info noted + Recorded

	Mechanic signature: Russell Levy	ID No. 99789411	Sta. DFW

Use Black Ball Point Pen-Ensure Both Copies Are Legible-See Coding Instructions

Figure 13.2 Sample aircraft maintenance logbook page from Delta Air Lines.

Let's look at each malfunction category a little more closely. Malfunctions, failures, or defects that occur during flight are defined by 121.703(b) as events that occur during the period from the moment the aircraft leaves the surface of the earth on takeoff until it touches down on landing. Specifically the FAA requires in 121.703 that each certificate holder report the occurrence or detection of each failure, malfunction, or defect *during flight* concerning:

(1) *Any fire and, when monitored by a related fire warning system, whether the fire warning system functioned properly;*

(2) *Any false warning of fire or smoke;*

(3) *An engine exhaust system that causes damage to the engine, adjacent structure, equipment, or components;*

(4) *An aircraft component that causes the accumulation or circulation of smoke, vapor, or toxic or noxious fumes;*

(5) *Any engine flameout or shutdown during flight or ground operations;*

(6) *A propeller feathering system or ability of the system to control overspeed;*

(7) *A fuel or fuel-dumping system that affects fuel flow or causes hazardous leakage;*

(8) *A landing gear extension or retraction, or the opening or closing of landing gear doors during flight;*

(9) *Any brake system component that results in any detectable loss of brake actuating force when the aircraft is in motion on the ground;*

(10) *Any aircraft component or system that results in a rejected takeoff after initiation of the takeoff roll or the taking of emergency actions, as defined by the aircraft flight manual or pilot's operating handbook;*

(11) *Any emergency evacuation system or component including any exit door, passenger emergency evacuation lighting system, or evacuation equipment found to be defective or that fails to perform the intended function during an actual emergency or during training, testing, maintenance, demonstrations, or inadvertent deployments; and*

(12) *Autothrottle, autoflight, or flight control systems or components of these systems.*

(13) *Aircraft components or systems that result in taking emergency actions during flight (except action to shut down an engine); and*

(14) *Aircraft structure that requires major repair.*

FAR 121.703(a)

The FAA also requires in 121.703(a) that each certificate holder report the occurrence or detection of each failure, malfunction, or defect that occurred or was detected on the ground. Specifically 121.703(a) requires reports for the following:

(1) *Brake system components that result in loss of brake actuating force when the airplane is in motion on the ground;*

(2) *Cracks, permanent deformation, or corrosion of aircraft structures, if more than the maximum acceptable to the manufacturer or the FAA;*

(3) *Emergency evacuation systems or components including all exit doors, passenger emergency evacuation lighting systems, or evacuation equipment that are found defective, or that fail to perform the intended functions during an actual emergency or during training, testing, maintenance, demonstrations, or inadvertent deployments.*

FAR 121.703(a)

The catchall paragraph is 121.703(c), which states a report is required for *any malfunction, failure, or defect in an aircraft at any time that, in the opinion of the certificate holder, has endangered or may endanger the safe operation of the aircraft used by it.*

Service difficulty reports (structural), covered in 121.704, are similar to operational reports but concern detection of defects or failures related to *aircraft structures*. Specifically, 121.704 requires a report be sent to the FAA for the following defects:

(1) *Corrosion, cracks, or disbonding that requires replacement of the affected part.*

(2) *Corrosion, cracks, or disbonding that requires rework or blendout because the corrosion, cracks, or disbonding exceeds the manufacturer's established allowable damage limits.*

(3) *Cracks, fractures, or disbonding in a composite structure that the equipment manufacturer has designated as a primary structure or a principal structural element.*

(4) *Repairs made in accordance with approved data not contained in the manufacturer's maintenance manual.*

(5) *Any other failure or defect in aircraft structure that occurs or is detected at any time if that failure or defect has endangered or may endanger the safe operation of an aircraft.*

FAR 121.704

If an aircraft structural failure or defect is detected by a FAA certificated repair station and *not* the air carrier, then the report required by 121.704(a) may be submitted by a certificated repair station when the reporting task has been assigned to that repair station by the air carrier certificate holder. However, the air carrier remains primarily responsible for ensuring compliance with the provisions of this section. The repair station is required to send the air carrier a copy of each report it has submitted to the FAA.

Paragraphs 121.703(d) and (e) and 121.704(c) cover when and how these reports are to be sent to the FAA. If a certificate holder has had a malfunction, failure, or defect and a report is required by 121.703(a) and (c) or 121.704(a) and (d), then the air carrier is required to send a report, in writing, to that air carrier's certificate-holding district office within 96 hours of the occurrence. This report must be sent within the 96 hour limit even though all required information might not be available. If additional information necessary to complete the report becomes available after the initial report was filed, the air carrier must expeditiously submit that additional information to the FAA. Also, each air carrier must make the report data available for 30 days for examination by the certificate-holding district office in a form and manner acceptable to the FAA Administrator or designated representative. The reports are required by 121.703(e) or 121.704(f) to include the following information:

(1) *The manufacturer, model, and serial number of the aircraft, engine, or propeller;*

(2) *The registration number of the aircraft;*

(3) *The operator designator;*

(4) *The date on which the malfunction, failure, or defect was discovered;*

(5) *The stage of flight or ground operation during which the malfunction, failure, or defect was discovered;*

(6) *The nature of the malfunction, failure, or defect;*

(7) *The applicable joint aircraft system/component code;*

(8) *The total cycles, if applicable, and total time of the aircraft, aircraft engine, propeller, or component;*

(9)   The manufacturer, manufacturer part number, part name, serial number, and location of the component that failed, malfunctioned, or was defective, if applicable;

(10) The manufacturer, manufacturer part number, part name, serial number, and location of the part that failed, malfunctioned, or was defective, if applicable;

(11) The precautionary or emergency action taken;

(12) Other information necessary for a more complete analysis of the cause of the failure, malfunction, or defect, including available information pertaining to type designation of the major component and the time since the last maintenance overhaul, repair, or inspection; and

(13) A unique control number for the occurrence, in a form acceptable to the Administrator.

FARs 121.703(e) and 121.704(f)

In order to avoid duplicate service difficulty reports being sent for the same event the FAA does not require a report if a malfunction, failure, or defect has already been reported by the certificate holder under the provision of FAR Part 21.3, which addresses certification procedures for products and parts or under the provisions of NTSB 830 concerning the notification and reporting of aircraft accidents or incidents.

Mechanical Interruption Summary Report

Every month an air carrier must submit a mechanical interruption summary report to the FAA. A mechanical interruption summary report is a detailed report of occurrences during the previous month that caused an interruption of an air carrier's normal service. The following events are discussed in 121.705(a) and require a mechanical interruption summary report:

- Interruption to a flight, unscheduled change of aircraft en route.
- Unscheduled stop or diversion from a route.
- Unscheduled engine removal caused by known or suspected mechanical difficulties or malfunctions that are not required to be reported as service difficulty reports (121.703 or 121.704).

Mechanical summary reports are to be submitted to the FAA before the tenth of every month for the previous month's mechanical interruptions.

Alteration and Repair

Whenever an air carrier performs a major alteration or major repair of an aircraft's airframe, engine, propeller, or other aircraft system it is required by 121.705 to submit an **alteration and repair report** of the work accomplished to the FAA. The air carrier must also maintain a copy of this report available for inspection by the air carrier's principal maintenance inspector.

Airworthiness Release or Aircraft Log Entry

FAR 121.709(a) requires that after maintenance, preventive maintenance, or alterations are performed on an aircraft, an ***airworthiness release*** logbook entry must be completed before an aircraft can be returned to service. The FAA allows only authorized certificated mechanics or repairmen to sign an airworthiness release, *except a certificated repairman may sign the release or entry only for the work for which he is employed and certificated [121.709(b)(3)].* An air carrier must have procedures set forth in the approved certificate holder's manual for preparing the airworthiness release or logbook entry. 121.709(b) and (d) specify that the signing of the airworthiness release by a qualified person's signature certifies that

> *(1) The work was performed in accordance with the requirements of the certificate holder's manual;*
> *(2) All items required to be inspected were inspected by an authorized person who determined that the work was satisfactorily completed;*
> *(3) No known condition exists that would make the airplane unairworthy.*
> *(4) So far as the work performed is concerned, the aircraft is in condition for safe operation.*

121.709(b)

Once an airworthiness release is completed and signed, the certificate holder must give a copy to the pilot in command. The way most air carriers comply with this provision is by including the airworthiness release in the aircraft maintenance logbook. Since the aircraft logbook is required to be on board the aircraft at all times, the pilot in command has access to the airworthiness release. Finally, 121.709(c) requires the air carrier to keep a record of that particular airworthiness release for at least 2 months.

Communication Records

Air carriers must comply with the two-way radio communication provision addressed in 121.99 which states

> *(a) Each certificate holder conducting domestic or flag operations must show that a two-way radio communication system or other means of communication approved by the Administrator is available at points that will ensure reliable and rapid communications, under normal operating conditions over the entire route (either direct or via approved point-to-point circuits) between each airplane and the appropriate dispatch office.*

FAR 121.99

The communication system used to comply with this regulation is required by 121.99(b) to be independent of any system operated by the U.S. government. An air carrier can maintain communication with each flight it operates via different means depending on where the aircraft may be situated (i.e., on the ground or in flight) and how the aircraft may be equipped. In the past, flight crews maintained a "listening watch" on a second or third VHF radio dedicated to a "company frequency" or commercially subscribed radio frequency (ARINC) in order to maintain contact with their company. While this satisfied the requirements of 121.99, it was inefficient and often distracting to the crewmember whose duty it was to listen to the company frequency and monitor simultaneously the air traffic control frequency. Some older aircraft still use this method of remaining in contact with the dispatch office.

Over the last 20 years air carriers have adopted a variety of methods by which they can maintain communications between the company dispatch office and the flight crews. One of the most popular is the automated communication and reporting system known as *ACARS*. This communication system is an aircraft-to-dispatcher data link transmitting over an assigned VHF frequency. The flight crew or the dispatcher uses a keypad to type a message, and with a push of a button that message is sent from the aircraft to the dispatcher or from the dispatcher to the aircraft. Another method of communication is via a satellite communication system or SATCOM. For obvious reasons this is particularly well suited to extended overwater operations.

This brings us to the **communication record** requirements for domestic and flag operations, which are covered in 121.711. An air carrier conducting domestic or flag operations is required to record each en route radio contact between the certificate holder and its pilots. To do this, the radio operator in the dispatch office maintains a logbook of all messages sent and received. Air carriers utilizing ACARS communications simply have the dispatcher print out every message it sends or receives or, if approved, may store the communication information on computer. Whether a communications logbook, ACARS printout, computer record, or some other approved means of recording communications is used, these records are required by 121.711 to be kept for at least 30 days.

Part 135 Record Keeping Requirements

Now let's take a look at the record keeping requirements for 135 operators. The bulk of the Part 135 record keeping requirements is covered in 135.63. The first requirement is that the following records must be kept at the certificate holder's principal business office or at other places approved by the FAA and shall be made available for inspection by the Administrator:

(a)   *The certificate holder's operating certificate.*
(b)   *The certificate holder's operations specifications.*
(c)   *A current list of aircraft used for Part 135 operations.*
(d)   *A record of each pilot.*
(e)   *A record of each flight attendant.*
(f)   *A completed aircraft load manifest (multi-engine aircraft only).*

FAR 135.63

Aircraft Records

As are 121 air carriers, Part 135 certificate holders are required by 135.63(a) to maintain a current list of aircraft used or available for use and the operations for which each is equipped. Furthermore, the certificate holder must keep this record for at least 6 calendar months.

Crewmember and Flight Attendant Record

Each certificate holder is required to keep an individual record of each pilot used in Part 135 operations for a period of at least 12 calendar months. This record must include the following information:

(1)   The full name of the pilot.
(2)   The pilot certificate (by type and number) and ratings that the pilot holds.
(3)   The pilot's aeronautical experience in sufficient detail to determine the pilot's qualifications to pilot aircraft in operations under this part.
(4)   The pilot's current duties and the date of the pilot's assignment to those duties.
(5)   The effective date and class of the medical certificate that the pilot holds.
(6)   The date and result of each of the initial and recurrent competency tests and proficiency and route checks required by this part and the type of aircraft flown during that test or check.
(7)   The pilot's flight time in sufficient detail to determine compliance with the flight time limitations found in 135.273.
(8)   The pilot's check pilot authorization, if any.
(9)   Any action taken concerning the pilot's release from employment for physical or professional disqualification.
(10) The date of the completion of the initial phase and each recurrent phase of the training required.

FAR 135.63(a)

An individual record for each flight attendant who is required under the applicable Part 135 regulations must also be maintained for a period of at least 12 months. This record must be of sufficient detail to determine compliance with the applicable portions of 135.273 concerning duty period limitations and rest requirements.

Load Manifest Record

Part 135.63(c) requires a certificate holder operating multi-engine aircraft to prepare an accurate load manifest in duplicate containing information concerning the loading of the aircraft. The pilot in command of an aircraft for which a load manifest must be prepared shall carry a copy of the completed load manifest in the aircraft to its destination. The certificate holder shall keep copies of completed load manifests for at least 30 days at its principal operations base or at another location used by it and approved by the FAA. The required load manifest must be prepared before each takeoff and must include

(1)   The number of passengers;
(2)   The total weight of the loaded aircraft;
(3)   The maximum allowable takeoff weight for that flight;
(4)   The center of gravity limits;
(5)   The center of gravity of the loaded aircraft, except that the actual center of gravity need not be computed if the aircraft is loaded according to a loading schedule or other approved method that ensures that the center of gravity of the loaded aircraft is within approved limits. In those cases, an entry shall be made on the manifest indicating that the center of gravity is within limits according to a loading schedule or other approved method;

(6)   *The registration number of the aircraft or flight number;*
(7)   *The origin and destination; and*
(8)   *Identification of crew members and their crew position assignments.*

FAR 135.63(c)

Reporting of Mechanical Irregularities

Each Part 135 certificate holder, like their Part 121 counterparts, is required by 135.65 to carry an aircraft maintenance log on board each aircraft for recording or deferring mechanical irregularities and their correction. The pilot in command must ensure that each mechanical irregularity that comes to the pilot's attention during flight time be entered into the aircraft maintenance log. If a previous maintenance irregularity is detected prior to flight, the pilot in command is required to determine the status of the irregularity entered in the maintenance log at the end of the previous flight.

As we've seen with the Part 121 maintenance logbook, the FAA requires a written record of any maintenance action made on the aircraft. If any mechanic or pilot completes a maintenance corrective action or defers maintenance concerning a reported or observed failure or malfunction of an airframe, power plant, propeller, rotor, or other aircraft equipment, that person is required by 135.65 to record the action taken in the aircraft maintenance log. Furthermore, each certificate holder's manual, which is required by 135.21 (policies and procedures), must include an approved procedure for keeping copies of the aircraft maintenance log in the aircraft for access by the appropriate personnel.

Summary

In this chapter we've discussed what records and reports the FAA requires 121 air carriers to create and maintain. As we've seen, records and reports are required to be kept for everything from employee training records, dispatch release forms, load manifests, flight plans, and *service interruption reports* to aircraft logbook entries and even en route aircraft to company communications. The FAA's primary reason for requiring these records is to allow it to better monitor and verify regulatory compliance.

Important Terms from this Chapter

Aircraft record
Airworthiness release
Alteration and repair report
Communication record
Crewmember and dispatcher records
Dispatch release
Flight release
Load manifest
Maintenance logbook
Service interruption report

Chapter 13 Exam

1. Air carriers operating under Part 121 are required to maintain current employee records of
   a. Certified airframe and power plant mechanics and flight crewmembers.
   b. Mechanics and repairmen authorized to complete an airworthiness release certificate.
   c. Aircraft dispatchers and security screening personnel.
   d. Aircraft dispatchers and crewmembers.

2. Air carriers operating under Part 121 must maintain a current list of each aircraft that:
   a. The certificate holder operates domestically and/or internationally.
   b. The certificate holder owns; leased aircraft are not required to appear on the list.
   c. The certificate holder operates in scheduled air transportation.
   d. The certificate holder operates in revenue operations.

3. What information is required to appear on a Part 121 domestic or flag operator's dispatch release form?
   a. Identification number of the aircraft, trip number, departure airport, intermediate stops, destination airport and alternate airports, a statement about the type of operation (e.g., VFR, IFR), minimum fuel supply, weather reports and forecasts.
   b. Company or organization name, make and model of aircraft, aircraft VIN number, flight number, name of each flight crewmember, departure airport, destination airport and alternate airports, minimum fuel supply, weather reports and forecasts.
   c. Aircraft VIN number, air carrier name, make and model of aircraft, trip number, name of the pilot in command, departure airport, destination airport and alternate airports, minimum fuel supply, weather reports and forecasts.
   d. Air carrier name, trip number, departure airport, intermediate stops, destination airport and alternate airports, a statement about the type of operation (e.g., VFR, IFR), weather reports and forecasts.

4. What is the main difference between the load manifest used in domestic and flag operations and the load manifest used in supplemental operations?
   a. Domestic, flag, and supplemental load manifests must contain identical information.
   b. Load manifests used in supplemental international operations may use metric measurements for weight and balance calculations.
   c. Load manifests used in supplemental international operations may use metric measurements for the calculation of fuel load only.
   d. None of the above.

5. What paperwork is the pilot in command required by 121 subpart V to carry aboard an airplane to its destination for domestic and flag operations?
   a. Completed load manifest, minimum fuel load calculations, flight plan.
   b. Completed load manifest, dispatch release, communications logbook.
   c. Completed load manifest, dispatch release, flight plan.
   d. Dispatch release, service interruption report, flight plan, crewmember records.

6. What additional paperwork items is the pilot in command required by 121 subpart V to carry aboard an airplane to its destination for supplemental operations?
    a. Pilot route certification, airworthiness release and a flight release instead of a dispatch release.
    b. Flight following paperwork, airworthiness release, and international route authority.
    c. Airworthiness release.
    d. None of the above.

7. The FAA requires an air carrier to maintain a record of each dispatch release or flight release for a period of
    a. 60 days
    b. 30 days
    c. 6 months
    d. 3 months

8. Air carriers are required to maintain a record of service difficulty reports for a period of
    a. 30 days
    b. 3 months
    c. 6 months
    d. 10 days

9. Who is allowed to sign an aircraft's airworthiness release certificate?
    a. Only the pilot in command or a certificated mechanic.
    b. The authorized certificated mechanic or repairman.
    c. A certificated repairman and the pilot in command.
    d. The air carrier's operations inspector or designated principal operations inspector.

10. An air carrier is required to maintain a record of each en route radio contact between the certificate holder and its pilots for what period of time?
    a. For a period of 90 days.
    b. For a period of 60 days.
    c. For a period of 2 years.
    d. For a period of 30 days.

11. A Part 135 certificate holder must maintain a current list of aircraft used or available for use and the operations for which each is equipped for how long?
    a. For a period of 90 days.
    b. For a period of 6 calendar months.
    c. For a period of 2 years.
    d. For a period of 30 days.

12. Each certificate holder is required to keep an individual record of each pilot or required flight attendant used in Part 135 operations for a period of:
    a. At least 3 calendar months.
    b. At least 60 days.
    c. At least 12 calendar months.
    d. At least 24 calendar months.

Maintenance

*No flying machine will ever fly from New York to Paris . . . [because]
no known motor can run at the requisite speed for four days without
stopping.*

—Orville Wright, 1908

In this chapter we will examine the requirements for maintenance that Part 121 places on air carriers. This is another area that is quite different in air carriage than what you may be familiar with from your previous exposure to Part 91 civilian training and operations. In Part 91 operations, for the most part, airworthiness is primarily the responsibility of a certificated airframe and power plant mechanic and the pilot flying the aircraft. In the case of an annual inspection or major repairs a certificated airworthiness inspector must also be involved. In Part 121 operations, the FAA is very much concerned about **process control**. That is, how does the air carrier maintain control of the maintenance procedures for which it is responsible.

Subpart L of Part 121 concerns maintenance, preventative maintenance, and alterations. It applies to all Part 121 certificate holders. With the "globalization" of the airline industry, it applies to carriers that have work done outside the United States by persons that do not hold U.S. airmen certificates. In that case, it puts the specific responsibility on the carrier to ensure that the foreign maintenance service providers or suppliers are subject to the same degree of surveillance that the FAA would perform within the United States. Further, the carrier is specifically responsible for assuring that all work performed is done in accordance with the carrier's maintenance and inspection manuals. This concept is very similar to that of operational control except applied to maintenance instead of flight operations.

The FARs are very clear that the certificate holder is responsible for the airworthiness of its aircraft and component parts. It must assure that the processes used are those approved in its maintenance manual. In 1979 a DC-10 aircraft was lost when the left engine separated from the aircraft. Subsequent investigation of the accident by the National Transportation Safety Board (NTSB) revealed that the carrier was using a procedure for removing the engine for maintenance that was not the one approved by the FAA and included in the carrier's maintenance manual. Although the procedures seemed similar in intent and result, an apparently minor difference in procedure repeatedly stressed the attach flange on the engine pylon, causing it eventually to break. In this case the carrier was held responsible for violating its own procedures in its own maintenance shop.

The same problem can arise in a different context. In 1996 ValueJet Flight 592 crashed in the Florida Everglades near Miami. The NTSB investigation revealed that this accident was directly caused by expired oxygen canisters that were improperly shipped in the aircraft's cargo hold; these canisters ignited and caused a major fire and loss of control of the aircraft. During the investigation an interesting question was posed to the senior ValueJet official in charge of maintenance. He was asked if he thought that the carrier could delegate the responsibility for compliance with FARs to the contract maintenance company that had worked on another of the carrier's DC-9s and shipped the expired canisters on a ValueJet aircraft. The answer stunned the hearing when he stated that yes, that responsibility could be delegated. That clearly is the incorrect answer.

FAR 121.363 makes it clear that a carrier may delegate the performance of any maintenance, preventative maintenance, or alteration to an outside contractor. However, this delegation of the work does not relieve the carrier of the responsibility to assure the airworthiness of its aircraft. That responsibility includes assuring compliance with manual procedures and company policies relating to airworthiness. This ***airworthiness responsibility***, like operational control, may never be delegated. Only the actual "wrench turning" can be delegated; all responsibility for assuring that the work was properly done and documented remains with the carrier. If the contractor makes a mistake in maintenance procedures or fails to properly document the work performed, it is the *carrier*, not the contractor, that FAA will hold accountable.

In order to assure that the company can actually do this, the FAA requires that the carrier have an adequate organization that is actually able to perform the required maintenance. This requirement is also extended to any contractors or subcontractors doing work for the carrier. The same organizational requirement is placed on the carrier or its contractors for the ***inspection function*** as well as the maintenance function. This inspection function brings us to one of the key differences between maintenance performed for Part 91 operators and Part 121 airlines.

Maintenance of Part 121 aircraft includes two interrelated components. First the aircraft must be *maintained*. For this think of the actual wrench turning. Then, the maintenance must be taken one step further. The aircraft must be inspected by an independent organization. The *inspection* of the work assures that whatever was to be done has actually been accomplished correctly and completely. It is this independent inspection that is designed to make sure things don't slip by or get overlooked. The airline must have separate maintenance functions and inspection functions. These two organizations must be separated (organizationally) at the operational level. That is, it must be separated at the level of the persons doing the actual work. The separation must occur below the level of administrative control at which overall responsibility for the required inspection functions and other maintenance and alteration functions is exercised.

As we've seen above, the Part 121 carrier's maintenance program is vested in a properly organized and staffed facility that assures that the carrier is able to exercise its airworthiness responsibility. To that end, 121.367 requires that the carrier must have in place the previously described programs that assure maintenance is performed in accord with its ***maintenance manual***. It must have adequate facilities and equipment to carry out the maintenance, and it must ensure that each aircraft that has been ***released to service*** has been properly maintained. Being released to service means that the carrier has assured that all required maintenance, repairs, and inspections have been performed and the documentation (records) prepared that assures the continuing airworthiness of the aircraft.

To assure that all personnel involved with maintenance have the information needed to perform their functions, FAA requires that the carrier have a maintenance manual (discussed above and previously in chapter 4). This manual must contain an organization chart (or description) for the maintenance and inspection functions as well as a list of any contractors or subcontractors that it uses to perform maintenance or inspections. It must contain descriptions and details of the programs of maintenance, inspection, and continuing airworthiness that must used by the carrier. These programs are normally drawn up starting with the aircraft manufacturer's maintenance manual and then adapted to the specific needs of the carrier. The maintenance program must include

tion chart (or description) for the maintenance and inspection functions as well as a list of any contractors or subcontractors that it uses to perform maintenance or inspections. It must contain descriptions and details of the programs of maintenance, inspection, and continuing airworthiness that must used by the carrier. These programs are normally drawn up starting with the aircraft manufacturer's maintenance manual and then adapted to the specific needs of the carrier. The maintenance program must include

- The method of performing routine and nonroutine maintenance (other than required inspections), preventive maintenance, and alterations.
- A designation of the items of maintenance and alteration that must be inspected (**required inspections**), including at least those that could result in a failure, malfunction, or defect endangering the safe operation of the aircraft if not performed properly or if improper parts or materials are used.
- The method of performing required inspections and a designation by occupational title of personnel authorized to perform each required inspection.
- Procedures for the reinspection of work performed pursuant to previous required inspection findings (**buy-back procedures**).
- Procedures, standards, and limits necessary for required inspections and acceptance or rejection of the items required to be inspected and for periodic inspection and **calibration of precision tools**, measuring devices, and test equipment.
- Procedures to ensure that all required inspections are performed.
- Instructions to prevent any person who performs any item of work from performing any required inspection of that work.
- Instructions and procedures to prevent any decision of an inspector, regarding any required inspection, from being countermanded by persons other than supervisory personnel of the inspection unit, or a person at that level of administrative control that has overall responsibility for the management of both the required inspection functions and the other maintenance, preventive maintenance, and alterations functions.
- Procedures to ensure that required inspections, other maintenance, preventive maintenance, and alterations that are not completed as a result of shift changes or similar work interruptions are properly completed before the aircraft is released to service.

FAA views the record keeping as being as important as the actual maintenance work. To that end, the carrier must provide (in its manual) for a suitable system that provides for preservation and retrieval of maintenance information (records) in an acceptable manner. This system of **maintenance records** must contain the following:

- A description of the work performed (this can be by way of a coding system),
- The name of the person performing the work if the work is performed by a person outside the organization of the certificate holder, and
- The name or other positive ID of the individual approving the work.

The records of each required maintenance task must include

(1) *All the records necessary to show that all requirements for the issuance of an airworthiness release under Section 121.709 have been met.* [See chapter 13.]
(2) *Records containing the following information:*
    (i) *The total time in service of the airframe.*
    (ii) *The total time in service of each engine and propeller.*

*(iii) The current status of **life-limited parts** of each airframe, engine, propeller, and appliance.*

(iv) The time since last overhaul of all items installed on the aircraft that are required to be overhauled on a specified time basis.

(v) The identification of the current inspection status of the aircraft, including the times since the last inspections required by the inspection program under which the aircraft and its appliances are maintained.

*(vi) The current status of applicable airworthiness directives (ADs), including the date and methods of compliance, and if the airworthiness directive involves recurring action (**recurring AD**), the time and date when the next action is required.*

(vii) A list of current major alterations to each airframe, engine, propeller, and appliance.

FAR 121.380(a)

These records must be maintained by the carrier and kept available for inspection by the FAA or the NTSB at the location(s) specified in its op specs. 121.380 requires the carrier to retain the required records for the following periods:

(1) Except for the records of the last complete overhaul of each airframe, engine, propeller, and appliance, the records required to show that all requirements for issuing an airworthiness release have been met shall be retained until the work is repeated or superseded by other work or for 1 year after the work is performed.

(2) The records of the last complete overhaul of each airframe, engine, propeller, and appliance shall be retained until the work is superseded by work of equivalent scope and detail.

FAR 121.380(c)

These records must be retained and transferred with the aircraft at the time the aircraft is sold. The purchaser of the aircraft may allow the seller to retain the records (for example if the seller is going to continue to perform the maintenance for the purchaser), but the purchaser is still responsible to provide these records to FAA and NTSB if required for surveillance or an investigation.

Who can perform the maintenance? The carrier may set up its own maintenance and inspection departments. If it does so under 121.379, then 121.378 requires each person *directly in charge* of maintaining or altering the carrier's aircraft must have an appropriate airman certificate. "Directly in charge of" means any person assigned to a position in which he or she is responsible for the work of a shop or station that performs the maintenance or alteration or any other function that affects airworthiness. This person who is directly in charge of a shop or station does not have to physically observe and direct each worker at that shop or station. Rather, he or she must be available for consultation and decision on matters that require instructions or decisions from a higher authority than that of the person actually performing the work. Further, any inspector must have an appropriate airman certificate.

An alternative method of certificating the operation is to rely on a certificate issued under Part 145 of the FAR. This part covers certification of repair stations (facilities). If the **maintenance repair organization (MRO)** is certificated under Part 145, then the FAA will look to that organization *as an organization* for the authority which allows it to perform maintenance and inspections for a carrier. In other words, a carrier may perform maintenance and alterations for itself or other carriers. In addition, it may contract out work to maintenance repair organizations certificated under Part 145. In any event, it may not contract out *responsibility* for maintaining the continuous airworthiness of its aircraft.

FAR 121.371 sets forth the requirements for the inspection personnel that are required for a carrier's inspection program. Inspectors must be appropriately certificated, properly trained, qualified, and authorized by the carrier to perform the inspections. The inspectors don't work individually on their own authority. Rather, the person performing inspections must be under the supervision and control of an inspection unit. This unit management will be held accountable by the FAA for any irregularities that occur. Of course the inspector may also be held accountable. A basic concept of inspection and one required by the FAA is that no person may perform a required inspection if he or she performed the item of work required to be inspected.

The FAA wants to be able to tell exactly who is responsible for inspections. Therefore, the inspection unit must maintain a current listing of persons who have been trained, qualified, and authorized to conduct required inspections. The persons authorized to perform inspections must be identified by name, occupational title, and the inspections that they are authorized to perform. If the inspections are contracted to third parties, then the carrier must assure that those third parties maintain this same information. The carrier (or person with whom it arranges to perform its required inspections) must give written information to each person authorized to perform inspections describing the extent of his or her responsibility and authority, and limits on his or her inspection authority. This information must be made available to the FAA upon request.

Once the maintenance and inspection programs have been set up, the FAA expects the carrier to perform continuing surveillance (or audits) of both its maintenance and its inspection programs. FAR 121.373 requires this ***continuing analysis and surveillance***. The purpose of these programs is to assure that if the programs start to produce unacceptable results, that fact will be picked up and corrected before any serious maintenance issues arise. It is the carrier's responsibility to continuously monitor its maintenance and inspection programs for the purposes of quality control. If the FAA finds that either of these programs is not adequately assuring that the requirements of Part 121 are being met, it may make any changes in the program(s) that it deems necessary to bring the program(s) back into compliance with Part 121. This process is subject to appeal by the carrier. Unless an emergency situation requiring immediate action exists, the carrier must be given a hearing to allow it to show that the programs were working as required.

FAR 121.375 requires that each carrier or person performing maintenance or preventive maintenance functions for it shall have a ***maintenance or inspection training program*** to ensure that each person (including inspection personnel) who determines the adequacy of work done is fully informed about procedures and techniques and new equipment in use and is competent to perform his duties.

As we saw earlier with pilots, flight attendants, and dispatchers, the FAA is concerned that safety sensitive workers such as mechanics are sufficiently rested so as not to be prone to fatigue related errors. FAR 121.377 says that within the United States, each carrier (or contractor performing maintenance functions for it) must relieve each person performing maintenance from duty for a period of at least 24 consecutive hours during any 7 consecutive days, or the equivalent thereof within any single calendar month. Note that due to jurisdictional issues, this provision only applies within the United States. This is one of the areas in Part 121 where serious conflict of national objectives occurs. On the one hand, the United States supports increased competition in the global marketplace by allowing maintenance work to be contracted to cheaper facilities outside the United States. On the other hand, these facilities are not subject to U.S. labor law and regulations, so we can't dictate the rest provisions. That makes these shops cheaper to operate and more competitive, but does it allow for the same level of safety as required for U.S. MROs? Is the competitive playing field level?

Summary

In this chapter we have looked at the structure of Part 121 air carrier maintenance. We have seen how it differs from the maintenance performed in Part 91 particularly in the organization, structure, inspections, and training required. This is done to assure the highest level of safety is achieved by air carriers.

Important Terms from this Chapter

Airworthiness responsibility

Buy-back procedures

Calibration of precision tools

Continuing analysis and surveillance

Inspection function

Life-limited parts

Maintenance manual

Maintenance or inspection training program

Maintenance records

Maintenance repair organization (MRO)

Process control

Recurring airworthiness directive (AD)

Released to service

Required inspections

Chapter 14 Exam

1. If repair work is "farmed out" to an outside maintenance repair organization under an approved contract, who is responsible for the airworthiness of the repair?
    a. The maintenance repair organization.
    b. The air carrier certificate holder.
    c. The FAA.
    d. Both A and B are jointly responsible.

2. The air carrier certificate holder may delegate the responsibility for the repair of its aircraft to
    a. Another Part 121 certificate holder repair station.
    b. A Part 145 FAA authorized repair station.
    c. Both A and B are permitted.
    d. Neither A nor B is permitted.

3. The air carrier certificate holder may delegate the responsibility for airworthiness of its aircraft to
    a. Another Part 121 certificate holder repair station.
    b. A Part 145 FAA authorized repair station.
    c. Both A and B are permitted.
    d. Neither A nor B is permitted.

4. Organizationally, the maintenance and inspection functions of a carrier
   a. Must be combined into a single department under the director of mainte-nance to assure control of the program.
   b. Must place the maintenance department under the inspection department to emphasize the relative importance of inspection vis-à-vis maintenance.
   c. May place the maintenance and inspection functions wherever is most feasi-ble for the company operations.
   d. Must place the maintenance function and the inspection function in sepa-rate organizations at the operational level of the company.

5. The maintenance program for each aircraft is described in the carrier's
   a. Ops specs.
   b. Maintenance manual.
   c. Management manual.
   d. Flight operations manual.

6. Records to show that all requirements for issuing a maintenance release have been met must be kept available for inspection for a period of
   a. 30 days.
   b. 90 days.
   c. 1 year.
   d. Forever and transferred with the aircraft if it is sold.

7. Records to show that the aircraft was overhauled must be kept for a period of
   a. 30 days.
   b. 90 days.
   c. 1 year.
   d. Forever and transferred with the aircraft if it is sold.

8. The mechanic for an airline (that has set up its maintenance under FAR 121.379) that changes a DC generator on an engine must hold
   a. An airframe certificate.
   b. A power plant certificate.
   c. An airframe and power plant certificate.
   d. He needn't hold any airman's certificate.

9. Maintenance and inspection training
   a. Is required at all Part 121 carriers.
   b. Is required only if the carrier has contracted its maintenance to a Part 145 maintenance repair facility.
   c. Is only suggested for Part 121 carriers but required for Part 145 facilities.
   d. None of the above.

10. If a Part 121 carrier contracts its maintenance work out to a foreign Part 145 mainte-nance facility, then that facility must provide its workers
    a. 1 day off every 7 days.
    b. 4 days off every calendar month.
    c. 1 week off every calendar year.
    d. It is not required to provide its workers any time off.

15 Appendices to Part 121

FAA regulations forbid drinking within 8 feet of the aircraft and smoking within 50 hours of flight. Or is it the other way around?

—Anon.

At the conclusion of the numbered sections of Part 121 there are several appendices to Part 121. These are supplemental materials to specific regulations and provide detail on how these things are to be done. For example, FAR 121.309 says that no Part 121 aircraft may be operated without *"First aid and emergency equipment and protective gloves . . . that meet . . . the specifications and requirements of Appendix A of this part"*. So the rule (121.309) requiring first aid kits makes an external reference to ***Appendix A: First Aid Kits and Emergency Medical Kits,*** which details exactly what must be in the first aid kits. There are a number of these rules that make this sort of external reference to the appendices of Part 121. In this final chapter we will review several of the appendices that are most likely to be encountered by air carrier employees in day to day operations.

Appendix B: Airplane Flight Recorder Specifications

Appendix B specifies exactly what parameters are included in an airplane flight data recorder (FDR) and the technical specifications applicable to that data. You may recall from our previous discussions about required equipment that the NTSB has been calling on the FAA to expand the number of data channels required to be recorded on the flight data recorders. Appendix B contains approximately 50 parameters that may be recorded on the flight data recorder. It is important to note that Appendix B doesn't set forth the requirement to have the flight data recorder or what data must be recorded. That was done in 121.343 and 121.344. What Appendix B does is set forth the specific technical standards applicable to that parameter. For example the first parameter is time. Time must be recorded in GMT (UTC) or on a frame counter as on a VCR. The range must be a 24 hour period and is required to be accurate to plus or minus 0.125 percent per hour. Time must be sampled (recorded) once every 4 seconds and resolvable down to 1 second.

Some items will refer to the range as being "as installed." This means that the system installation standards can recognize the inherent differences of different systems. For example, groundspeed readout calls for the range to be as installed. If one aircraft has a groundspeed potential of 0–300 knots and another from 0–600 knots, the FDR channel may record this differing range.

Appendix E: Flight Training Requirements

Appendix E contains a table of the maneuvers and procedures required by Section 121.424 for pilot initial, transition, and upgrade flight training and the maneuvers that are in the carrier's approved low altitude windshear flight training program. The appendix indicates whether these maneuvers must be performed in flight or, as in the case of windshear maneuvers and procedures, in an authorized airplane simulator. Certain other maneuvers and procedures may be performed in an airplane visual simulator, a nonvisual airplane simulator, a training device, or a static airplane as indicated by the appropriate symbol in the table of maneuvers. Whenever a maneuver or procedure is authorized to be performed in a nonvisual simulator, it may be performed in a visual simulator; when it is authorized to be performed in a training device, it may be performed in a visual or nonvisual simulator, and in some cases, a static airplane. When the requirement may be performed in either a training device or a static airplane, that is indicated in the appendix

If you refer to the table in Appendix E you will find that it is broken into three vertical sections. These sections are applicable to initial, transition, and upgrade training, respectively. Within each column, it is indicated where the maneuver may be performed and for which crewmembers it is required. Appendix E should be particularly helpful to new hires going for initial training as it is a clear, unambiguous roadmap of what is going to be done in training. At the conclusion of training, you will be evaluated using the proficiency check requirements of Appendix F.

Appendix F: Proficiency Check Requirements

The contents and format of *Appendix F* are very similar to those of Appendix E. This appendix contains a list of all the maneuvers that must be performed for a proficiency check and indications of whether the maneuver must be performed in the airplane or may be performed in the simulator. Note that windshear training and checking is always performed in the simulator. Again, for the new hires, your simulator and airplane check ride at the conclusion of initial training will come right out of Appendix F. You can study it beforehand and be confident as you go through training that you are preparing for everything to be done on the check. Your examiner will be using a form very similar to the layout of Appendix F, which indicates exactly what tasks must be performed.

Appendix H: Advanced Simulation Plan

The FAA has encouraged and, now, even mandated the use of advanced flight simulators in air carrier training. In Part 91 the word *simulator* is widely misused to mean any device that is a cockpit mock-up—realistic or not. This is actually a misnomer. The FAA has two classes of training devices. These are flight training devices (FTDs) and flight simulators. These two classes are further divided into subcategories. FTDs are classified from Level 1 through Level 6 and include everything from cockpit procedures trainers

(CPTs) to nonmotion, aircraft specific, flight-training devices. Simulators that you are likely to encounter in your airline training program are classified from Level A to Level D and must be approved by the FAA for use in the training program. This approval oversight is conducted by the National Simulator Evaluation Team based in Atlanta.

The use of the simulator in training and checking is determined by the level of simulation, that is, Level A through Level D. To be used under *Appendix H* training, the simulator must be a Level B through Level D simulator. What are the differences in the levels of simulation? The differences are outlined below.

Level B

Simulator Requirements

For the *Level B simulator* the following are required:

- Aerodynamic programming to include
    - ➢ Ground effect—for example, roundout, flare, and touchdown. This requires data on lift, drag, and pitching moment in ground effect.
    - ➢ Ground reaction—Reaction of the airplane upon contact with the runway during landing to include strut deflections, tire friction, and side forces.
    - ➢ Ground handling characteristics—steering inputs to include crosswind, braking, thrust reversing, deceleration, and turning radius.
- Minimum of three-axis freedom of motion systems.
- Level B landing maneuver test guide to verify simulator data with actual airplane flight test data, and provide simulator performance tests for Level B initial approval.
- Multichannel recorders capable of recording Level B performance tests.

Visual System Requirements

- Visual system compatibility with aerodynamic programming.
- Visual system response time from pilot control input to visual system output shall not exceed 300 milliseconds more than the movement of the airplane to a similar input. Visual system response time is defined as the completion of the visual display scan of the first video field containing different information resulting from an abrupt control input.
- A means of recording the visual response time for comparison with airplane data.
- Visual cues to assess sink rate and depth perception during landings.
- Visual scene to instrument correlation to preclude perceptible lags.

Level C

Simulator Requirements

For the *Level C simulator* the following are required:

- Representative crosswind and three-dimensional windshear dynamics based on airplane related data.
- Representative stopping and directional control forces for at least the following runway conditions based on airplane related data:

> Dry,
> Wet,
> Icy,
> Patchy wet,
> Patchy icy, and
> Wet on rubber residue in touchdown zone.

- Representative brake and tire failure dynamics (including antiskid) and decreased brake efficiency due to high brake temperatures based on airplane related data.
- A motion system which provides motion cues equal to or better than those provided by a six-axis freedom of motion system.
- Operational principal navigation systems, including electronic flight instrument systems, INS, and OMEGA, if applicable.
- Means for quickly and effectively testing simulator programming and hardware.
- Expanded simulator computer capacity, accuracy, resolution, and dynamic response to meet Level C demands. Resolution equivalent to that of at least a 32-bit word length computer is required for critical aerodynamic programs.
- Timely permanent update of simulator hardware and programming subsequent to airplane modification.
- Sound of precipitation and significant airplane noises perceptible to the pilot during normal operations and the sound of a crash when the simulator is landed in excess of landing gear limitations.
- Aircraft control feel dynamics shall duplicate the airplane simulated. This shall be determined by comparing a recording of the control feel dynamics of the simulator to airplane measurements in the takeoff, cruise, and landing configuration.
- Relative responses of the motion system, visual system, and cockpit instruments shall be coupled closely to provide integrated sensory cues. These systems shall respond to abrupt pitch, roll, and yaw inputs at the pilot's position within 150 milliseconds of the time, but not before the time, when the airplane would respond under the same conditions. Visual scene changes from steady state disturbance shall not occur before the resultant motion onset but within the system dynamic response tolerance of 150 milliseconds. The test to determine compliance with these requirements shall include simultaneously recording the analog output from the pilot's control column and rudders, the output from an accelerometer attached to the motion system platform located at an acceptable location near the pilots' seats, the output signal to the visual system display (including visual system analog delays), and the output signal to the pilot's attitude indicator or an equivalent test approved by the Administrator. The test results in a comparison of a recording of the simulator's response to actual airplane response data in the takeoff, cruise, and landing configuration.

Visual Requirements

- Dusk and night visual scenes with at least three specific airport representations, including a capability of at least 10 levels of occulting, general terrain characteristics, and significant landmarks.
- Radio navigation aids properly oriented to the airport runway layout.
- Test procedures to quickly confirm visual system color, RVR, focus, intensity, level horizon, and attitude as compared to the simulator attitude indicator.
- For the approach and landing phase of flight, at and below an altitude of 2,000 feet height above the airport (HAA) and within a radius of 10 miles from the airport, weather representations including the following:

- ➤ Variable cloud density,
- ➤ Partial obscuration of ground scenes, that is, the effect of a scattered to broken cloud deck,
- ➤ Gradual break out,
- ➤ Patchy fog,
- ➤ The effect of fog on airport lighting, and
- ➤ Category II and III weather conditions.
- Continuous minimum visual field of view of 75 degrees horizontal and 30 degrees vertical per pilot seat. Visual gaps shall occur only as they would in the airplane simulated or as required by visual system hardware. Both pilot seat visual systems shall be able to be operated simultaneously.
- Capability to present ground and air hazards such as another airplane crossing the active runway or converging airborne traffic.

Level D

Simulator Requirements
Level D simulators require the following:

- Characteristic buffet motions that result from operation of the airplane (for example, high speed buffet, extended landing gear, flaps, nose-wheel scuffing, stall) and can be sensed at the flight deck. The simulator must be programmed and instrumented in such a manner that the characteristic buffet modes can be measured and compared to airplane data. Airplane data are also required to define flight deck motions when the airplane is subjected to atmospheric disturbances such as rough air and cobblestone turbulence. General purpose disturbance models that approximate demonstrable flight test data are acceptable.
- Aerodynamic modeling for aircraft for which an original type certificate is issued after June 1, 1980, including low-altitude, level-flight ground effect, mach effect at high altitude, effects of airframe icing, normal and reverse dynamic thrust effect on control surfaces, aeroelastic representations, and representations of nonlinearities due to side slip based on airplane flight test data provided by the manufacturer.
- Realistic amplitude and frequency of cockpit noises and sounds, including precipitation, static, and engine and airframe sounds. The sounds shall be coordinated with the weather representations required in visual requirement for special weather representations (see below).
- Self-testing for simulator hardware and programming to determine compliance with Level B, C, and D simulator requirements.
- Diagnostic analysis printout of simulator malfunctions sufficient to determine MEL compliance. These printouts shall be retained by the operator between recurring FAA simulator evaluations as part of the daily discrepancy log required under Section 121.407(a)(5).

Visual Requirements
- Daylight, dusk, and night visual scenes with sufficient scene content to recognize a specific airport, the terrain, and major landmarks around that airport and to successfully accomplish a visual landing. The daylight visual scene must be part of a total daylight cockpit environment which at least represents the amount of light in the cockpit on an overcast day. For the purpose of this rule, daylight visual system

is defined as a visual system capable of producing, as a minimum, full color presentations, scene content comparable in detail to that produced by 4,000 edges or 1,000 surfaces for daylight and 4,000 light points for night and dusk scenes, 6 foot lamberts of light at the pilot's eye (highlight brightness), 3 arc minutes resolution for the field of view at the pilot's eye, and a display which is free of apparent quantization and other distracting visual effects while the simulator is in motion. The simulation of cockpit ambient lighting shall be dynamically consistent with the visual scene displayed. For daylight scenes, such ambient lighting shall neither wash out the displayed visual scene nor fall below 5 foot lamberts of light as reflected from an approach plate at knee height at the pilot's station and/or 2 foot lamberts of light as reflected from the pilot's face.

- Visual scenes portraying representative physical relationships that are known to cause landing illusions in some pilots, including short runway, landing over water, runway gradient, visual topographic features, and rising terrain.
- Special weather representations which include the sound, visual, and motion effects of entering light, medium, and heavy precipitation near a thunderstorm on takeoff, approach, and landings at and below an altitude of 2,000 feet HAA and within a radius of 10 miles from the airport.
- Level C visual requirements in daylight as well as dusk and night representations.
- Wet and, if appropriate for the operator, snow-covered runway representations, including runway lighting effects.
- Realistic color and directionality of airport lighting.
- Weather radar presentations in aircraft where radar information is presented on the pilot's navigation instruments.

The differences in the different levels of flight simulation are summarized in Figure 15.1, which is taken from AC 120-40B.

Training and Checking Permitted

Appendix H also specifies the training and checking that may be accomplished in each level of simulation under an approved simulator training program.

Level B
- Regency of experience (Sec. 121.439).
- Night takeoffs and landings (Part 121, Appendix E).
- Landings in a proficiency check without the landing on the line requirements (Sec. 121.441).

Level C
- For all pilots, transition training between airplanes in the same group, and for a pilot in command the certification check required by Section 61.153(g).
- Upgrade to pilot-in-command training and the certification check when the pilot
  - ➢ Has previously qualified as second in command in the equipment to which the pilot is upgrading;
  - ➢ Has at least 500 hours of actual flight time while serving as second in command in an airplane of the same group; and
  - ➢ Is currently serving as second in command in an airplane in this same group.

General Requirements for Simulators by Level

					Flight Simulators (AC 120-40 B)				
Simulator Level	Control Loading	Visual Scenes	Motion	Visual Field of View (Note 4)	Ground Handing Package	Runway Contaminates	Sound	Buffets	Radar
A	Static	Night	3 Axis	45 × –30					
B	Static	Night	3 Axis	45 × 30	Yes			Yes	
C	Static and Dynamic	Night and Dusk	6 Axis	75 × 30	Yes	feel	Cockpit Noise	Yes	
D	Static and Dynamic	Night, Dusk, and Day	6 Axis	75 × 30	Yes	Feel and See	Realistic Cockpit Noise	Characteristic, Compliance Statement, and Test Required	Operating Radar (Note 5)

Figure 15.1 General requirements for simulator by level. *Notes:* 1. For training, testing, or checking credits, consult the appropriate Pratical Test Standards appendices and the regulation that the training, testing, or checking is to be conducted under. 2. Copies of the Practical Test Standards may be found at *http://www.mmacicbi.gov/afs/afs600/akt.htim.* 3. Copies of the Federal Aviation Regulations may be found at *http://www.faa.gov/avr/afs/FARS/FAR-IDX.HTM.* 4. Per pilot simultaneously. 5. When display is on pilot's navigation display.

- Initial pilot-in-command training and the certification check when the pilot
  - Is currently serving as second in command in an airplane of the same group;
  - Has a minimum of 2,500 flight hours as second in command in an airplane of the same group; and
  - Has served as second in command on at least two airplanes of the same group.
- For all second-in-command pilot applicants who meet the aeronautical experience requirements of Section 61.159 of this chapter (14 CFR) in the airplane, the initial and upgrade training and checking required by Part 121, and the certification check requirements of Section 61.153 of this chapter (14 CFR).

Level D
Except for the line check required by Section 121.440 and the static airplane requirements of Appendix E to Part 121, and the operating experience requirements of Section 121.434, all pilot flight training and checking required by Part 121 and the certification check requirements of Section 61.153(g) may be done in a Level D simulator. The exceptions must be performed in an actual airplane.

Appendix I: Drug Testing Program

The drug testing required for Part 121 carriers is found in *Appendix I*. This provision sets the requirements and standards for all drug testing of air carrier *and* other employees.

Who must be tested? Here is a big surprise for some Part 91 operators. Part 91 operators probably aren't even aware of the existence of Part 121, Appendix I. Why should they be? That applies to airlines, right? Well, not completely. To find the applicability of Appendix I (and Appendix J) to Part 91 operators we must look not to Part 91 but to part 135! FAR 135.1, the applicability section for Part 135, says:

(c)   For the purpose of (the drug and alcohol testing requirements) **operator** means any person or entity conducting nonstop sightseeing flights for compensation or hire in an airplane or rotorcraft that begin and end at the same airport and are conducted within 25 statute mile radius of that airport.

FAR 135.1

So here we have the excluded activities from Part 135 for nonstop sightseeing flights placed back under Part 135 for drug and alcohol testing. Where do you find the requirements for the testing? FARs 135.249 through 135.255 direct you to Part 121 Appendix I and J! So, the individual or small flight school that conducts sightseeing flights without a drug and alcohol testing program is in violation of Part 121!

Other than these sightseeing flights, air carrier employees who perform a **safety-sensitive function** directly or by contract for an air carrier (including Part 135 carriers) must be tested pursuant to an FAA approved anti-drug program. These positions include

- Flight crewmembers,
- Flight attendants,
- Flight instructors,
- Aircraft dispatchers,

- Aircraft maintenance personnel,
- Ground security coordinators, and
- Aviation screeners.

The drug testing must be done in accordance with approved DOT procedures as outlined in 49 CFR Part 40. The laboratory used to perform the analysis must be a Department of Health and Human Service (HHS) approved laboratory and comply with all procedures required by HHS and the DOT. The program must be approved by the FAA prior to implementation and is subject to annual review. The program must accomplish seven types of testing. These are *pre-employment testing, periodic testing, random testing, post-accident testing and testing based on reasonable cause, return to duty testing, and follow-up testing.*

Pre-employment Testing

Under pre-employment testing, an applicant/employee must be drug tested (screened) prior to the first time he or she performs a safety-sensitive function for an employer. The employer must advise each individual applying to perform a safety-sensitive function at the time of application that he will be required to undergo a pre-employment test to determine the presence of marijuana, cocaine, opiates, phencyclidine (PCP), and amphetamines, or a metabolite of those drugs in the individual's system. An employer must not allow an individual required to undergo pre-employment testing to perform a safety-sensitive function unless the employer has received a verified negative drug test result for the individual. Pre-employment also applies to employees that previously performed safety-sensitive functions and are now returning to perform a safety-sensitive function.

Periodic Testing

Each employee, such as pilots, that is required to undergo a medical examination under Part 67 of this chapter (14 CFR) shall submit to a periodic drug test. The employee shall be tested for the presence of marijuana, cocaine, opiates, phencyclidine (PCP), and amphetamines, or a metabolite of those drugs during the first calendar year of implementation of the employer's anti-drug program. The tests shall be conducted in conjunction with the first medical evaluation of the employee or in accordance with an alternative method for collecting periodic test specimens detailed in an employer's approved anti-drug program. An employer may discontinue periodic testing of its employees after the first calendar year of implementation of the employer's anti-drug program when the employer has implemented an unannounced testing program based on random selection of employees.

Random Testing

The basic rule for random testing is that the minimum annual percentage rate for random drug testing must be 50 percent of covered employees. However, the airline industry has shown that the incidence of drug use is so low among the employees in the industry that it has successfully gotten the FAA to lower the actual random testing rate. This reduction of the percentage rate for random drug testing is based on the reported positive rate for the entire industry. All information used for this determination is drawn from the statistical reports required of the airlines. Each year the FAA publishes in the Federal Register the minimum annual percentage rate for random drug testing of covered employees for the next year. When the minimum annual percentage rate for random drug testing is 50 percent, the Administrator may lower this rate to 25 percent of all covered employees if the he or she determines that the data received under the reporting requirements for 2 consecutive calendar years indicate that the reported positive rate is less than 1.0 percent. When the minimum annual percentage rate for random drug testing is 25 percent and the data received under the reporting requirements for any calendar year indicate that the reported positive rate is equal to or greater than 1.0 percent, the Administrator will increase the minimum annual percentage rate for random drug testing to 50 percent of all covered employees.

As the name suggests, this is a random selection of employees for random drug testing. It must be made by a scientifically valid method, such as a random-number table or a computer based random number generator that is matched with employees' Social Security numbers, payroll identification numbers, or other comparable identifying numbers. Under the selection process used, each covered employee shall have an equal chance of being tested each time selections are made. These tests must ensure that the random drug tests are unannounced and that the dates for administering random tests are spread reasonably throughout the calendar year. Expect one day to be returning from a flight and be invited to "make a deposit" before you leave the terminal building.

Post-accident Testing

Post-accident testing is required of each employee who performs a safety-sensitive function if that employee's performance either contributed to an accident or cannot be completely discounted as a contributing factor to the accident. The employee shall be tested as soon as possible but not later than 32 hours after the accident. The decision not to administer a test under this appendix must be based on a determination, using the best information available at the time of the determination, that the employee's performance could not have contributed to the accident. The employee must submit to post-accident testing under this appendix.

Testing Based on Reasonable Suspicion

Testing based on reasonable suspicion is required of each employee who performs a safety-sensitive function and who is reasonably suspected of using a prohibited drug. An employer may test an employee's specimen for the presence of other prohibited drugs or drug metabolites only in accordance with Appendix I and the DOT Procedures for Transportation Workplace Drug Testing Programs (49 CFR Part 40). At least two of the employee's supervisors, one of whom is trained in detection of the symptoms of possible drug use, shall substantiate and concur in the decision to test an employee who is reasonably suspected of drug use. (In the case of an employer other than a Part 121 certificate holder who employs 50 or fewer employees who perform safety-sensitive functions, one supervisor who is trained in detection of symptoms of possible drug use may substantiate the decision to test an employee who is reasonably suspected of drug use.) The decision to test must be based on a reasonable and articulable belief that the employee is using a prohibited drug on the basis of specific contemporaneous physical, behavioral, or performance indicators of probable drug use.

Return to Duty Testing

Each employer must ensure that before an individual is returned to duty to perform a safety-sensitive function after refusing to submit to a drug test or receiving a verified positive drug test result, the individual shall undergo a drug test. No employer shall allow an individual required to undergo return to duty testing to perform a safety-sensitive function unless the employer has received a verified negative drug test result for the individual.

Follow-up Testing

Follow-up testing is required for any individual that has been hired to perform or who has been returned to the performance of a safety-sensitive function after refusing to submit to a required drug test or after receiving a verified positive drug test result. The number and frequency of these tests will be established by the employer's ***medical review officer (MRO).*** (The medical review officer is a person qualified in accordance with 49 CFR Part 40 who performs the functions set forth in 49 CFR Part 40 and Appendix I. If the employer does not have a qualified individual on staff to serve as MRO, then it may contract for the provision of MRO services as part of its drug testing program.)

In the case of a person who is evaluated under Appendix I and determined to be in need of assistance in resolving problems associated with illegal use of drugs, follow-up testing shall consist of at least six tests in the first 12 months following the employee's return to duty. The employer may direct the employee to undergo testing for alcohol, in addition to drugs, if the medical review officer determines that alcohol testing is necessary for the particular employee. Any such alcohol testing must also be conducted in accordance with the provisions of 49 CFR Part 40. This follow-up testing may not exceed 60 months after the date the individual begins to perform or returns to the performance of a safety-sensitive function. The medical review officer may terminate the requirement for follow-up testing at any time after the first six tests have been conducted, if he or she determines that such testing is no longer necessary.

Finally, let's note the harshness of penalties for violations of this program. An employee who has verified positive drug test results on two required drug tests is *permanently precluded* from performing for any employer the safety-sensitive duties that he or she performed prior to the second drug test. Also, an employee who has engaged in prohibited drug use during the performance of a safety-sensitive function is also permanently precluded from performing that safety-sensitive function for any employer.

Employee Assistance Plan (EAP)

Each employer must provide an ***employee assistance plan (EAP)*** for its employees. The employer may establish the EAP as a part of its internal personnel services or the employer may contract with an entity that will provide EAP services to an employee. The program includes education and training on drug use for employees and training for supervisors making determinations for testing of employees based on reasonable cause. The program must include a ***drug education program*** that includes at least the following elements: display and distribution of informational material; display and distribution of a community service hot-line telephone number for employee assistance; and display and distribution of the employer's policy regarding drug use in the workplace. The employer's policy shall include information regarding the consequences under the rule of using drugs while performing safety-sensitive functions, receiving a verified positive drug test result, or refusing to submit to a drug test required under the rule.

The employee assistance program must also include a ***drug training program.*** This must be a reasonable program of initial training for employees. The employee training program must include at least the following elements: the effects and consequences of drug use on personal health, safety, and work environment; the manifestations and behavioral cues that may indicate drug use and abuse; and documentation of training given to employees and employer's supervisory personnel.

The employer's supervisory personnel who will determine when an employee is subject to testing based on reasonable cause must receive specific training on specific, contemporaneous physical, behavioral, and performance indicators of probable drug use in addition to the training specified above. The employer shall ensure that supervisors who will make reasonable cause determinations receive at least 60 minutes of initial training. The employer shall implement a reasonable recurrent training program for supervisory personnel making reasonable cause determinations during subsequent years. The employer shall identify the employee and supervisor EAP training in the employer's drug testing plan submitted to the FAA for approval.

Appendix J: Alcohol Misuse Prevention Program

The FAA also requires an alcohol abuse prevention program, described in ***Appendix J,*** that is somewhat similar to the drug testing program of Appendix I. This program is to help prevent accidents and injuries resulting from the misuse of alcohol by employees who perform safety-sensitive functions in aviation. The same employees are covered as are covered by the drug testing provisions of Appendix I. There are seven types of alcohol testing performed. These include *pre-employment testing, post-accident testing, random testing, reasonable suspicion testing, return to duty testing, follow-up testing, and **retesting of covered employees with an alcohol concentration of 0.02 or greater but less than 0.04.***

Pre-employment Testing

An employer may, but is not required to, conduct pre-employment alcohol testing under this part. If it chooses to conduct pre-employment alcohol testing, it must comply with the following requirements:

- It must conduct a pre-employment alcohol test before the first performance of safety-sensitive functions by every covered employee (whether a new employee or someone who has transferred to a position involving the performance of safety-sensitive functions).
- It must treat all safety-sensitive employees performing safety-sensitive functions the same for the purpose of pre-employment alcohol testing (i.e., it must not test some covered employees and not test others).
- It must conduct the pre-employment tests after making a contingent offer of employment or transfer, subject to the employee passing the pre-employment alcohol test.
- It must conduct all pre-employment alcohol tests using the alcohol testing procedures of 49 CFR Part 40.
- It must not allow a covered employee to begin performing safety-sensitive functions unless the result of the employee's test indicates an alcohol concentration of less than 0.04.

Post-accident Testing

Post-accident testing is required as soon as practicable following an accident. The employer must test each surviving covered employee for alcohol if that employee's performance of a safety-sensitive function either contributed to the accident or cannot be completely discounted as a contributing factor to the accident. The decision not to administer a test under this section shall be based on the employer's determination, using the best available information at the time of the determination, that the covered employee's performance could not have contributed to the accident.

If a required post-accident alcohol test is not administered within 2 hours following the accident, the employer shall prepare and maintain on file a record stating the reasons the test was not promptly administered. If a test required by this section is not administered within 8 hours following the accident, the employer shall cease attempts to administer an alcohol test and shall prepare and maintain the same record. Records shall be submitted to the FAA upon request of the Administrator or his or her designee.

A covered employee who is subject to post-accident testing shall remain readily available for such testing or may be deemed by the employer to have refused to submit to testing. However, this doesn't require the employee to delay receipt of necessary medical attention for injured people following an accident or to prohibit a covered employee from leaving the scene of an accident for the period necessary to obtain assistance in responding to the accident or to obtain necessary emergency medical care.

Random Testing

Random testing for alcohol follows essentially the same rules as those for the random testing for drugs. The selections must be on a statistically sound basis and cover a specified percentage of employees.

Reasonable Suspicion Testing

The testing provisions for reasonable suspicion are very similar to those for reasonable cause testing for drugs. The most significant difference between the two is the recognition of the fact that alcohol metabolizes much more quickly, so there are time limits set on when the testing may be performed. The employer must require a covered employee to submit to an alcohol test when the employer has reasonable suspicion to believe that the employee has violated the alcohol misuse prohibitions. The employer's determination that reasonable suspicion exists to require the covered employee to undergo an alcohol test shall be based on specific, contemporaneous, articulable observations concerning the appearance, behavior, speech, or body odors of the employee. The required observations must be made by a supervisor who is trained in detecting the symptoms of alcohol misuse. The supervisor who makes the determination that reasonable suspicion exists cannot conduct the breath alcohol test on that employee.

Alcohol testing is authorized if the observations required above are made during, just preceding, or just after the period of the work day that the covered employee is required to be in compliance with this rule. An employee may be directed by the employer to undergo reasonable suspicion testing for alcohol only while the employee is performing safety-sensitive functions, just before the employee is to perform safety-sensitive functions, or just after the employee has ceased performing such functions.

If a test required by this appendix is not administered within 2 hours following the determination of reasonable suspicion, the employer shall prepare and maintain a record stating the reasons the test was not promptly administered. If a test required by this appendix is not administered within 8 hours following the determination of reasonable suspicion, the employer shall cease attempts to administer an alcohol test and shall state in the record the reasons for not administering the test. Even in the absence of a reasonable suspicion alcohol test, no covered employee shall report for duty or remain on duty requiring the performance of safety-sensitive functions while the employee is under the influence of or impaired by alcohol, as shown by the behavioral, speech, or performance indicators of alcohol misuse. The employer may not permit the covered employee to perform or continue to perform safety-sensitive functions until

- An alcohol test is administered and the employee's alcohol concentration measures less than 0.02; or
- The start of the employee's next regularly scheduled duty period, but not less than 8 hours following the determination that there was reasonable suspicion that the employee had violated the alcohol misuse provisions.

Return to Duty Testing

An employer must ensure that before a covered employee returns to duty requiring the performance of a safety-sensitive function after engaging in conduct that constitutes misuse of alcohol, the employee shall undergo a return to duty alcohol test with a result indicating an alcohol concentration of less than 0.02.

Follow-up Testing

Following a determination that a covered employee is in need of assistance in resolving problems associated with alcohol misuse, each employer must ensure that the employee is subject to unannounced follow-up alcohol testing as directed by a substance abuse professional. A covered employee must be tested under this paragraph only while the employee is performing safety-sensitive functions, just before the employee is to perform safety-sensitive functions, or just after the employee has ceased performing such functions.

Retesting of Covered Employees with an Alcohol Concentration of 0.02 or Greater but Less than 0.04

Each employer must retest a covered employee to ensure that the employee has an alcohol concentration of less than 0.02 if the employer chooses to permit the employee to perform a safety-sensitive function within 8 hours following the administration of an alcohol test indicating an alcohol concentration of 0.02 or greater but less than 0.04.

The provisions of Appendix J, like the drug testing provisions of Appendix I, provide for the establishment of an employee assistance plan and training for supervisors in identifying the symptoms of alcohol misuse.

Summary

In this chapter we have reviewed several of the appendices to Part 121. They are developed to be incorporated by reference into the regulations in the subparts of Part 121. An employee of a 121 carrier must at least be aware of the existence of these appendices, and in some case even Part 91 operators/employees need to be aware of the rules found in Part 121.

Important Terms or Concepts from this Chapter

Appendix A: First Aid Kits and Emergency Medical Kits

Appendix B: Airplane Flight Recorder Specifications

Appendix E: Flight Training Requirements

Appendix F: Proficiency Check Requirements

Appendix H: Advanced Simulation Plan

Appendix I : Drug Testing Program

Appendix J: Alcohol Misuse Prevention Program

Drug education program

Drug training program

Employee assistance plan (EAP)

Follow-up testing

Level B simulator

Level C simulator

Level D simulator

Medical review officer (MRO)

Operator

Periodic testing

Post-accident testing and testing based on reasonable cause

Pre-employment testing

Random testing

Retesting of covered employees with an alcohol concentration of 0.02 or greater but less than 0.04

Return to duty testing

Safety-sensitive function

Chapter 15 Exam

1. If a new-hire pilot wished to know what maneuvers would be covered in his initial aircraft training, a good place to look would be
    a. The relevant provisions of Part 61: Certification of Airmen.
    b. The relevant provisions of Part 121: Subpart N: Air Carrier Training Requirements.
    c. The relevant provisions of Part 121: Subpart O: Crewmember Qualification.
    d. Part 121 Appendix E: Flight Training Requirements

2. Which level of simulation has the greatest degree of fidelity to the aircraft?
    a. Level B.
    b. Level C.
    c. Level D.
    d. None of the above.

3. Which level of simulation may be used to meet the training requirements for landings?
    a. Level B.
    b. Level C.
    c. Level D.
    d. All of the above.

4. If you are a flight instructor for a small flight school and it conducts sightseeing flights for hire, must you have a drug testing program?
    a. Yes.
    b. No.
    c. Insufficient information to determine.

5. Which of the following require drug testing at a Part 121 carrier?
    a. Flight attendants.
    b. Ground security coordinators.
    c. Pilots.
    d. All of the above.

6. Pre-employment drug testing is required by the FAA of
    a. All newly hired pilots.
    b. All newly hired customer service agents.
    c. Airport ticket office manager.
    d. All of the above.

7. Reasonable cause drug testing
    a. Can be instituted at any time by the carrier.
    b. Requires at least two of the employee's supervisors to concur in the testing decision.
    c. Requires a medical review officer to concur in the testing decision.
    d. Is unavailable unless the employee has a documented history of drug abuse.

8. If a pilot fails two drug tests
    a. He must undergo drug rehabilitation for at least 1 year before returning to duty.
    b. He must undergo 6 months of rehabilitation and peer counseling and review.
    c. He is forbidden to act as pilot in command until he has been drug free for 6 months.
    d. He is forever barred from acting as a commercial pilot for any company.

9. The blood alcohol concentration that is considered as operating under the influence of alcohol for FAR purposes is
    a. 0.04.
    b. 0.4.
    c. 0.8.
    d. 1.0.

10. After an accident, the employer must administer an alcohol test to any relevant employees within
    a. 1 hour after the accident.
    b. 2 hours after the accident.
    c. 4 hours after the accident.
    d. 8 hours after the accident.

Answers to End of Chapter Exams

Is this going to be on the test?

—Students, from time immemorial.

Chapter 1

1. The concept of common carriage is derived from
   a. Federal Aviation Regulations.
   b. Federal statutes.
   c. British common law.
   d. State statutes.

   Answer (c): Common carriage derives from the early application of British common law to the transportation and hospitality (hotel/inn) industries. It has carried into United States legal concepts through American common law.

2. Private carriage is distinguished from common carriage primarily by
   a. The lack of an exchange of money for transportation (carriage).
   b. The amount of money charged for the transportation (carriage).
   c. Contracts between parties as opposed to carriage on an individual basis.
   d. Transportation (carriage) of only one or very small numbers of parties.

   Answer (d): Private carriage is that transportation (carriage) arranged between one party (or some other small number of parties) and the carrier. As the number of parties being provided carriage increases, the likelihood of common carriage increases.

3. Which of the following is not an element of common carriage?
   a. Having a license or certificate.
   b. Performing carriage for anyone (persons or goods).
   c. From place to place.
   d. For compensation or hire.

   *Answer (a): It is not necessary that the carrier be licensed or certificated in order to be determined to be a **common** carrier. It is only necessary that it hold out to the public that it is willing to perform carriage for anyone from place to place for compensation or hire.*

4. Holding out to the public would include
   a. Advertising.
   b. Flyers in a campus student union.
   c. Statements on a web page.
   d. All of the above.

Answer (d): Holding out as an air carrier can be done in any of a number of ways. The key element is an indication to the public at large of a willingness to perform transportation.

5. In analyzing a situation where a private pilot is accused of acting illegally as a common carrier, the FAA will, among other tests, look to see if the pilot
   a. Was paid only for the fuel, oil, and aircraft rental.
   b. Had an independent interest in taking the trip.
   c. Advertised the availability of his or her services.
   d. Used his or her personal aircraft or paid money for a rental aircraft.

Answer (b): While there are tests that partially involve pro rating fuel, oil, rental, and airport fees, and whether the pilot held out to the public, answers a and c are both incomplete statements of the tests applied to determine if the pilot was acting as a common carrier. The independent interest test looks specifically at whether the pilot had an independent interest in taking the trip or was only interested in going if he or she received money for the trip.

6. As a commercial pilot, acting individually and without further certificates, you may
   a. Charge a hunter to take him to the deep north woods of Alaska.
   b. Charge a fellow student half of the costs to take him home to visit his girlfriend.
   c. Charge a gas company to perform pipeline aerial spotter patrols.
   d. Charge an acquaintance to take her to the Atlantic City casinos.

Answer (c): Answers a, b, and d all involve carrying people for hire. Without an air carrier certificate (or meeting one of the small exceptions allowed for private pilots) you would not be legal to perform these missions. Pipeline patrol is one of the specific activities excluded from certification requirements by operation of 14 CFR 119(e)(4)(vi).

7. A company must operate under 14 CFR 121 if it is
   a. A domestic operation.
   b. A commuter operation.
   c. An on-demand operation.
   d. None of the above.

Answer (a): A domestic, flag, or supplemental operation must be conducted under Part 121 rules. Commuter and on-demand operations are conducted under Part 135 rules.

8. A company operating small corporate size jets between Los Angeles and Mexico City on a scheduled basis would need to hold
   a. A domestic operating certificate.
   b. A flag operating certificate.
   c. A supplemental operating certificate.
   d. An on-demand operating certificate.

Answer (b): Scheduled operation of turbojet aircraft outside the 48 contiguous United States or between points in Alaska and Hawaii and outside of Alaska and Hawaii require a flag operating certificate. If this operation was performed on a nonscheduled basis it would require an on-demand certificate.

9. Assume you were operating as an on-demand air carrier but didn't have an operating certificate. The potential penalty for this would be a $10,000 fine for
   a. Each flight conducted for compensation or hire.
   b. Conducting flights without a certificate.
   c. Each section of Part 135 for each flight conducted.
   d. You wouldn't be fined; you would be required to obtain a certificate before continuing and your pilot certificate could be suspended.

Answer(c): The rules applicable to unauthorized operators act as if to give you a certificate for the sole purpose of holding you responsible for all things a certificate holder is responsible for. You would then be fined for every section you were not complying with for each and every flight conducted. This could easily amount to hundreds of thousands of dollars (or more) of potential fines.

10. Operational control is the concept that
    a. The carrier, not the crew, is the final determinant of how the aircraft is operated.
    b. The carrier knows where all of its aircraft are and relies on the crew to advise it of what they intend to do.
    c. The crew, acting for the carrier, determines how best to operate the flight.
    d. The pilot in command is solely responsible for the conduct of the flight.

Answer (a): The carrier, not the crew, determines how its flights are to be operated. It is a collaborative process, but ultimately, the company controls its operations through personnel authorized to exercise operational control.

Chapter 2

1. The purpose of operations specifications (or ops specs) is to
   a. Identify to FAA and itself how it will specifically comply with various provisions of the FARs.
   b. Identify to the employees how the company will accomplish certain operations.
   c. Identify for operational management how it is to manage the carrier.
   d. None of the above.

Answer (a): The purpose of the operations specifications (ops specs) is to identify to the FAA and itself how a company intends to comply with specific provisions of the FARs. It is available as guidance to all affected employees, management, and FAA.

2. Ops specs must contain
   a. Authorizations.
   b. Limitations.
   c. Certain procedures.
   d. All of the above.

Answer (d): FAR 119.7 provides that an operator must obtain operations specifications that contain the authorizations, limitations, and procedures under which each kind of operation must be conducted.

3. Operating under 14 CFR Part 121
    a. Eliminates the carrier's requirement to comply with Part 91.
    b. Requires only that the carrier comply with parts 119 and 121.
    c. Requires the carrier to comply with Part 91 as well as Part 121 unless the requirements under Part 121 are more stringent than the Part 91 requirements.
    d. None of the above.

Answer (c): All operators must comply with the general operating rules contained in Part 91. In addition, air carriers must also comply with the much more stringent rules contained in Part 121.

4. Which of the following is *not required* to be in a domestic carrier's ops specs?
    a. Names and addresses of the five largest shareholders.
    b. Registration markings of each aircraft.
    c. Other business names under which the carrier may be operating.
    d. Any authorized deviations or exemptions granted by FAA.

Answer (a): FAR 119.49(a) sets forth the required contents of the operations specifications. The list is very specific as to what must be included and it does include the names and addresses of any of the shareholders of the company.

5. Production of ops specs are now automated by FAA using what amounts to a punch card system. By doing this, the FAA intends that the ops specs of each carrier be
    a. Identical to other carriers of the same size.
    b. Tailored to suit the individual, specific needs of each carrier.
    c. Completely up to the carrier what procedures it wants to include.
    d. None of the above.

Answer (b): The automated ops specs program is intended to provide uniformity to the ops specs of various carriers while, at the same time, allowing the ops specs to be "custom fit" to the specific needs of each carrier. There will be uniformity for similar provisions, but each carrier can decide what provisions it will need in order to operate.

6. The starting point for a new Part 121 domestic carrier in setting up ops specs is to
    a. First contact a representative of the national certification team.
    b. First contact a representative of the regional certification team.
    c. First contact a representative of the local FSDO certification team.
    d. First contact the principal operations inspector assigned to that carrier.

Answer (a): The first step for a Part 121 domestic carrier is to contact the national air carrier certification team.

7. A copy of the ops specs must be maintained by the carrier at
    a. All locations where it conducts business.
    b. All locations where crew bases are located.
    c. Its general counsel's office.
    d. Its principal base of operations.

Answer (d): FAR 119.43(a) requires that the carrier keep a copy of its approved ops specs at its principal base of operations. It must also place the material into its manual and indicate that the material comes from the ops specs and that therefore compliance is mandatory.

8. A domestic carrier's ops specs are valid
    a. For 1 year from date of issue.
    b. For 2 years from date of issue.
    c. Until the carrier fails to conduct the kind of approved operation for 30 days and doesn't give FAA 5 days notice before resuming operations.
    d. Permanently, once issued.

Answer (c): Ops specs, once issued, are generally valid until suspended, surrendered, or revoked by the FAA. The one exception to this is that if a carrier fails to conduct the kind of operation approved by the ops specs for 30 days. If that happens, FAR 119.63 requires that the carrier give the FAA at least 5 working days notice and make itself available for a full inspection before resuming service.

9. A domestic carrier must get an air carrier certificate prior to operations. This is
    a. An economic approval required by the Civil Aeronautics Board.
    b. An economic approval required by DOT.
    c. A safety issue required by international treaty.
    d. A safety issue required by the FAA.

Answer (d): The air carrier operating certificate is no longer required for economic reasons. It is now only required for safety issues and is issued by the FAA.

10. If you were a ramp service supervisor for Aeromech Airlines, where would you look to find the loading instructions (procedures) for how to load a particular A-320-232 aircraft? (Refer to Aeromech Ops Specs E096.)
    a. Aeromech's ops specs.
    b. Volume 2 of the flight crew operations manual (FCOM).
    c. Volume 3 of the flight crew operations manual (FCOM).
    d. Aeromech Weight and Balance Manual revision 00.

Answer (c): Section E of Aeromech's ops specs contains information on weight and balance control. The loading schedule instructions are found in several documents. Volume 2 of the flight crew operations manual (FCOM) gives the data for the loading to be used by the weight and balance agent or flight crew. Volume 3 gives the procedures.

Chapter 3

1. As per the Part 121 requirements found in FAR 119.65, what five specific management positions are required for a Part 121 air carrier?
    a. Director of maintenance, director of quality assurance, chief pilot, director of operations and chief counsel.
    b. Director of safety, director of operations, director of maintenance, chief pilot and chief inspector.
    c. Director of operations, chairman of the board of directors, director of inflight, chief pilot, chief inspector.

d. Chief pilot, chief inspector, director of maintenance, director of safety and director of inflight.

Answer (b): Management personnel required for operations conducted under Part 121 are (1) director of safety, (2) director of operations, (3) chief pilot, (4) director of maintenance, and (5) chief inspector [FAR 119.65 (A)].

2. As per the Part 135 requirements found in FAR 119.69, what three specific management positions are required for a Part 135 air carrier?
   a. Director of safety, director of maintenance and chief pilot.
   b. Director of operations, director of safety and director of maintenance.
   c. Director of inspections, chief pilot and director of maintenance.
   d. Director of operations, chief pilot and director of maintenance.

Answer (c): Management personnel required for operations conducted under Part 135 are (1) director of operations, (2) chief pilot, and (3) director of maintenance.

3. What two required management positions, for both Part 121 and Part 135 air carriers, must be filled by a pilot holding an air transport pilot certificate (ATP)?
   a. Chief pilot and the chief inspector.
   b. Chief pilot and the director of safety.
   c. Director of operations and the chief pilot.
   d. Chief director and chief pilot.

Answer (c): The positions of chief pilot and the director of operations must be filled by a pilot holding an air transport pilot certificate [FAR 119.65(a) and (b) Part 121 and FAR 119.69(a) Part 135].

4. What minimum required management positions must be filled by a mechanic holding an airframe and power plant certificate (A&P)?
   a. Director of maintenance and the chief inspector.
   b. Chief inspector, director of safety and the director of maintenance.
   c. Director of maintenance, director of operations and the chief inspector.
   d. Director of maintenance and the director of safety.

Answer (a): The director of maintenance and the chief inspector positions must be filled by a mechanic holding an airframe and power plant certificate [FAR 119.65(a),(c), and (d) and FAR 119.69(a) and (e)].

5. What required management position is responsible for the overall *operational control* of an air carrier's flight?
   a. Chief pilot.
   b. Director of operations.
   c. Pilot in command.
   d. Director of inflight.

Answer (b): The director of operations provides operational control of all flight operations for the air carrier.

6. Which department serves to specifically implement the concept of operational control?

    a. The dispatch center.
    b. The inflight center.
    c. The maintenance control center.
    d. The director of operations office.

Answer (c): The dispatch department serves to specifically implement the concept of operational control. Dispatchers have the responsibility to plan the details of each specific flight and maintain communications with the flight at all times to keep it appraised of things such as weather, NOTAMs, operational limitations, and so forth.

7. The director of safety is required to hold which FAA certificates?
    a. Air transport pilot certificate (ATP) and airframe and power plant certificate (A&P).
    b. ATP only.
    c. A&P only.
    d. None.

Answer (d): There is no requirement for the director of safety to hold an ATP or A&P certificate.

8. FAR Part 1 defines *operational control* as?
    a. Ensuring only crewmembers trained and qualified in accordance with the applicable regulations are assigned to conduct a flight.
    b. Ensuring each flight has complied with the conditions specified for release before it is allowed to depart.
    c. The exercise of authority over initiating, conducting, and terminating a flight.
    d. Designating a pilot in command.

Answer (c): FAR 1.1 defines operational control as "the exercise of authority over initiating, conducting, and terminating a flight."

Chapter 4

1. What manuals are required to be carried aboard an air carrier aircraft operated under Part 121?

FAR 121.141 requires the AFM to be carried aboard an aircraft during Part 121 operations. Also, 121.137 requires crewmembers to have the specific parts of the manual required in 121.133 pertaining to flight operations easily accessible while performing their duties (e.g., flight operations manual including weight and balance information, performance analysis, minimum equipment list provisions).

2. What manuals are required to be carried aboard a Part 121 air carrier aircraft in supplemental operations?

FAR 121.139 requires supplemental air carriers to carry the entire manual and/or all subparts.

3. What manuals are required to be carried aboard an air carrier aircraft operated under Part 135?

FAR 135.21(g) requires a certificate holder to carry an operations manual when conducting aircraft inspections or maintenance at stations where it does not keep an approved inspection program manual. FARs 135.81 and 135.83 require the operator of an aircraft to provide an aircraft operating manual containing normal, abnormal, and emergency checklists. The manual must also include instructions on the operation of fuel, hydraulic, electrical, and mechanical systems and emergency operation of instruments and controls. Also, FAR 91.31(b) requires an FAA-approved AFM be carried aboard each aircraft for the guidance of crewmembers when conducting flight operations.

4. What parts of the manual are required to be in printed form?

   Except for the portion of the manual pertaining to maintenance, all portions must be in a paper "manual" format (FAR 121.133).

5. When is a Part 121 or Part 135 air carrier required to carry a maintenance manual onboard the aircraft?

   If a certificate holder conducts aircraft inspections or maintenance at stations where it does not keep the approved inspection manual, the maintenance manual is required to be carried aboard the aircraft.

6. When is a Part 121 supplemental air carrier required to carry a maintenance manual onboard the aircraft?

   FAR 121.139 requires supplemental air carriers to have a copy of the entire manual aboard the aircraft for use by the contract personnel at those locations. By the nature of supplemental operations, these air carriers don't operate to the same locations on a repetitive basis, so this ensures a manual will be accessible to maintenance personnel.

Chapter 5

1. What positions in an air carrier require an FAA airman's certificate?
    a. Captain, first officer and flight follower.
    b. Flight crew, flight attendants, mechanics.
    c. Cockpit crewmembers, dispatchers, mechanics.
    d. Captain, chief executive officer, dispatchers.

   Answer (c): Cockpit crewmembers, dispatchers, and mechanics require an FAA certificate (FARs 121.383, 63.3, 65.5, 65.111).

2. Which air carrier personnel are required to carry a FAA Airman's Certificate on his/her person when performing the tasks which require the certificate?
    a. Cockpit crewmembers, flight attendants, and mechanics.
    b. Mechanics, captains, first officers, head flight attendant, and dispatchers.
    c. Cockpit crewmembers, mechanics, and dispatchers.
    d. Cockpit crewmembers, dispatchers, and chief operating officer.

   Answer (c): Cockpit crewmembers, mechanics, and dispatchers are required to carry, on their person, the appropriate FAA certificate when engaged in operations covered under 121/135 (FARs 121.383, 63.3, 65.5, 65.111).

3. The mandatory retirement age for all required cockpit crewmembers is?
    a. No person may serve as a cockpit crewmember on an airplane engaged in operations under Part 121 if that person has reached his/her sixtieth birthday.
    b. No person may serve as a pilot on an airplane engaged in operation under Part 121 if that person has reached his/her sixty-second birthday.
    c. No person may serve as a pilot on an airplane engaged in operations under Part 121 if that person has reached his/her sixtieth birthday.
    d. No person may serve as a flight engineer on an airplane engaged in operations under Part 121 if that person has reached his/her sixtieth birthday.

Answer (c): No person may serve as a pilot on an airplane engaged in operations under Part 121 if that person has reached his/her sixtieth birthday [FAR 121.383(c)].

4. What is the minimum pilot crew operating under Part 121?
    a. 1
    b. 2
    c. 3
    d. 4

Answer (b): The minimum pilot crew is two pilots and the certificate holder shall designate one pilot as pilot in command and the other second in command [121.385(c)].

5. What is the minimum pilot crew operating under Part 135 in a Category II operation?
    a. 1
    b. 2
    c. 3
    d. 4

Answer (b): No person may operate an aircraft in a Category II operation unless there is a second in command of the aircraft [FARs 135.111, 121.385(c)].

6. Which is an untrue statement?
    a. An aircraft, equipped with less than 10 passenger seats, may be flown under Part 135 without a second in command if the aircraft is equipped with an operative and approved autopilot system and the use of that system is authorized by the appropriate operations specifications.
    b. An aircraft, equipped with less than 10 passenger seats, may be flown under Part 135 without a second in command if the certificate holder applies for an amendment of its operation specifications authorizing the use of an autopilot system in place of a second in command.
    c. An aircraft, equipped with less than 10 passenger seats, may be flown under Part 135 without a second in command if the certificate holder can supply proof of insurance for such 135 operations.
    d. An aircraft, equipped with less than 10 passenger seats, may be flown under Part 135 without a second in command if the pilot in command has at least 100 hours PIC time in the make and model of aircraft to be flown and has met all other applicable 135 requirements.

Answer (c): Minimum flight crew composition is determined by the approved aircraft operating limitations or aircraft flight manual and the FAA Administrator (FARs 135.99, 135.105).

7. If an aircraft is certificated with 149 seats, but only 99 passengers are aboard for a particular flight, how many flight attendants are required?
   - a. 2
   - b. 3
   - c. 4
   - d. 5

Answer (b): Three flight attendants are required (FAR 121.391).

8. If an aircraft is certificated with 275 seats, but only 249 passengers are aboard for a particular flight, how many flight attendants are required?
   - a. 7
   - b. 6
   - c. 5
   - d. 4

Answer (b): Six flight attendants are required (FAR 121.391).

9. How many flight attendants are required for an aircraft that has a payload capacity of less than 7,500 pounds and is equipped with 19 passenger seats?
   - a. 3
   - b. 2
   - c. 1
   - d. 0

Answer (d): Zero flight attendants are required (FAR 121.391).

10. During boarding and deplaning of originating and terminating flights, the FAA requires how many flight attendants be onboard the aircraft?
   - a. Two less flight attendants than the minimum number of flight attendants required for dispatch.
   - b. One less flight attendant than the minimum number of flight attendants required for dispatch.
   - c. The FAA minimum number of flight attendants required for dispatch must be onboard the aircraft during boarding and deplaning.
   - d. The FAA minimum number of flight attendants required for a stopover must be onboard during boarding and deplaning.

Answer (c): The FAA minimum number of flight attendants required for dispatch must be onboard the aircraft during boarding and deplaning (FAR 121.393).

Chapter 6

1. For the purpose of the training regulations, airplanes are broken down into three categories of aircraft called?
   - a. Group I, Group II, and Group III.
   - b. Piston aircraft, turbofan aircraft, and turbojet aircraft.
   - c. Piston aircraft, turboprop aircraft, and turbojet aircraft.
   - d. Group A, Group B, Group C.

Answer (c): For the purpose of the training regulations, airplanes are broken down into three categories of aircraft: piston, turboprop, and turbojet (FAR 121.400).

2. What type of training would be required for crewmembers that have qualified and served in the same capacity on another airplane in the same group?
    a. Programmed training.
    b. Differences training.
    c. Initial operating training.
    d. Transition training.

Answer (d): The type of training required for crewmembers who have qualified and served in the same capacity on another airplane in the same group is called transition training (FAR 121.400).

3. What type of training ensures each crewmember or dispatcher is adequately trained and currently proficient with respect to the type of airplane s/he is crewing or dispatching?
    a. Requalification training.
    b. Remedial training.
    c. Recurrent training.
    d. Initial training.

Answer (c): Recurrent training ensures each crewmember or dispatcher is adequately trained and currently proficient with respect to the type of airplane and crewmember position involved (FAR 121.427).

4. If a pilot completes initial training as a second in command (first officer) on a piece of equipment in March when would be the latest this pilot could complete recurrent training?
    a. Recurrent must be completed by the end of March of the next year.
    b. Recurrent must be completed before the 1st March of the next year.
    c. Recurrent must be completed before the end of April of the next year.
    d. Recurrent must be completed before the end of September of the same year.

Answer (c): A crewmember may complete recurrent training either during the month before or the month after the calendar month in which that training or check is required [FAR1 21.401(b)].

5. Who may conduct the required Part 121 training?
    a. Any authorized Part 141 flight school or the Part 121 training center.
    b. Either the 121 certificate holder or a company holding a FAR 142 flight training certificate may conduct the required training.
    c. Either a Part 141 flight school or Part 142 flight training center may conduct the required training.
    d. Only a company holding a FAR 142 flight training certificate.

Answer (b): The required training may be conducted by either the 121 certificate holder or a company holding a FAR 142 flight training certificate (FAR 121.402).

6. What is the recency of experience requirement for a flight engineer?
    a. A flight engineer must have at least 50 hours of flight engineer time in the same make/model aircraft within the preceding 6 months.

b. A flight engineer must have at least 50 hours of flight engineer (turbojet) time in Group II aircraft within the preceding 6 months.

c. A flight engineer must have at least 50 hours of flight engineer time in the same make/model aircraft within the preceding 120 days.

d. A flight engineer must have at least 100 hours of flight engineer time in the same make/model aircraft within the preceding 6 months.

Answer (a): A flight engineer must have at least 50 hours of flight engineer time in the same make/model aircraft within the preceding 6 months (FAR 121.453).

7. No person may serve as a pilot in command unless that pilot has received a line check within?

a. The preceding 6 calendar months.

b. The preceding 24 calendar months.

c. The preceding 120 days.

d. The preceding 12 calendar months.

Answer (d): No person may serve as a pilot in command unless that pilot has satisfactorily completed a line check within the preceding 12 calendar months.

8. When the visibility is below what value must the pilot in command make all takeoffs and landings when flying with a second in command who has less than 100 hours in the type of airplane to be flown?

a. When the visibility is below the standard takeoff minimums of 1 statute mile or 5,000 RVR.

b. When the visibility is below 3/4 statute mile or 4,000 RVR for the runway to be used.

c. When the visibility is below 1/2 statute mile or 1,800 RVR for the runway to be used.

d. When the visibility is below published Category I landing minimums.

Answer (b): If the second in command has fewer than 100 hours of flight time as second in command in operations under this part in the type airplane to be flown and the pilot in command is not a check airman, the pilot in command must make all takeoffs and landings when the visibility is below 3/4 statute mile or 4,000 RVR for the runway to be used.

9. How many hours is an aircraft dispatcher required to observe flight operations from the flight deck within the preceding 12 calendar months? May observing simulator training satisfy this requirement?

a. 5 hours, yes.

b. 12 hours, no.

c. 10 hours, no.

d. 5 hours, no.

Answer (a): An aircraft dispatcher must have, within the preceding 12 calendar months, observed flight operations from the flight deck for at least 5 hours in one of the types of aircraft in each group to be dispatched (FAR 121.463). The requirement may be satisfied by observing 5 hours of simulator training [FAR 121.463(c)].

10. How often must a pilot serving as pilot in command satisfactorily complete a proficiency check?

a. Within the preceding 24 calendar months.
b. Within the preceding 6 calendar months, also must complete a special airport qualification.
c. Must complete a proficiency check every 12 calendar months.
d. Within the preceding 12 calendar months, must also complete either simulator training or a proficiency check within the preceding 6 calendar months.

Answer (d): A pilot in command must satisfactorily complete a proficiency check or an approved simulator course within the preceding 12 calendar months and must also complete either simulator training or a proficiency check within the preceding 6 calendar months.

Chapter 7

1. A pilot is scheduled to fly for 6 consecutive days. May that pilot be scheduled to deadhead on the seventh day? Furthermore, may the pilot additionally be assigned a training period on the seventh day? Could the pilot then be required to ferry an aircraft to some destination in order to position the aircraft for some future revenue service?

Yes, to all three questions. The 7 day rest requirement or "1 in 7 rule" exists as a scheduled flight time limitation only. There is no restriction placed on consecutive days of duty. The air carrier is only required to assure a 24 consecutive hour rest period is granted before the pilot may again be used in scheduled air transportation. Regarding the ferry flight, as long as the ferry flight is conducted under FAR Part 91, the Part 121 7 day rest limitation does not apply.

2. A pilot is scheduled to deadhead on the first day of a trip. May the pilot be scheduled to fly for the next 6 days? Is the time a pilot spends en route deadheading considered rest?

Since the time spent deadheading is not considered rest, under FARs 121.471(f), 121.491, and 121.519 the pilot may not be scheduled to fly for the next 6 days unless there is a 24 consecutive hour rest period in the pilot's schedule prior to the seventh day on duty.

3. A pilot is originally scheduled for a minimum rest period of 8 hours; because of weather delays this pilot's flight has been delayed. In this circumstance would an air carrier be allowed to schedule a pilot for less than an 8 hour rest period?

No, the minimum 8 hour reduced rest period may not be further reduced. In this case, the pilot's next departure time must be delayed in order to provide an 8 hour period free from duty. A pilot must always be able to look back 24 hours and find at least an 8 hour rest period.

4. A flight crew is scheduled for a 7:45 flight. Prior to departure the company adjusts the flight time to 8:10 to compensate for headwinds. Is this flight a legal assignment?

Yes, weather conditions are beyond the control of the air carrier and the FAA does give the air carrier relief from the 8 hour schedule limitation.

5. A pilot is given the minimum reduced rest the first night of a 3 day trip. How soon must the pilot be given the required compensatory rest?

   FAR 121.471(c)(1) states: A required compensatory rest period must begin no later than 24 hours after the commencement of the reduced rest period.

6. A flight crew, because of a prior reduced rest period, is scheduled to receive compensatory rest beginning at 2130 hours. The flight crew is scheduled to complete the last leg of the day at 2115 hours; because of a ground stop ATC delay the flight crew will arrive at the final destination at 2145 hours. Can the flight crew legally depart on this last leg?

   No, the flight crew may not depart. The FAA offers no relief from the time the compensatory rest period is required to begin. If the historic block time plus any anticipated delays will have the crew arrive at the destination after 2130 hours the flight crew may not depart.

7. Is it legal for a company to require a normally scheduled pilot to be available to answer a phone call or pager during designated rest period? What if the pilot is "sitting reserve" for the month but in a designated rest period?

   The FAA defines a rest period in FAR 121.471(e). The FAA has determined rest as a continuous period of time a flight crewmember is free from all duty requirements. These duty requirements include answering the phone, pager, or email or in any way remaining in contact with the company for the reason of being available for assignment if the need arises. Also, time spent deadheading to or from a duty assignment may not be considered a rest period [FAR 121.471(f) Domestic Operations, 121.491 Flag Operations, 121.519 Supplemental Operations].

8. If during a pilot's designated rest period, the company calls to notify the pilot of an adjustment to the departure time, does this require the pilot to "reset" the clock and begin a new rest period?

   No, the pilot is not required to answer the phone during his rest period. The pilot may choose to answer the phone; this, however, would not require the company to start a new rest period.

9. A pilot is scheduled to fly 97 hours for this month (at fifteen 6.5 hour flight days). Due to circumstances beyond the control of the company, the pilot has accumulated 96 hours prior to the last scheduled duty day of the month. Is it legal for the pilot to fly the last 6.5 hour assignment?

   No, the pilot is not legal to begin the last scheduled flight day. The company would be required to alter the pilot's schedule to keep the pilot being scheduled to exceed the 100 hour per month limitation. In this example the pilot could be scheduled for a 3 hour flight day. If during the last day the pilot was delayed again and was projected to go over the scheduled 3 hours this would then be legal. Remember the "legal to start, legal to finish rule."

10. A domestically assigned pilot is scheduled to fly 97 hours for this month (at fifteen 6.5 hour flight days). Due to circumstances beyond the control of the company, the

pilot has accumulated 96 hours prior to the last scheduled duty day of the month. Is it legal for the pilot to be assigned to deadhead home on a 6.5 hour flight?

Yes, since deadhead time does not count as flight time any amount of deadhead time would be legal.

11. What is the maximum flight time allowable for a two pilot crew for the following time periods in domestic, flag, or supplemental operations? 12 calendar months? Calendar month or 30 consecutive days? 7 consecutive days? Between rest periods?

Domestic operations limitations:
1. Calendar year	*1,000 flight hours maximum*
2. Calendar month	*100 flight hours maximum*
3. 7 consecutive calendar days	*30 flight hours maximum*
4. Between rest periods	*8 flight hours maximum*

Flag operation limitations:
1. 12 calendar months	*1,000 flight hours maximum*
2. Calendar month	*100 flight hours maximum*
3. 7 consecutive day period	*32 flight hours maximum*
4. 24 consecutive hours	*8 flight hours maximum (without a rest period)*

Supplemental operation limitations:
1. Calendar year	*1,000 flight hours maximum*
2. 30 consecutive days	*100 flight hours maximum*
3. Between rest periods	*8 to <10 flight hours maximum*

12. What is the maximum duty day for a pilot in a two pilot crew flying in supplemental operations?

The maximum on duty limit is 16 hours in a 24 hour period. A pilot must always be able to look back over the last 24 hour period and find at least 8 hours of rest. Therefore, a pilot cannot exceed a 16 hour duty day.

13. Can a pilot in a two pilot crew flying in domestic operations exceed more than 8 hours of flying in a 24 hour period?

Yes, the 8 hour limitation is based on rest periods; a pilot may not fly more than 8 hours between rest periods.

14. Is a rest period required for a pilot given a domestic reserve assignment? How about an international pilot sitting reserve?

Yes, since December 1999 the FAA has required a reserve pilot to be able to look back for a scheduled rest period of at least 8 hours. If the pilot cannot find a scheduled rest period of at least 8 hours the flight assignment is not legal. International pilots are not protected by the look-back provision.

15. What is the maximum duty day for a pilot in a domestic operation?

The maximum on duty limit is 16 hours in a 24 hour period. A pilot must always be able to look back over the last 24 hour period and find at least 8 hours of rest. Therefore, a pilot cannot exceed a 16 hour duty day.

16. What is the maximum amount of duty an aircraft dispatcher may be scheduled for?

    No air carrier may schedule an aircraft dispatcher for more than 10 hours of duty.

17. What is the maximum number of hours a pilot in supplemental operations, on a three pilot crew, may be scheduled in a 24 consecutive hour period?

    No air carrier conducting supplemental operations may schedule a pilot for more than 8 hours in any 24 consecutive hour period.

18. What is the maximum number of hours a pilot assigned flying in supplemental operations may be aloft in any 30 consecutive day period, as a member of a flight crew consisting of two pilots and one additional flight crewmember?

    No air carrier conducting supplemental operations may schedule a pilot for more than 120 hours aloft during any 30 consecutive day period.

19. What is the maximum number of hours an air carrier may schedule a pilot to fly in flag operations, having two pilots and one additional flight crewmember?

    No air carrier conducting flag operations may schedule a pilot to fly for more than 12 hours during any 24 consecutive hour period.

20. What type of flying counts towards a pilot's annual, monthly, and weekly flight time limitations?

    All commercial flight time, except military, in any flight crewmember position.

Chapter 8

1. All aircraft operated by FAR 121 carriers must either be U.S. registered aircraft or
    a. Foreign aircraft operated under wet lease to the U.S. carrier.
    b. Foreign aircraft, approved under U.S. type design and operated under dry lease to the U.S. carrier.
    c. Foreign aircraft, approved under ICAO type design and operated under dry lease to the U.S. carrier.
    d. Foreign aircraft may not be operated by U.S. carriers.

    Answer (b): Airplanes operated by U.S. carriers must either be U.S. registered aircraft or foreign aircraft registered in an ICAO country and of a type design that is approved under a U.S. type certificate. Furthermore, it must comply with all airworthiness standards that would apply if it were a U.S. registered aircraft.

2. Proving tests are required of new type designs. If the design has never been proved under Part 121, it must be operated for

    a. 25 hours including 10 at night.
    b. 50 hours including 10 at night.
    c. 100 hours including 10 at night.
    d. 200 hours including 10 at night.

Answer (c): If the aircraft type has never been proven in Part 121 operations, then the carrier must perform at least 100 hours of proving flights into representative destinations and operations. The proving flights must include at least 10 hours of night flights and the total number may be reduced in some instances where an equivalent level of safety may be demonstrated to the FAA.

3. V_1, or takeoff decision speed, is the
    a. Maximum speed in the takeoff at which the pilot must first take action to stop.
    b. Maximum speed in the takeoff at which the pilot must decide to take action to stop.
    c. Maximum speed in the takeoff where a takeoff may still be initiated.
    d. Minimum speed in the takeoff where it is possible to get airborne.

Answer (a): V_1, takeoff decision speed, is the speed by which the pilot must have first taken action to stop the aircraft and still be able to do so in the remaining runway. The name is a bit misleading as it implies the decision to stop may be made anytime up to that speed and still be able to stop. This does not consider the reaction time and would result in not being able to stop on the remaining runway.

4. In the event of an engine failure at or above V_1, the pilot should achieve and maintain V_2, until
    a. 35 feet above the runway surface.
    b. The landing gear is retracted.
    c. Acceleration altitude.
    d. The airplane is established (configured) for en route climb.

Answer (c): Part 25 requires that on takeoff, in the event of an engine failure, the crew must be able to achieve a 2.4 percent climb gradient from the point the aircraft landing gear is retracted (and airspeed is at V_2) until it reaches acceleration altitude, normally 400 feet above the takeoff surface. At that point the aircraft is accelerated to allow the flaps to be retracted and the aircraft configured for en route climb.

5. Net takeoff flight path is used in computing takeoff/climb performance capability of the aircraft. What is net takeoff flight path?
    a. The climb performance of the aircraft as determined in certification testing.
    b. The climb performance of the aircraft as determined in certification testing reduced by 8 feet per 1,000 feet traveled.
    c. The climb performance of the aircraft as determined in certification testing reduced by the loss of performance in the event of an engine failure.
    d. All of the above.

Answer (b): The net takeoff flight path of the aircraft for performance planning is the actual climb performance of the airplane reduced by a "fudge factor" of 0.8 percent or 8 feet per 1,000 feet. This gives an extra margin of safety in the climb as the actual climb is slightly better than the minimum required and is increasing throughout the climb.

6. Takeoff run must be accomplished
    a. Within the length of the runway.
    b. Within the length of the runway plus stopway.
    c. Within the length of the runway plus stopway plus clearway.
    d. Within the length of the runway plus clearway (except clearway may only be counted up to one-half the length of the runway).

Answer (a): The takeoff run is analogous to the takeoff roll for light aircraft and must be accomplished within the confines of the runway surface.

7. Takeoff distance must be accomplished
    a. Within the length of the runway.
    b. Within the length of the runway plus stopway.
    c. Within the length of the runway plus stopway plus clearway.
    d. Within the length of the runway plus clearway (except clearway may only be counted up to one-half the length of the runway).

Answer (d): The takeoff distance is analogous to the total distance to clear a 50 foot obstacle for light aircraft and must be accomplished within the confines of the runway surface plus any clearway, except you may only consider clearway up to one-half the runway length.

8. Runway limit weight guarantees that an aircraft may
    a. Accelerate to V_1, lose an engine, and stop on the remaining runway.
    b. Accelerate to V_1, lose an engine, and stop on the remaining runway plus stopway.
    c. Accelerate to V_1, lose an engine, and continue the flight.
    d. None of the above.

Answer (c): Runway limit weight is the maximum weight that allows for stopping the aircraft if an engine failure occurs below V_1, and allows flight to continue if the engine failure occurs at or above V_1.

9. The maximum weight at which an air carrier aircraft may depart is limited to
    a. The maximum weight that will assure compliance with engine out climb limits.
    b. The maximum weight that will guarantee en route OEI terrain clearance.
    c. The maximum weight that will assure landing below maximum landing weight.
    d. All of the above.

Answer (d): It is important to understand that the maximum takeoff weight must consider a number of variables any one of which may be controlling (limiting). For example, on a short runway and a hot day, the runway limit may be controlling; on a hot day, the climb limit might control; and on an IFR day with a short stage length and a quite distant alternate, landing weight limits may control.

10. A turbine aircraft is scheduled into a runway that is 8,600 feet in length. May our aircraft (which will require 5,100 feet to land) land there on a wet day?
    a. Yes.
    b. No.
    c. Insufficient information to determine.

Answer (b): If our turbine aircraft requires 5,100 feet to land, then the runway must be a minimum of (5,100/0.60) = 8,500 feet. On a dry day, this would be sufficient. On a wet day, we must multiply the landing distance by 1.15 for a total distance required of 9,775 feet.

Chapter 9

1. In order to carry cargo on the passenger level in a passenger aircraft, the cargo
    a. Must be approved by the ramp services agent responsible for the flight.
    b. Must be on pallets that are securely strapped to the flooring of the aircraft.
    c. Must be secured in bins that can withstand 1.15 times the emergency landing g loads.
    d. Must be smaller than 15 pounds.

Answer (c): FAR 121.285(b) requires that passenger carrying aircraft that are used to carry cargo as well as passengers must have the cargo in approved bins that can with-stand "G" forces equal to 1.15 times the load factors applicable to emergency landing conditions. Alternatively, the cargo may be properly restrained behind a bulkhead.

2. Landing gear aural warning devices must sound a warning if
    a. A landing is attempted with the gear not locked down.
    b. Throttles are reduced for landing with the gear not locked down (only).
    c. Flaps are set for landing with the gear not locked down (only).
    d. None of the above.

Answer (a): The present regulations require that the aural warning be given at any time a landing is attempted and the gear is not locked down. The old regulation required only that the throttle position be tested.

3. To be used in Part 121 operations, aircraft with more than 44 seats must be shown to be able to conduct an evacuation in
    a. 60 seconds or less.
    b. 90 seconds or less.
    c. 120 seconds or less.
    d. No time is specified for conducting evacuations.

Answer (b): FAR 121.291 requires that Part 121 passenger aircraft with more than 44 seats be capable of being evacuated in 90 seconds or less.

4. Transport category aircraft elevators typically
    a. Are interconnected but may be operated separately in an emergency.
    b. Are rigidly interconnected and operate together as a unit.
    c. Are only connected to the control columns by electrical circuits.
    d. Are a single unit that may be operated from either the pilot or copilot seat.

Answer (a): This is one of the major design differences of Part 25 aircraft and Part 23 aircraft. The transport category aircraft must preclude the possibility of a control cir-cuit jam. One way of doing this is to use separate controls for each half of the elevator structure (ailerons and rudder as well) and allow, in emergency conditions, for these controls to be separated and operated independently.

5. The takeoff warning system of a transport category aircraft must operate from the initial portion of the takeoff (application of takeoff power) until
    a. The aircraft passes the takeoff decision speed.
    b. The aircraft passes through 500 feet on the takeoff.
    c. The aircraft is rotated for takeoff.
    d. The warning system must operate until the aircraft is properly configured.

Answer (c): The takeoff warning system must sound an alarm that is automatically activated if a takeoff is attempted and the aircraft is not properly configured for take-off. It sounds from application of takeoff power until the configuration is changed to allow for a safe takeoff, the takeoff is terminated, the warning is deactivated by the pilot, or the airplane is rotated for takeoff.

6. Under normal operating conditions the pressurized cabin of a Part 121 aircraft must maintain a maximum cabin pressure altitude of
    a. 8,000 feet
    b. 10,000 feet
    c. 12,500 feet
    d. 15,000 feet

Answer (a): Part 25 requires that pressurized compartments and cabins maintain a maximum cabin pressure altitude of 8,000 feet at the maximum operating altitude of the aircraft.

7. Which cargo compartment on a passenger airplane has fire extinguishing equipment built into the compartment that is controllable from the cockpit?
    a. Class A.
    b. Class B.
    c. Class C.
    d. Class D.

Answer (c): A Class C compartment must have both an approved smoke/fire detector system and a built-in fire extinguishing or suppression system. It is the only class compartment to require extinguishing equipment.

8. An aircraft with 254 passenger seats would require
    a. 1 fire extinguisher.
    b. 2 fire extinguishers.
    c. 3 fire extinguishers.
    d. 4 fire extinguishers.

Answer (d): Aircraft with seating capacity of 7 to 30 require one fire extinguisher; those with from 31 through 60 seats require two extinguishers; those with from 61 to 200 require three extinguishers; and those with from 201 through 300 passenger seats require four fire extinguishers.

9. A blue cockpit annunciator light would indicate
    a. Warning.
    b. Caution.
    c. Status.
    d. Exit.

Answer (c): A warning light is red, a caution light is yellow, a safe light is green, and other colors may be used (if there is no chance of confusion) for other purposes such as status of a system.

10. Cockpit voice recorders are required to continuously record the
    a. Last 15 minutes of each flight.
    b. Last 30 minutes of each flight.
    c. Last 45 minutes of each flight.
    d. Last 1 hour of each flight.

Answer (b): Cockpit voice recorders (CVRs) are required to record continuously for 30 minutes.

Chapter 10

1. The rule requiring all required, installed equipment to be operative is violated when
   a. The aircraft is started.
   b. The aircraft is taxied.
   c. The aircraft takes off.
   d. The aircraft lands.

Answer (c): The rule reads that no person may take off an aircraft with inoperative instruments or equipment installed. Of course in air carrier operations this is substantially modified by the availability of minimum equipment list relief provisions.

2. In passenger-carrying airplanes, at least two of the fire extinguishers must
   A. Be of the Halon 1211 (or equivalent) type.
   B. Be of the CO_2 type.
   C. Be of the water/pressure type.
   D. Be of the dry chemical type.

Answer (a): FAR 121.309 requires that at least two fire extinguishers aboard passenger-carrying aircraft be of the Halon 1211 type.

3. In considering the need for escape slides or similar evacuation means, the aircraft is assumed to be
   a. On the ground with collapsed landing gear.
   b. On the ground with a single collapsed landing gear.
   c. On the ground with the nose gear collapsed.
   d. On the ground with all landing gear extended.

Answer (d): FAR 121.310 requires that an approved means of evacuating the passengers be available if the emergency exit (other than over-the-wing exits) are more than 6 feet above ground with the airplane on the ground and the landing gear extended.

4. Emergency lighting for interior or exterior use must be able to be controlled at the
   a. Flight crew's station in the cockpit.
   b. A position in the passenger compartment.
   c. Both of the above.
   d. Neither of the above.

Answer (c): FAR 121.310 provides that each emergency light required for interior exit lights or exterior exit lighting be operable manually from both the flight crew station and a point in the passenger compartment that is readily accessible to a normal flight attendant seat.

5. During ground operations, it is
   a. Suggested, but not required, that each passenger be seated with his seat belt fastened.
   b. Required that each passenger be seated and belts fastened only when taking the runway.
   c. Required that each passenger be seated and belts fastened only when taking off.
   d. Required that each passenger be seated and belts fastened during all movement on the surface.

Answer (d): FAR 121.311 requires that each person on board an air carrier airplane must occupy an approved seat or berth with a separate safety belt properly secured about him or her during movement on the surface, takeoff, or landing.

6. The crew uses checklist procedures that are provided by the
   a. FAA.
   b. Manufacturer of the aircraft.
   c. Operator of the aircraft.
   d. Pilot's union.

Answer (c): FAR 121.315 provides that each certificate holder must provide flight crews with an approved cockpit check procedure for each type of aircraft that it operates.

7. Flight crewmembers must be provided and use oxygen when
   a. The cabin pressure altitude exceeds 10,000 feet.
   b. The cabin pressure altitude exceeds 12,500 feet.
   c. The cabin pressure altitude exceeds 14,000 feet.
   d. he cabin pressure altitude exceeds 15,000 feet.

Answer (a): FAR 121.329 provides that anytime the aircraft is above 10,000 feet, the flight crew must be provided and use oxygen. Answers b, c and d are the various altitudes regarding oxygen use in Part 91 operations.

8. If one pilot leaves his station at the controls, it is necessary for the other pilot to don his or her oxygen mask if the aircraft is above
   a. 12,500 feet.
   b. Flight level 250.
   c. Flight level 350.
   d. Flight level 410.

Answer (b): FAR 121.333 provides that if for any reason at any time it is necessary for one pilot to leave his station at the controls of the airplane when operating a flight altitudes above flight level 250, the remaining pilot at the controls shall put on and use his oxygen mask until the other pilot has returned to his duty station.

9. In the event of cabin pressurization failure, the crew must be provided with oxygen that allows for a total of

a. 10 minutes operation allowing descent to 10,000 feet altitude.
b. 110 minutes total operation.
c. 120 minutes total operation.
d. None of the above.

Answer (c): FAR 121.133 provides for the emergency descent after loss of pressurization. It requires that the pilots be supplied enough oxygen to comply with FAR 121.329 but not less than a 2 hour supply. This consists of enough oxygen to descend from the maximum certificated altitude to 10,000 feet in 10 minutes and then to fly at 10,000 feet for 110 minutes thereafter.

10. The flight recorder must continuously record
    a. 30 minutes of continuous data.
    b. 1 hour of continuous data.
    c. 24 hours of continuous data.
    d. 25 hours of continuous data.

Answer (d): FAR 121.343 requires that aircraft certificated for flight above 25,000 feet be equipped with flight recorders. The flight data recorder must operate continuously from the instant the aircraft begins its takeoff roll until it has completed its landing roll at an airport. The data must be kept until the aircraft has operated for at least 25 hours of operating time.

11. Traffic Alert and Collision Avoidance System—II (TCAS II) equipment is required for
    a. All Part 121 carrier aircraft.
    b. All large Part 121 aircraft.
    c. Part 121 aircraft with more than 10 seats.
    d. Part 121 aircraft with more than 30 seats.

Answer (d): FAR 121.356 provides that all air carrier aircraft that have a passenger seating configuration of more than 30 seats must be equipped with TCAS II equipment. Smaller aircraft (10 to 30 seats) need only have a less capable TCAS system.

12. The cockpit voice recorder (CVR) is required to operate starting at
    a. Engine start.
    b. Application of ground or aircraft power to the aircraft.
    c. First use of a checklist.
    d. From the time the crew is seated in the cockpit.

Answer (c): FAR 121.359 requires that the cockpit voice recorder (CVR) be operated continuously from the start of the first use of the checklist until the completion of the final checklist at the termination of the flight.

Chapter 11

1. In the case of domestic flights *each* flight must be dispatched, unless the flight was originally included in the dispatch of a multi-leg flight and the aircraft doesn't spend more than how many hours on the ground?
    a. 4 hours.
    b. 3 hours.

    c. 2 hours.

    d. 1 hour.

Answer (d): In the case of domestic flights each flight must be dispatched, unless the flight was originally included in the dispatch of a multi-leg flight and the aircraft doesn't spend more than 1 hour on the ground.

2. What information is required to appear on a Part 121 domestic or flag operator's dispatch release form?

    a. Company or organization name, make and model of aircraft, aircraft VIN number, flight number, name of each flight crewmember, departure airport, destination airport and alternate airports, minimum fuel supply, and weather reports and forecasts.

    b. Identification number of the aircraft, trip number, departure airport, intermediate stops, destination airport and alternate airports, a statement about the type of operation (e.g., VFR, IFR), minimum fuel supply, and weather reports and forecasts.

    c. Aircraft VIN number, air carrier name, make and model of aircraft, trip number, name of the pilot in command, departure airport, destination airport and alternate airports, minimum fuel supply, and weather reports and forecasts.

    d. Air carrier name, trip number, departure airport, intermediate stops, destination airport and alternate airports, a statement about the type of operation (e.g., VFR, IFR), and weather reports and forecasts.

Answer (b): The information that is required to appear on a Part 121 domestic or flag operator's dispatch release form is identification number of the aircraft, trip number, departure airport, intermediate stops, destination airport and alternate airports, a statement about the type of operation (e.g., VFR, IFR), minimum fuel supply, and weather reports and forecasts.

3. What is the main difference between the load manifest used in domestic and flag operations and the load manifest used in supplemental operations?

    a. Domestic, flag, and supplemental load manifests must contain identical information.

    b. Load manifests used in supplemental international operations may use metric measurements for weight and balance calculations.

    c. Load manifests used in supplemental international operations may use metric measurements for the calculation of fuel load only.

    d. None of the above.

Answer (a): Domestic, flag, and supplemental load manifests must contain identical information (121.693).

4. FAR 121.613 says an air carrier may not dispatch an IFR flight under Part 121 unless the weather reports and forecasts indicate that at the time of arrival at the destination airport

    a. The ceiling will be at least 1,500 feet above the lowest published instrument approach minimum for at least 1 hour before and 1 hour after the estimated time of arrival at the destination airport.

    b. The visibility and RVR will be greater than the standard takeoff minimums of 1/2 statute mile visibility or 2,400 feet RVR (runway visual range) for three or more engine airplanes and 1 statute mile visibility or 5,000 feet RVR for twin engine aircraft.

c. Conditions will be at or above the authorized landing minimums.

d. Conditions will be at or above the authorized landing minimums for at least 1 hour before and 1 hour after the estimated time of arrival at the destination airport.

Answer (c): FAR 121.613 states that no flight may be dispatched unless appropriate weather reports or forecasts, or any combination thereof, indicate that the weather conditions will be at or above the authorized landing minimums at the estimated time of arrival at the airport or airports to which the flight is dispatched or released.

5. When is a departure airport alternate airport required prior to the departure of a flight operating under 121?

a. When weather conditions are greater than the standard takeoff minimums of 1/2 statute mile visibility or 2,400 feet RVR (runway visual range) for three or more engine aircraft.

b. When weather conditions are such that an aircraft departs an airport with takeoff minimums below the departure airport's landing minimums in the certificate holder's ops specs.

c. When weather conditions are forecast to be, for at least 1 hour before and 1 hour after the estimated time of arrival at the destination airport, at or above the authorized landing minimums.

d. When the appropriate weather reports or forecasts indicate the ceiling will be at least 1,500 feet above the lowest published instrument approach minimum or lowest circling MDA.

Answer (b): When weather conditions are such that an aircraft departs an airport with takeoff minimums below the departure airport's landing minimums in the certificate holder's ops specs (FAR 121.617).

6. How are alternate airport weather minimums derived for an airport with *one* operational navigational facility providing a straight-in nonprecision approach procedure, or a straight-in precision approach procedure, or a circling maneuver from an instrument approach procedure?

a. A ceiling is derived by adding 200 feet to the authorized Category I HAT or HAA, and a visibility is derived by adding 1 statute mile to the authorized Category I landing minimum.

b. A ceiling is derived by adding 400 feet to the authorized Category I HAT or HAA, and a visibility is derived by adding 1 statute mile to the authorized Category I landing minimum.

c. A ceiling is derived by adding 200 feet to the authorized Category I HAT or HAA, and a visibility is derived by adding 1/2 statute mile to the authorized Category I landing minimum.

d. A ceiling is derived by adding 400 feet to the authorized Category I HAT or HAA, and a visibility is derived by adding 1/2 statute mile to the authorized Category I landing minimum.

Answer (b): A ceiling is derived by adding 400 feet to the authorized Category I HAT or HAA, and a visibility is derived by adding 1 statute mile to the authorized Category I landing minimum (Paragraph C.055 of an air carrier's op specs).

7. How are alternate airport weather minimums derived for an airport with at least two operational navigational facilities, each providing a straight-in nonprecision approach procedure or a straight-in precision approach procedure to different, suitable runways?

    a. A ceiling is derived by adding 200 feet to the authorized Category I HAT or HAA, and a visibility is derived by adding 1 statute mile to the authorized Category I landing minimum.

    b. A ceiling is derived by adding 400 feet to the authorized Category I HAT or HAA, and a visibility is derived by adding 1 statute mile to the authorized Category I landing minimum.

    c. A ceiling is derived by adding 200 feet to the authorized Category I HAT or HAA, and a visibility is derived by adding 1/2 statute mile to the authorized Category I landing minimum.

    d. A ceiling is derived by adding 200 feet to the higher Category I HAT of the two approaches used, and a visibility is derived by adding 1/2 statute mile to the higher authorized Category I landing minimum of the two approaches used.

Answer (d): A ceiling is derived by adding 200 feet to the higher Category I HAT of the two approaches used, and a visibility is derived by adding 1/2 statute mile to the higher authorized Category I landing minimum of the two approaches used (Paragraph C.055 of an air carrier's op specs).

8. In Part 121 domestic operations, when is a destination alternate airport required?

    a. When the destination weather is not forecast to be, from 1 hour before until 1 hour after scheduled arrival time, at least 1/2 statute mile visibility or 2,400 feet RVR (runway visual range) for three or more engine airplanes and 1 statute mile visibility or 5,000 feet RVR for twin engine aircraft.

    b. When the weather is not forecast to be better than 1,500 feet higher than the lowest published instrument minimums or 2,000 feet above airport elevations, whichever is greater. The visibility must be at least 3 miles or at least 2 miles added to the lowest published minimum visibility, whichever is greater.

    c. When the destination weather is not forecast to be, from 1 hour before scheduled arrival until 1 hour after, a ceiling of 2,000 feet and 3 statute miles visibility.

    d. When the destination weather is not forecast to be, from 1 hour before scheduled arrival until 1 hour after, a ceiling of 3,000 feet and 2 statute miles visibility.

Answer (c): Remember the "1-2-3 rule" FAR 121.619 requires that from 1 hour before scheduled arrival until 1 hour after, the weather shall be forecast to be at least a 2,000 foot ceiling and 3 statute miles visibility.

9. What are the mandatory fuel requirements for Part 121 domestic operations?

    a. A flight may not depart unless it has enough fuel to fly to the airport to which it is dispatched, then fly to the most distant alternate (if required), then fly for 45 minutes at normal cruising fuel consumption rates.

    b. A flight may not depart unless it has enough fuel to fly to the airport to which it is dispatched, then fly to the closest alternate (if required), then fly for 30 minutes at normal cruising fuel consumption rates.

    c. A flight may not depart unless it has enough fuel to fly to and land at the airport to which it is dispatched plus an additional 15 percent of the required fuel load (from departure airport to destination airport).

    d. A flight may not depart unless it has enough fuel to fly to and land at the airport to which it is dispatched plus 90 minutes of contingency fuel, if no destination alternate is required.

Answer (a): FAR 121.619 states a flight may not depart unless it has enough fuel to fly to the airport to which it is dispatched, then fly to the most distant alternate (if required), then fly for 45 minutes at normal cruising fuel consumption rates.

10. Repair "B" on a minimum equipment list requires inoperative items to be repaired within what time interval?
    a. Repair category "B" shall be repaired within the *time interval specified* in the remarks column of the certificate holder's approved MEL.
    b. Repair category "B" inoperative items shall be repaired within *3 consecutive calendar days (72 hours)* **excluding** the calendar day the malfunction was recorded in the aircraft maintenance log and/or record.
    c. Repair category "B" inoperative items shall be repaired before midnight on the *third consecutive calendar day (72 hours)* **including** the calendar day the malfunction was recorded in the aircraft maintenance log and/or record.
    d. Repair category "B" inoperative items shall be repaired within *10 consecutive calendar days (240 hours)* **excluding** the calendar day the malfunction was recorded in the aircraft maintenance log and/or record.

Answer (b): Repair category "B" inoperative items shall be repaired within 3 consecutive calendar days (72 hours) excluding the calendar day the malfunction was recorded in the aircraft maintenance log and/or record (Paragraph D.095 of an air carrier's op specs).

Chapter 12

1. Operational control may be defined as
    a. The supervision of the dispatching of flight crew by the crew scheduling department.
    b. The exercise of the FAA's inspection authority over U.S. certificated air carriers.
    c. The exercise of authority over initiating, conducting, or terminating a flight.
    d. The exercise of an air carrier's maintenance inspection authority granted under Part 145.

Answer (c): Operational control is defined as the exercise of authority over initiating, conducting, or terminating a flight (FAR 1.1).

2. Typically the authority to dispatch or release a flight is held by which position(s)?
    a. An air carrier's director of operations (DO), aircraft dispatcher, and/or pilot in command.
    b. An air carrier's chief financial officer, chief flight instructor, or principal operations inspector (POI).
    c. The pilot in command, who may delegate this authority to the aircraft dispatcher.
    d. An air carrier's crew scheduling supervisor.

Answer (a): The authority to dispatch or release a flight is held by an air carrier's director of operations, who typically delegates this duty to both the aircraft dispatcher and pilot in command (FARs 121.533, 121.535, and 121.537).

3. Prior to flight who is responsible for airplane security?
   a. The air carrier security marshal.
   b. The ground security coordinator.
   c. The airport security marshal.
   d. The ramp supervisor.

Answer (b): Prior to flight the ground security coordinator (GSC) is responsible for airplane security (FAR Part 108).

4. What is the definition of a critical phase of flight?
   a. That period during ground or flight operations anytime the cockpit-to-cabin door is closed.
   b. That period of flight involving takeoff, landing, and all flight operations conducted below 10,000 feet.
   c. That period of flight including all ground operations involving taxi, takeoff, landing, and all other flight operations conducted below 10,000 feet, unless in level cruise.
   d. That period of flight or ground operations involving taxi, takeoff, landing, and all other flight operations.

Answer (c): The FAA has established critical phases of flight to include all ground operations involving taxi, takeoff, and landing and all other flight operations conducted below 10,000 feet, unless in level cruise flight [FAR 121.542 (c)].

5. What credential(s) must an FAA air carrier inspector possess to gain access to the flight deck?
   a. Two forms of government photo ID, FAA form 110A (FAA inspector's ID card), and a driver's license or military ID .
   b. FAA form 121-548 jumpseat authorization letter, and a photo ID.
   c. An air carrier's standard jumpseat authorization form (DOT form 121-548).
   d. FAA form 110A (FAA inspector's ID card) and FAA form 8430-13 jumpseat form.

Answer (d): An FAA air carrier inspector on official duty must present FAA form 110A (FAA inspector's ID card) and FAA form 8430-13 (jumpseat form) (FAR 121.548).

6. The pilot in command of a passenger-carrying airplane that has a lockable cockpit-to-cabin door must ensure the door is closed and locked during which period of aircraft operations?
   a. The cockpit-to-cabin door must be closed during taxi, takeoff, and landing.
   b. The cockpit-to-cabin door must be closed prior to aircraft pushback and for the duration of aircraft operations.
   c. The cockpit-to-cabin door must be closed and locked during flight.
   d. The cockpit-to-cabin door must be closed and locked prior to any aircraft movement.

Answer (c): The pilot in command of a passenger-carrying airplane that has a lockable flight crew compartment door must ensure that the door is closed and locked during flight [FAR 121.587(a)].

7. What precautions must an air carrier take when transporting a passenger that requires medical oxygen?
   a. The carrier must ensure the passenger's personal oxygen canisters were manufactured in accordance with DOT 4166 oxygen safety requirements.
   b. The carrier must inspect the passenger's personal oxygen canisters to ensure they comply with the approved types authorized in the carrier's op specs.
   c. An air carrier may allow a passenger to carry and operate oxygen equipment as long as that carrier supplies the necessary equipment.
   d. The carrier must ensure the passenger's personal oxygen canisters were manufactured after December 31, 1999.

   Answer (c): An air carrier may allow a passenger to carry and operate oxygen equipment as long as that carrier supplies the necessary equipment [FAR 121.574(a)(1i)].

8. When a twin engine aircraft suffers engine failure or an engine is shut down in flight as a precautionary measure to prevent possible damage, the pilot in command is required to do what two things?
   a. Inform air traffic control of the engine failure or in flight shutdown and contact the person responsible for operational control for instructions.
   b. Land the airplane at the nearest suitable airport, in nautical miles, at which a safe landing can be made and notify the appropriate ATC facility as soon as practicable after the engine failure or in flight shutdown.
   c. Inform air traffic control of the engine failure or in flight shutdown and request immediate clearance to nearest airport with appropriate maintenance facilities.
   d. Land the airplane at the nearest suitable airport, *in point of time*, at which a safe landing can be made, and notify the appropriate ATC facility as soon as practicable after the engine failure or in flight shutdown.

   Answer (d): When a twin engine aircraft suffers engine failure or an engine is shutdown in flight as a precautionary measure to prevent possible damage, the pilot in command is required to land the airplane at the nearest suitable airport, in point of time, at which a safe landing can be made, and notify the appropriate ATC facility as soon as practicable after the engine failure or in flight shutdown.

Chapter 13

1. Air carriers operating under Part 121 are required to maintain current employee records of:
   a. Certified airframe and power plant mechanics and flight crewmembers.
   b. Mechanics and repairmen authorized to complete an airworthiness release certificate.
   c. Aircraft dispatchers and security screening personnel.
   d. Aircraft dispatchers and crewmembers.

   Answer (d): Air carriers operating under Part 121 are required to maintain current records of aircraft dispatchers and crewmembers (121.683).

2. Air carriers operating under Part 121 must maintain a current list of each aircraft that

a. The certificate holder operates domestically and/or internationally.
b. The certificate holder owns; leased aircraft are not required to appear on the list.
c. The certificate holder operates in scheduled air transportation.
d. The certificate holder operates in revenue operations.

Answer (c): Air carriers operating under Part 121 must maintain a current list of each aircraft that the certificate holder operates in scheduled air transportation (FAR 121.685).

3. What information is required to appear on a Part 121 domestic or flag operator's dispatch release form?
    a. Identification number of the aircraft, trip number, departure airport, intermediate stops, destination airport and alternate airports, a statement about the type of operation (e.g., VFR, IFR), minimum fuel supply, weather reports and forecasts.
    b. Company or organization name, make and model of aircraft, aircraft VIN number, flight number, name of each flight crewmember, departure airport, destination airport and alternate airports, minimum fuel supply, weather reports and forecasts.
    c. Aircraft VIN number, air carrier name, make and model of aircraft, trip number, name of the pilot in command, departure airport, destination airport and alternate airports, minimum fuel supply, weather reports and forecasts.
    d. Air carrier name, trip number, departure airport, intermediate stops, destination airport and alternate airports, a statement about the type of operation (e.g., VFR, IFR), weather reports and forecasts.

Answer (a): The information that is required to appear on a Part 121 domestic or flag operator's dispatch release form is identification number of the aircraft, trip number, departure airport, intermediate stops, destination airport and alternate airports, a statement about the type of operation (e.g., VFR, IFR), minimum fuel supply, and weather reports and forecasts.

4. What is the main difference between the load manifest used in domestic and flag operations and the load manifest used in supplemental operations?
    a. Domestic, flag and supplemental load manifests must contain identical information.
    b. Load manifests used in supplemental international operations may use metric measurements for weight and balance calculations.
    c. Load manifests used in supplemental international operations may use metric measurements for the calculation of fuel load only.
    d. None of the above.

Answer (a): Domestic, flag, and supplemental load manifests must contain identical information (FAR 121.693).

5. What paperwork is the pilot in command required by 121 subpart V to carry aboard an airplane to its destination for domestic and flag operations?
    a. Completed load manifest, minimum fuel load calculations, flight plan.
    b. Completed load manifest, dispatch release, communications logbook.
    c. Completed load manifest, dispatch release, flight plan.
    d. Dispatch release, service interruption report, flight plan, crewmember records.

Answer (c): The pilot in command is required by 121 Subpart V to carry aboard an airplane to its destination a completed load manifest, dispatch release, and flight plan (FAR 121.695).

6. What additional paperwork items is the pilot in command required by 121 subpart V to carry aboard an airplane to its destination for supplemental operations?
    a. Pilot route certification, airworthiness release and a flight release instead of a dispatch release.
    b. Flight following paperwork, airworthiness release, and international route authority.
    c. Airworthiness release.
    d. None of the above.

Answer (a): Additionally the pilot in command of an aircraft in supplemental operations is required by 121 Subpart V to carry aboard an airplane to its destination pilot route certification paperwork, airworthiness release, and a flight release instead of a dispatch release (FAR 121.697).

7. The FAA requires an air carrier to maintain a record of each dispatch release or flight release for a period of
    a. 60 days.
    b. 30 days.
    c. 6 months.
    d. 3 months.

Answer (d): Certificate holders are required by FARs 121.695(b) and 121.697(e) to maintain copies of the dispatch release or flight release, load manifest, and flight plan for a period of 3 months.

8. Air carriers are required to maintain a record of service difficulty reports for a period of
    a. 30 days.
    b. 3 months.
    c. 6 months.
    d. 10 days.

Answer (a): Air carriers are required to maintain a record of service difficulty reports for a period of 30 days [FARs 121.703(d) and 121.704(c)].

9. Who is allowed to sign an aircraft's airworthiness release certificate?
    a. Only the pilot in command or a certificated mechanic.
    b. The authorized certificated mechanic or repairman.
    c. A certificated repairman and the pilot in command.
    d. The air carrier's operations inspector or designated principal operations inspector.

Answer (b): An airworthiness release may be signed by an authorized certificated mechanic or repairman except that a certificated repairman may sign the release or entry only for the work for which he is employed and certificated.

10. An air carrier is required to maintain a record of each en route radio contact between the certificate holder and its pilots for what period of time?

    a. For a period of 90 days.
    b. For a period of 60 days.
    c. For a period of 2 years.
    d. For a period of 30 days.

Answer (d): An air carrier is required to maintain a record of each en route radio contact between the certificate holder and its pilots for a period of 30 days (FAR 121.711).

11. A Part 135 certificate holder must maintain a current list of aircraft used or available for use and the operations for which each is equipped for how long?
    a. For a period of 90 days.
    b. For a period of 6 calendar months.
    c. For a period of 2 years.
    d. For a period of 30 days.

Answer (b): As are 121 air carriers, Part 135 certificate holders are required by FAR 135.63(a) to maintain a current list of aircraft used or available for use and the operations for which each is equipped. Furthermore, the certificate holder must keep this record for at least 6 calendar months.

12. Each certificate holder is required to keep an individual record of each pilot or required flight attendant used in Part 135 operations for a period of
    a. At least 3 calendar months.
    b. At least 60 days.
    c. At least 12 calendar months.
    d. At least 24 calendar months.

Answer (c): Each certificate holder is required to keep an individual record of each pilot used in Part 135 operations for a period of at least 12 calendar months. An individual record for each flight attendant who is required under the applicable Part 135 regulations must also be maintained for a period of at least 12 months [FAR 135.63(a)].

Chapter 14

1. If repair work is "farmed out" to an outside maintenance repair organization under an approved contract, who is responsible for the airworthiness of the repair?
    a. The maintenance repair organization.
    b. The air carrier certificate holder.
    c. The FAA.
    d. Both A and B are jointly responsible.

Answer (b): The FARs are very clear that the certificate holder is responsible for the airworthiness of its aircraft and, further, that this responsibility may not be delegated.

2. The air carrier certificate holder may delegate the responsibility for the repair of its aircraft to
    a. Another Part 121 certificate holder repair station.
    b. A Part 145 FAA authorized repair station.
    c. Both A and B are permitted.
    d. Neither A nor B is permitted.

Answer (c): While the carrier may not delegate the responsibility for assuring airworthiness of its aircraft, it may delegate the actual maintenance work to be done. It may delegate the work to either another Part 145 carrier or to an FAA approved Part 145 maintenance facility.

3. The air carrier certificate holder may delegate the responsibility for airworthiness of its aircraft to
   a. Another Part 121 certificate holder repair station.
   b. A Part 145 FAA authorized repair station.
   c. Both A and B are permitted.
   d. Neither A nor B is permitted.

Answer (d): As stated above, the carrier may not delegate the responsibility for airworthiness to any other party.

4. Organizationally, the maintenance and inspection functions of a carrier
   a. Must be combined into a single department under the director of maintenance to assure control of the program.
   b. Must place the maintenance department under the inspection department to emphasize the relative importance of inspection vis-à-vis maintenance.
   c. May place the maintenance and inspection functions wherever is most feasible for the company operations.
   d. Must place the maintenance function and the inspection function in separate organizations at the operational level of the company.

Answer (d): The maintenance and inspection functions must be separated (organizationally) at the operational level. The separation must occur below the level of administrative control at which overall responsibility for the required inspection functions and other maintenance and alteration functions is exercised.

5. The maintenance program for each aircraft is described in the carrier's
   a. Ops specs.
   b. Maintenance manual.
   c. Management manual.
   d. Flight operations manual.

Answer (b): The ops specs provide the general outline of responsibility for the maintenance program while the approved maintenance manual of the airline provides the detailed information of how specific tasks are to be performed.

6. Records to show that all requirements for issuing a maintenance release have been met must be kept available for inspection for a period of
   a. 30 days.
   b. 90 days.
   c. 1 year.
   d. Forever and transferred with the aircraft if it is sold.

Answer (c): Minor repairs such as those needed to return an aircraft to service (issue a maintenance release) must be retained until the work is repeated or 1 year, whichever is longer.

7. Records to show that the aircraft was overhauled must be kept for a period of
    a. 30 days.
    b. 90 days.
    c. 1 year.
    d. Forever and transferred with the aircraft if it is sold.

Answer (d): Records of major repairs such as an airframe overhaul must be kept forever and must be transferred with the aircraft when it is sold.

8. The mechanic for an airline (that has set up its maintenance under FAR 121.379) that changes a DC generator on an engine must hold
    a. An airframe certificate.
    b. A power plant certificate.
    c. An airframe and power plant certificate.
    d. He needn't hold any airman's certificate.

Answer (d): Since the carrier has set up its maintenance under FAR 121.379 it is operating as a repair station. In that case, the individual person doing the work need not hold an airman certificate. Rather, the person supervising the maintenance must hold the appropriate airman certificate. In this case we are relying on the certificate of the carrier for accountability.

9. Maintenance and inspection training
    a. Is required at all Part 121 carriers.
    b. Is required only if the carrier has contracted its maintenance to a Part 145 maintenance repair facility.
    c. Is only suggested for Part 121 carriers but required for Part 145 facilities.
    d. None of the above.

Answer (a): Maintenance and inspection training is part of the ongoing quality assurance programs required by the FAA.

10. If a Part 121 carrier contracts its maintenance work out to a foreign Part 145 maintenance facility, then that facility must provide its workers
    a. 1 day off every 7 days.
    b. 4 days off every calendar month.
    c. 1 week off every calendar year.
    d. It is not required to provide its workers any time off.

Answer (d): The foreign repair station is subject to the U.S. FAA's aviation regulations but is not subject to U.S. labor laws. There is no specific requirement under U.S. law that the repair station provide days off. Of course the facility is subject to its own local labor laws.

Chapter 15

1. If a new-hire pilot wished to know what maneuvers would be covered in his initial aircraft training, a good place to look would be

a. The relevant provisions of Part 61: Certification of Airmen.
b. The relevant provisions of Part 121: Subpart N: Air Carrier Training Requirements.
c. The relevant provisions of Part 121: Subpart O: Crewmember Qualification.
d. Part 121 Appendix E: Flight Training Requirements

Answer (d): Appendix E to Part 121 contains all of the required training for pilot initial, upgrade, and transition training. It is a very useful document for the newly hired pilot to use because he can become familiar with the scope of training to be performed.

2. Which level of simulation has the greatest degree of fidelity to the aircraft?
   a. Level B.
   b. Level C.
   c. Level D.
   d. None of the above.

Answer (c): Referring to figure 15.1, you can see that the highest level of fidelity available in a certificated flight simulator is found in a Level D simulator.

3. Which level of simulation may be used to meet the training requirements for landings?
   a. Level B.
   b. Level C.
   c. Level D.
   d. All of the above.

Answer (d): Refer to Appendix H. This appendix specifies all of the training and checking that can be performed in a simulator. Levels B, C, and D may all be used for some (or all) of the required landings.

4. If you are a flight instructor for a small flight school and it conducts sightseeing flights for hire, must you have a drug testing program?
   a. Yes.
   b. No.
   c. Insufficient information to determine.

Answer (a): This is one of the most surprising requirements in the FAR! FAR 135.1 requires small, Part 91 operators that give sightseeing rides (using the 25 mile exception to Part 135) to perform Part 121 Appendix I drug testing! Read the regulations carefully!

5. Which of the following require drug testing at a Part 121 carrier?
   a. Flight attendants.
   b. Ground security coordinators.
   c. Pilots.
   d. All of the above.

Answer (d): All safety-sensitive positions require drug and alcohol testing. All of the above positions are included on the list in Appendix I of safety-sensitive employees.

6. Pre-employment drug testing is required by the FAA of
   a. All newly hired pilots.
   b. All newly hired customer service agents.

c. Airport ticket office manager.
d. All of the above.

Answer (a): Of the above listed positions, only the pilots are carried as safety sensitive for purposes of Appendix I. While a company may elect to test the other individuals, it may do so only as permitted by local law. It is not exempted from local laws for non–safety related employees.

7. Reasonable cause drug testing
   a. Can be instituted at any time by the carrier.
   b. Requires at least two of the employee's supervisors to concur in the testing decision.
   c. Requires a medical review officer to concur in the testing decision.
   d. Is unavailable unless the employee has a documented history of drug abuse.

Answer (b): Reasonable cause drug testing may be performed only after at least two of the employee's supervisors have seen acts leading to suspicion of drug usage. At least one of these supervisors must have been trained in detection in the symptoms of drug use.

8. If a pilot fails two drug tests
   a. He must undergo drug rehabilitation for at least 1 year before returning to duty.
   b. He must undergo 6 months of rehabilitation and peer counseling and review.
   c. He is forbidden to act as pilot in command until he has been drug free for 6 months.
   d. He is forever barred from acting as a commercial pilot for any company.

Answer (d): This is the capital punishment of airline employees, especially pilots. If a pilot fails two drug tests, he can never again work for any employer in the same safety-sensitive position.

9. The blood alcohol concentration that is considered as operating under the influence of alcohol for FAR purposes is
   a. 0.04.
   b. 0.4.
   c. 0.8.
   d. 1.0.

Answer (a): Refer to Appendix J. The level of blood alcohol content that triggers a determination of alcohol usage is 0.04 percent.

10. After an accident, the employer must administer an alcohol test to any relevant employees within
    a. 1 hour after the accident.
    b. 2 hours after the accident.
    c. 4 hours after the accident.
    d. 8 hours after the accident.

Answer (b): Appendix J gives the employer up to 2 hours to test an employee for alcohol after an accident. If it doesn't do so, it must establish and maintain records that show why the testing was not performed.

Glossary of Terms

The following glossary defines terms used in this book. Other definitions may be found in the *FAR Part 1, Definitions and Abbreviations*, the *Aeronautical Information Manual* and *The Air Transportation Operations Inspector's Handbook* (chapter 4).

ACARS: An automated communication and reporting system allowing an aircraft-to-company automated data link. This system enables data transmissions between the airplane and a ground station using a VHF network.

Accelerate/stop distance: The amount of runway distance required to accelerate the aircraft to a point *immediately prior* to V_1, lose an engine, take the first action to stop the airplane and come to a complete stop on the remaining runway and stopway.

Acceleration altitude: The minimum altitude during departure (usually 400 feet above the takeoff surface) to which the airplane must be climbed before pitch may be lowered for the purpose of accelerating to a speed at which takeoff flaps may be raised.

Administrator: The Federal Aviation Administrator or any person to whom he has delegated his authority.

Advanced qualification program (AQP): A type of voluntary training program that offers an alternative to the traditional Part 121 crewmember training and checking requirements. AQP curriculum covers indoctrination, qualification, and continuing qualification training.

Age 60 rule: The rule that prohibits the use of pilots in Part 121 operations after they reach the age of 60 years old.

Air carrier: A person who undertakes directly by lease, or other arrangement, to engage in air transportation.

Air carrier district office (Old term): An FAA field office serving an assigned geographical area, staffed with Flight Standards personnel serving the aviation industry and general public on matters of scheduled air carriers and other large aircraft operations.

Air commerce: Interstate, overseas, or foreign air commerce or the transportation of mail by aircraft or any operation or navigation of aircraft within the limits of any federal airway, or any operation or navigation of aircraft which directly affects or which may endanger safety in interstate, overseas, or foreign air commerce.

Airplane flight manual (AFM): A manual prepared by the manufacturer and approved by the FAA. The AFM is designed to give a flight crew all of the operational and performance information it needs in order to operate the aircraft safely.

Air transportation: Interstate, overseas, or foreign air commerce or the transportation of mail by aircraft.

Airways navigation facilities: Those ICAO standard navigation aids (VOR, VOR/DME, and/or NDB) which are used to establish the en route airway structure. These facilities are also used to establish the degree of navigation accuracy required for air traffic control and Class I navigation.

Airworthiness directive (AD): An airworthiness directive is a form of communication used by the FAA to notify aircraft owners and operators of unsafe conditions that may exist because of design defects, maintenance, or other cases and to specify the conditions under which the product may continue to be operated. An AD is a regulatory requirement, just like any FAR.

Airworthiness release: A required logbook entry returning an aircraft to service after maintenance, preventive maintenance, or alterations were performed on an aircraft.

Airworthiness responsibility: Responsibility by an air carrier for assuring compliance with manual procedures and company policies relating to airworthiness. This responsibility may not be delegated by the air carrier.

Alternate airport: An airport which the aircraft dispatcher, flight follower, or captain may designate to be used if weather conditions at the departure or intended destination are less than required or if a landing at the intended airport becomes inadvisable. When an alternate is required for a flight, that airport designated as an alternate for destination or as a takeoff alternate must meet the requirements for alternate airports in the operations specifications paragraph C55.

Alternate airport (weather) minimums: The minimum forecast ceiling and visibility required to permit an airport to be listed (filed) as an alternate airport in a flight plan. (See *standard alternate minimums* and *derived alternate (weather) minimums*.)

Alternate fuel: The fuel necessary for a flight to make a missed approach at the destination airport, fly from the destination to the most distant alternate airport, make an IFR approach (if available forecasts indicate conditions will be below VFR minimums), and make a landing.

Auto flight guidance system (AFGS): Aircraft systems, such as an autopilot, autothrottles, displays, and controls, that are interconnected in such a manner so as to allow the crew to automatically control the aircraft's lateral and vertical flight path and speed. A flight management system is sometimes associated with an AFGS.

Balanced field length: The amount of runway and stopway that allows an aircraft to accelerate to V_1, lose an engine, and then either stop on the remaining runway or continue with guaranteed obstacle clearance.

Basic FAR Part 135 operator: A basic FAR Part 135 operator is a certificate holder who will use more than one pilot in command and will be authorized, because of the operator's limited size and scope, certain deviations from the manual content, management personnel, and training program curriculum requirements of FAR Part 135. Normally, a deviation will not be granted to operators intending to use more than five pilots, including seconds in command; or more than five aircraft; or more than three different types of aircraft; or who intend to use check airmen; or aircraft type-certificated for more than nine passenger seats; conduct Category II or III approach operations; or conduct operations outside the United States, Canada, Mexico, and the Caribbean.

Cargo compartment classification: A system of classifying cargo compartments according to the fire detection and protection capabilities installed.

Category I instrument approach: Any authorized precision or nonprecision instrument approach which is conducted with a minimum height for IFR flight not less than 200 feet above the touchdown zone and a minimum visibility of not less than 1/2 statute mile.

Ceiling: The height above the ground or water of the base of the lowest layer of clouds that is reported as broken, overcast, or obscuration, and not classified as "thin" or "partial." Partial obscuration (-X), thin broken (-BKN), and thin overcast (-OVC) do not constitute a ceiling.

Certificate holder: A person holding an FAA operating certificate when that person engages in scheduled passenger or public charter passenger operations or both.

Certificate-holding district office: The flight standards district office that has responsibility for administering the certificate and is charged with the overall inspection of the certificate holder's operations.

Chief executive officer: The CEO's primary duty is the relationship between the air carrier and the board of directors of the company and the oversight of senior financial matters.

Chief operating officer: Ensures a successful working relationship is maintained between various top air carrier management positions.

Chief pilot: Position responsible for the supervision of all the air carrier's pilots.

Class I navigation: Any en route flight operation or portion of an operation that is conducted entirely within the operational service volumes of ICAO standard airway navigation facilities. Class I navigation also includes en route flight operations over routes designated with an "MEA GAP" (or the ICAO equivalent).

Class II navigation: Any en route flight operation which is not defined as Class I navigation. Class II navigation is any en route operation that takes place outside the service volume of ICAO standard airway navigation facilities. Class II navigation does not include operations within an "MEA GAP."

Clearway: An area beyond the runway, not less than 500 feet wide, centrally located about the extended centerline of the runway and under the control of the airport authorities.

Climb limit weight: The maximum weight that still guarantees an aircraft can proceed from the point 35 feet above the runway to 1,500 feet above the runway surface (or specified higher altitude) while maintaining required climb gradients in order to achieve adequate obstacle clearance.

Commercial operator: A person who, for compensation or hire, engages in the carriage by aircraft in air commerce of persons or property.

Common carriage: Any operation for compensation or hire in which an operator holds itself out (by advertising or any other means) as willing to furnish transportation for any member of the public who seeks the services that the operator is offering. The operator openly offers service for a fee to any member of the public.

Commuter operation: A common carriage passenger-carrying operation using aircraft having a maximum seating configuration of 30 seats or less, excluding any required pilot-in-command seat, and a maximum payload capacity of 7,500 pounds or less, with a frequency of operations of at least five round trips per calendar week on at least one route between two or more points.

Company flight manual: An airplane flight manual (AFM) developed by and/or for a specific operator.

Configuration deviation list (CDL): Similar to an aircraft's minimum equipment list (MEL), an FAA-approved CDL contains allowances and limitations for aircraft to operate without secondary airframe or engine parts while still being considered airworthy.

Contingency fuel: The increment of fuel necessary for a flight to compensate for any known traffic delays and to compensate for any other condition that may delay the landing of the flight.

Crewmember: A person assigned to perform duty in an aircraft during flight time.

Crew resource management (CRM) training: Training that focuses on the interrelationships between crewmembers, dispatch, maintenance, FAA, and other agencies. It is especially designed to help crewmembers learn to communicate effectively and to use all available resources when dealing with in flight problems or emergencies.

Cockpit voice recorder (CVR): A device which records the words of each flight crewmember, the radio communications, and the general ambient cockpit noises and speech.

Decision altitude (height) [DA/(H)]: With respect to the operation of aircraft, the specified minimum altitude at which a decision must be made, during an ILS or PAR instrument approach, to either continue the approach or execute a missed approach.

Derived alternate (weather) minimums: A method by which the weather minimums required to file an airport as an alternate airport may be reduced from the standard requirements of 600 feet and 2 statute miles for a precision approach and 800 feet and 2 miles for a nonprecision approach.

Deviation authority: The authority granted by the FAA to operate an aircraft outside of FAR compliance in order to perform operations under a military contract or emergency circumstance.

Differences training: The training required for crewmembers and dispatchers who have qualified and served on a particular type airplane when the FAA determines that differences training is necessary before a crewmember serves in the same capacity on a particular variation of that airplane (e.g., a pilot qualified on the 767-200 for a given company must receive training on the differences of a 767-400 before flying that new model).

Direct air carrier: Defined in FAR 119.3 as a person who provides or offers to provide air transportation and who has operational control over the operational functions performed in providing that transportation.

Director of maintenance: Position responsible for all air carrier maintenance and inspection personnel.

Director of operations: Position responsible for ensuring all flight operations are conducted safely and in compliance with all FARs, op specs, and company policies.

Director of safety: Position responsible for the overall safety functions required of a Part 121 air carrier. Conducts safety reviews of all functions including public safety, security, maintenance, and flight operation.

Dispatcher: An airline employee who is responsible for authorizing the departure of an aircraft. The dispatcher must ensure, among other things, that the aircraft's crew has all the proper information necessary for their flight and that the aircraft is in proper mechanical condition. The dispatcher shares responsibility with the pilot in command for the dispatch of every flight.

Dispatcher resource management (DRM) training: Training that focuses on the interrelationships between crewmembers, dispatch, maintenance, FAA, and other agencies. It is especially designed to help dispatchers learn to communicate effectively and to use all available resources when dealing with in flight problems or emergencies.

Dispatch release: A document to be carried on board an air carrier's flight containing at least the following information: identification number of the aircraft, trip or flight number, departure airport, destination airport, alternate airport, any intermediate stops, a statement concerning type of flight (e.g., IFR/VFR), and minimum fuel supply.

Domestic operation: Any scheduled passenger-carrying operation conducted between any points within the 48 contiguous states of the United States and the District of Columbia by any U.S. citizen engaged in common carriage using airplanes having a passenger seating configuration of more than 30 seats, excluding any required crewmember seat, or a payload capacity of more than 7,500 pounds.

Driftdown altitude: The lowest altitude where an aircraft can maintain a net flight path that allows the aircraft to clear all terrain and obstructions within 5 statute miles by at least 2,000 feet vertically and with a positive slope at 1,500 feet above the airport.

Dry lease: An aircraft leased without a crew.

En route fuel: The fuel necessary for a flight to reach the airport to which it is dispatched and to conduct one instrument approach.

Essential air service: Government subsidized airline service to rural areas of the United States, which continued after the Airline Deregulation Act of 1978.

ETA: The estimated time of arrival of a flight at its intended destination.

Evacuation demonstration: Operators of aircraft with 44 or more seats must demonstrate that the carrier is able to evacuate the entire aircraft in 90 seconds or less.

Extended overwater operations: Those flights conducted at a horizontal distance of more than 50 nautical miles from the nearest shoreline.

Extended-range twin-engine operations (ETOPS): ETOPS certification allows a twin-engine aircraft to operate over routes devoid of any suitable alternate/diversionary airports within 120 to 180 minutes flying time.

FARs: Federal Aviation Regulations, Title 14 of the U.S. Code of Federal Regulations.

First segment climb: Begins at brake release and ends at a point after takeoff where the speed is V_2 and the landing gear has finished retracting. This will be at an altitude of more than 35 feet above the runway surface and at an airspeed of V_2. During first segment climb the aircraft is only required to demonstrate a *positive rate of climb* after liftoff. During this portion of the departure, the crew is not expected nor required to do anything except fly the airplane.

Flag operation: Any scheduled passenger-carrying operation conducted to any point outside the 48 contiguous states of the United States and the District of Columbia by any U.S. citizen engaged in common carriage using airplanes having a passenger seating configuration of more than 30 seats, excluding any required crewmember seat, or a payload capacity of more than 7,500 pounds.

Flight control: Similar to a dispatch office, a flight control office is responsible for operational control of all aircraft, including monitoring the status and activity of each individual airplane.

Flight crewmember: A pilot, flight engineer, or flight navigator assigned to duty in an aircraft during flight time.

Flight follower: A person who performs the duties required to exercise operational control over a supplemental air carrier or Part 135 operator's flight.

Flight following: The exercise of performing operational control over a supplemental air carrier or Part 135 operator's flight.

Flight management system (FMS): An integrated system used by flight crews for flight planning, navigation, performance management, aircraft guidance, and flight progress monitoring. [Also called a flight management computer system (FMCS).]

Flight operations quality assurance (FOQA): A program air carriers use to collect and analyze digital flight data of actual line aircraft operations.

Flight plan: A required planning document that covers the expected operational details of a flight such as destination, route, fuel onboard, and so forth. It is filed with the appropriate FAA air traffic control facility.

Flight recorder: An instrument or device that records information about the performance of an aircraft in flight or about conditions encountered in flight.

Flight standards district office (FSDO): An FAA field office serving an assigned geographical area and staffed with Flight Standards personnel who serve the aviation industry and general public on matters relating to the certification and operation of air carrier and general aviation aircraft.

Flight time: Pilot time that commences when an aircraft moves under its own power for the purpose of flight and ends when the aircraft comes to rest at the next point of landing.

Fourth segment climb: Begins with the climb configuration and airspeed set and ends (normally) at 1,500 feet above the surface. During fourth segment climb a twin-engine aircraft must be able to maintain a net takeoff flight path *minimum climb gradient of 1.2 percent or 12 feet per 1,000 feet traveled.*

Free flight: A flight capability in which operators have the freedom to select a path and speed in real time. Air traffic restrictions are imposed only to ensure separation, to preclude exceeding airport capacity, to prevent unauthorized flight through special use airspace, and to ensure safety of flight. Restrictions are limited in extent and duration to correct the identified problem.

Fuel burn: The total burnoff of fuel from the departure airport to the destination airport and to land. Included in this figure is precomputed fuel for taxi to and from a given runway. An air carrier uses some precomputed fuel burns for frequently flown routes.

General maintenance manual (GMM): The GMM is prepared by the air carrier or aircraft manufacturer and covers the airworthiness information for a particular model of aircraft.

General operations manual (GOM): The GOM is a company manual that contains flight operations material not related specifically to a particular aircraft's operation. The GOM includes information such as policies, procedures, and guidance necessary for flight operations personnel to perform their duties with the highest degree of safety.

Global positioning system (GPS) landing system (GLS): GLS is a differential GPS-based landing system providing both vertical and lateral position fixing capability.

Ground proximity warning system (GPWS): A device that can detect certain hazardous conditions and warn the crew. Conditions such as too rapid closure to the ground (sink rate), being too close to the ground (terrain), or going below the approach flight path (glide slope) will be called to the crew's attention through a verbal annunciator.

Group I airplanes: For the purposes of 121 Subpart N, Group I airplanes are piston or turboprop airplanes.

Group II airplanes: For the purposes of 121 Subpart N, Group II airplanes are turbofan or turbojet airplanes.

HAZMAT: Hazardous materials. There are many state and federal regulations and company policies addressing acceptance, handling, and documentation of hazardous materials.

High minimums captain: A captain with less than 100 hours of pilot in command time in the type of aircraft s/he is operating. A high minimums captain must add 100 feet and 1/2 statute mile to the landing minimums appearing in the operator's op specs.

Holding out: A term used to describe offering to the public the carriage of persons and property for hire either intrastate or interstate (e.g., advertising, using a booking agent).

Indoctrination training: The initial training a crewmember receives as a new hire. *"Indoc"* includes training on the subject of company policies, procedures, and paperwork.

Initial operating experience (or IOE): A period of time that a new crewmember (new to the operation, not necessarily the company) flies while under the direct supervision of a qualified check pilot.

Initial training: The training required for crewmembers and dispatchers who have not qualified and served in the same capacity on another airplane of the same group.

JAA JAR-OPS-1: European Joint Aviation Authorities (JAA) Joint Aviation Requirements (JAR) operational agreements (OPS). The European JAA adopted common operational guidance for all member states in order to harmonize the rules within those states. JAR-OPS-1 is Part 1 of the operational agreement applicable to commercial air transportation fixed wing aircraft.

Landing gear aural warning device: An aural warning device that functions continuously or is periodically repeated if a landing is attempted when the landing gear is not locked down.

Landing minimums: The necessary visibility for an instrument approach for a particular runway. This value controls whether an air carrier may initiate or complete an instrument approach under existing weather conditions.

Line check: Routine evaluation of a crewmember's skills while operating live, line flights. These check rides are conducted in the normal course of business by company check airmen and consist of observations of one or more legs.

Line oriented flight training (LOFT): Flight training designed to instill a team attitude on the flight deck and evaluate an entire crew's performance instead of individual crewmembers.

Load manifest: A document containing the weight of a loaded aircraft, total weight computed under approved procedures, evidence the aircraft is loaded within center of gravity limits, and names of passengers unless that list is maintained by the air carrier.

Low-level windshear advisory system: Airborne windshear detection, warning, and avoidance equipment.

Maintenance: Includes inspection, overhaul, repair, preservation, and the replacement of parts, but excludes preventive maintenance.

Maintenance ferry flight: A maintenance ferry flight operating under the authority of the director of maintenance or his representative and applicable FARs. Such a flight must be issued a maintenance ferry flight authorization specifying the limitations and conditions under which it is to operate. A maintenance ferry flight is not to be confused with a repositioning flight.

Maintenance repair organization (MRO): An air carrier repair station certificated under Part 145, allowing it to perform maintenance and alterations for itself or other carriers.

Maintenance training program: A training program designed to ensure all maintenance personnel are fully informed about procedures and techniques and new equipment in use and are competent to perform the required duties.

Mechanical interruption summary report: A detailed report of occurrences during flight that causes a disruption of an air carrier's normal service.

Medical certificate: Acceptable evidence of physical fitness on a form prescribed by the Administrator.

Minimum descent altitude (MDA): The lowest altitude, expressed in feet above mean sea level, to which descent is authorized on final approach or during circle-to-land maneuvering in execution of a standard instrument approach procedure where no glide slope is provided.

Minimum equipment list (MEL): A FAA-approved list of aircraft equipment that are not essential to an aircraft's airworthiness and may be deferred for limited periods of time.

Minimum fuel: The minimum allowable fuel for an aircraft's release on a particular flight segment. This includes fuel to destination, then to the most distant required alternate, required reserves, contingency, and fuel for start and taxi. Known delays, diversions, and so forth are considered in this figure. Also included is fuel for acceleration, climb, cruise, descent, one instrument approach and missed approach, and the landing.

Minimum navigation performance standards (MNPS): *See* required navigation performance.

Net takeoff flight path: The actual flight path of the aircraft as determined during design and certification.

Nonscheduled operation: Any passenger-carrying operation that is other than a scheduled operation or any all-cargo operation, including on-demand and supplemental operations.

On-demand operation: An operation conducting nonscheduled operations in aircraft of 30 seats or less if common carriage or 20 seats or less if non–common carriage.

1 in 7 rule: The rule requiring an air carrier to give a pilot 1 day (24 consecutive hours) free from all duty in each 7 day period.

1-2-3 rule: A rule for determining the destination alternate requirement. From 1 hour before scheduled arrival until 1 hour after, a domestic operator must have at least a 2,000 foot ceiling and 3 statute miles visibility.

Operational control: With respect to a flight, the exercise of authority over initiating, conducting, or terminating a flight.

Operational service volume: That volume of airspace surrounding a NAVAID which is available for operational use and within which a signal of usable strength exists and where that signal is not operationally limited by co-channel interference.

Operations specifications (op specs): The document created by the carrier and FAA wherein the carrier specifically explains (or identifies) how it will conduct operation of its aircraft in accord with Federal Aviation Regulations.

Outsourced training: Any training, testing, or checking activity that an air carrier certificate holder provides by way of a contract arrangement with another party.

Overwater operations: Those flights conducted over any body of water beyond that point at which an aircraft is unable to glide to the shoreline of land when all engines fail.

Passenger-carrying operation: Any aircraft operation carrying any person other than a crewmember, company employee, authorized government representative, or person accompanying a shipment.

Passenger seating configuration: The total number of seats for which the aircraft is type certificated that can be made available for passenger use aboard a flight.

Performance objectives: A statement describing the behavior a crewmember must demonstrate to be able to successfully perform a crewmember's task.

Pilot in command: The person who has final authority and responsibility for the operation and safety of the flight; has been designated as pilot in command before or during the flight; and holds the appropriate category, class, and type rating, if appropriate, for the conduct of the flight.

Planned redispatch or rerelease en route: Any flag operation (or international supplemental operation) that is planned, before takeoff, to be redispatched or rereleased while in flight to a destination airport other than the original destination airport.

Portable electronic device (PED): Devices such as AM/FM radios, CD players, cellular phones, and laptop computers may interfere with an aircraft's electronics systems. For this reason, FAA regulations prohibit airline passengers from using PEDs except during cruise flight or when the flight crew determines it is safe to do so.

Principal base of operations: The primary operating location of a certificate holder as designated by the Administrator.

Principal maintenance inspector (PMI): An FAA maintenance inspector assigned the regulatory oversight of a particular air carrier's maintenance activities.

Principal operations inspector (POI): An FAA safety inspector assigned the regulatory oversight of a particular air carrier's flight operations.

Private carriage: Does not involve offering or holding out by the operator through advertising or any other means.

Private charter: Any charter for which the entity chartering the airplane engages the total capacity of an airplane for the carriage of passengers in civil or military air movements conducted under contract with the government of the United States of the government of a foreign country; or passengers invited by the charterer, the cost of which is borne entirely by the charterer and not directly or indirectly by the individual passengers.

Procedures for Air Navigation Services—Aircraft Operations (PANS-OPS): ICAO document outlining procedure standards for terminal instrument procedures. In the United States, these procedures are covered in the United States Standards for Terminal Instrument Procedures (TERPS).

Process control: The control of maintenance procedures required by the air carrier.

Programmed hours: Training hours specified in Part 121 for certain categories of training (e.g., initial new hire, transition, requalification, and recurrent).

Protective breathing equipment (PBE): A portable protective self-contained breathing unit conveniently located on the flight deck or at other points throughout the aircraft. A PBE protects against the effects of smoke, carbon dioxide, or other harmful gases or an oxygen deficient environment caused by other than an airplane depressurization.

Proving tests: Dry run operated by an air carrier to show the suitability of the aircraft for the operations it contemplates performing.

Public charter: Any charter that is not a private charter.

Qualified local observer: A person who provides weather, landing area, and other information as required by the carrier and has been trained by the carrier under an approved training program.

Recurrent training: Training that ensures each crewmember or dispatcher is adequately trained and currently proficient with respect to the type of airplane s/he is crewing or dispatching (FAR 121.427).

Reliable fix: With respect to air navigation, the passage of a VOR, a VORTAC, or NDB. It also includes a VOR/DME fix or a VOR intersection, an NDB intersection, and a VOR/NDB intersection.

Repair category: A classification of inoperative items on board an aircraft; each repair category contains the time interval that inoperative items must be repaired.

Repositioning flight: Relates to the movement of an aircraft on which no payload is carried, the purpose of which is to locate the aircraft at a point where passengers and/or cargo are to be boarded for revenue service. The aircraft may carry a full crew complement and other nonrevenue passengers, as approved, but will not carry revenue payload under this classification. A repositioning flight is normally operated under FAR Part 91. A repositioning flight is not to be confused with a maintenance ferry flight. The only correct reference to a ferry flight is when the authorization to operate is in accordance with a special ferry permit.

Requalification training: The training required for crewmembers previously trained and qualified, but who have become unqualified due to not having had the recurrent training required under FAR 121.427 or not having taken a proficiency check required by FAR 121.441.

Required navigation performance (RNP): A statement of navigation performance necessary for operations within a defined airspace such as the North Atlantic Minimum Navigation Performance Standards (MNPS) Airspace.

Rest period: A continuous period of time a flight crewmember is free from all duty requirements.

Rest records: Records kept to show how much rest a crewmember or dispatcher has received during the previous 24 hour period.

Runway limit weight: The maximum weight, at existing conditions, that will guarantee the aircraft meets the balanced field length requirements.

RVR (runway visual range): A specific measurement of visibility taken by a device placed alongside a runway for the purpose of measuring runway visibility. Measurements are expressed in hundreds of feet. They may be placed at the approach end of the runway (touchdown RVR), in the middle of the runway (mid-RVR), or at the far end of the runway (rollout RVR), or all three positions.

Scheduled passenger operations: The holding out to the public of air transportation service for passengers from identified air terminals at a set time announced by timetable or schedule published in a newspaper, magazine, or other advertising medium.

Second in command: A pilot who is designated to be second in command of an aircraft during flight time.

Second segment climb: Begins at the point where the aircraft achieves gear retraction at a speed of V_2 and ends at acceleration altitude (normally 400 feet). During this segment of the departure, in the event of an engine failure the crew is only expected to do the immediate items required to fly the airplane. This would include feathering an inoperative turboprop propeller and assuring landing gear retraction. The aircraft must maintain a minimum climb gradient of 2.4 percent or 24 feet per 1,000 feet traveled. No turning or banking of the aircraft is permitted prior to 50 feet above the runway surface. A maximum 15 degree bank is permitted after that.

Service difficulty reports: A report of certain aircraft equipment malfunctions, failures, or structural defects that must be sent to the FAA.

Single pilot-in-command operator: A single pilot-in-command FAR Part 135 operator is a certificate holder who will use only one pilot in command in FAR Part 135 operations. The single pilot in command shall be identified by name on the certificate holder's operations specifications. Using "freelance" pilots or temporary pilot employees in place of the pilot in command named on the operations specifications is not authorized. The certificate holder may be authorized to use no more than three individuals as second-in-command pilots. These individuals will be identified by name on the certificate holder's operations specifications and shall meet all the requirements of FAR Part 135 to serve as second in command. Single pilot-in-command operators are not authorized to operate aircraft type-certificated for more than nine passenger seats, conduct Category II or III approach operations, or conduct operations outside the United States, Canada, Mexico, or the Caribbean.

Single pilot operator: A single pilot FAR Part 135 operator is a certificate holder who will use only one pilot in FAR Part 135 operations. The single pilot shall be identified by name on the certificate holder's operations specifications. Using "freelance" pilots or temporary pilot employees in place of the pilot named on the operations specifications is not authorized. FAR Part 135 does not require single pilot FAR Part 135 operators to maintain manuals, training programs, or management positions.

Single visit training program: A program that allows air carriers to place all flight crewmembers on the same recurrent training cycle.

Special airport qualifications: Airports requiring that each pilot in command make an actual entry into that airport within the last 12 months or qualify using pictorial means to train for the unusual circumstances affecting that airport.

Standard alternate (weather) minimums: The standard minimum ceiling and visibility that must be forecast in order to list an airport as an alternate airport. Standard minimums for a precision (ILS, MLS, or GLS) approach are 600 foot ceiling and 2 statute miles visibility. Standard minimums for a nonprecision (VOR, VOR/DME, LOC, NDB, etc.) approach are 800 foot ceiling and 2 statute miles visibility. These minimums apply unless a carrier has received approval in its ops specs to use lower than standard derived alternate minimums. (*See* derived alternate (weather) minimums.)

Sterile area: An airport area to which access is controlled by the inspection of persons and property in accordance with an approved security program.

Stopway: An area beyond the takeoff runway, no less wide than the runway and centered upon the extended centerline of the runway, able to support the airplane during an aborted takeoff without causing structural damage to the airplane and designated by the airport authorities for use in decelerating the airplane during an aborted takeoff.

Supplemental operations: Any nonscheduled passenger-carrying operation or any all-cargo operation conducted under FAR Part 121.

Takeoff warning system: A warning system which provides an aural warning that is automatically activated during the initial portion of the takeoff roll if the airplane is in a configuration that would not allow a safe takeoff. Also known as takeoff configuration warning system (TOCWS).

TERPS: The United States Standards for Terminal Instrument Procedures that outlines the methods for certifying terminal procedures (approaches) in the United States. The TERPS is similar in concept to the ICAO PANS-OPS and the JAA-JAR-OPS-1 documents.

Third segment climb: Begins at acceleration altitude and continues until the aircraft is cleaned up and established in the cruise climb configuration at the cruise climb airspeed. During this segment of departure the aircraft is accelerated, flaps are retracted, any emergency checklists are run, and maximum continuous or cruise climb power is set. The aircraft must maintain a net takeoff flight path *minimum climb gradient of 1.2 percent or 12 feet per 1,000 feet traveled*. The minimum gradient is 1.5 percent for three engine aircraft (15 feet per 1,000 feet traveled), and 1.7 percent for four-engine aircraft (17 feet per 1,000 feet traveled).

30 in 7 rule: The rule that limits a pilot's flight time to 30 hours in a 7 day period.

Traffic alert collision avoidance system (TCAS): Equipment that provides traffic alerts of conflicting traffic. In the case of collision threat, it also issues resolution advisories.

Transition training: The training required for crewmembers and dispatchers who have qualified and served in the same capacity on another airplane in the same group.

Upgrade training: The training required for crewmembers who have qualified and served as second in command or flight engineer on a particular airplane type, before they serve as a pilot in command or second in command, respectively, on that airplane.

V_1: The maximum speed in the takeoff at which the pilot must take first action (e.g., apply brakes, reduce thrust, deploy speed brakes) to stop the airplane within the accelerate-stop distance. V_1 also means the minimum speed in the takeoff, following a failure of the critical engine at V_{EF}, at which the pilot can continue the takeoff and achieve the required height above the takeoff surface within the takeoff distance. V_1 is the end of the go/no-go decision process.

V_{EF}: The speed at which the critical engine is assumed to fail. The aircraft continues to accelerate from the instant an engine fails until the instant the pilot recognizes and reacts to the engine failure by activating the first deceleration device.

V_{LOF}: The speed at which the aircraft will leave the ground if rotation is begun at V_R and the correct rate of rotation is used.

V_{MC}: The airspeed at which, when the critical engine is suddenly made inoperative, it is possible to maintain control of the airplane with that engine still inoperative and maintain straight flight with an angle of bank of not more than 5 degrees.

V_{MCG}: The minimum control speed on the ground and the airspeed during takeoff run at which, when the critical engine is suddenly made inoperative, it is possible to maintain control of the airplane using rudder control alone (without the use of nose-wheel steering).

V_{MC} **limit:** A minimum weight limit used in aircraft where reduced power takeoffs are used. This minimum weight is designed to control V_{MC} from being too high on takeoff.

V_R: The rotation speed or the speed at which the nose may be raised to initial climb attitude.

V_2: The single-engine takeoff safety speed. In the event of an engine failure on takeoff, this is the minimum speed to be maintained to at least 400 feet above the takeoff surface. V_2 is analogous to the best single engine rate of climb (V_{YSE}) for a light twin-engine aircraft.

WAT limit charts: Weight, altitude, temperature limit charts are takeoff performance planning charts (*see also* runway limit, climb limit definitions).

Bibliography

American Airlines Flight Department. 1971. *Boeing 727 Operating Manual,* Fort Worth, TX, American Airlines Flight Academy.

Black's Law Dictionary, 4th Edition. 1968. St. Paul, MN, West Publishing Company.

Dave English et al. 2000. *Slipping the Surly Bounds.* New York: McGraw Hill Publishing.

Federal Aviation Administration. 24 April 1986. *Advisory Circular 120-12A; Private Carriage Versus Common Carriage of Persons or Property,* U.S. Government Printing Office.

George E. Hopkins. 2000. *Flying the Line,* Vol. 2, Washington D.C., Airline Pilots Association, International.

Greg N. Brown, Mark J. Holt. 2001. *The Turbine Pilot's Flight Manual,* 2nd Edition, Ames, IA, Iowa State University Press.

Office of the Federal Register. 1988. *Air Transportation Operations Inspectors Handbook Order 8400.10,* Department of Transportation, Federal Aviation Administration, Washington D.C., U.S. Government Printing Office.

Office of the Federal Register. 2 October 1990. *Special Federal Aviation Regulation 58— Advanced Qualification Program,* Federal Register, Vol. 55, No. 91, Rules and Regulations (pp.40262-40352), Washington D.C., National Archives and Records Administration.

Office of the Federal Register. 2001. *Airman's Information Manual/Federal Aviation Regulations,* edited by Charles F. Spence, Washington D.C., McGraw-Hill.

Office of the Federal Register. 2001. *Federal Air Regulations for Flight Crew,* edited by Jackie Spanitz, Newcastle, WA, Aviation Supplies and Academics.

William L. Prosser. 1974. *Law of Torts,* St. Paul, MN, West Publishing Company.

A